iPhone 4 Made Simple

Martin Trautschold
and
Gary Mazo

Apress®

iPhone 4 Made Simple

ISBN-13 (pbk): 978-1-4302-3192-9

ISBN-13 (electronic): 978-1-4302-3193-6

Printed and bound in the United States of America 9 8 7 6 5 4 3 2 1

President and Publisher: Paul Manning
Lead Editor: Steve Anglin
Development Editor: James Markham
Editorial Board: Clay Andres, Steve Anglin, Mark Beckner, Ewan Buckingham, Gary Cornell, Jonathan Gennick, Jonathan Hassell, Michelle Lowman, Matthew Moodie, Duncan Parkes, Jeffrey Pepper, Frank Pohlmann, Douglas Pundick, Ben Renow-Clarke, Dominic Shakeshaft, Matt Wade, Tom Welsh
Coordinating Editor: Laurin Becker
Copy Editor: Mary Behr, Mary Ann Fugate, Heather Lang, Patrick Meador, Ralph Moore, Kim Wimpsett
Technical Reviewer: Rene Ritchie
Compositor: MacPS, LLC
Indexer: BIM Indexing & Proofreading Services
Artist: MacPS, LLC and Rod Hernandez
Cover Designer: Anna Ishchenko

Distributed to the book trade worldwide by Springer Science+Business Media, LLC., 233 Spring Street, 6th Floor, New York, NY 10013. Phone 1-800-SPRINGER, fax (201) 348-4505, e-mail orders-ny@springer-sbm.com, or visit www.springeronline.com.

For information on translations, please e-mail rights@apress.com, or visit www.apress.com.

Apress and friends of ED books may be purchased in bulk for academic, corporate, or promotional use. eBook versions and licenses are also available for most titles. For more information, reference our Special Bulk Sales–eBook Licensing web page at www.apress.com/info/bulksales.

This book is dedicated to our families—to our wives, Julie and Gloria, and to our kids, Sophie, Livvie and Cece, and Ari, Dan, Sara, Billy, Elise and Jonah.

Without their love, support, and understanding, we could never take on projects like this one. Now that the book is done, we will gladly share our iPhones with them – for a little while!

Contents at a Glance

Contents

About the Authors

Martin Trautschold is the founder and CEO of Made Simple Learning, a leading provider of Apple iPad, iPhone, iPod touch, BlackBerry, and Palm webOS books and video tutorials. He has been a successful entrepreneur in the mobile device training and software business since 2001. With Made Simple Learning, he helped to train thousands of BlackBerry Smartphone users with short, to-the-point video tutorials. Martin has now co-authored sixteen "Made Simple" guide books. He also co-founded, ran for 3 years, and then sold a mobile device software company. Prior to this, Martin spent 15 years in technology and business consulting in the US and Japan. He holds an engineering degree from Princeton University and an MBA from the Kellogg School at Northwestern University. Martin and his wife, Julia, have three daughters. He enjoys rowing and cycling. Martin can be reached at martin@madesimplelearning.com.

Gary Mazo is Vice President of Made Simple Learning and is a writer, a college professor, a gadget nut, and an ordained rabbi. Gary joined Made Simple Learning in 2007 and has co-authored the last thirteen books in the Made Simple series. Along with Martin, and Kevin Michaluk from CrackBerry.com, Gary co-wrote *CrackBerry: True Tales of BlackBerry Use and Abuse*—a book about BlackBerry addiction and how to get a grip on one's BlackBerry use. The second edition of this book will be published by Apress this fall. Gary also teaches writing, philosophy, technical writing, and more at the University of Phoenix. Gary has been a regular contributor to CrackBerry.com—writing product reviews and adding editorial content. He holds a BA in anthropology from Brandeis University. Gary earned his M.A.H.L (Masters in Hebrew Letters) as well as ordination as Rabbi from the Hebrew Union College-Jewish Institute of Religion in Cincinnati, Ohio. He has served congregations in Dayton, Ohio, Cherry Hill, New Jersey and Cape Cod, Massachusetts. Gary is married to Gloria Schwartz Mazo; they have six children. Gary can be reached at: gary@madesimplelearning.com.

About the Technical Reviewer

 **Rene Ritchie** is editor of TiPb.com, the iPhone and iPad blog, which covers the full range of news, how-tos and app, game, and accessory reviews. Part of the Smartphone Experts network, TiPb also provides a full range of help and community forums and has a thriving YouTube channel (http://www.youtube.com/theiphoneblog/), Facebook page (http://www.facebook.com/tipbcom/) and Twitter following (http://twitter.com/tipb). A graphic designer, web developer, and author, Rene lives and works in Montreal. He can be reached via rene@tipb.com or @reneritchie on Twitter.

Acknowledgments

A book like this takes many people to successfully complete. We would like to thank Apress for believing in us and our unique style of writing.

We would like to thank our Editors, Jim and Laurin, and the entire editorial team at Apress.

We would like to thank our families for their patience and support in allowing us to pursue projects such as this one.

Part I

Quick Start Guide

In your hands is one of the most exciting devices to hit the market in quite some time: the iPhone 4. This Quick Start Guide will help get you and your new iPhone 4 up and running in a hurry. You'll learn all about the buttons, switches, and ports, and how to use the innovative and responsive touch screen and multitask with the new App Switcher bar. Our App Reference Tables introduce you to the apps on your iPhone 4—and serves as a quick way to find out how to accomplish a task.

Getting Around Quickly

This Quick Start Guide is meant to be just that—a tool that can help you jump right in and find information in this book, as well as learn the basics of how to get around and enjoy your iPhone right away.

We'll start with the nuts and bolts in our "Learning Your Way Around" section, which covers what all the keys, buttons, switches, and symbols mean and do on your iPhone. In this section, you'll see some handy features such as multitasking by double-clicking the **Home** button. You'll also learn how to interact with the menus, submenus, and set switches—tasks that are required in almost every application on your iPhone. You'll also find out how to read your connectivity status and what to do when you travel on an airplane.

> **TIP:** Check out Chapter 2, "Typing Tips, Copy/Paste and Search" for great typing tips and more.

In the "Touch Screen Basics" section, we will help you learn how to touch, swipe, flick, zoom, and more.

Later, in the "App Reference Tables," section, we've organized the app icons into general categories, so you can quickly browse through the icons and jump to a section in the book to learn more about the app a particular icon represents. This guide also includes several handy tables designed to help you get up and running with your iPhone quickly:

- Getting Started (Table 2)
- Stay Organized (Table 3)
- Be Entertained (Table 4)
- Stay Informed (Table 5)
- Network Socially (Table 6)
- Be Productive (Table 7)

So let's get started!

Learning Your Way Around

To help you get comfortable with your iPhone, we start with the basics—what the buttons, keys, and switches do—and then move into how you start apps and navigate the menus. Probably the most important status indicator on your iPhone, besides the battery, is the one that shows network status in the upper right corner. Understand what these status icons do is crucial to getting the most out of your iPhone.

Keys, Buttons, and Switches

Figure 1 shows all the things you can do with the buttons, keys, switches, and ports on your iPhone. Go ahead and try out a few things to see what happens. Swipe left to search, swipe right to see more icons, try double-clicking the **Home** button to bring up the multitasking App Switcher bar, and press and hold the **Power/Sleep** key. Have some fun getting acquainted with your device.

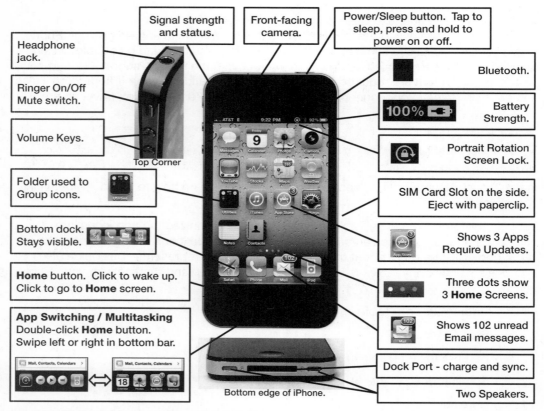

Figure 1. *The iPhone's buttons, ports, switches and keys.*

Switching Apps (AKA Multitasking)

One of the great new features introduced with the iPhone 4 is the ability to multitask or jump between applications (see Figure 2).

Double-click the **Home** button to bring up the **App Switcher** bar in the bottom of the screen. Next, swipe right to see more icons and tap any icon of any app you want to start. If you don't see the icon you want, then single-click the **Home** button to see the entire **Home** screen. Repeat these steps to jump back to the app you just left. The nice thing is that the app you just left is always shown as the first app on the **App Switcher** bar.

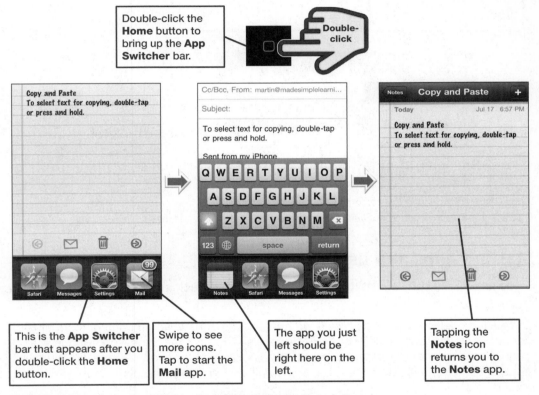

Double-click the **Home** button to bring up the **App Switcher** bar.

Double-click

This is the **App Switcher** bar that appears after you double-click the **Home** button.

Swipe to see more icons. Tap to start the **Mail** app.

The app you just left should be right here on the left.

Tapping the **Notes** icon returns you to the **Notes** app.

Figure 2. *Multitasking or App Switching by double-clicking the Home button.*

iPod Controls and Portrait Screen Rotation Lock

You will see a few more icons if you swipe from left to right in the **App Switcher** bar. You can lock the screen rotation by tapping the left-most icon, and the middle buttons control the currently playing music or video. The last icon on the right will start your iPod (see Figure 3).

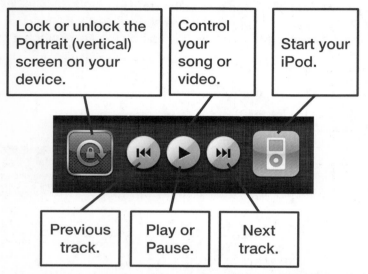

Lock or unlock the Portrait (vertical) screen on your device.

Control your song or video.

Start your iPod.

Previous track.

Play or Pause.

Next track.

Figure 3. *The Screen Rotation Lock button, iPod controls, and the iPod icon in the App Switcher bar.*

Starting Apps and Using Soft Keys

Some apps have soft keys at the bottom of the screen, such as the **iPod** app shown in Figure 4.

To see and use the soft keys in the **iPod** app, you must have some content (e.g., music, videos, podcasts, and so on) on your iPhone. See Chapter 3: " Sync Your iPhone with iTunes" for help with syncing your music, videos, and more to your iPhone. Follow these steps to launch the **iPod** app and become familiar with using the soft keys to get around:

1. Tap the **iPod** icon to start the **iPod** app.

2. Touch the **Albums** soft key at the bottom to view your albums.

3. Touch the **Artists** soft key to view a list of your artists.

4. Try all the soft keys in **iPod**.

5. In some apps, such as the **iPod** app, you will see the **More** soft key in the lower right corner. Tap this key to see additional soft keys or even rearrange your soft keys.

TIP: You know which soft key is selected because it is highlighted—usually with a color. The other soft keys are gray, but can still be touched.

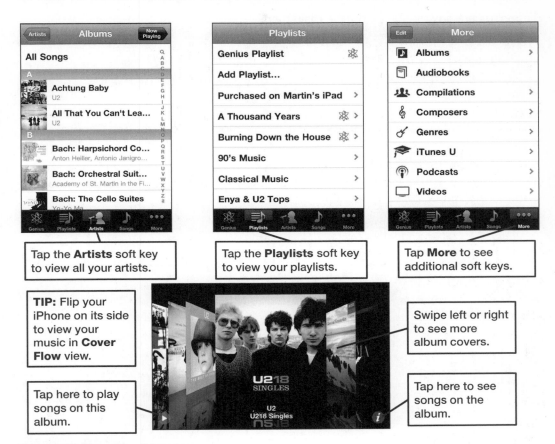

Tap the **Artists** soft key to view all your artists.

Tap the **Playlists** soft key to view your playlists.

Tap **More** to see additional soft keys.

TIP: Flip your iPhone on its side to view your music in **Cover Flow** view.

Swipe left or right to see more album covers.

Tap here to play songs on this album.

Tap here to see songs on the album.

Figure 4. *Working with soft keys in apps.*

Menus, Submenus, and Switches

Once you are in an app, you can select any menu item by simply touching it. Using the Settings app as an example, tap **General**, and then tap **Auto-Lock**, as shown in Figure 5.

Submenus are any menus below the main menu.

> **TIP:** You know there is a submenu or another screen if you see the greater than symbol next to the menu item (**>**).

How do you get back up to the previous screen or menu? Tap the button in the top of the menu. If you're in the **Auto-Lock** menu, for example, you'd touch the **General** button.

You'll see a number of switches on the iPhone, such as the one next to **Airplane Mode** shown in Figure 5. To set a switch (e.g., change the switch from **OFF** to **ON**), just touch it.

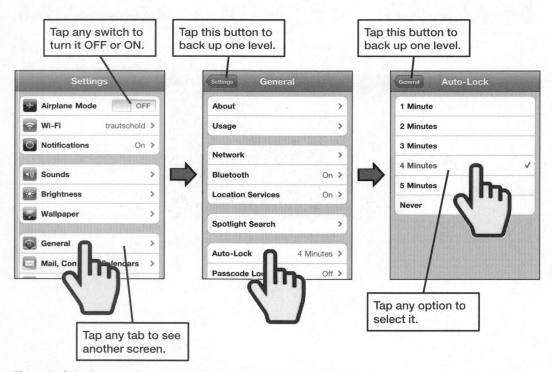

Figure 5. *Selecting menu items, navigating submenus, and setting switches.*

Reading the Connectivity Status Icons

Most of the functions on your iPhone work only when you are connected to the Internet (e.g., email, your browser, the **App Store**, **iTunes**, and so on), so you need to know when you're connected. Understanding how to read the status bar can save you time and frustration.

Cellular Data Signal Strength (1-5 bars):

Strong   Weak Radio Off – Airplane Mode

Wi-Fi Network Signal Strength (1-3 symbols):

Strong  Weak Off

You can tell whether you are connected to a network, as well as the general speed of the connection, by looking at the left end of your iPhone's **Top** status bar. Table 1 shows typical examples of what you might see on this status bar.

Table 1. *How to Tell When You Are Connected.*

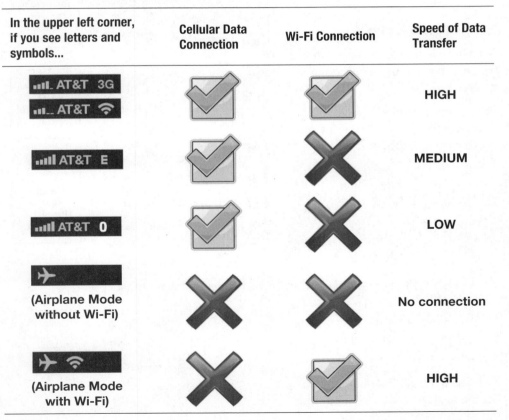

In the upper left corner, if you see letters and symbols...	Cellular Data Connection	Wi-Fi Connection	Speed of Data Transfer
AT&T 3G / AT&T (wifi)	✓	✓	HIGH
AT&T E	✓	✗	MEDIUM
AT&T O	✓	✗	LOW
(Airplane Mode without Wi-Fi)	✗	✗	No connection
(Airplane Mode with Wi-Fi)	✗	✓	HIGH

Chapter 5: "Wi-Fi and 3G Connectivity" shows you how to connect your iPhone to a Wi-Fi or 3G Cellular Data Network.

Flying On An Airplane – Airplane Mode

Often when you are flying on an airplane, the flight crew will ask you to turn off all portable electronic devices for takeoff and landing. Then, when you get to altitude, they say "all approved electronic devices" can be turned back on.

> **TIP:** Check out the "International Travel" section of Chapter 5: "Wi-Fi and 3G Connectivity" for many money saving tips you can take advantage when you travel overseas with your iPhone.

If you need to turn off your iPhone completely, press and hold the **Power** button on the top right edge, and then **Slide to Power Off** your iPhone with your finger.

Follow these steps to enable **Airplane Mode**:

1. Tap the **Settings** icon.

2. Set the switch next to **Airplane Mode** in the top of the left column to **ON.**

3. Notice that the Wi-Fi is automatically turned **Off** and that the **Phone** will not work.

> **TIP:** Some airlines do have in-flight Wi-Fi networks. On those flights, you may want to turn your Wi-Fi back **On** at the appropriate time.

You can turn your Wi-Fi connection **Off** or **On** by following these steps:

1. Tap the **Settings** icon.

2. Tap **Wi-Fi** near the top of the screen.

3. To enable the Wi-Fi connections, set the switch next to **Wi-Fi** at the top of the page to **ON.**

4. To disable the Wi-Fi, set the same switch to **OFF**.

5. Select the Wi-Fi network and follow the steps the flight attendant provides to connect to in-flight Wi-Fi.

Touch Screen Basics

In this section, we will describe how to interact with the iPhone's touch screen.

Touch Screen Gestures

The iPhone has an amazingly sensitive and intuitive touch screen. Apple, renowned for making its iPad, iPod touch, and iPod devices easy-to-use, has come up with an excellent, even higher resolution, highly responsive touch screen.

If you are used to a physical keyboard and a trackball or trackpad, or even an iPod's intuitive scroll wheel, then this touch screen will take a little effort to master. With a little practice, though, you'll soon become comfortable interacting with your iPhone.

You can do almost anything on your iPhone by using a combination of the following:

- Touch screen "gestures"
- Touching icons or soft keys on the screen
- Clicking the **Home** button at the bottom

The following sections describe the various gestures you can use on your iPhone 4.

Tapping and Flicking

To start an app, confirm a selection, select a menu item, or select an answer, simply tap the screen. To move quickly through contacts, lists, and the music library in **List** mode, flick from side to side or up and down to scroll through items. Figure 6 shows both of these gestures.

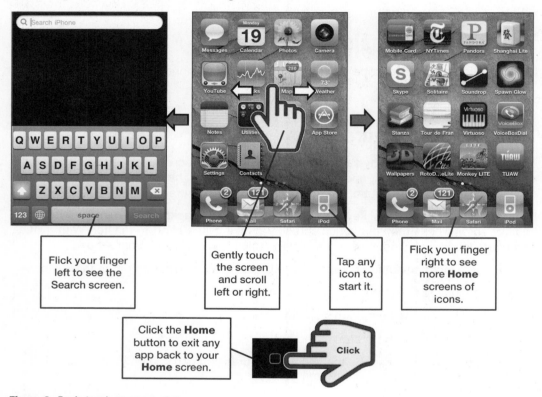

Flick your finger left to see the Search screen.

Gently touch the screen and scroll left or right.

Tap any icon to start it.

Flick your finger right to see more **Home** screens of icons.

Click the **Home** button to exit any app back to your **Home** screen.

Click

Figure 6. *Basic touch-screen gestures.*

Swiping

To swipe, gently touch and move your finger as shown in Figure 7. You can also do this to move between open **Safari** web pages and pictures. Swiping also works in lists, such as the **Contacts** list.

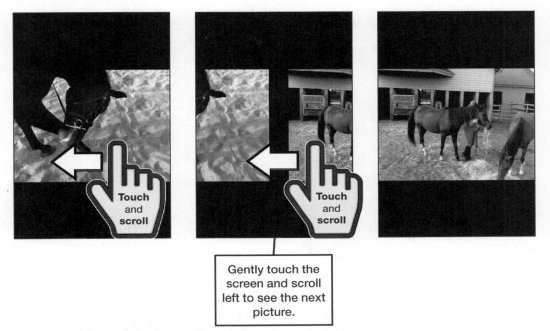

Gently touch the screen and scroll left to see the next picture.

Figure 7. *Touch and swipe to move between pictures and web pages.*

Scrolling

Scrolling is as simple as touching the screen and sliding your finger in the direction you want to scroll (see Figure 8). You can use this technique in messages (email), the **Safari** web browser, menus, and more.

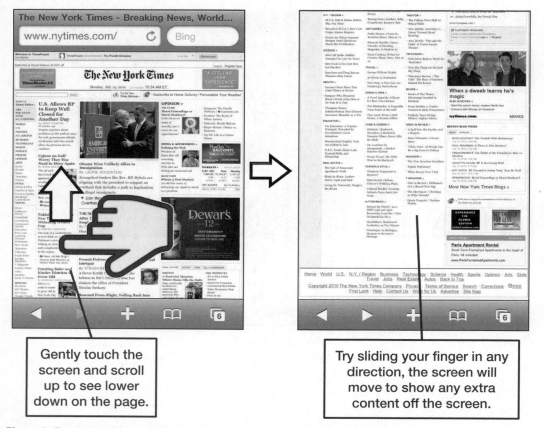

Gently touch the screen and scroll up to see lower down on the page.

Try sliding your finger in any direction, the screen will move to show any extra content off the screen.

Figure 8. *Touch and slide your finger to scroll around a web page, a zoomed picture, and more.*

Double-Tapping

You can double-tap the screen to zoom in and then double-tap again to zoom back out.
This works in many places, such as web pages, mail messages, and pictures (see Figure 9).

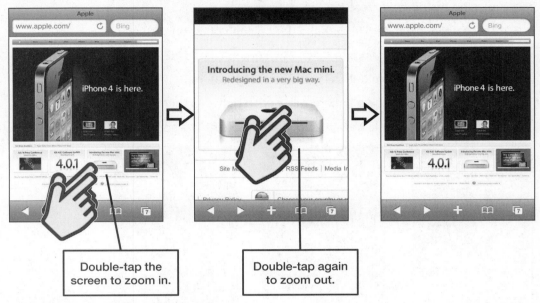

Double-tap the
screen to zoom in.

Double-tap again
to zoom out.

Figure 9. *Double-tapping to zoom in or out.*

Pinching

You can also pinch open or closed to zoom in or out. This works in many places, including web pages, mail messages, and pictures (see Figure 10). Follow these steps to zoom in using the *pinching* feature:

1. To zoom in, place two fingers that touch each other on the screen.

2. Gradually slide your fingers open. The screen zooms in.

Follow these steps to zoom out using the pinching feature.

1. To zoom out, place two fingers with space between them on the screen.

2. Gradually slide your fingers closed, so they touch. The screen zooms out.

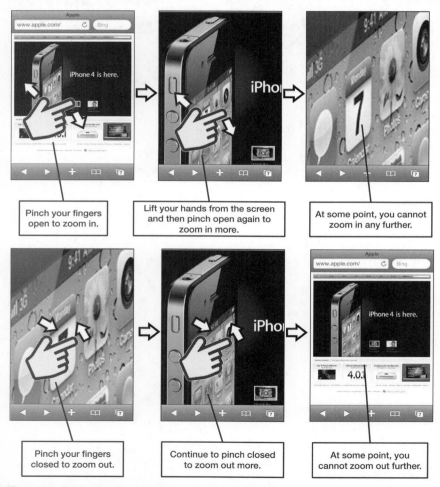

Figure 10. *Pinch open to zoom in and pinch closed to zoom out.*

App Reference Tables

This section gives you a number of handy reference tables that group the various apps that are pre-installed on your iPhone by their functionality. Also included in the tables are other useful apps you can download from the **App Store**. Each table gives you a brief description of the app and tells you where you can find more information about it in this book.

Getting Started

Table 2 provides some quick links to help you connect your iPhone to the Web (using Wi-Fi or 3G); buy and enjoy songs or videos (using the **iTunes** and **iPod** apps); make your iPhone sleep or power off; unlock your iPhone; use the electronic **Picture Frame**; and more.

Table 2. *Getting Started.*

To Do This...	Use This...		Where to Learn More
Turn the iPhone on or off.		The **Power/Sleep** button: Press and hold this key on the right of the top edge of the iPhone.	Getting Started – Ch. 1
Adjust settings and connect to the Internet (via Wi-Fi or 3G).		**Settings > Wi-Fi** or **Settings > General > Network**	Wi-Fi & 3G – Ch. 5
Return to Home screen.		The **Home** button	Getting Started – Ch. 1
Unlock the iPhone.		Slide your finger to unlock your iPhone.	Getting Started – Ch. 1
Completely power down your iPhone.	Press and hold the power key	Slide this button to power the device off.	Getting Started – Ch. 1
Sync music, videos, pictures, addresses, calendar, e-mail, and notes with your computer.	**iTunes (for Windows** and **Apple Mac)** **MobileMe Sync Service** **Google/Exchange Sync**		iTunes Sync – Ch. 3 Other Sync Methods – Ch. 4
Set a really amazing new wallpaper.		**3D Wallpapers**	Personalize – Ch. 9

Stay Connected and Organized

Table 3 provides links for everything from organizing and finding your contacts to managing your calendar, working with email, sending messages, getting driving directions, calling people, and more.

Table 3. *Staying Connected and Organized.*

To Do This...	Use This...		Where to Learn More
Manage your contact names and numbers.		**Contacts**	Contacts – Ch. 19
Manage your calendar.		**Calendar**	Calendar – Ch. 20
Surf the Web		**Safari**	Safari – Ch. 17
Call your friends.		**Phone**	Phone – Ch. 10
Use video conferencing.		**FaceTime**	Video Conferencing – Ch. 12
Control your iPod and iPhone with your voice. (Press and hold the **Home** button.)		**Voice Control**	Multitasking and Voice Control – Ch. 8

To Do This...	Use This...		Where to Learn More
Dial and search by simply speaking.		**VoiceBox Dialer**	Phone – Ch. 10
Send text, picture, and video messages.		**Messages**	SMS and MMS – Ch. 11
View and send email.		**Mail**	Email – Ch. 18
Find just about anything, get directions, avoid traffic, and more.		**Maps**	Maps – Ch. 22

Be Entertained

You can have lots of fun with your iPhone; Table 4 shows you how. For example, you can use your iPhone to buy or rent movies, check out free Internet radio with **Pandora**, or buy a book and enjoy it in a whole new way using **iBooks**. If you already use a **Kindle**, you can sync all your **Kindle** books to your iPhone and enjoy them right away. You can also choose from more than 200,000 apps from the **App Store** to make your iPhone even more amazing, fun, and useful. You can also rent a movie from **Hulu** or **iTunes**, downloading it immediately for later viewing (say on an airplane or train).

Table 4. *Being Entertained.*

To Do This...	Use This...	Where to Learn More
Buy music, videos, podcasts, and more.	**iTunes on your iPhone**	iTunes on iPhone – Ch. 25
Use your computer to sync, buy music apps, and listen to music and other content.	**iTunes on your Computer**	iTunes User Guide – Ch. 30
Browse and download apps right to your iPhone	**App Store**	App Store – Ch. 26
See playlists, artists,songs, albums, audiobooks, videos, and more.	**iPod**	Music – Ch. 13 Videos & TV – Ch. 16
Listen to free Internet radio.	**Pandora**	Music – Ch. 13
Read a book anytime, anywhere.	**iBooks**	iBooks & E-Books – Ch. 14

To Do This...	Use This...		Where to Learn More
Read your Kindle books.		**Kindle**	iBooks & E-Books – Ch. 14
Look at, zoom in on, and organize your pictures.		**Camera**	Photography – Ch. 21
Look at, zoom in on, and organize your pictures.		**Photos**	Photography – Ch. 21
Rent a movie.		**Hulu Plus**	Videos & TV – Ch. 16
Watch a video from YouTube.		**YouTube**	Videos & TV – Ch. 16
Play a game.		**Games Icons**	Games & Fun – Ch. 27
Work on a crossword puzzle by tapping your finger.		**Times Crosswords**	App Store – Ch. 26
Interact with comics in a whole new way.		**Marvel Comics**	New Media – Ch. 15

Stay Informed

You can also use your iPhone to read your favorite magazine or newspaper with up-to-the-minute vibrant pictures and videos (see Table 5). Or, you can use it to check out the latest weather reports.

Table 5. *Staying Informed.*

To Do This...	Use This...		Where to Learn More
Check your favorite radio news program.		NPR News	App Store – Ch. 26
Read the newspaper.		New York Times	New Media – Ch. 15
Check the weather.		The Weather Channel	App Store – Ch. 26
Check out the latest headlines.		AP Mobile	App Store – Ch. 26

Network Socially

You can also use your iPhone to connect and stay up-to-date with friends, colleagues, and professional networks using the social networking tools on your iPhone (see Table 6).

Table 6. *Networking Socially.*

To Do This...	Use This...		Where to Learn More
Skype.		**Skype**	Video Messaging and Skype – Ch. 12
Network on LinkedIn.		**LinkedIn**	Social Networking – Ch. 28
Stay connected with friends on Facebook.		**Facebook**	Social Networking – Ch. 28
Follow your favorites on Twitter.		**Twitter**	Social Networking – Ch. 28

Be Productive

An iPhone can also help you be more productive. You can use it to access and read just about any PDF file or other document with the **GoodReader** app. You can take notes with the basic **Notes** app, or step up to the advanced **Evernote** app, which has amazing capabilities for integrating audio, pictures, and text notes, and as well as syncing everything to a web site. You can also use your iPhone to set an alarm, calculate a tip, see what direction you are walking in, and record a voice memo (see Table 7).

Table 7. *Being Productive.*

To Do This...	Use This...		Where to Learn More
Access and read almost any document .		**GoodReader**	New Media – Ch. 15
Take notes, store your grocery list, and more.		**Notes**	Notes – Ch. 23
Take and organize your notes in a whole new way.		**Evernote**	Notes – Ch. 23
Use folders to organize your icons.		**Folders**	Move Icons and Work with Folders – Ch. 7
Set an alarm, countdoun timer, and more.		**Clock**	Utilities – Ch. 24
Calculate a tip or find the cosine of 30 degrees.		**Calculator**	Utilities – Ch. 24

To Do This...	Use This...		Where to Learn More
Find out whether you are walking north.		**Compass**	Utilities – Ch. 24
Take a note without using your hands or typing.		**Voice Memos**	Utilities – Ch. 24

Part II

Introduction

Welcome to your new iPhone 4—and to the book that tells you what you need to know to get the most out of it. In this part we show you how the book is organized and where to go to find what you need. We even show you how to get some great tips and tricks sent right to your iPhone 4 via short e-mail messages.

Introduction

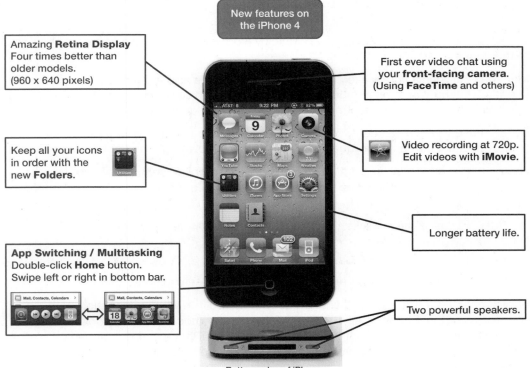

New features on the iPhone 4

Amazing **Retina Display** Four times better than older models. (960 x 640 pixels)

First ever video chat using your **front-facing camera**. (Using **FaceTime** and others)

Keep all your icons in order with the new **Folders**.

Video recording at 720p. Edit videos with **iMovie**.

Longer battery life.

App Switching / Multitasking Double-click **Home** button. Swipe left or right in bottom bar.

Two powerful speakers.

Bottom edge of iPhone.

Congratulations on Your New iPhone 4!

You hold in your hands perhaps the most powerful and elegant smartphone available, a phone that is also a media player, e-book reader, gaming machine, life organizer, and just about everything else available today: the iPhone 4.

The iPhone 4 can do more than just about any other smartphone on the market. In a beautiful and elegantly designed package, the iPhone 4 will have you surfing the web, checking email, and organizing your busy life in no time.

> **NOTE**: Take a look at Chapter 12, where we show you how to use the **Skype** iPhone app and the new **FaceTime** video chat feature on your iPhone 4!

With your iPhone 4, you can view your photos and interact with them using intuitive touch-screen gestures. You can pinch, zoom, rotate, and email your photos—all by using simple gestures.

Interact with your content like never before. News sites and web sites look and read like never before due to the incredibly clear and crisp retina display. Flip through stories, videos, and pictures, and interact with your news.

For the first time, really feel as though you are reading a book when you read on an electronic device. Pages turn slowly or quickly (you can even see the words on the back of the pages when you turn them).

Manage your media library like never before. The **iTunes** app features a beautiful interface, letting you choose music, watch videos, organize playlists, and more—all in an effortless and fun way on the iPhone 4's high definition–quality screen.

Do you have a Netflix account? You will soon be able to manage your content, organize your queue, and stream high-quality movies and TV shows right on your iPhone 4.

Hulu + is available now, and it allows you to watch complete seasons of your favorite TV shows right on your iPhone (see Chapter 16 for more information).

> **NOTE**: The Netflix app was not out at the time of writing of this book, but we were assured it will be out by the end of summer, 2010.

Update your **Facebook** status and receive push alerts—all on your iPhone 4.

Stay connected to the web and your email with the built-in Wi-Fi connection or the 3G connection of the iPhone 4. All the latest high-speed protocols are supported, so you can always be in touch and get the latest content. The iPhone 4 also includes a "horizontal" keyboard to type out emails and notes when you use the device in **Landscape** mode.

Getting the Most out of *iPhone 4 Made Simple*

Read this book cover-to-cover if you choose, but you can also peruse it in a modular fashion, by chapter or topic. Maybe you just want to check out the **App Store** app, try **iBooks**, set up with your email or contacts, or just load up your phone with music. You can do all this and much more with our book.

You will soon realize that your iPhone 4 is a very powerful device. There are, however, many secrets "locked" inside, which we help you "unlock" throughout this book.

Take your time—this book can help you understand how to best use, work, and have fun with your new iPhone 4. Think back to when you tried to use your first Windows or Mac computer. It took a little while to get familiar with how to do things. It's the same with the iPhone 4. Use this book to help you get up to speed and learn all the best tips and tricks more quickly.

Also remember that devices this powerful are not always easy to grasp—at first.

You will get the most out of your iPhone 4 if you can read a section and then try out what you read. We all know that reading and then doing an activity gives us a much higher retention rate than simply reading alone.

So, in order to learn and remember what you learn, we recommend the following:

Read a little, try a little on your iPhone 4, and repeat!

How This Book Is Organized

Knowing how this book is organized will help you quickly locate things that are important to you. Here we show you the main organization of this book. Remember to take advantage of our abridged table of contents, detailed table of contents, and our comprehensive index. All of these elements can help you quickly pinpoint items of interest to you.

Day in the Life of an iPhone 4 User

Located inside the front and back covers, the "Day in the Life of an iPhone 4 User" reference is an excellent guide to your phone's features, providing ideas on how to use your iPhone and lots of easy-to-access, cross-referenced chapter numbers. So, if you see something you want to learn, simply thumb to that page and learn it—all in just a few minutes.

Part 1: Quick Start Guide

Touch Screen Basics: This book's many practical and informative screen shots will help you quickly learn how to touch, swipe, flick, zoom, and more with your iPhone 4 touch screen.

App Reference Tables: Quickly skim the icons or apps grouped by category. Get a thumbnail of what all the apps do on your iPhone 4, including a pointer to the relevant chapter numbers, so you can jump right to the details of how to get the most out of each app in this book.

Part 2: Introduction

You are here now . . .

Part 3: You and Your iPhone 4

This is the meat of the book, organized in 30 easy-to-understand chapters, all of them packed with loads of pictures to guide you every step of the way.

Part 4: iPhone 4's Soulmate, iTunes

As a special bonus for our readers, we have provided an extensive iTunes Bonus Guide in Chapter 30. This special bonus chapter walks you through many of the **iTunes** app's best features, showing you how to maximize, not just the features of **iTunes**, but the iPhone 4 itself. The more comfortable you can get with the **iTunes**, the more you can arrange and use content from your computer on your iPhone 4—making a great and enjoyable user experience even more so.

Quickly Locating Tips, Cautions, and Notes

If you flip through this book, you can instantly see specially formatted **TIPS**, **CAUTIONS**, and **NOTES** that highlight important facts about using the iPhone 4. For example, if you want to find all the special tips relevant to using the iPhone's Calendar, you can flip to the Calendar chapter and search for these highlighted nuggets of information.

> **TIP**: **TIPS**, **CAUTIONS**, and **NOTES** are all formatted like this, with a gray background, to help you see them more quickly.

Free iPhone 4 Email Tips

Finally, check out the author's web site at www.madesimplelearning.com for a series of very useful "bite-sized" chunks of iPhone 4 tips and tricks. We have taken a selection of the great tips out of this book and even added a few new ones. Click the "Free Tips" link and register for your tips in order to receive a tip right in your iPhone 4 inbox about once a week. Learning in small chunks is a great way to master your iPhone 4!

Part III

You and Your iPhone 4 . . .

This is the heart of *iPhone 4 Made Simple*. In this section, you'll find clearly labeled chapters—each explaining the key features of your iPhone 4. You'll see that most chapters focus on an individual app or a specific type of application. Many of the chapters discuss applications that come with your iPhone 4, but we also include some fun and useful apps you can download from the App Store. Sure, the iPhone 4 is for fun, but it's for a whole lot more, too. We finish with some handy troubleshooting tips that can help if your iPhone 4 isn't working quite right.

Chapter 1

Getting Started

In this chapter we will take you on a step-by-step tour of your new iPhone 4 and everything you get in the box. We will also look at the ins and outs of charging it and how to make your battery last longer. In order to get started with your iPhone, you need to connect it to iTunes to get it activated and registered. In our iPhone Basics section at the end of this chapter, we will show you the basics of how to maneuver on your iPhone so you can get up and running quickly.

Getting to Know Your iPhone

In this section we show you how to use everything you get in the box with your iPhone 4. We also give you some iPhone battery and charging tips, and then talk about how to determine if your iPhone is already activated and the **Slide to Unlock** feature.

What Is Included in the Box

While the box may seem skimpy to most people new to iPhones, it does contain everything you need to get started and enjoy your iPhone, except for a good manual—which is why we wrote this book!

iPhone: On the very top, as soon as you open it, you see your new iPhone.

Paper folder: Under the plastic holder for the iPhone you will find a paper folder, which contains the following:

> **Finger Tips**: A 4.5" x 2.5" small fold-out booklet with 19 panels of basic information on your iPhone

> **iPhone 4 Product Information Guide**: A 4.5" x 2.5" booklet with font that is way too small to read, containing all the legal terms, conditions, warnings, and disclaimers related to your iPhone

> **Apple Logo Stickers**: You get two of those nice white Apple logos that you sometimes see on car windows. Enjoy!

In the bottom of the box you will find the following, as shown in Figure 1–1.

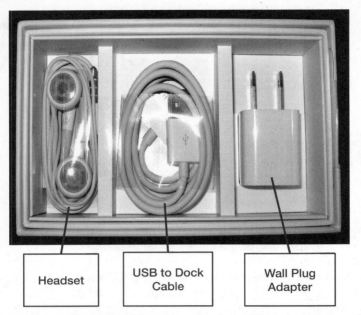

Figure 1–1. *The headset, USB cable, and wall plug adapter in the bottom of the box.*

iPhone Headset

The headset consists of two white earphones for listening to music, videos, or phone calls, and a small controller attached to the wire to the right earphone. Plug this into the hole on the top left edge of your iPhone. Make sure it is all the way inserted—it can be a little tough to press in.

As the image here shows, the controller has a plus (+) and minus (-) key as well as a **Center** button. You can increase or decrease volume with the (+) and (-) keys and use the **Center** button to answer or hang up phone calls.

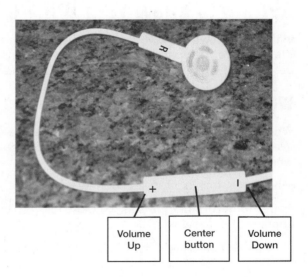

NOTE: You can move between songs with two or three clicks of the **Center** button. Double-click to go to the next track. Triple-click to go to the previous track.

The included headset also contains a small microphone for phone calls.

USB to Dock Cable

This is your cable to connect to your computer, and it also doubles as your power cable.

Wall Plug Adapter

This has a USB socket on one end and a plug on the other end to plug into an electrical outlet socket. Just connect the USB cable to your iPhone and the other end to the wall plug to charge your iPhone from the wall.

How to Remove or Install the SIM Card

In order to place or receive phone calls, you need to have a SIM card (Subscriber Identity Module card) installed in your iPhone. Every new iPhone should already have a SIM card pre-installed.

NOTE: iPhone 4 uses the new MicroSIM standard, like the iPad—not the MiniSIM, like previous iPhones.

There may be times when you want to remove and replace the SIM card—for example, if you are travelling internationally, or if you just received a replacement iPhone and want to swap SIM cards from your old one.

TIP: When you travel internationally, using a local SIM card in your iPhone may save money. With international voice and data roaming rates, international travel with your iPhone can be surprisingly expensive. Check out the "Travelling Internationally" section of Chapter 5, "Wi-Fi and 3G Connectivity," for more information.

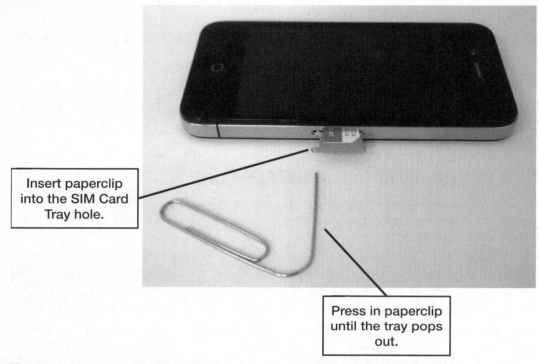

Insert paperclip into the SIM Card Tray hole.

Press in paperclip until the tray pops out.

Figure 1–2. *Insert a paperclip into the SIM Card Tray hole to eject and remove the SIM Card*

1. Insert the paperclip into the hole on the right side of your iPhone. See Figure 1–2.

2. Press the paperclip straight into the hole until the **SIM Card Tray** pops out.

3. Remove the tray so you can remove or replace the SIM card.

4. When inserting a SIM card, make sure the SIM card is installed with the notch facing the top right of the holder. It should sit flush in the holder with the metal contacts facing the bottom of the holder.

5. Slide the **SIM Card Tray** back into the iPhone until it clicks into place.

Antenna Issues with iPhone 4

There is an issue that exists (and has been acknowledged by Apple) that results in a decrease of the wireless signal strength bars when you hold the iPhone in a certain manner. The problem is located around the gap between the two sections of the metal antenna on the lower left hand side of the phone.

How to resolve this issue?

■   Try not to press hard (don't death grip it) when you hold the phone on a call.

- Don't make contact between your hand and the line that separates the antenna on the left hand side of the phone.

- Get a free case that using the **Case Program** app from Apple. (see next section.)

- Purchase a case that covers the metal antenna.

Using the Free Apple Case Program App

To get your free case, use the Case Program from the App Store.

> **NOTE:** You must use this free case program within 30 days of your iPhone purchase and you must purchase your iPhone before September 30, 2010.

1. Do a search in the App Store for "iPhone 4 case" to locate the Case Program.

2. Download and install the free **Case Program** app.

3. Tap the **Case Program** icon to start it.

4. Tap the Get Started button and log in with your iTunes password.

5. Tap any case to view details and images of each case option.

6. Tap the **Photo Gallery** tab to see pictures of the case.

7. If you like the case, tap the **Select** button.

8. Verify your shipping address and tap the **Place Order** button from the top of the page.

9. Finally, you will see an order confirmation saying estimated time to ship. At publishing time, the lead time was about 3-5 weeks.

Charging Your iPhone and Battery Life Tips

Your iPhone may already have some battery life, but you might want to charge it completely so you can enjoy uninterrupted hours of use after you get it set up. This charging time will give you a chance to check out the rest of this chapter, install or update iTunes, or check out all the cool iPhone apps in Chapter 26, "The Amazing App Store."

Charging from the Power Outlet

The fastest way to charge your iPhone is to plug it directly into the wall outlet. You use the same USB connection cable used to connect your iPhone to your computer. As shown here, plug the wide end of the cable into the port at the bottom of your iPhone (next to the **Home** button) and the USB cable end into the **Wall Plug Adapter**. Then plug into any wall outlet.

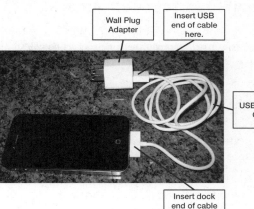

You know your iPhone is charging by looking at the screen. You will see a lightning bolt or plug icon inside the battery indicator in the upper right corner.

The main battery icon will show your charge level. See the image here, which shows a charging iPhone with an almost-full battery.

> **TIP:** Some newer cars have built-in power outlets just like in your home, where you can plug in your iPhone power cord. Some also have a Dock option that allows you to control the **iPod** app from your car radio headset. These outlets are sometimes buried in the middle console behind the front seat.

Charging from Your Computer

You can also charge your iPhone when you plug it into your computer, albeit a little slower than when directly connected to the wall charger.

> **TIP:** Try different USB ports of your computer. Some USB ports share a bus and have less power, while others have their own bus and more power.

For best charging, you should have your computer plugged into the wall outlet. If your computer is not connected to the wall power outlet, your iPhone will charge, but at a slower rate.

Keep in mind that if your laptop computer goes to sleep or you close the screen, your iPhone will stop charging.

> **TIP:** You can show the actual percentage of battery life remaining. To do this, tap your **Settings** icon, then **General**, then **Usage**, and turn **Battery Percentage** to **On**.

Charging from Other Accessories

Some accessories designed to work with your iPhone will also charge it. The most common of these are iPhone/iPod music docks. These are speaker systems that you plug into your iPhone to listen to your music. The only time your iPhone will not charge is when you see the warning message on your screen saying, "Charging is not supported with this accessory." This occurs on older accessories, or those not designed specifically for your iPhone.

> **TIP:** A Case and External Battery Combined.
>
> Some cases actually have external batteries built into the case. There are several manufacturers available. One provider, Mophie (www.mophie.com), has produced such cases for previous iPhone models and is currently developing an iPhone 4 battery with case called a "Juice Pack."

Expected Battery Life

Apple says the iPhone 4 battery should last longer than the iPhone 3Gs with its bigger battery and advanced technology. See Table 1–1.

Table 1–1. *Battery Life Specifications from Apple.*

Talk Time	7 hours of talk time on 3G
(Talking on the phone or using FaceTime video chat)	14 hours of talk time on 2G
	TIP: To use 2G instead of 3G, you have to turn off 3G. Go to **Settings** > **General** > **Network** > Set **Enable 3G** to **Off**. See Chapter 5 for more details on using 3G, 2G, and Wi-Fi.
Internet Use	6 hours of Internet use on 3G
(Browsing the Internet with Safari)	10 hours of Internet use on Wi-Fi
Video Playback	10 hours of video playback
Audio Playback	40 hours of audio playback
Standby Time	300 hours when in Sleep mode

These battery life durations are in ideal conditions with a new, fully charged battery. You will notice that over time, your actual battery life will diminish.

Battery and Charging Tips

The key question is, how do you get the most out of your battery life and make sure your iPhone is charged and ready for you when you need it? In this section we cover a few tips to help you accomplish this.

Getting More Out of Each Charge

To extend your battery life, try some of the following tips.

1. **Lower your screen brightness**: Tap **Settings** and then **Brightness**. Use the slider bar to lower your brightness to a level less than halfway across that still works for you.

2. **Turn off Location Services**: If you don't need your actual location to be transmitted to your apps, you can turn this off. Tap **Settings**, then **General**, and **Location Services**. Set **Location Services** to **Off**. If you go into an app that wants your location, then you will be reminded to turn it back on.

3. **Set a Shorter Auto-Lock**: Shortening the time your iPhone takes to turn off the screen when not being used and go into sleep mode can help save your battery. To do this, tap **Settings**, then **General**, and **Auto-Lock**. Set **Auto-Lock** as short as possible—you can set as short as **1 minute** if you like.

4. **Turn off push email** and push notifications.

5. Learn more about battery life tips from the Apple web site at `http://www.apple.com/batteries/iphone.html`.

Making the Battery Last Longer

The iPhone uses a rechargeable battery that will lose its ability to maintain a charge over time and has only a limited number of cycles during its useful life. You can extend the life of your iPhone battery by making sure you run it down completely at least once a month. The rechargeable battery will last longer if you do this complete draining once a month.

Finding More Places to Charge Up

No matter what you do, if you really use your iPhone a lot, you will want to find more places and more ways to charge it up. Besides using your power cord or connecting it to your computer, Table 1–2 shows you some other options.

Table 1–2. *Other Places and Ways to Charge Your iPhone*

Airport Charging Station	Most airports have wall sockets available today where you can top-off your iPhone while you are waiting for your flight. Some airports have labeled "charging stations," and others simply have wall sockets that may even be hidden behind chairs or other objects. You may have to do a bit of hunting to beat out all those other power-hungry travelers!
External Battery Pack	This accessory allows you to extend the life of your iPhone battery by five times or more. You can buy them for about US $40–65. Do a web search for "external iPhone battery" to find all the latest and greatest options.
Car Charger	If you are using your iPhone heavily for phone calls during the day, you may want to invest in a car charger or another way to give your iPhone a little more juice in the middle of a long day. These chargers plug directly into the cigarette lighter socket in your car. These run about US $15–25.
Car Power Inverter	If you are taking a long car trip, you can buy a power inverter to convert your 12V car power outlets into a power outlet where you can plug in your iPhone charger. Do a web search for "power inverter for cars" to find many options for under US $50. This is a small price to pay for hours of enjoyment on your iPhone!
Charge in Other Accessories	As we mentioned, you can also charge your iPhone in many accessories designed to do other things, like play your music over speakers. You need to look for the plug or lightning bolt icons to make sure your iPhone is charging in these accessories.

iTunes and Your iPhone

Now that you know some of the basics about your iPhone and how to get the most out of your battery, you are ready to start enjoying it. Connecting it to iTunes is the next step. iTunes allows you to activate and register your iPhone and tie it to your Apple ID (iTunes account). Once you do that, you can buy songs, movies, books, and just about anything else right from your iPhone or in iTunes on your computer.

You can also use iTunes to load up your music and videos and even backup your iPhone and later restore it. If you don't have iTunes, you will need to install the latest version (9.2 at time of writing).

Knowing If You Need to Activate Your iPhone

You need to connect your iPhone to iTunes to activate it if you see the black screen similar to the one here, showing the USB cable plugging into iTunes, and only emergency calls are allowed.

Skip to the "iTunes and Your iPhone" section later in this chapter to find out how to get your iPhone going.

Slide to Unlock and Your Home Screen

Once your iPhone has been activated, you will see the Slide to Unlock screen, as shown in Figure 1–3. Touch your finger to the screen and follow the path of the arrow to slide the unlock button to the right.

Once you do that, you will see your Home screen.

Notice that the four icons locked in the Bottom Dock (Figure 1–3, bottom-right) do not move while the rest of the icons can move back and forth in "pages." Learn how to move your favorite icons into the Bottom Dock in our "Moving Icons" section in Chapter 7.

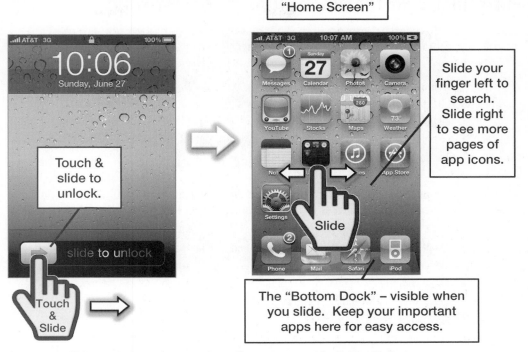

Figure 1–3. *Slide to unlock, moving around your Home screen and the Bottom Dock*

Install or Upgrade iTunes on Your Computer

If you do not have iTunes loaded on your computer, then open a web browser and go to www.itunes.com/download. Download the software from the link provided.

TIP: We have detailed instructions showing you how to install iTunes in the "How to Download and Install iTunes" section and also how to upgrade iTunes in the "iTunes Upgrade" section in Chapter 30, "iTunes User Guide."

If you already have iTunes installed on your computer, you should check to see if an updated version is available. Version 9.2 was the latest at publishing time.

1. Start iTunes.

2. If you are a Windows user, select **Help** from the menu, and then **Check for Updates**.

3. If you are a Mac user, select **iTunes** from the menu, and then **Check for Updates**.

4. If an update is available, then follow the instructions to update iTunes.

Connecting Your iPhone to iTunes the First Time

Once you have installed or upgraded to iTunes version 9.2 or higher, you are ready to connect your iPhone to iTunes on your computer.

> **TIP:** Using the iTunes Home Sharing feature, you can share your purchased content from the same iTunes account (music, apps, videos, iBooks, and more) across authorized computers on your home network. Also, any of the same content can be synced to any iPod/iPhone/iPhone under the same iTunes account. Learn more about syncing content using iTunes in Chapter 3, "Sync with iTunes," and learn about Home Sharing in Chapter 30, "iTunes User Guide."

By connecting your iPhone to iTunes, you will register or associate your iPhone (via the device serial number) to a particular iTunes account (Apple ID).

> **TIP:** The bonus of this approach is that if you have purchased apps for another iPhone or iPod touch and other content (music, videos, and more), then you can run all those apps on your new iPhone! Note that all content you sync to your iPhone has to originate from a single computer. So you need to select your "main" computer to sync with your iPhone.

If you do not yet have an iTunes Account (Apple ID), we will show you how to create one.

Start Up iTunes

If iTunes is not already running, double-click the **iTunes** icon on your desktop.

- Mac users, you may have to click the **Finder** icon, select the **Go** menu, and then select **Applications** to look for iTunes. (The Mac shortcut is **Shift**+**Command**+**A** to get to Applications.)

- Windows users, click on the **Start** menu or **Windows logo** in the lower left corner, select **All Programs**, and then select **iTunes**.

After you start iTunes, it should open, with the left and main window nav bars looking similar to the image shown in Figure 1–4. The main window content may look quite different.

Figure 1–4. *iTunes software main window (selections shown: iTunes Store and App Store)*

NOTE: What is shown in the main window on your iTunes will look quite different depending on what you select in the left navigation bar and the top navigation bar. In Figure 1–4, the **iTunes Store** is selected in the left nav bar and the **App Store** is selected in the main nav bar so we see **App Store**–related content in the main window.

Registering or Activating Your iPhone the First Time

Once you have iTunes installed or updated on your computer, you are ready to connect your iPhone for the first time and get it registered or activated so you can start using it.

NOTE: If your iPhone has already been registered (you see the "Slide to Unlock" message or your Home screen of icons when you tap the **Home** button on the bottom of your device), then you can skip this Registration section and jump to the "Set Up Your iPhone" section later in this chapter.

1. Start up iTunes on your computer.

2. Connect your iPhone to your computer, as shown in Figure 1–5. Plug in the wide end of the white USB cable to the bottom port on your iPhone and the small USB connector end into an available USB port on your computer.

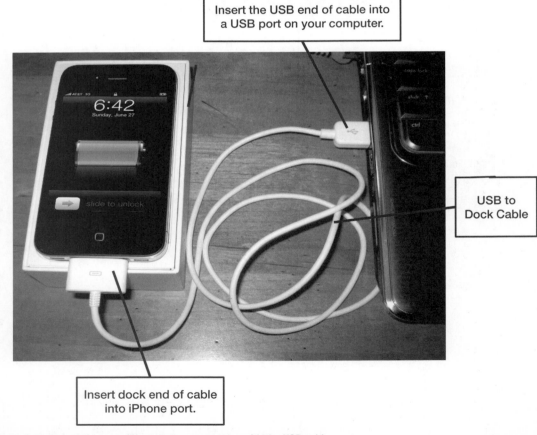

Insert the USB end of cable into a USB port on your computer.

USB to Dock Cable

Insert dock end of cable into iPhone port.

Figure 1–5. *Connecting your iPhone to your computer with the USB cable*

NOTE: You need to use the USB cable instead of Bluetooth or Wi-Fi to connect your iPhone to iTunes on your computer.

3. When you connect your iPhone to your computer the first time, your Windows computer should automatically install the necessary drivers. If you are on a Mac computer, you may see messages recommending you upgrade to the latest version of the operating system before using your iPhone. Follow the steps shown on the screen to complete the process.

4. In order to see the Setup screen you may need to click **iPhone** under **DEVICES** in the left nav bar. Then you should see the new iPhone Setup screen, as shown in Figure 1–6.

Figure 1–6. *iPhone first time setup window in iTunes after clicking on "iPhone" in the left navigation bar*

5. Click the **Continue** button to see the Apple iPhone License Agreement, as shown in Figure 1–7.

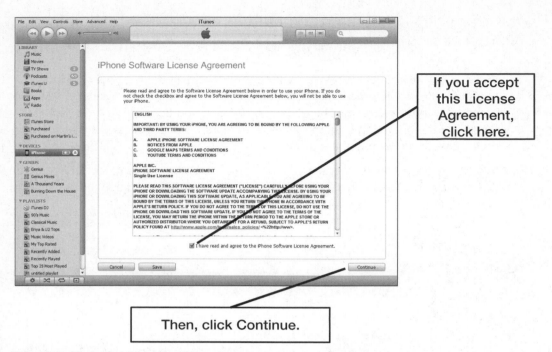

Figure 1–7. *iPhone first time setup License Agreement screen*

6. In order to continue, check the box under the license agreement and click the **Continue** button.

7. You will then be given the opportunity to sign in using your Apple ID or create a new Apple ID (Figure 1–8).

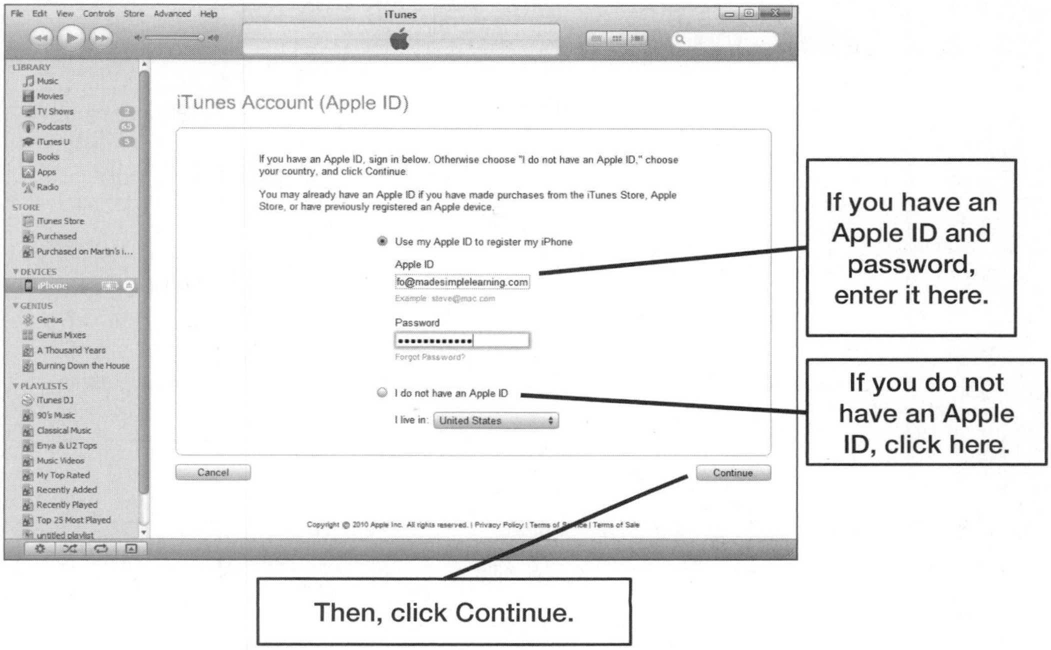

Figure 1–8. *iPhone first time setup login or create Apple ID*

8. Enter your Apple ID and password or click I do not have an Apple ID and select your country.

9. Then click the Continue button.

   ■ If you tried to enter your Apple ID and password and received an error message about "additional security information is required," then read the "Troubleshooting: Fixing the Apple ID Security Error" section in Chapter 30, "iTunes User Guide."

10. You should now see the Registration screen shown in Figure 1–9.

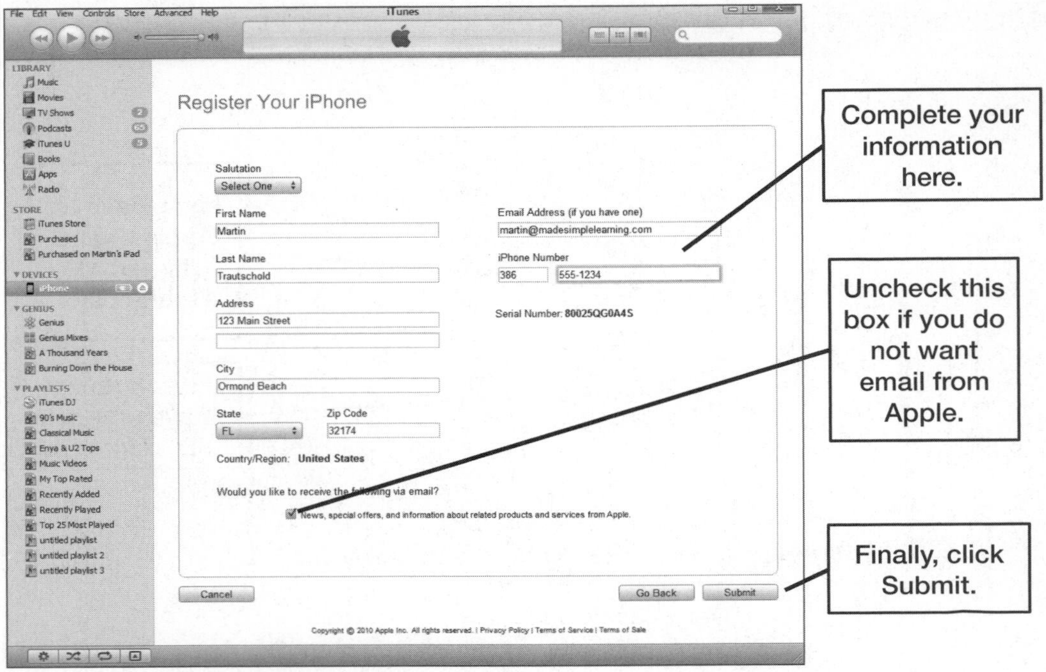

Figure 1–9. *iPhone Registration screen, without an Apple ID*

11. Type in your information and click **Submit** to complete your registration.

If everything has been entered correctly, you will see either the MobileMe ad (Figure 1–10) or the Set Up Your iPhone screen (Figure 1–11).

Apple's MobileMe Sync Service

After registering your iPhone for the first time, you will probably see a screen advertising MobileMe, as shown in Figure 1–10.

Figure 1–10. *iTunes MobileMe ad page (usually appears after registering your iPhone)*

To keep setting up your iPhone, click the **No Thanks** button to continue to the next screen.

What is MobileMe?

MobileMe is free for a limited time (currently 60 days), and then it costs US $99.00 for a single user or US $149.00 for a family plan. MobileMe provides a way to keep your email, contacts, calendar, web bookmarks shared across all your computers and mobile devices. You can even use MobileMe to locate a missing iPhone! At publishing time, photo sharing is limited to Mac computers with MobileMe iPhoto folders. See our MobileMe Tour section in Chapter 5, "Other Sync Methods."

Set Up Your iPhone

After your registration is complete, the first time you connect your iPhone, you will see the screen shown in Figure 1–11.

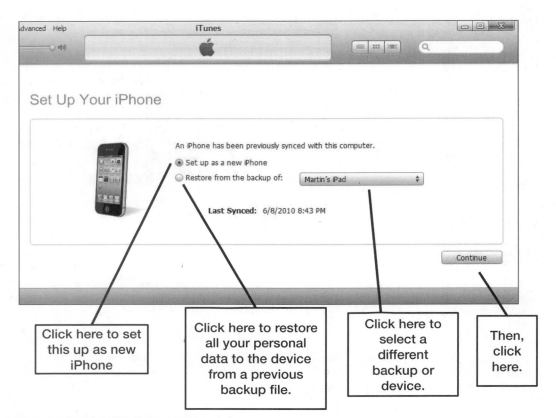

Figure 1–11. *Set Up Your iPhone screen*

1. If you would like to set this up as a new iPhone, do the following:

   a. Click the selection next to Set up as a new iPhone.

   b. Click the Continue button and skip to Step 3.

   NOTE: If you want to keep your existing iPhone and/or iPod touch and set up your new iPhone, then you should select **Setup a New iPhone**, as shown.

2. If you would like to restore from a backup of another iPhone or device (iPad/iPod touch), do the following:

CAUTION: We have heard of people experiencing problems (lock-ups, lower battery life, etc.) when they restored a backup from a non-iPhone (iPad/iPod touch) to the iPhone. Also, selecting **Restore** here assumes you have first made a backup of your old device (iPad/iPod touch) in order to restore the latest information to your new iPhone.

    a. Click the button next to Restore from the backup of.

    b. Select the particular backup file from the drop-down menu.

    c. Click the **Continue** button to restore data to your iPhone from the backup file.

    d. Now you are done with the initial setup of your iPhone.

3. As shown in Figure 1–12, you have the option of naming your iPhone and setting up basic sync options in iTunes.

4. Give your iPhone a **Name**. Each time you plug in your iPhone—to this or any other computer—your iPhone will show the name you choose here. In this case, we will call this one **Martin's iPhone**.

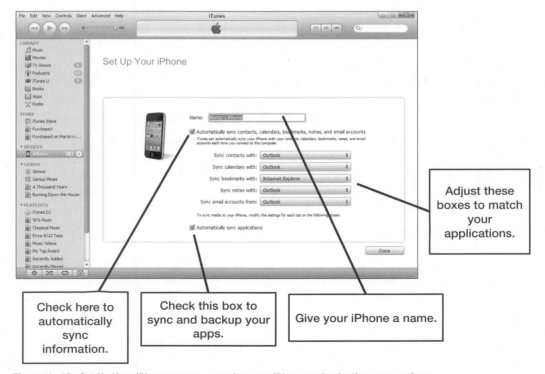

Figure 1–12. *Set Up Your iPhone screen—naming your iPhone and selecting sync options*

TIP: To Get Moving Quickly and Not Sync Anything

The first sync to your iPhone can take a long time (15 minutes or more). If you want to start playing with your new iPhone quickly, uncheck both boxes shown in Figure 1–12 and click **Done**. Don't worry—you can check or uncheck these boxes in iTunes later. We show you the details in Chapter 3, "Sync Your iPhone with iTunes."

5. To use iTunes to sync information between your computer and your iPhone, leave the box checked next to Automatically sync contacts, calendars, bookmarks, notes and email accounts.

6. To adjust the application selected to sync or turn off the sync, click the drop-down next to the item and select the appropriate action. In the image shown here, we are changing our bookmarks sync to **none** because we don't want to sync bookmarks.

CAUTION: Your iPhone does not have as much memory as your computer, so be careful selecting **automatically sync** when you have thousands of songs, photos, or videos in your computer iTunes library.

7. Leave the box checked next to **Automatically sync applications**, if you would like applications you purchase on your iPhone backed up to your computer. We recommend leaving this checked. This option allows you to update apps from iTunes on your computer and be able to manage and arrange your app icons and Home screens using iTunes on your computer.

8. Click **Done** to complete the Set Up screen.

Setup Complete: The iPhone Summary Screen

Once you confirm your choices and click **Done** (Figure 1–12), you will be taken to the main Summary screen (Figure 1–13).

Figure 1–13. *iPhone Summary screen in iTunes*

Maintaining Your iPhone

Now that you have set up your iPhone with iTunes, you will want to know how to safely clean the screen and then keep it protected with various cases.

Cleaning Your iPhone Screen

After using your iPhone a little while, you will see that your fingers (or other fingers besides yours) have left smudges and oil on the formerly pristine screen. You will want to know how to safely clean the screen. One way to keep the screen cleaner throughout the day is to place a protective screen cover on the iPhone, which may also have the added benefit of cutting down on glare (discussed in the next section).

We also recommend the following:

1. Turn off your iPhone by pressing and holding the **Sleep/Power** key on the top edge, and then use the slider to turn it off.

2. Remove any cables, such as the USB sync cable.

3. Rub the screen with a dry soft lint-free cloth (like a cloth supplied to clean eyeglasses or something similar).

4. If the dry cloth does not work, then try adding a very little bit of water to dampen the cloth. If you use a damp cloth, try not to get any water in the openings.

> **CAUTION:** Never use household cleaners, abrasive cleaners such as SoftScrub, or ammonia-based cleaners such as Windex, alcohol, aerosol sprays, or solvents.

Cases and Protective Covers for Your iPhone

Once you have your iPhone in your hands you will notice how beautifully it is constructed. You will also notice that it can be fairly slippery and could slip out of your hands, rock around a bit, or have the back get scratched when you are typing on it.

We recommend buying a protective case for your iPhone. Average cases run about US $10–40 and fancy leather cases can cost US $100 or more. Spending a little to protect your iPhone, which costs $200 or more, makes good sense.

Where to Buy Your Covers

You can purchase your iPhone protective cover at any of the following locations.

- Amazon.com (www.amazon.com)
- The Apple Accessory Store: (http://store.apple.com)

- iLounge: (http://ilounge.pricegrabber.com)
- TiPB – The iPhone + iPad Blog Store (http://store.tipb.com/)

You could also do a web search for "iPhone cases" or "iPhone protective covers."

> **TIP:** You *may* be able to use a case designed for another type of smartphone for your iPhone. If you go this route in order to save some money, just make sure your iPhone fits securely in the case or cover.

What to Buy . . .

The following sections provide some types of cases and price ranges to choose from.

> **TIP:** Get a free case from Apple if you purchase your iPhone before September 30, 2010 and you use the Case app within 30 days of purchase. See the "Using the Free Apple Case Program App" section earlier in this chapter. This is because of the antenna reception issue also noted earlier in this chapter.

Rubber / Silicone Cases ($10–30)

What these do: Provide a cushioned grip, absorb iPhone bumps and bruises, and isolate the edges of the phone (antennas) from your fingers.

Pros: Inexpensive, colorful and comfortable to hold. Prevent your fingers from interfering with the iPhone antennas, which are the metal edges of the phone

Cons: Not as professional as a leather case

Combined Cases with External Battery Packs ($50-80)

What these do: They combine the protective features of a hard shell case with a rechargeable external battery pack.   Manufacturers such as Mophie and Case-Mate are busy working on iPhone 4 versions of these cases, hopefully by the time you read this book, they are available.

Pros: Protect your iPhone; receive a tremendous boost in your battery life – some boast 50% or more battery life.

Cons: Adds weight and bulk to the phone.

Waterproof Cases ($10–40)

What these do: Provide waterproof protection for your iPhone and allow you to safely use the iPhone near water (in the rain, at the pool, at the beach, on the boat, etc.)

TIP: If you like to row or paddle, then you will want a waterproof case. Check out the **SpeedCoach Mobile** app. You can buy this app for about $65 from the App Store.

Pros: Provide good water protection

Cons: May make the touch screen harder to use, usually do not protect from drops or bumps

Hard Plastic / Metal Case ($20–40)

What these do: Provide hard, solid protection against scratches and bumps and short drops

Pros: Provide good protection

Cons: Add some bulk and weight. You may need to remove when charging because the iPhone might become overheated.

Leather or Special Cases ($50–100+)

What these do: Provide more of a luxury feel and protect the iPhone

Pros: Leather luxury feel, protects the front and the back

Cons: More expensive, add bulk and weight

Screen Glass and Back Glass Protectors ($5–40)

What these do: Protect the screen and back of the iPhone from scratches

Pros: Help prolong life of your iPhone, protect against scratches, most decrease screen glare

Cons: Some may increase glare or may affect touch sensitivity of the screen.

iPhone Basics

Now that you have your iPhone charged, with a clean screen, registered, and decked out with a new protective case, let's take a look at some of the basics to help you get around with the software.

Powering On/Off and Sleep/Wake

To power on your iPhone, press and hold the **Power/Sleep** button on the top edge of the iPhone for a few seconds (Figure 1–14). Simply tapping this button quickly won't power on the iPhone if it is completely off—you really need to hold it until you see the iPhone power on.

When you are no longer using your iPhone, you have two options: you can either put it into sleep mode or turn it off completely.

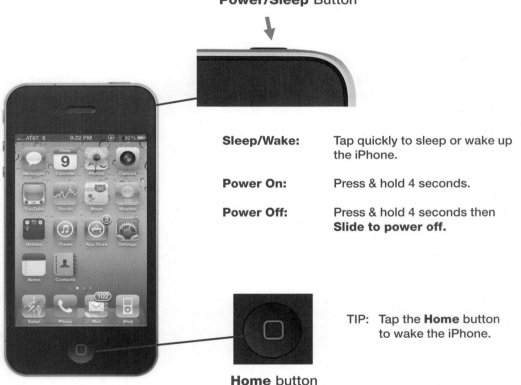

Power/Sleep Button

Sleep/Wake: Tap quickly to sleep or wake up the iPhone.

Power On: Press & hold 4 seconds.

Power Off: Press & hold 4 seconds then **Slide to power off.**

TIP: Tap the **Home** button to wake the iPhone.

Home button

Figure 1–14. *Power/Sleep button and Home button*

The advantage of sleep mode is that when you want to use your iPhone again, just a quick tap of the **Power/Sleep** button or the **Home** button will bring your iPhone back awake. According to Apple, the iPhone has up to a month of stand-by power.

If you want to maximize your battery or if you know you won't be using your iPhone for quite some time—say when you go to sleep—you should turn it off completely. The way to do this is to press and hold the **Power/Sleep** button until you see the **Slide to Power Off** bar appear. Just slide the bar to the right and the iPhone will power off.

Moving Around Inside Apps and Your Settings Screens

Getting around the screens inside the apps on your iPhone is as simple as tapping on the screen. See Figure 1–15.

1. Tap any icon to start the app. Tap the **Settings** icon to start the **Settings** app.

2. Touch **General** to see the General settings.

3. Touch **Network** to see Network settings.

4. Any switch is set by tapping it. So, next to **Data Roaming**, touch the **OFF** switch to turn it **On**.

5. To go back a level in the screens, you touch the button in the upper left corner. In this case you would touch the **General** button to get out of the Network Settings screen.

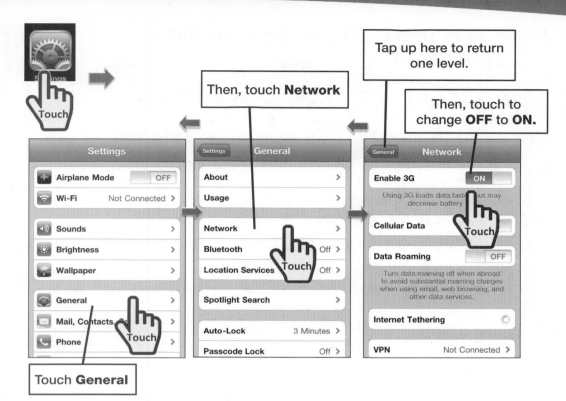

Figure 1–15. *Navigating around icons and settings screens*

The Home Button

 The button you will use most often is your **Home** button (Figure 1–14). This button will begin everything you do with your iPhone and also jump out of every app back to your Home screen. If your iPhone is sleeping, press the **Home** button once to wake up your iPhone (assuming it is in sleep mode).

Pressing the **Home** button will take you out of any application program and bring you back to your Home screen.

TIP: Double-tapping your **Home** button launches the fast app switcher. If the phone is locked and playing music, a double tap will launch the iPod controls.

Multitask by Double-Clicking the Home Button

To multitask, you simply double-click the **Home** button.

> **TIP:** We have more details on multitasking in Chapter 8, "Multitasking and Voice Control."

1. While in any app or from the Home screen, try double-clicking the **Home** button. See Figure 1–16.

2. You will see a small bar of icons appear in the bottom row. These represent the apps that you have started since you powered on your iPhone.

3. Tap any icon to return to that app.

4. Swipe your finger left or right to see more icons.

5. Swipe all the way to the left to see an additional set of controls for the iPod and to lock the screen in Portrait (vertical) orientation.

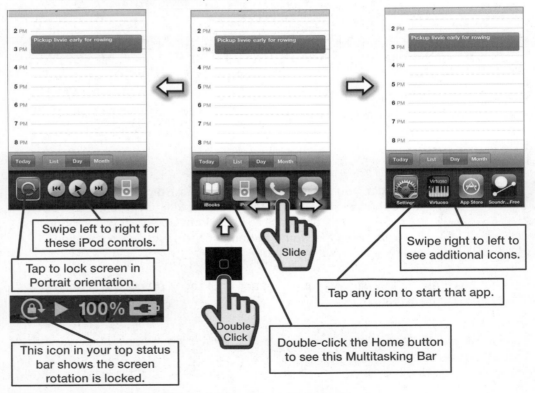

Figure 1–16. *Double-clicking the Home button to see the multitasking bar*

Volume Keys for Ringer and Audio/Video Playback

Located on the upper left-hand side of the iPhone (Figure 1–17), these are simple **Volume Up/Volume Down** keys that you will find very handy.

Ringer Volume

If you are not playing a song, video, or other content, pressing these **Volume** keys will adjust the volume of your phone ringer.

Muting the Phone Ringer

You have a switch just above the **Volume** keys on the left side of your iPhone. Slide the **Ringer Mute** switch to the back of the iPhone to turn it on. You will see a little orange next to the switch when the mute is on. To turn off the mute, simply slide the switch back toward the front of the iPhone. See Figure 1–17.

Adjusting Playback or Phone Voice Volume

When you are listening to music, video, or other content, or when you are on a phone call, you can use the **Volume** keys to raise or lower the volume. When listening to music or videos, you can also use the on-screen slider bar to adjust volume. See Figure 1–17.

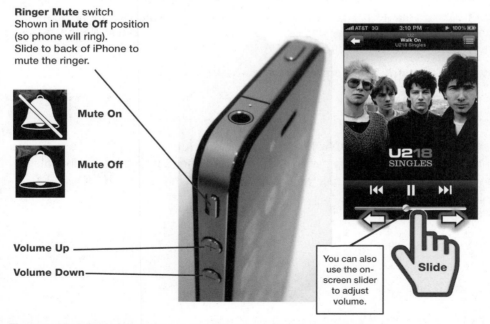

Ringer Mute switch
Shown in **Mute Off** position
(so phone will ring).
Slide to back of iPhone to
mute the ringer.

Mute On

Mute Off

Volume Up

Volume Down

You can also use the on-screen slider to adjust volume.

Slide

Figure 1–17. *Adjusting the volume on your iPhone or muting the phone ringer*

Locking Your Screen in Portrait (Vertical) Orientation

As you tilt your iPhone on its side, in some apps, you will notice that the iPhone screen rotates to horizontal or landscape orientation. You might want this in order to get the larger landscape keyboard for typing. There may be times when you don't want your screen to rotate from portrait orientation when you turn your iPhone on its side. For these occasions, you can lock the screen in portrait orientation. See Figure 1–16.

1. Double-click the **Home** button.

2. Swipe left to right to see the iPod and screen lock controls.

3. Touch the **Portrait Orientation Lock** button in the left end of icons.

4. To disable the lock, tap the same button again.

> **TIP:** This is a great way to read iBooks in bed. If you prefer the larger page view in portrait mode, enable Portrait Orientation Lock. This way when you set your iPhone on your lap or hold it almost flat, the screen will not accidentally rotate to landscape mode. Check out Chapter 14, "iBooks and e-Books," for more.

Adjust or Disable the Auto-Lock Time-Out Feature

You will notice that your iPhone will auto-lock and go into sleep mode with the screen blank after a short amount of time. You can change this time or even disable this feature altogether inside the **Settings** icon.

1. Touch the **Settings** icon from your Home screen.

2. Touch **General**.

3. Touch **Auto-Lock**.

4. You will see your current Auto-Lock setting next to Auto-Lock on this page (Figure 1–18). The default setting is that the iPhone locks after 3 minutes of sitting idle (to save battery life.) You can change this to **1**, **2**, **3**, **4**, **5** minutes, or **Never**.

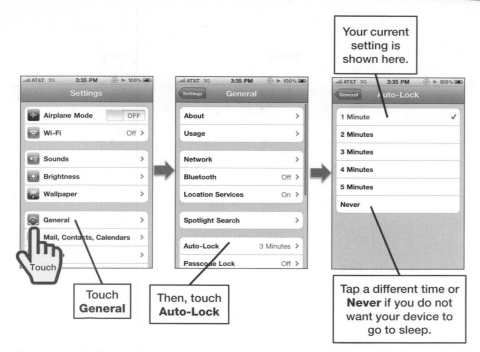

Figure 1–18. *Settings to adjust or remove the time-out for the Auto-Lock feature*

5. Touch the desired setting to select it—you know it's selected when you see the checkmark next to it.

6. Then, touch the **General** button in the upper left-hand corner to get back to the General screen. You should see your change now reflected next to **Auto-Lock**.

> **BATTERY LIFE TIP:**
> Setting the Auto-Lock shorter (e.g., 1 minute) will help you save battery life.

Adjusting the Date, Time, Time Zone, and 24-Hour Format

Usually, the date and time is either set for you or adjusts when you connect your iPhone to your computer, which we cover in Chapter 3, "Sync Your iPhone with iTunes." You can, however, manually adjust your date and time quite easily. You may want to do this when you are traveling with your iPhone and need to adjust the time zone when you land.

1. Touch the **Settings** icon.

2. Touch **General**.

3. Scroll down and touch **Date & Time** to see the Date & Time settings screen.

4. If you prefer to see **09:30** and **14:30** instead of **9:30 AM** and **2:30 PM**, respectively, then tap the **24-Hour Time** setting switch to **On**.

5. To set the date and time manually, you have to turn off the automatic time setting feature. Tap the switch next to **Set Automatically** and set it to **Off**.

6. To set your time zone, tap **Time Zone** and type in the name of a major city in your time zone. The iPhone will show you matching city names as you type.

7. When you see the correct city in your time zone, tap it to select it. In the image here, we typed the first few letters of **Chicago** until we saw it appear. Then we tapped **Chicago, U.S.A.** to select it.

8. After selecting the city, you are brought back to the main Date & Time screen with your selected city shown next to **Time Zone**.

9. Tap **Set Date & Time** to adjust your date and time.

10. On this screen you can set the date and time.

11. To adjust the date, tap the date at the top of the screen.

12. To adjust the time, tap the time at the top of the screen.

13. Adjusting the date and time is then done by touching and sliding the wheels up or down as shown in the image here.

14. When you are done, tap the **Date & Time** button in the upper left corner.

Adjusting the Brightness

Your iPhone has an **Auto-Brightness** control available, which is turned on by default. This uses the built-in light sensor to adjust the brightness of the screen. When it is darker outside or nighttime, then the auto-brightness control will dim the screen. When it is bright and sunny, the screen will be automatically brightened so it is easier to read. Generally, we advise that you keep this set to **On**.

If you want to adjust the brightness, use the controls in your **Settings** app.

1. From your Home screen, touch the **Settings** icon.

2. Then touch **Brightness**.

3. Move the slider control to adjust the brightness.

4. Set the switch next to Auto-Brightness to turn it **On** or **Off**.

TIP: Setting the brightness lower will help you save battery life. A little less than halfway across seems to work fine.

Chapter 2

Typing Tips, Copy/Paste and Search

In this chapter, we show you some good ways to type and save valuable time typing on your iPhone, whether you use the portrait (vertical/smaller) keyboard or the landscape (horizontal/larger) keyboard. You will learn how to select different language keyboards, how to type symbols, and other tips.

Later in this chapter, we will show you about the spotlight search and the Copy and Paste function. Copy and Paste will save you lots of time as well as increase accuracy when working with your iPhone.

Typing on Your iPhone

You will quickly find two on-screen keyboards on your iPhone: the smaller one visible when you hold your iPhone in a vertical orientation, and the larger landscape keyboard when you hold the iPhone in a horizontal orientation. The nice thing is that you can choose whichever keyboard works best for you.

Typing on the Screen with Two Thumbs

You will find when you first start out with your iPhone that you can most easily type with one finger—usually your index finger—while holding the iPhone with the other hand.

After a little while, you should be able to experiment with thumb typing (like you see so many people doing with other phones such as the BlackBerry smartphones). Once you practice a little, typing with two thumbs instead of a single finger will really boost your speed. Just be patient, it does take practice to become proficient typing quickly with your two thumbs.

You will actually notice after a while that the keyboard touch sensitivity assumes you are typing with two thumbs. What this means is that the letters on the left side of your keyboard are meant to be pressed on their left side, and the keys on the right are meant to be touched/pressed on their right side (Figure 2–1).

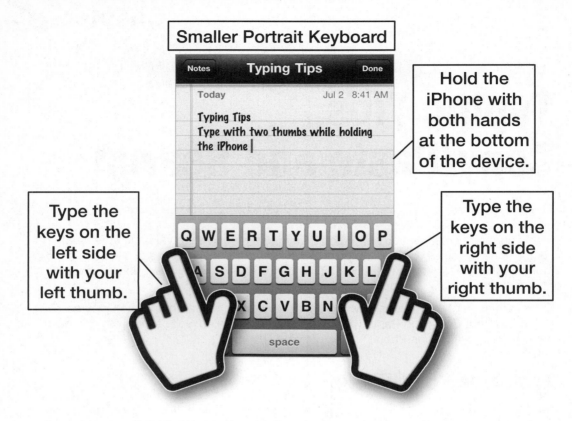

Smaller Portrait Keyboard

Hold the iPhone with both hands at the bottom of the device.

Type the keys on the left side with your left thumb.

Type the keys on the right side with your right thumb.

Figure 2–1. *Typing with two thumbs while holding the iPhone vertically.*

TIP: If you have larger hands and find typing on the smaller vertical keyboard challenging, then flip your iPhone on its side to get the larger, landscape keyboard (see Figure 2–2).

Simply turn the iPhone sideways in many apps and the keyboard will change to a larger, landscape keyboard to make it easier to type (see Figure 2–2).

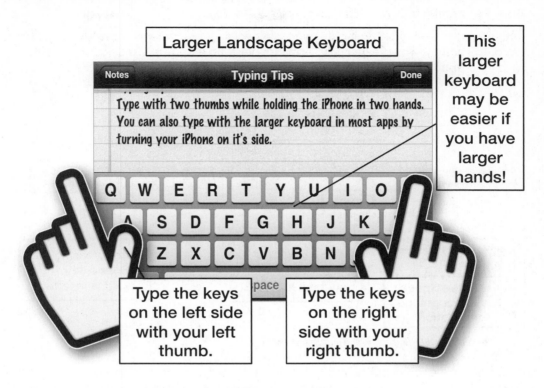

Figure 2–2. *Turn your iPhone on its side to type with the larger Landscape keyboard.*

Saving Time with Auto-Correction

When you are typing for a while, you will begin to notice a little pop-up window directly below some of the words you are typing—this is called Auto-Correction.

NOTE: If you never see the Auto-Correction pop-up window, then you will have to enable Auto-Correction by going into your **Settings** app > **General** > **Keyboard** > Set **Auto-Correction** to **ON**.

You can save yourself time when you see the correct word guessed by just pressing the **Space** key at the bottom of the keyboard to select that word.

In this example, we start typing the word "especially," and when we get to the c in the word, the correct word "especially" appears below in a pop-up. To select it, we simply press the **Space** key at the bottom (see Figure 2–3).

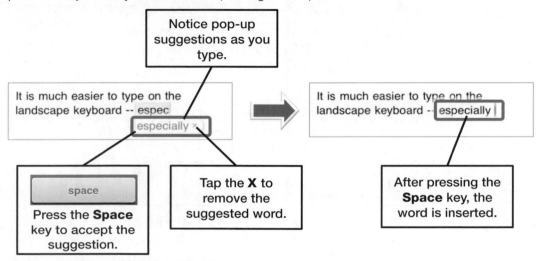

Figure 2–3. *Using Auto-Correction and suggested words.*

Your first inclination might be to tap the pop-up word, but that simply erases it from the screen. It is ultimately faster to keep typing or press the **Space** key when you see the correct word, as there will be more situations in which the word is either correct or will become correct as you keep typing—less finger travel in the long run.

> **TIP:** The Auto-Correction also looks through your **Contacts** list to make suggestions. For example, if Martin Trautschold was in your **Contacts** list, you would see "Trautschold" come up as an Auto-Correction suggestion after typing "Trauts."

After you learn to use the **Space** key, you will see that this pop-up guessing can be quite a time saver. After all, you were going to have to type a space at the end of the word anyway.

Sometimes the Auto-Correction word is incorrect; in this case, you simply need to press the **Backspace** key 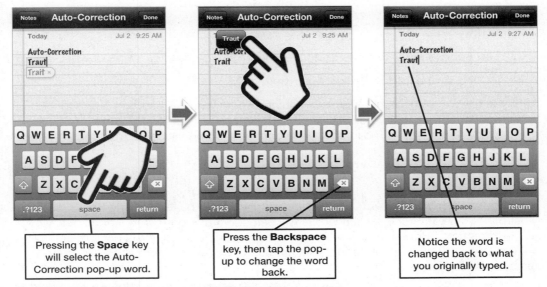 and then you will see a pop-up appear with the original word before the Auto-Correction changed it. See Figure 2-4

Pressing the **Space** key will select the Auto-Correction pop-up word.

Press the **Backspace** key, then tap the pop-up to change the word back.

Notice the word is changed back to what you originally typed.

Figure 2–4. *Dealing with Auto-Correction words that are not correct.*

TIP: With Auto-Correction, you can save time by avoiding typing the apostrophe in many common contractions, such as "wont" and "cant." Auto-Correction will show you a little pop-up window with the contraction spelled correctly; all you need to do to select the correction is to press the **Space** key.

Cc/Bcc, From: gary@madesimplelearnin…

Subject: Change in plans

Hi Martin,
I wont
won't ×

With some words, you have to add an extra character for the Auto-Correction to figure out:

Type "Weree" to get **We're**.

Type "Welll" to get **We'll**.

Hearing Auto-Correction Words Out Loud

You can set your iPhone to speak out the Auto-text and Auto-Correction words as they appear. This might be helpful to selecting the correct word. To enable this type of speaking:

1. Tap the **Settings** icon.

2. Tap **General**.

3. Tap **Accessibility** near the bottom of the page (you need to swipe down).

4. Set the switch next to **Speak Auto-text** to **On**.

After you enable this feature, whenever you are typing, you will hear the Auto-Correction word that pops up. If you agree with the word you hear, press the **Space** key to accept it; otherwise, keep typing. It can save you some time from looking up from the keyboard.

Spell Checker

Working together with the Auto-Correction feature is your built-in iPhone Spell Checker. Most of the time, your misspelled words will be caught and corrected automatically by Auto-Correction. Sometimes, a word will not be corrected, but still is misspelled. You will see any words that the iPhone thinks are misspelled underlined with a red dotted line as in Figure 2-5.

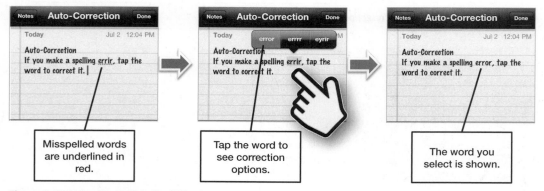

Figure 2–5. *Using the Built-In Spell Checker.*

> **TIP:** If your Spell Checker has too many incorrect words, then you can give it a fresh start by clearing out all the custom words. To do this: 1. Tap your **Settings** icon. 2. Tap **General**. 3. Tap **Reset** near at the bottom. 4. Tap **Reset Keyboard Dictionary**. 5. Tap **Reset Dictionary** to confirm. This will clear out all custom words added to your iPhone dictionary.

Accessibility Options

There are a number of useful features on the iPhone to help with accessibility. The VoiceOver option will read to you from the screen. It will tell you what you tap on, what buttons are selected, and all the options. It will read entire screens of text as well. If you like to see things larger, you can also turn on the **Zoom** feature, as described after the next section.

Getting Your iPhone to Speak To You (VoiceOver)

One cool feature of the iPhone is that you can turn on the VoiceOver feature so that the iPhone will speak anything on the screen. You can even get it to read to you from any e-mail, text document, or even an iBook page.

TIP: Use your headphones when VoiceOver is on and you are in a public place to better hear what is said and to avoid bothering others.

To enable **VoiceOver**:

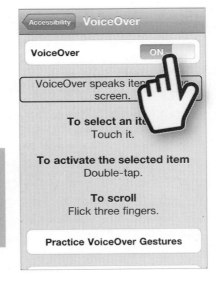

1. Tap the **Settings** icon.

2. Tap **General**.

3. Tap **Accessibility** near the bottom of the page.

4. Tap **VoiceOver**.

5. Set the **VoiceOver** switch to **On**.

CAUTION: As shown on the screen to the right, the VoiceOver gestures are different from the normal gestures. Tap the **Practice VoiceOver Gestures** button to get used to them.

Scroll down the VoiceOver screen to see more settings.

Adjust whether or not hints are spoken by changing the setting for **Speak Hints.**

When you type with **VoiceOver**, by default every character you type will be spoken. You can change it by tapping **Typing Feedback.** On the next screen you can set feedback to **Characters, Words, Characters and Words**, or **Nothing**.

On this setting screen, you can also adjust the **Speaking Rate** by sliding the bar.

You can adjust whether **Phonetics** and **Pitch Change** are used by setting the switches.

Accessibility	**VoiceOver**
Speak Hints	ON
Speaking Rate	
Typing Feedback	Characters... >
Use Phonetics	ON
Use Pitch Change	ON
Braille	>
Web Rotor	>

To have an entire page read to you in the **Notes** or **iBooks** app, you need to simultaneously tap the bottom and top of the block of text on the screen. If you tap in the text with one finger, only a single line is read to you.

Using Zoom to Magnify the Entire Screen

You may want to turn on the Zoom feature if you find that the text, icons, buttons, or anything on the screen is a little too hard to see. With the Zoom turned on, you can zoom the entire screen to almost twice the size. Everything is much easier to read.

NOTE: You cannot use VoiceOver and Zoom at the same time; you need to choose one or the other. Instead of magnifying the entire screen, you can also increase just the font sizes for your major apps using the **Large Text** feature. We show you how in the "Use Larger Text Size for Easier Reading" section below.

To enable **Zoom**:

1. Tap the **Settings** icon.

2. Tap **General**.

3. Tap **Accessibility** near the bottom of the page.

4. Tap **Zoom**.

5. Set the switch next to **Zoom** to **On**.

Similar to **VoiceOver**, **Zoom** uses the three-fingered gestures. Make sure to take note of them before you leave the screen.

Accessibility	Zoom

Zoom ON

Zoom magnifies the entire screen.

To zoom
Double-tap with three fingers.

To move around the screen
Drag three fingers while zoomed.

To change zoom
With three fingers, double-tap and drag up or down.

White on Black

If the contrast and colors are difficult to see, then you might want to turn on the **White on Black** setting. To change this setting:

1. Get into the **Accessibility** screen in the **Settings** app, as shown previously.

2. Set the **White on Black** switch to **On**.

    With this setting **On**, everything that was light on the screen becomes black, and everything that was dark or black becomes white.

Use Larger Text Size for Easier Reading

You can really expand the size of your font in **Contacts**, **Mail**, **Messages** and **Notes** using the **Large Text** feature.

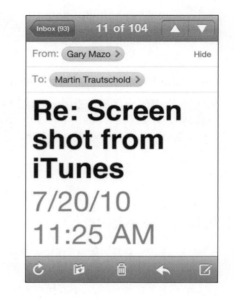

1. Tap the **Settings** icon.

2. Tap **General**.

3. Tap **Accessibility** near the bottom of the page (you need to swipe down).

4. Tap **Large Text**. You will then see a screen of font size options going from Off, 20pt text, 24pt, 32pt, 40pt, 48pt and 56pt text. Tap the size you want to use. The image shown to the right is using 48pt font.

5. Tap the **Accessibility** button in the upper left corner to return to the previous screen, then tap the **Home** button to exit **Settings**.

Triple-Click Home Button Options

You can set a triple-click of the **Home** button to do various things related to Accessibility.

1. Get into the **Accessibility** screen in the **Settings** app, as shown previously.

2. Tap **Triple-click the Home Button** near the bottom of the page.

3. Choose from **Off**, **Toggle VoiceOver**, **Toggle White on Black**, or **Ask**.

Magnifying Glass for Editing Text/Placing the Cursor

How many times have you been typing something and wanted to move the cursor precisely between two words, or between two letters?

This can be hard to do until you figure out the Magnifying Glass trick. What you do is this: Touch and hold your finger on the place where you want the cursor (see Figure 2–6). After a second or two, you will see the magnifying glass appear. Then, while you hold your finger on the screen, slide it around to position the cursor. When you let go, you will see the Copy/Paste pop-up menu, but you can ignore it.

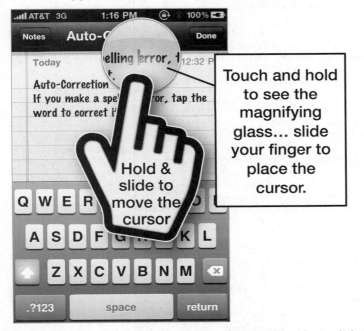

Figure 2–6. *Touch and hold the screen to see the magnifying glass and place the cursor.*

Typing Numbers and Symbols

How do you type a number or a symbol using the on-screen keyboard on the iPhone? When you are typing, tap the **123** key in the lower left corner to see numbers and common symbols such as $! ~ & = # . _ - +. If you need more symbols, from the number keyboard, tap the **#+=** key just above the **ABC** key in the lower left corner (see Figure 2–7).

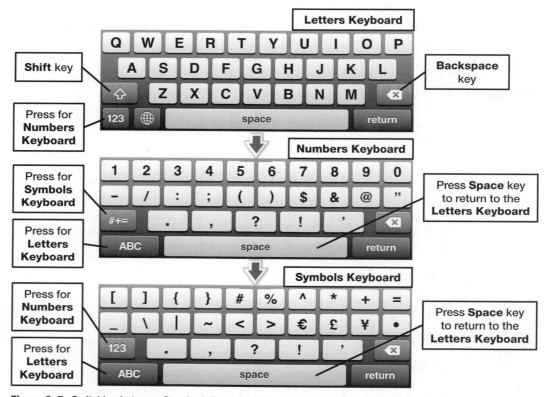

Figure 2–7. *Switching between Standard, Numbers & Basic Symbols, and Advanced Symbols keyboards.*

TIP: Notice that the Number & Basic Symbols keyboard will stay active until you either hit the **Space** key or press the key for another keyboard, such as **ABC**.

Touch and Slide Trick

These tips are courtesy of Rene Ritchie from the iPhone Blog (www.tipb.com).

Typing Uppercase Letters

Normally to type uppercase letters, you would press the **Shift** key then press the letter.

The faster way to type single uppercase letters and symbols that require the **Shift** key is to press the **Shift** key, keep your finger on the keyboard, slide over to the key you want, and release.

For example, to type an uppercase "D," press the right **Shift** key, then slide over to the "D" key and release.

Touch Shift and slide to the letter.

Rapidly Typing a Single Number

If you have to type just a single number, then press the **123** key and slide your finger up to the number. However, to type several numbers in a row, it's best to press the **123** key, let go, and then press each number.

Press and Hold Keyboard Shortcut for Typing Symbols and More

What about symbols not shown on the keyboard?

TIP: You can type more symbols than are shown on the screen.

All you do is press and hold a letter, number, or symbol that is related to the symbol you want.

For example, if you wanted to type the YEN symbol (¥), you would press and hold the **$** key until you saw the other options, slide up your finger to highlight, and then let go on the YEN symbol.

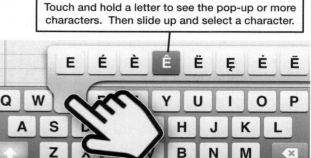

Touch and hold a letter to see the pop-up or more characters. Then slide up and select a character.

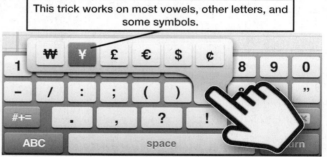

This trick works on most vowels, other letters, and some symbols.

This tip also works with the **.com** key in the Safari web browser and when typing e-mail addresses by pressing and holding the **Period** (.) key. You can get additional web site suffixes by pressing and holding the **.com** or **Period** keys.

You see on the screen **.co.uk**, **.ie**, **.de, .ca, .eu,** which are not on the standard US keyboard. These are present because we have installed additional international keyboards. See how to enable international keyboards in the "Typing In Other Languages—International Keyboards" section later in this chapter.

> **TIP: A few more useful, but hidden symbols.**
>
> There is a good bullet point character on the **Advanced Symbols** keyboard just above the **Backspace** key. You can also get a **degree** symbol if you press and hold the **Zero** key (0). Also, press and hold the **?** and **!** keys to get their Spanish inverted cousins.

Caps Lock

You double-press the **Shift** key to get turn on **Caps Lock**. You know it's turned on when the key turns blue.

To turn off Caps Lock, simply press the **Shift** key again.

Quickly Selecting and Deleting or Changing Text

If you need to quickly change or delete some text you are typing, the quickest way is to first select it.

1. Begin selecting the text by double-tapping it.

2. Adjust the selection by dragging the blue handles.

3. To erase the selected text, press the **Backspace** key.

4. To replace the text, simply start typing. The text will be instantly replaced by the letters you type.

Keyboard Options & Settings

There are a few keyboard options to make typing on your iPhone easier. The keyboard options are located in the **General** tab of your **Settings**.

1. Tap the **Settings** icon.

2. Tap **General**.

3. Swipe up, then tap **Keyboard** near the bottom of the page.

Auto-Correction ON/OFF

Using the built-in dictionary, **Auto-Correction** will automatically make changes to commonly misspelled words. For example, if you type in "wont," Auto-Correction will change it to "won't" on the fly. You need to make sure it is **ON** if you want this feature to work. (This is the default setting.)

Auto-Capitalization

When you start a new sentence, words will automatically be capitalized if **Auto-Capitalization** is **ON**.

Also, common proper nouns will be correctly capitalized. For example, if you typed "New york," you would be prompted to change it to "New York"—again, just pressing the **Space** key will select the correction. If you backspace over a capital letter, the iPhone will assume the new letter you type should be capital as well. This is also set to **ON** by default.

Enable Caps Lock

Sometimes when you type, you may want to lock the caps by double-tapping the **Cap** key. Enabling **Caps Lock** will allow you to do this.

This is set to **OFF** by default.

".." Shortcut

If you are a former BlackBerry user or had an older iPhone, you might be familiar with the feature that will automatically put in a period at the end of the sentence when you double-press the **Space** key. This is exactly the same feature that you can enable on the iPhone. By default, this is also set to **ON**.

Typing In Other Languages—International Keyboards

At publishing time, the iPhone enables you to type in over a dozen different languages, including languages from Dutch to Spanish. Some of the Asian languages, such as Japanese and Chinese, offer two or three keyboards for different typing methods.

Adding a New International Keyboard

To enable various language keyboards, follow these steps:

1. Touch the **Settings** icon (refer to Figure 2–8).

2. Tap **General**.

3. Tap **Keyboard** near the bottom of the page.

4. Tap **International Keyboards**.

5. Tap **Add New Keyboard**.

6. Tap any keyboard/language listed to add that keyboard.

7. Now you will see the keyboard listed on the available keyboards.

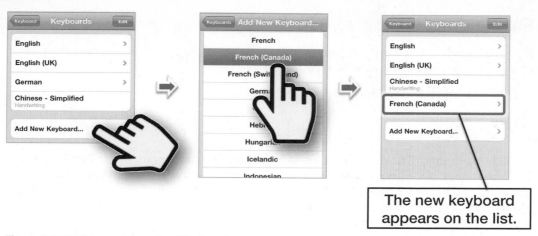

The new keyboard appears on the list.

Figure 2–8. *Adding new international keyboards.*

Editing, Re-Ordering, or Deleting Keyboards

You may want to adjust options for a keyboard, re-order, or simply remove a keyboard that you no longer use.

1. Follow steps 1-4 under Adding a New International Keyboard earlier to view the list of International Keyboards.

2. To adjust options for a specific, tap the listed keyboard. In our example, we tapped **French (Canada)**.

3. Change the **Software Keyboard Layout** by tapping the choice in that section.

4. Adjust the **Hardware Keyboard Layout** by tapping a choice in that section.

5. Tap the **Keyboards** button in the upper left corner to save your choices and return to the list of keyboards.

6. To re-order or delete a keyboard, tap the **Edit** button in the upper right corner.

7. To change the order of keyboards, touch and drag the right edge of the keyboard with the three gray bars up or down.

Touch and drag to re-order the keyboards.

8. To delete a keyboard, tap the **red minus sign** so it swings to the vertical position, then tap **Delete**.

9. To finish editing your keyboards, tap the **Done** button in the upper right corner.

You will now notice a little Globe key appear when you install at least one international keyboard. Press the **Globe** key to cycle between all the languages (see Figure 2–9).

TIP: You can press and hold the **Globe** key to see a list of available keyboards. Then you can quickly select the keyboard you wish to use.

Japanese, Chinese, and some other languages provide several keyboard options to meet your typing preferences.

In some of the languages (such as Japanese), you will see the letters typed change into characters or you can draw characters. You may also see a row of other character combinations above the keyboard. When you see the combination you want, tap it.

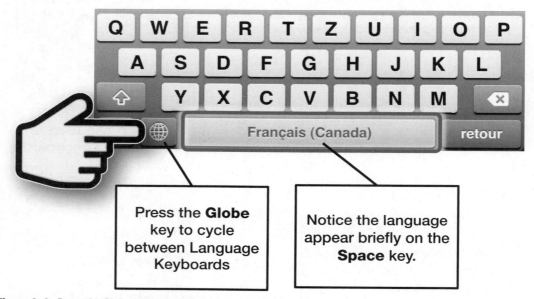

Press the **Globe** key to cycle between Language Keyboards

Notice the language appear briefly on the **Space** key.

Figure 2–9. *Press the **Globe** key to cycle between International Keyboards.*

Copy and Paste

Copy and Paste is very useful for saving time and increasing your accuracy. You can use it for taking text from your email (such as meeting details) and pasting it into your Calendar, or you may want to simply copy an e-mail address from one place in a form into another to save yourself some time re-typing It. (We show you this technique in the "Setup Exchange/Google Account" in Chapter 4, "Other Ways to Sync.") There are lots of places to use Copy and Paste; the more comfortable you are with it, the more you will use it. You can even copy text or images from your Safari web browser and paste them into a Note or a Mail message.

Selecting Text with Double-Tap

If you are reading or typing text, you can double-tap to start selecting text for the copy. This works well in Mail, Messages, and Notes.

You will see a box with blue dots (handles) at opposite corners. Just drag the handles to select the text you wish to highlight and copy, as shown in Figure 2–10.

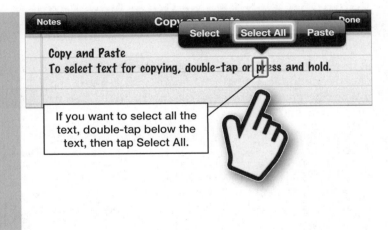

Exactly position the cursor with this magnifying window

Double-tap to start selecting text

Drag the blue dot to expand the selection

Figure 2–10. *Double-tap to start selecting text, then drag the blue dots to expand the selection.*

TIP: If you want to select all the text, tap and hold the screen on the text or double-tap the screen above or below the text. Then you should see a pop-up showing you Select or Select All. Tap **Select** to select a word. Tap **Select All** to highlight all the text.

If you want to select all the text, double-tap below the text, then tap Select All.

Selecting Text with Two-Finger Touch

The other way to select text requires that you touch the screen simultaneously with two fingers. This seems to work best if you are holding your iPhone with one hand and use your thumb and forefinger from your other hand to touch the screen. You can also set the iPhone down on the table and touch with a finger from both hands.

1. Touch the screen simultaneously at the beginning and end of the text you want to select. Don't worry if you cannot get the selection exactly on the first touch.

2. After the two-finger touch, use the blue handles to drag the beginning and end of the selection to the correct position, as shown in Figure 2–11.

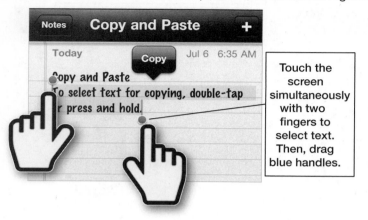

Figure 2–11. *Select text by touching the screen at the same time with two fingers.*

Selecting Web Site or Other Non-Editable Text with Touch and Hold

In the Safari web browser and other places where you cannot edit the text, hold your finger on some text and the paragraph will become highlighted with handles at each of the corners.

Drag the handles if you want to select even more text.

NOTE: If you drag smaller than a paragraph, the selector will switch to fine-text mode and give you the blue handles on both ends of the selection to pick just the characters or words you want. If you drag your finger beyond a paragraph, you get the gross-text selector with which you can drag up or down to select whole reams of text and graphics.

Cut or Copy the Text

Once you have the text that you wish

to copy highlighted, just touch the **Copy** tab at the top of the screen. The tab will turn blue, indicating that the text is on the clipboard.

> **NOTE:** If you have previously cut or copied text, then you will also see the Paste option, as shown.

Once you have selected the text, then tap Cut, Copy, or Paste.

Jumping Between Apps/App Switching/Multitasking

After you copy text, you may want to paste it into another app. The easiest way to jump between apps is to use the App Switcher.

1. Copy or cut your text.

2. Double-tap the **Home** button to bring up the App Switcher on the bottom of your screen (see Figure 2-12).

3. If you just left an app running in the background, you will be able to find it in the App Switcher bar.

4. Swipe right or left to find the app you want and tap it.

5. If you don't see the app you want in the App Switcher bar, then tap the **Home** button and start it from the **Home** screen.

6. Now, paste the text by pressing and holding the screen and selecting **Paste** from the pop-up.

7. Double-tap the **Home** button again and tap the app you just left to jump back to it.

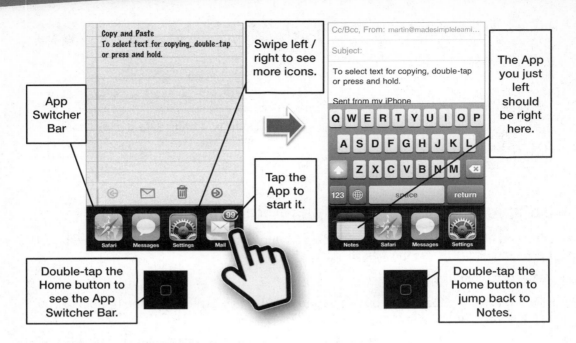

Figure 2–12. *Select text by touching the screen at the same time with two fingers.*

Pasting the Text

If you are pasting the text into the same Note or Mail message:

1. Use your finger to move the cursor to where you want to paste the text. Remember the Magnifying Glass trick (as we showed earlier in this chapter) to help you position the cursor.

2. Once you let go of the screen, you should see a pop-up asking you to **Select**, **Select All**, or **Paste**.

3. If you don't see this pop-up, then double-tap the screen.

4. Select **Paste** to paste your selection.

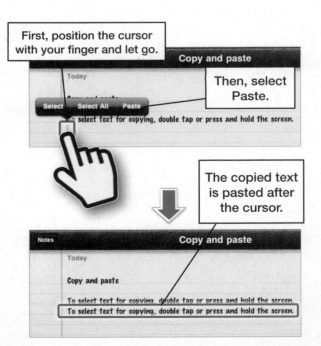

Pasting Text or an Image into Another Icon

To paste the text or image you have copied into another icon:

1. Tap the **Home** button (refer to Figure 2–13).

2. Tap the icon into which you want to paste the text. In this case, let's tap **Mail**.

3. Tap the **Compose** icon 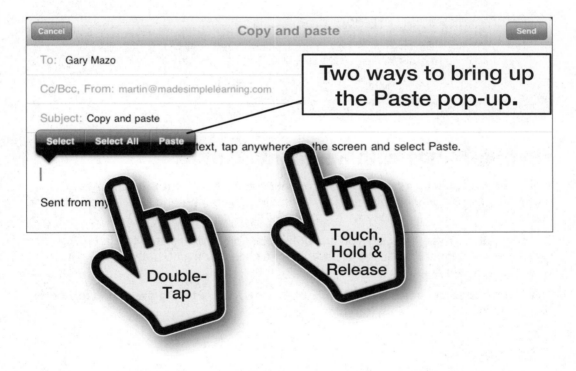 to write a new e-mail.

4. Double-tap anywhere in the body of the message.

5. Tap **Paste**.

Figure 2–13. *Bring up the Paste command by either double-tapping or touching, holding, and releasing.*

Move the cursor to the body of the text and either double-tap or touch, hold, and release your finger and you will see the Paste pop-up. Tap **Paste** and the text on the clipboard will be pasted right into the body of the e-mail.

Shake to Undo Paste or Typing

One of the great new features in Copy and Paste is the ability to undo either typing or the Paste you just completed.

All you have to do is shake the iPhone after the paste. A new pop-up appears giving you the option to undo what you have just done.

Tap **Undo Typing** or **Undo Paste** to correct the mistake.

> **TIP: Quickly Delete Text by Selecting, Then Pressing Backspace**
>
> If you ever want to delete a number of lines of text, a paragraph, or even all the text you just typed quickly with one or two taps, this tip is for you. Use the techniques described previously to
>
> select the text you want to delete. Then, simply press the **Delete** key [x] in the lower left corner of the keyboard to delete all the selected text.

Finding Things with Spotlight Search

A great feature on your iPhone to find information is the **Spotlight Search**—Apple's proprietary search method for a global search through your iPhone for a name, event, or subject.

The concept is simple; let's say you are looking for something related to Martin. You cannot remember if it was an e-mail, a Note, or a Calendar event, but you do know it was related to Martin.

This is the perfect time to use the **Spotlight Search** feature to find everything related to Martin on your iPhone.

Activating Spotlight Search

First, you need to get into the **Spotlight Search**, which resides to the left of the first page of the **Home** screen.

On the left side of the first circle (indicating the first page of your **Home** screen) is a very small magnifying glass.

Swipe your finger from left to right on the first page of icons to see the **Spotlight Search** page.

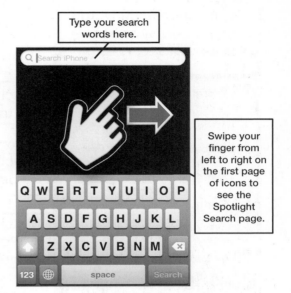

Type your search words here.

Swipe your finger from left to right on the first page of icons to see the Spotlight Search page.

1. On the **Spotlight Search** page (see Figure 2-14), type in one or a few words for your search.

2. Tap the **Search** button in the lower right corner to execute your search.

> **TIP:** If you are looking for a person, type their full name to more accurately find items from only that person (for example, "Martin Trautschold"). This will eliminate any other Martins who might be in your iPhone and make sure you find items only related to Martin Trautschold.

3. In the search result, you'll see all e-mails, appointments, meeting invitations, and contact information found. Swipe down to see more results.

4. Tap one of the results in the list to view its contents.

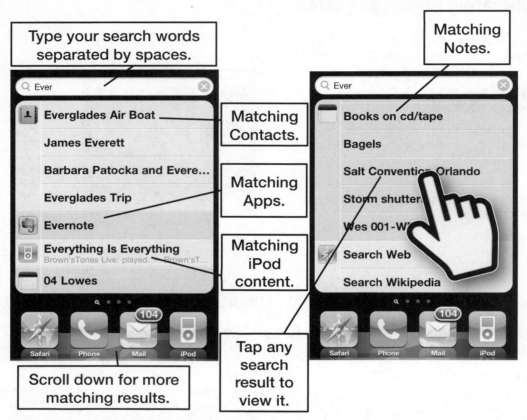

Figure 2–14. *Spotlight Search Results pages.*

Your search results stay there until you clear them, so you can go back to **Spotlight Search** once again by swiping to the right from your **Home** screen.

To clear the search field, just touch the **X** in the search bar. To exit **Spotlight Search**, just press the **Home** key or swipe to the left.

Search Web or Search Wikipedia

After you perform a Spotlight Search, you will notice at the very bottom of the results are shown **Search Web** and **Search Wikipedia**.

Tap either of these to execute your search on the Web or in Wikipedia.

Customizing Spotlight Search

You can customize your Spotlight Search by removing certain apps or types of data from the search. You can even change the order in which each type of data is searched. This might be useful if you want to search only your **Contacts** and **Mail** messages, but nothing else. Or, if you know that you always want to search **Mail** first, then **Calendar**, then **Music**, you could set those items in the proper order.

1. Tap the **Settings** icon.

2. Tap **General**.

3. Tap **Spotlight Search**.

4. To change the order of the items searched, touch and drag the right edge of the item with the three gray bars up or down.

5. To remove a specific item from the search, tap it to remove the check mark next to it. Unchecked items are not searched by **Spotlight Search**.

6. Tap the **General** button in the upper left corner to return to the **Settings**.

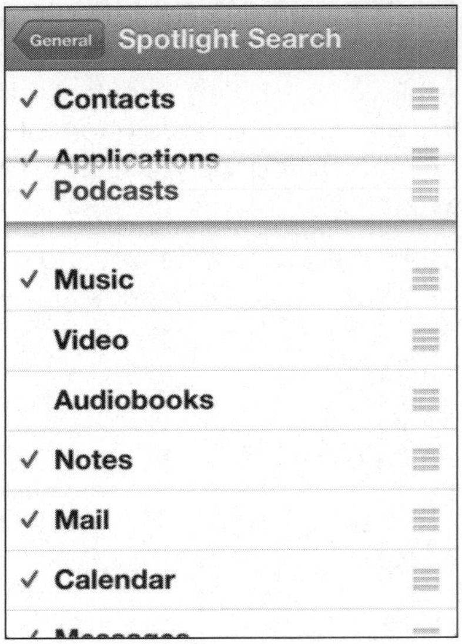

General	Spotlight Search
✓ **Contacts**	≡
✓ **Applications**	≡
✓ **Podcasts**	≡
✓ **Music**	≡
Video	≡
Audiobooks	≡
✓ **Notes**	≡
✓ **Mail**	≡
✓ **Calendar**	≡
✓ **Messages**	≡

Chapter 3

Sync Your iPhone with iTunes

In this chapter we will show you how to set up or adjust the synchronization of information between your iPhone and your Windows or Mac computer using iTunes.

We'll also take a look at what to consider before you sync and how to set up both automatic and manual sync of your personal information. With iTunes, you can sync or transfer contacts, calendar, notes, apps, music, videos, iBooks, documents, and picture libraries.

Moreover, as you'll see, iTunes will automatically back up your iPhone whenever you connect it to your computer. And, because nothing ever works right all the time, we'll show you a few simple troubleshooting tips. Finally, you'll see how to check for updates and install updated operating system software for your iPhone.

> **TIP:** iTunes can do so much more than just syncing—organize your music, create playlists, buy songs and videos, and it includes the Home Sharing and Genius features. To learn about all of ITune's features and capabilities—especially if you're new to iTunes—please check out Chapter 30: "iTunes User Guide."

Before You Set Up Your iTunes Sync

There are a few things you need before you can start using iTunes to sync. We cover the prerequisites and answer a few common questions about the reasons to use iTunes. We also help you understand what happens if you own another Apple device, such as an iPad or iPod, and start syncing with your iPhone.

Prerequisites

There are just a few things you need to do before you sync your iPhone with iTunes.

TIP: If you followed all the steps in Chapter 1: "Getting Started," chances are you've already completed the steps listed below and the initial sync of your contacts, calendar, bookmarks, notes, and email accounts to your iPhone. If so, you may want to skip ahead to the "Apps: Sync and Manage Them" section later in this chapter.

1. Make sure you've installed version 9.2 or higher of iTunes on your computer. For help with installing or updating iTunes, see Chapter 30: "iTunes User Guide."

2. Create an iTunes account (Apple ID); see the "Create iTunes Account" section in Chapter 30.

3. Get the white sync cable that came with your iPhone. One end plugs into the bottom of your iPhone near the **Home** button and the other plugs into the USB port on your computer.

Can I Sync iTunes with an iPod or iPad *and* My iPhone?

Yes! As long as you are syncing to the same computer, you can sync several Apple devices (Apple says up to five, but we've heard of people syncing more) to the same iTunes account on a single computer.

CAUTION: You can't sync the same iPhone, iPad, or iPod to two different computers. If you attempt to do this, you'll see a message like: "Would you like to wipe this device (iPhone, iPad, iPod) and resync the new library?" If you answer **Yes**, any music and videos on the device will be erased.

There Are Other Sync Options (MobileMe and Exchange/Google)—Should I Use iTunes?

There are other ways to synchronize your personal information and email, such as Exchange/Google and MobileMe, which we cover in Chapter 4: "Other Sync Methods." Keep in mind, however, that even if you choose one of these, you'll still need to use iTunes to

- Backup and restore your iPhone
- Update the iPhone operating system software

- Sync and manage your applications (apps)

- Sync your music library and playlists

- Sync movies, TV shows, podcasts, and iTunes U content

- Sync books

- Sync photos

Wireless Sync versus iTunes Desktop Sync

Ideally, your personal information (contacts, calendar, and notes) are all synced wirelessly and automatically to your iPhone. With a wireless sync, you don't need to plug your iPhone into your computer to do the sync, everything happens over the airwaves. Depending on your environment, you may or may not be able to use a wireless sync for all your information. For example, if you use Google, then for a full wireless sync of calendar and contacts, you need to use the Exchange sync option (not iTunes sync).

Table 3–1 summarizes the synchronization options. What you choose to use for synchronization should be driven by where you currently store your email, contacts, and calendar—your environment and whether or not you want to have a wireless sync.

NOTE: As you can see, with some environments, you can wirelessly sync your contacts and calendars to your iPhone.

Table 3–1. *Synchronization Options for Your Personal Information*

Your Environment	Wireless Sync Using	Desktop Sync Using	Notes
Google for email, calendar, and contacts	Settings ➤ Mail,Contacts,Calendar ➤ Add Account ➤ Microsoft Exchange	iTunes	This is free.
Google for email, calendar, notes	(Cannot wirelessly sync contacts this way) Settings ➤ Mail,Contacts,Calendar ➤ Add Account ➤ Gmail	iTunes required to sync Google Contacts	This is free.
Email, calendar and contacts on Microsoft Exchange Server	Settings ➤ Mail,Contacts,Calendar ➤ Add Account ➤ Microsoft Exchange	iTunes	This is free.

Your Environment	Wireless Sync Using	Desktop Sync Using	Notes
Email, calendar and contacts in Yahoo!	Wireless sync for email, calendar, notes (not for contacts): Settings ➤ Mail,Contacts,Calendar ➤ Add Account ➤ Yahoo!	iTunes required to sync Yahoo! Contacts	This is free.
Email, calendar, and contacts on various platforms. You are subscribed to the MobileMe service.	Settings ➤ Mail,Contacts,Calendar ➤ Add Account ➤ MobileMe	MobileMe	This is free for 60 days, then US$99 for one user, US$149 for a family plan. (Pricing is valid as of publication time.)
Email, calendar, and contacts in AOL	Wireless sync for email, calendar, notes (not for contacts): Settings ➤ Mail,Contacts,Calendar ➤ Add Account ➤ AOL	iTunes required to sync AOL Contacts	This is free.
LDAP (Lightweight Directory Access Protocol) contacts	Settings ➤ Mail,Contacts,Calendar ➤ Add Account ➤ Other ➤ Add LDAP Account	Not available.	This is free.
CalDAV calendar account	Settings ➤ Mail,Contacts,Calendar ➤ Add Account ➤ Other ➤ Add CalDAV Account	Not available.	This is free. Must have access to CalDAV account in this format cal.server.com with a username and password.
Subscribed calendar at your work	Settings ➤ Mail,Contacts,Calendar ➤ Add Account ➤ Other ➤ Add Subscribed Calendar	Not available.	This is free. Must have access to a subscribed calendar (web address, username, and password). Access to server is in this format: myserver.com/cal.ics

Set Up Your iTunes Sync

Now that you've thought about the other options, you're ready to get started setting up your iTunes sync. We show you all the steps for both automated syncs and manual transfers of information to your iPhone using iTunes.

The iPhone Summary Screen (Manually Manage Music, Update, Restore, and More)

The Summary tab in iTunes is where you see and update your version of your iPhone operating system software and an important switch related to syncing music, video and other content. It is also where you can select to automatically open iTunes (to sync) whenever you connect your iPhone to your computer.

As Figure 3-1 shows, once you connect your iPhone to your computer, you can see important information, like your iPhone's memory capacity, installed software version, and serial number. You can also check for updates to the software version, restore data to your iPhone, and choose from the several options available on this screen.

In particular, you can decide whether you want to **Manually manage music and videos** using the checkbox at the bottom of this screen.

Figure 3-1. The iPhone **Summary** screen in iTunes

To see the **Summary** screen:

1. Start the iTunes software on your computer.

2. Connect your iPhone to your computer with the white USB cable supplied with the device. Plug one end into the bottom of the iPhone near the **Home** button and the other end into a USB port on your computer.

3. If you've successfully connected your iPhone, you should see your iPhone listed under **DEVICES** in the left nav bar.

4. Click on your iPhone in the left nav bar, then click on the **Summary** tab on the top left edge of the main window.

5. If you want to be able to drag and drop music and videos onto your iPhone, check the box next to **Manually manage music and videos**.

6. If you want to have iTunes open and sync your iPhone automatically whenever you connect it to your computer, check the box next to **Open iTunes when this iPhone is connected.**

> **TIP:** If this iTunes software is not installed on your primary computer (the one you use for syncing). It could be installed on a second computer which you use for charging your iPhone. If so, you should check the box next to **Manually manage music and videos** and uncheck the box next to **Open iTunes when this iPhone is connected**

iTunes Navigation Basics

Get a feel for the left nav bar. Click on various items in this left nav bar and notice that the main display window changes.

The top nav bar inside the main window also changes based on what you have selected in the left nav bar. For example, when you click on your iPhone in the left nav bar, you'll see tabs across the top of the main window that show information related to your device. When you click on the iTunes store in the left nav bar, you see tabs related to the store in the main window.

Getting to the Sync Setup Screen (Info Tab)

Your first step is to get to the setup screen for syncing your contacts, calendar, email and so forth. You follow the same steps described above for getting to the **Summary** screen, except now you click the **Info** tab at the top to see the Contacts (and other sync settings) in the main iTunes window, as shown in Figure 3–2.

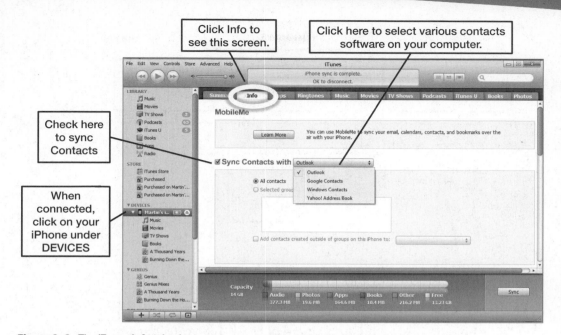

Figure 3–2. *The iTunes Info tab where you set up contacts, calendar, bookmarks, and more.*

Sync Your Contacts

Let's start by setting up syncing of your contacts.

1. Check the box next to **Sync Contacts with** and adjust the pull-down menu to the software or service where your contacts are stored. At publication time, on a Windows computer these are Outlook, Google Contacts, Windows Contacts, and Yahoo! Address Book, as shown in Figure 3–3.

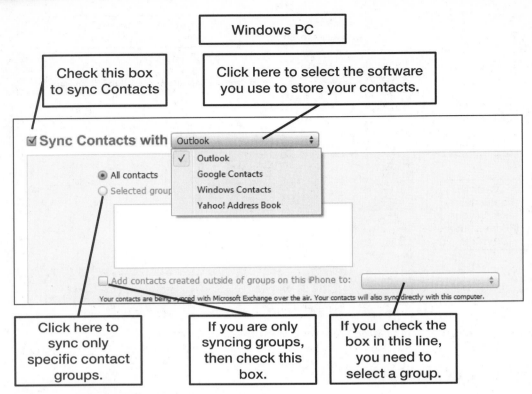

Windows PC

Check this box to sync Contacts

Click here to select the software you use to store your contacts.

☑ Sync Contacts with [Outlook ⬦]

          ✓ Outlook

              Google Contacts

  ● All contacts   Windows Contacts

  ○ Selected grou   Yahoo! Address Book

☐ Add contacts created outside of groups on this iPhone to: [⬦]

Your contacts are being synced with Microsoft Exchange over the air. Your contacts will also sync directly with this computer.

Click here to sync only specific contact groups.

If you are only syncing groups, then check this box.

If you check the box in this line, you need to select a group.

Figure 3–3. *Selecting software for syncing contacts (Windows)*

CAUTION: Whenever you switch between software and services in these sync settings screens (called the **sync provider**), it affects every one of the mobile devices connected to your iTunes account. For example, if you sync contacts to your iPad or iPod touch, these changes will also affect MobileMe. You will be changing the way contacts sync for any other devices connected to your iTunes account.

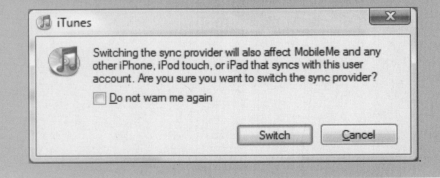

iTunes

Switching the sync provider will also affect MobileMe and any other iPhone, iPod touch, or iPad that syncs with this user account. Are you sure you want to switch the sync provider?

☐ Do not warn me again

[Switch]   [Cancel]

Google Contacts Sync:

If you select Google Contacts, you'll be prompted to enter your Google ID and password, as shown in Figure 3–4.

Figure 3–4. *Login screen for syncing Google Contacts*

To change your Google ID or password, click the **Configure** button next to the **Sync Contacts with** option you saw at the top of this section.

Yahoo! Address Book Sync:

If you select Yahoo! Contacts, you'll be prompted to enter your Yahoo! ID and password, as shown in Figure 3–5.

Figure 3–5. *Yahoo! Address Book sync login screen*

To change your Yahoo! ID or password, click the **Configure** button next to the **Sync Contacts with** option you saw at the top of this section.

NOTE: The options you see in this and other drop-down boxes on the **Info** tab will vary slightly depending on the software installed on your computer. For example, on a Mac, the contacts sync does not have a drop-down list; instead the other services, such as Google Contacts and Yahoo!, are shown as separate check boxes (see Figure 3–6).

2. Select either of these options:

a. **All Contacts,** to sync all contacts in your address book (this is the default).

b. **Selected Groups,** to sync contacts only within specific groups that you check in the window below.

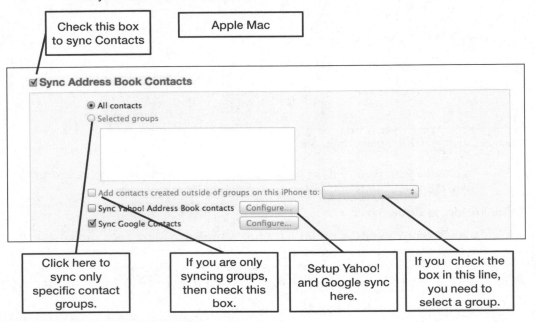

Figure 3-6 labels:

Check this box to sync Contacts

Apple Mac

☑ **Sync Address Book Contacts**

⦿ All contacts
◯ Selected groups

☐ Add contacts created outside of groups on this iPhone to:
☐ Sync Yahoo! Address Book contacts   Configure...
☑ Sync Google Contacts   Configure...

Click here to sync only specific contact groups.

If you are only syncing groups, then check this box.

Setup Yahoo! and Google sync here.

If you check the box in this line, you need to select a group.

Figure 3–6. *Setting up Contacts sync groups on the Apple Mac*

NOTE: These groups can't be created here—they must be created in the application or service where your contacts are stored (Outlook, Google, Yahoo!, Entourage, etc.).

3. In Figure 3-6, the third from the bottom check box that says **Add contacts created outide of groups on this iPhone to** (select a group from the drop down list) lets you specify a new group for any new contacts you add on your iPhone that you don't explicitly assign to a group.

4. To continue setting up your calendar, email, and more, scroll down the page.

5. If you don't want to set anything else up for syncing, click the **Apply** button in the lower-right corner of the iTunes screen to start the sync.

NOTE: Depending on how many contacts you have, the initial sync could take longer than 10 minutes, and may even require 30 or more minutes. So you may want to do this sync when you can let your iPhone sit for as long as it takes (during lunch, after dinner, etc.).

Sync Your Calendar

1. Within the same **Info** tab, scroll down to see the calendar sync set up, as shown in Figure 3–7.

2. Check the box next to **Sync Calendars with** and adjust the pull-down menu to the software or service that stores your calendars. This might be Outlook or another application on a Windows computer, and iCal on a Mac.

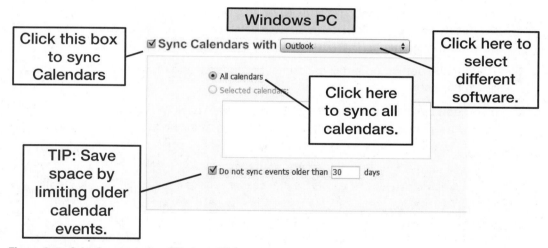

Figure 3–7. *Calendar sync set up (Windows PC)*

3. Select either of these options (see Figure 3–8):

    a. **All Calendars** to sync all calendars (this is the default).

    b. **Selected Calendars** to sync only calendars you've checked in the window below.

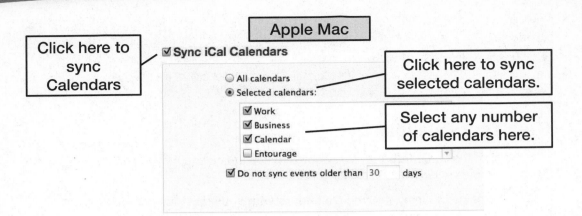

Figure 3–8. *Calendar sync setup (Apple Mac)*

4. If you want to save space on your iPhone, click the check box next to **Do not sync events older than 30 days.** You can adjust the days up or down to fit your needs.

5. To continue setting up email accounts, bookmarks and more, scroll down the page.

6. If you don't want to set anything else up for sync, click the **Apply** button in the lower-right corner of the iTunes screen to start the sync.

> **NOTE:** If you're a Mac user who uses Microsoft Entourage, you'll need to enable Entourage to sync with iCal. To do this, go into the **Preferences** settings in Entourage, then go to **Sync Services** and check the boxes for synchronizing with iCal and Address book, as shown in Figure 3–9.

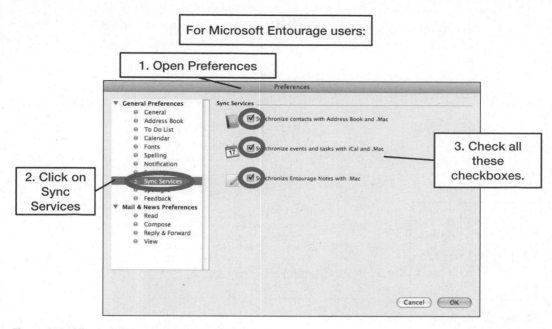

Figure 3–9. *Microsoft Entourage settings (Apple Mac)*

NOTE: As of the writing of this book, Entourage, unlike iCal, can't handle multiple calendars.

Sync Email Account Settings

It is important to keep in mind that the **Sync Mail Accounts** settings should really be called **Sync Mail Account Settings (without your password or mail)**. What this means is that only the email account settings are transferred to your iPhone during the sync. This helps you in that you won't have to actually type all the settings on the iPhone itself.

NOTE: After syncing the email account settings to your iPhone, you'll still have to enter your password for each email account in the **Settings ➤ Mail, Contacts, Calendars** for each email account. You have to do this only once on your iPhone for each account.

1. Scroll down below the Calendar settings on the same **Info** tab in iTunes to see the **Mail** account settings.

2. Check the box next to **Sync Mail Accounts from** and adjust the pull-down menu to the software or service that stores your email (Figure 3–10). This might be Outlook on a Windows computer, or Entourage or Mail on a Mac.

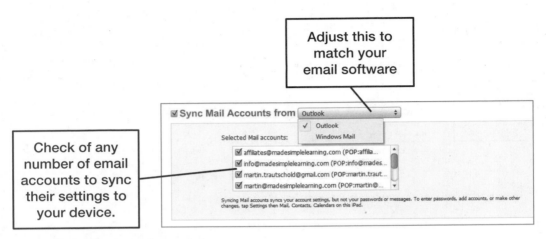

Figure 3–10. *Setting up email accounts to sync*

3. To continue setting up bookmarks, notes, and more, scroll down the page.

4. If you do not want to set anything else up for sync, then click the **Apply** button in the lower-right corner of the iTunes screen to start the sync.

Sync Bookmarks and Notes

One great feature of the iTunes sync is that you can sync the browser bookmarks from your computer to your iPhone. This allows you to start browsing on your iPhone with all your favorite sites immediately. You can also sync your notes from your computer to your iPhone and keep them up-to-date in both places using iTunes.

NOTE: As of publication time, iTunes supports only two web browsers for sync: Microsoft Internet Explorer and Apple Safari. If you use Mozilla Firefox or Google Chrome, you can still sync your bookmarks, but you'll have to install free bookmark sync software (e.g., www.xmarks.com) to sync from Firefox or Chrome to Safari or Explorer. Then you can sync your browser bookmarks in a two-step process.

1. Scroll down below the email settings on the same **Info** tab in iTunes to see the **Other** settings.

2. To sync your browser bookmarks, check the box next to **Sync bookmarks with** and adjust the pull-down menu to the web browser you use (see Figure 3–11). At this time, you can select only Internet Explorer or Safari.

3. To sync your notes, check the box next to **Sync notes with** and select the software or service where your notes are stored.

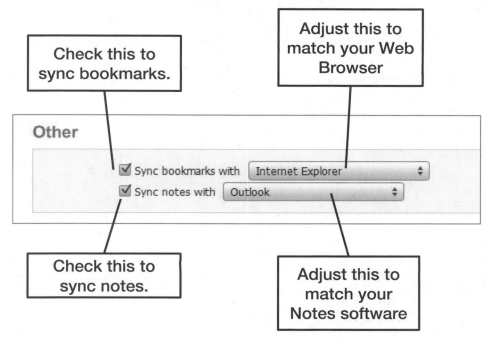

Figure 3–11. *Browser bookmarks and notes sync setup*

4. Click the **Apply** button in the lower-right corner of the iTunes screen to start the sync.

Syncing Your iPhone with iTunes

The syncing is normally automatic when you plug in your iPhone to your computer's USB port. The only exception is if you have disabled the automatic sync.

Keeping Track of the Sync

At the top of iTunes, inside the Status window, you can see what is happening with the sync. You may see **"Syncing contacts with "Martin's iPhone"** or **Syncing calendars with "Martin's iPhone"...**, which lets you see what is currently being synced.

iTunes

Syncing contacts with "Martin's iPhone"...

Handling Sync Conflicts

Sometimes, the iTunes sync will detect conflicts between the data in your computer and on your iPhone, such as the same contact entry with two different company names, or the same calendar entry with two different notes. Handling these conflicts is fairly straightforward.

1. In the **Conflict Resolver** window, click on the information that is correct. This turns the background a light blue, while the side not selected is white. See Figure 3–12.

2. If there are any more conflicts, click the **Next** button until you finish resolving all conflicts.

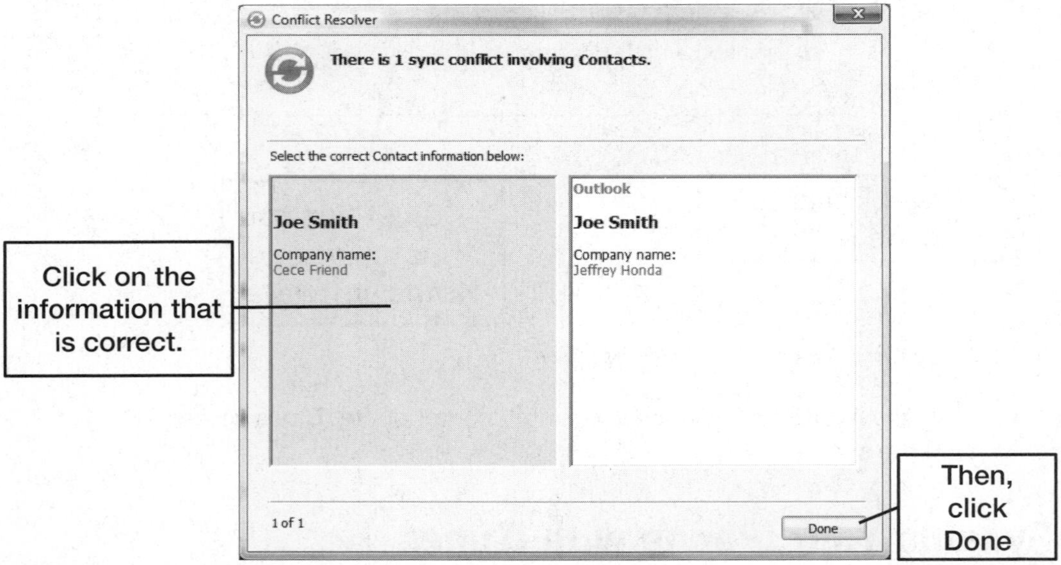

Conflict Resolver

There is 1 sync conflict involving Contacts.

Select the correct Contact information below:

Outlook

Joe Smith   **Joe Smith**

Company name: Company name:
Cece Friend   Jeffrey Honda

Click on the information that is correct.

1 of 1   Done

Then, click Done

Figure 3–12. *iTunes sync Conflict Resolver*

3. Click **Done** to close the window.

4. All your selections will be applied to the next sync with your iPhone. As Figure 3-13 shows, the next screen gives you the choice to **Sync Now** or **Sync Later**.

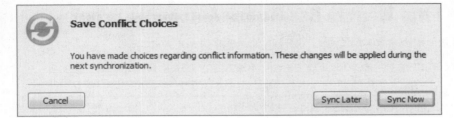

Figure 3–13. *Conflict Resolver final screen*

NOTE: Conflicts can cause the sync to stop in mid-process. Contacts are synced first, then the Calendar. So if a Contacts sync conflict is found, the Calendar will not sync until the Contacts conflict is resolved. Make sure to resync your iPhone after you resolve conflicts to complete the sync.

Cancelling a Sync in Progress

You can cancel a sync from iTunes or from your iPhone.

To cancel the sync from iTunes on your computer:

Click the **X** inside the sync status window, as shown in Figure 3–14.

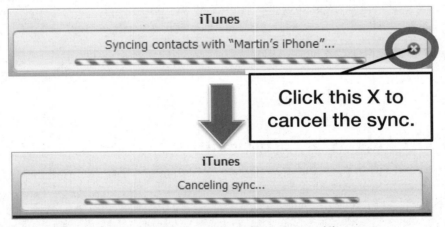

Figure 3–14. *Clicking the X in the status window in iTunes to cancel the sync*

To cancel the sync from the iPhone:

Slide the slider bar at the bottom of the screen that says **Slide to Cancel.** This is in the same place as the normal **Slide to Unlock** message.

Why Might I Not Want to Use iTunes Automatic Sync?

There could be a few reasons to sync manually instead of automatically:

1. You don't want to fill up your iPhone with too many music and video files.

2. The sync and backup process takes a long time, so you don't want it to happen every time you connect your iPhone to your computer.

3. You plug your iPhone into various computers to charge it up, but don't want to be asked if you want to erase and resync your music every time.

> **NOTE:** If you want to drag and drop music and videos, you need to make sure to check the box next to **Manually manage music and videos** in the **Summary** tab in iTunes.

Manually Stopping the Auto Sync Before It Starts

There may be times you want to connect your iPhone to your computer without the auto sync starting up. This could be because you don't have much time and want to quickly drag and drop a few new songs to your iPhone without syncing everything else.

To stop the normal auto sync of your iPhone, you can press certain keys on your computer keyboard while connecting your iPhone to your computer.

On a Windows PC:

Press and hold **Shift** + **Ctrl** while connecting your iPhone to your computer.

On a Mac:

Press and hold **Command** + **Option** while connecting your iPhone.

Turning Off the Auto Sync Permanently

You can turn off the auto sync permanently in iTunes. You might want to do this if you prefer to have manual control over all the sync processes.

> **CAUTION:** Turning off the auto sync also disables the automatic backup of your iPhone every time you connect it to your computer. This setting is best for a secondary computer, which you might use to charge your iPhone but would never want to sync.

To turn off the auto sync in iTunes, follow these steps:

1. From the iTunes menu, select **Edit** and then **Preferences**.

2. Click on the **Devices** tab at the top.

3. Check the box next to **Prevent iPods, iPhones and iPads from syncing automatically** (see Figure 3–15).

4. Click the **OK** button to save your settings.

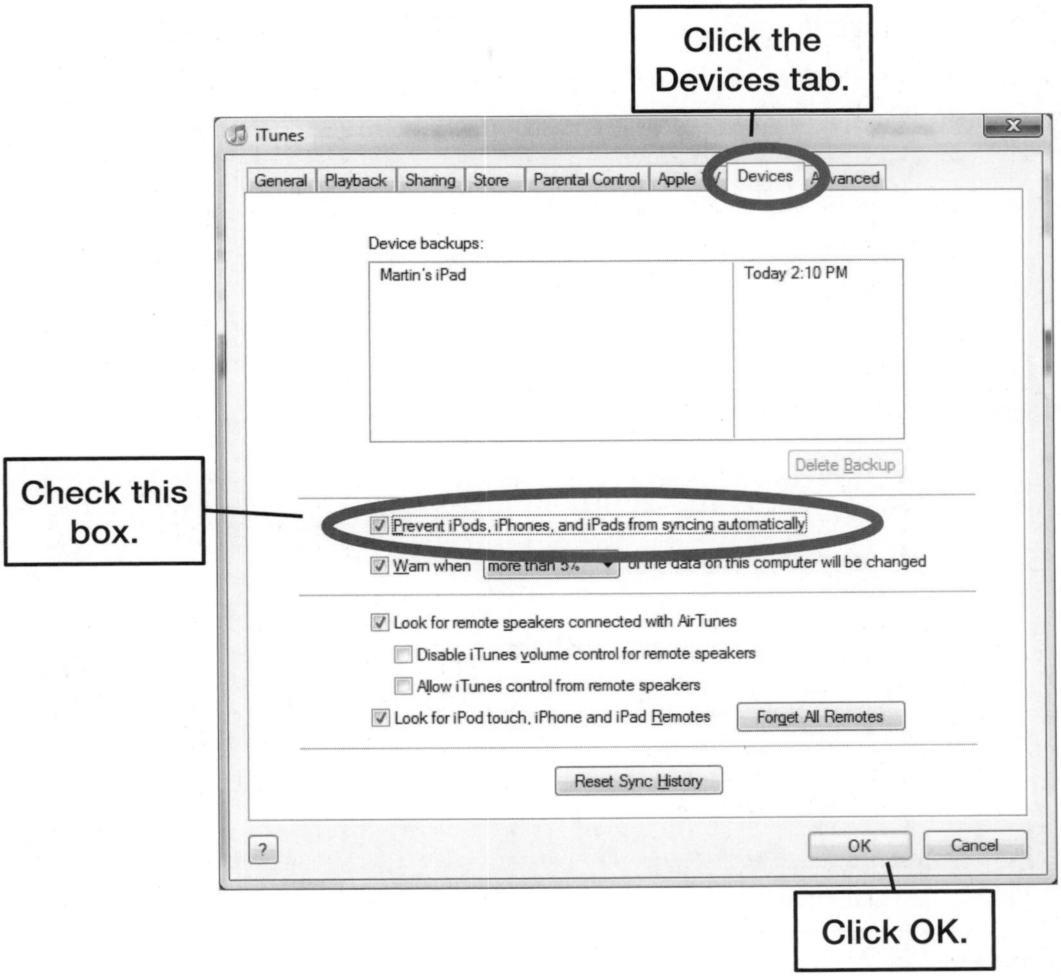

Figure 3–15. *Disabling auto sync in iTunes*

Getting a Clean Start with the Sync

Sometimes you'll have issues with the sync and just need to get a fresh start. There are a few things you can do in this regard with iTunes: you can erase or reset the sync history so iTunes thinks it is syncing for the first time with your iPhone, and you can force all information on the iPhone to be replaced with information from your computer.

Reset Sync History (Make iTunes Think It Is Syncing for the First Time)

To reset your sync history in iTunes, follow these steps:

1. Select the **Edit** menu and then click on **Preferences**.

2. Click the **Devices** tab at the top of the iTunes Preferences window.

3. Click the **Reset Sync History** button at the bottom, as shown in Figure 3–16.

4. Confirm your selection by clicking **Reset Sync History** in the pop-up window.

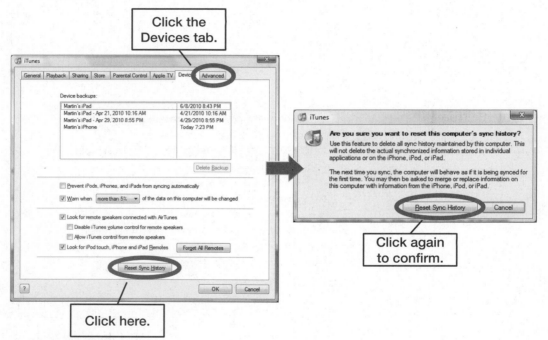

Figure 3–16. *Resetting sync history in iTunes*

Replace All Information on the iPhone (Next Sync Only)

Sometimes you may need to get a fresh start with your iPhone information. For whatever reason, you want to get rid of all the information on your iPhone in one or all the synced apps and just start over. Follow steps.

1. As you did to set up the sync previously, connect your iPhone to your computer, start iTunes, click on your **iPhone** in the left nav bar, and click the **Info** tab at the top of the main window.

2. Scroll all the way down to the **Advanced** section (see Figure 3–17).

3. Check one, some, or all of the boxes as you desire.

Check any boxes to erase all current information on the iPhone and replace it with the information from your computer.

Advanced

Replace information on this iPhone
- ☑ Contacts
- ☑ Calendars
- ☐ Mail Accounts
- ☐ Bookmarks
- ☑ Notes

During the next sync only, iTunes will replace the selected information on this iPhone with information from this computer.

Capacity	Audio	Photos	Apps	Books	Other	Free
14 GB	377.3 MB	25.4 MB	164.6 MB	10.4 MB	217.9 MB	13.22 GB

Cancel

Apply

Figure 3–17. *In the **Advanced** area, select the information you want to replace.*

4. When you are ready, click the **Apply** button in the lower-right corner. The sync should happen immediately. All of the information for the apps you have checked will be erased from the iPhone and replaced with the information from these your computer.

Apps: Sync and Manage Them

With iTunes, you can sync and manage your apps on your iPhone. It's easy to drag and drop your app icons around on a particular **Home** screen page or even between pages on your iPhone.

Sync Apps in iTunes

Follow these steps to sync and manage apps:

1. As you did to set up the sync previously, connect your iPhone to your computer, start iTunes, and click on your **iPhone** in the left nav bar.

2. Click the **Apps** tab on the top of the main window.

3. Click the check box next to **Sync Apps** to see all apps stored on your iPhone and your **Home** screens, as shown in Figure 3–18.

NOTE: To see what happens when you turn your iPhone to horizontal mode while it is connected to iTunes, look at Figure 3–18, which shows the vertical layout with the **Home** screens along the right.

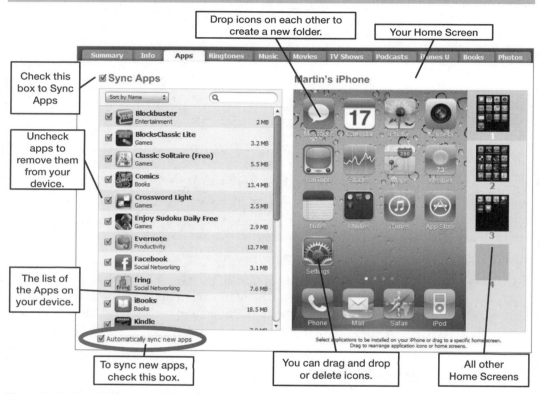

Figure 3–18. *Sync Apps screen in iTunes*

Move Apps, Work with Folders or Delete App Icons

It is very easy to move around and organize your application icons in this screen in iTunes, as Figure 3–19 shows.

To move an app within a screen: Click on it and drag it around the screen.

To move an app between Home screen pages: Click and drag it to the new page in the right column. The new page will expand in the main screen. Drop the icon in the main screen.

To dock an app on the bottom dock: Click and drag it down to drop it on the bottom dock. If there are already four icons on the bottom dock, you'll need to drag one off to make room for the new icon. Only four icons are allowed.

To create a new folder: Drag and drop one icon onto another icon.

To move an app into an existing folder: Drag and drop the icon onto the folder icon.

To move an app out of a folder: Click on the folder to open it. Then, drag and drop the icon outside of that folder.

To view another Home screen page: Click on that page in the right column.

To delete an app: Click on it, and then click the little **X** in the upper-left corner. You can only delete apps you have installed. You won't see an X on preinstalled apps like iTunes.

To delete a folder: Remove all apps from that folder (drag them out) and it will disappear.

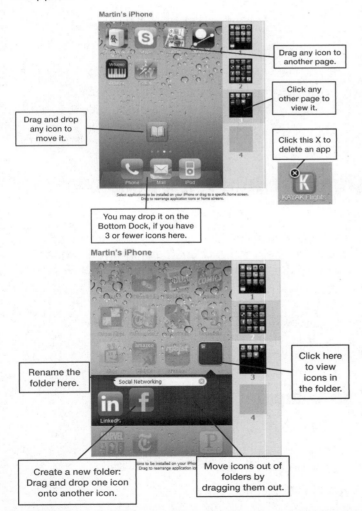

Figure 3–19. *Moving app icons, working with folders, or deleting apps in iTunes*

Remove or Reinstall Apps

To remove an app from your iPhone, simply uncheck the box next to it and confirm your selection, as shown in Figure 3–20.

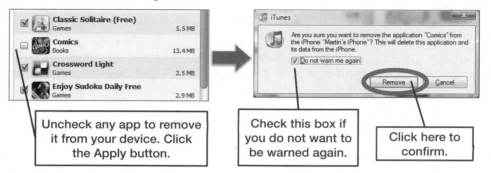

Figure 3–20. *Unchecking an app to delete it from your iPhone*

> **TIP:** Even if you delete an app from your iPhone, if you have chosen to sync apps as shown, you can still reinstall that app by rechecking the box next to it. The app will be reloaded onto your iPhone during the next sync.

File Sharing (File Transfer) Between iPhone and Computer

As long as you have an app installed that works with files, such as GoodReader or Stanza, you can use iTunes to transfer files between your computer and your iPhone. You perform this file transfer using the bottom of the **Apps** tab in iTunes—below all the application icon screens.

> **TIP:** Some apps, such as GoodReader, come with wireless methods for transferring and sharing files. Check out the GoodReader section in Chapter 15: "New Media," for more information.

Copying Files from Your Computer to Your iPhone

To copy files from your computer to your iPhone, follow these steps.

1. As you did to set up the previous sync, connect your iPhone to your computer, start iTunes, and click on your **iPhone** in the left nav bar.

2. Click the **Apps** tab on the top of the main window.

3. Scroll down to the **File Sharing** section below the apps.

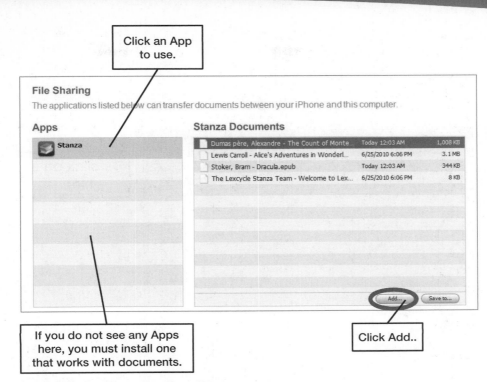

Click an App to use.

File Sharing

The applications listed below can transfer documents between your iPhone and this computer.

Apps

Stanza

Stanza Documents

Dumas père, Alexandre - The Count of Monte...	Today 12:03 AM	1,008 KB
Lewis Carroll - Alice's Adventures in Wonderl...	6/25/2010 6:06 PM	3.1 MB
Stoker, Bram - Dracula.epub	Today 12:03 AM	344 KB
The Lexcycle Stanza Team - Welcome to Lex...	6/25/2010 6:06 PM	8 KB

Add...   Save to...

If you do not see any Apps here, you must install one that works with documents.

Click Add..

Figure 3–21. *Transferring files to your iPhone*

4. Click on any app to use in the left column, and then click the **Add** button in the lower-right corner (see Figure 3–21).

5. A window will pop up, to let you select a file to transfer and click the **Open** button, as shown in Figure 3–22. The file will be transferred immediately to your iPhone.

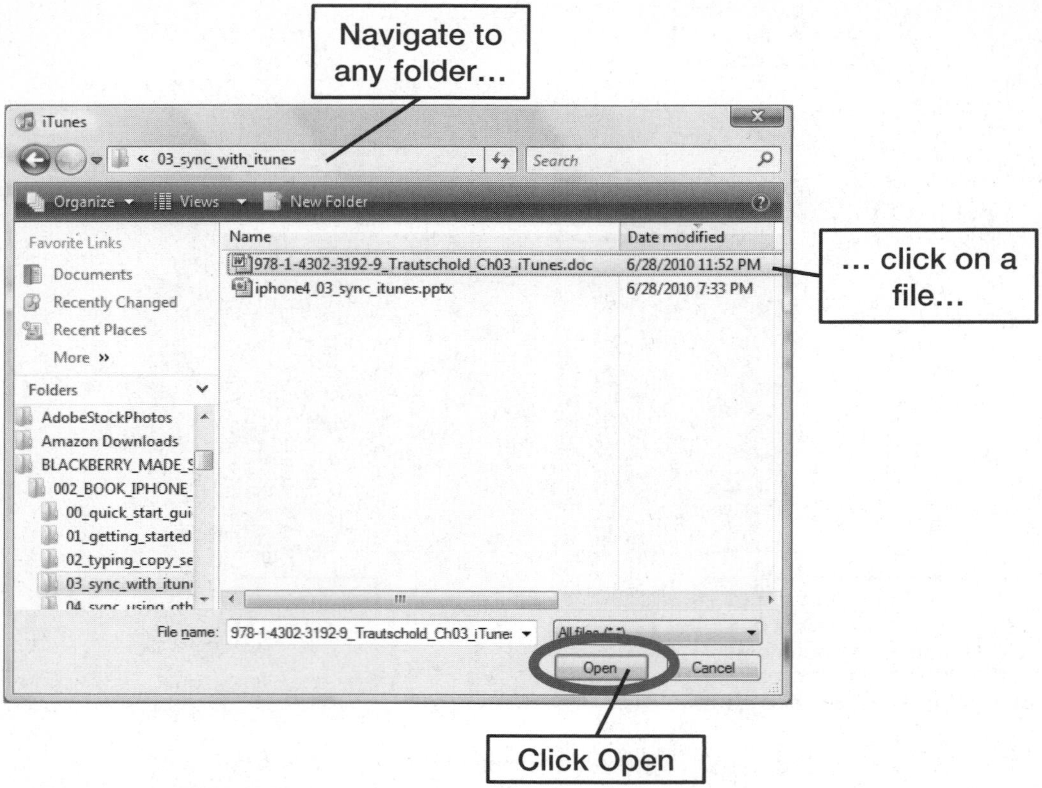

Figure 3–22. *Selecting a file to transfer to your iPhone*

Copying Files from Your iPhone to Your Computer

To copy files from your iPhone to your computer, follow these steps.

1. Connect your iPhone to your computer, start iTunes, and click on your **iPhone** in the left nav bar.

2. Click the **Apps** tab at the top of the main window.

3. Scroll down to the **File Sharing** section below the apps (see Figure 3–23).

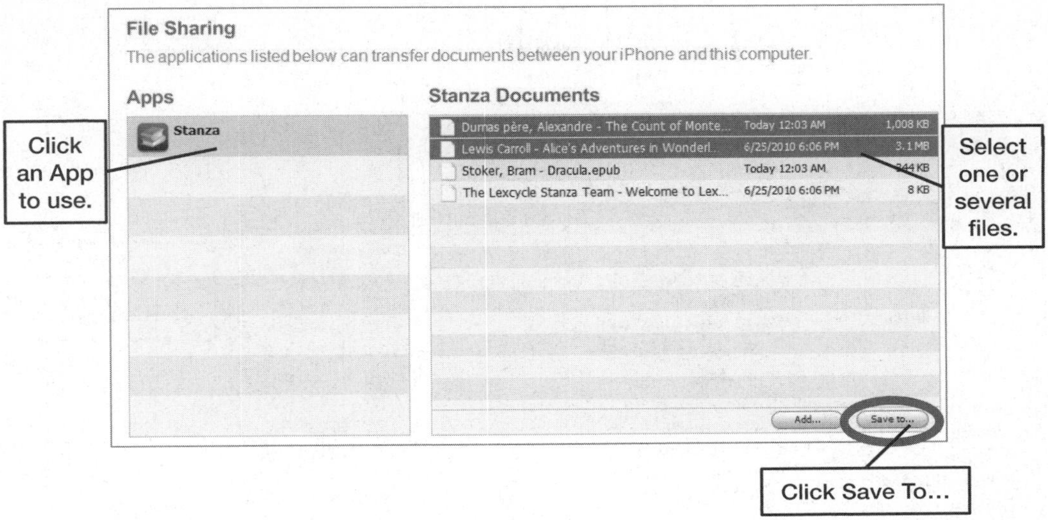

Figure 3–23. *Transferring files from your iPhone*

4. Click on any app from which you want to transfer the files in the left column.

5. Select one or several files using any of these methods:

   a. Click on a single file.

   b. Hold the **Control** key (Windows) or **Option** key (Mac) and click on any number of files.

   c. Hold the **Shift** key and click on the top and bottom file in a list to select all files in that list.

6. After the file(s) are selected, click the **Save To** button in the lower-right corner.

7. A window will pop up asking you to select a folder on your computer to receive the files from your iPhone. Locate and click on the folder, and then click the **Select Folder** button, as shown in Figure 3–24. The file(s) will be transferred immediately to your computer.

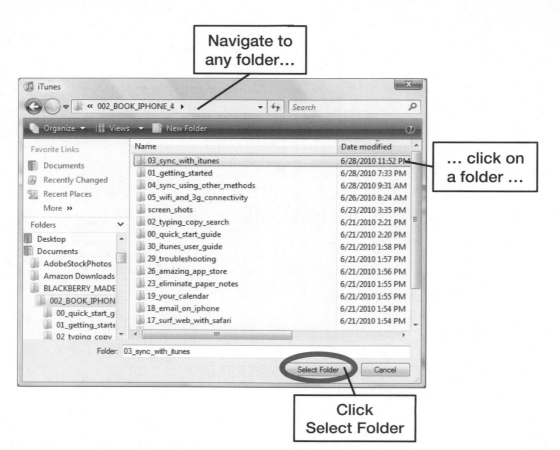

Figure 3–24. *Selecting a folder on your computer to receive files from your iPhone*

Sync Media and More

Now let's look at how to set up an automatic sync for music, movies, iBooks, iTunes U content, and more.

> **CAUTION:** Make sure you're logged into iTunes with the same iTunes account you want to use on your iPhone as Digital Rights Management (DRM)-protected content (music, videos, and more) won't sync unless both accounts match. You can log out and log in to iTunes on both your desktop and your iPhone if you have to to make sure you are logged into the right accounts.

Syncing Ringtones

When you click the **Ringtones** tab, you can choose to sync your entire ringtone library or selected items.

1. Connect your iPhone to your computer, start iTunes, and click on your iPhone in the left nav bar.

2. Click the **Ringtones** tab at the top of the main window.

3. Check the box next to **Sync Ringtones,** shown to the right.

| Summary | Info | Apps | **Ringtones** | Music |

☑ **Sync Ringtones**

⦿ All ringtones
◯ Selected ringtones

4. The default is to sync **All ringtones**. To sync only specific ones, click the radio button next to **Selected ringtones**.

5. When you are done with your selections, click the **Apply** button to start the ringtone sync.

> **TIP:** Learn how to assign ringtones to your contacts, purchase custom ringtones and create your own ringtones from your music in Chapter 10: "Using Your iPhone as a Phone."

Syncing Music

When you click the **Music** tab, you can choose to sync your entire music library or selected items.

> **CAUTION:** If you have manually transferred some music, music videos, or voice memos to your iPhone already, you'll receive a warning message that all existing content on your iPhone will be removed and replaced with the selected music library from your computer.

To sync music from your computer to your iPhone, follow these steps.

1. Connect your iPhone to your computer, start iTunes, and click on your **iPhone** in the left nav bar.

2. Click the **Music** tab on the top of the main window.

3. Check the box next to **Sync Music** (see Figure 3–25).

4. Click next to **Entire music library** only if you are *sure* your music library will not be too large for your iPhone.

5. Click next to **Selected playlists, artists, and genres** if you are unsure whether your music library is too large, or if you want to sync only specific playlists or artists.

 a. You can choose whether to include music videos and voice memos by checking those boxes.

 b. You can also automatically fill free space with songs.

> **CAUTION:** We don't recommend checking this option because it will take up all the space in your iPhone and leave no room for all those cool apps!

 c. Now check off any of the playlists or artists in the two columns on the bottom of the screen. You can even use the search box at the top of the **Artists** column to search for particular artists.

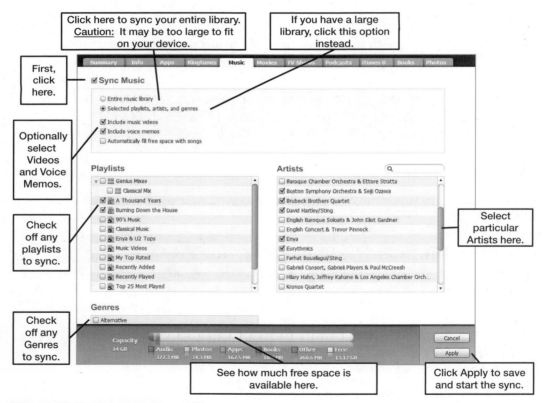

Figure 3–25. *Syncing music with your iPhone*

6. When you are done with your selections, click the **Apply** button to start the music sync.

Syncing Movies

When you click the **Movies** tab, you can choose to sync specific, recent, or unwatched movies, or all of them.

To sync movies from your computer to your iPhone, follow these steps.

1. Connect your iPhone to your computer, start iTunes, and click on your **iPhone** in the left nav bar.

2. Click the **Movies** tab on the top of the main window.

3. Check the box next to **Sync Movies** (see Figure 3–26).

4. If you'd like to sync recent or unwatched movies, check the box next to **Automatically include** and use the pull-down to select **All, 1 most recent, All unwatched, 5 most recent unwatched**, etc.

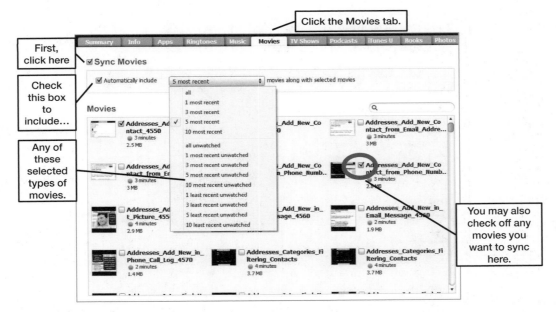

Figure 3–26. *Configuring movie sync to automatically include selections*

5. If you selected any item besides **All**, you have the choice to sync specific movies or videos to your iPhone. Simply check the boxes next to the movies you want to include in the sync.

6. When you are done choosing movies, click the **Apply** button to save your settings and start the sync.

Syncing TV Shows

When you click the **TV Shows** tab, you can choose to sync specific, recent, or unwatched TV shows, or all of them.

To sync TV shows from your computer to your iPhone, follow these steps.

1. Connect your iPhone to your computer, start iTunes, and click on your **iPhone** in the left nav bar.

2. Click the **TV Shows** tab on the top of the main window.

3. Check the box next to **Sync TV Shows** (see Figure 3–27).

4. If you'd like to sync recent or unwatched TV shows, check the box next to **Automatically include** and use the pull-down to select **All, 1 newest, All unwatched, 5 oldest unwatched**, **10 newest unwatched**, etc.

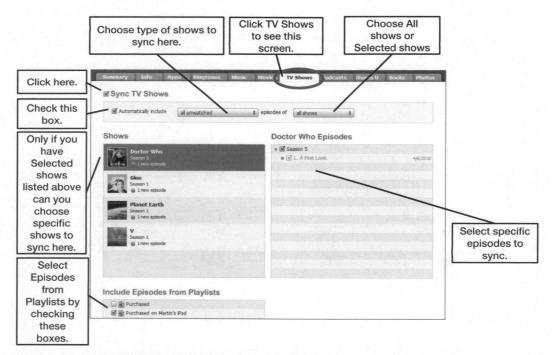

Figure 3–27. *Configuring TV show sync to automatically include selections*

5. Choose **All Shows** or **Selected Shows** next to **episodes of**.

6. If you choose **Selected Shows**, you can choose individual shows and even individual episodes in the two sections in the middle of the screen.

7. If you have playlists of TV shows, you can select those for inclusion by checking the boxes in the bottom section of the screen.

8. When you are done choosing individual TV shows, click the **Apply** button to save your settings and start the sync.

Syncing Podcasts

When you click the **Podcasts** tab, you can choose to sync specific, recent, or unplayed podcasts, or all of them.

TIP: Podcasts are audio or video shows that are usually regularly scheduled (e.g., daily, weekly, or monthly). Most are free to subscribe to in the iTunes store. When you subscribe and set up the auto sync as shown in this section, you'll receive all your favorite podcasts on your iPhone.

Many of your favorite radio shows are recorded and broadcast as podcasts. We encourage you to check out the **Podcast** section of the iTunes store to see what might interest you. You'll find podcasts of movie reviews, news shows, law school test reviews, game shows, old radio shows, educational content, and much more.

To sync podcasts from your computer to your iPhone, follow these steps.

1. Connect your iPhone to your computer, start iTunes, and click on your **iPhone** in the left nav bar.

2. Click the **Podcasts** tab on the top of the main window.

3. Check the box next to **Sync Podcasts** (see Figure 3–28).

4. If you'd like to sync recent or unplayed podcasts, check the box next to **Automatically include** and use the pull-down to select **All, 1 newest, All unplayed, 5 newest, 10 most recent unplayed**, etc.

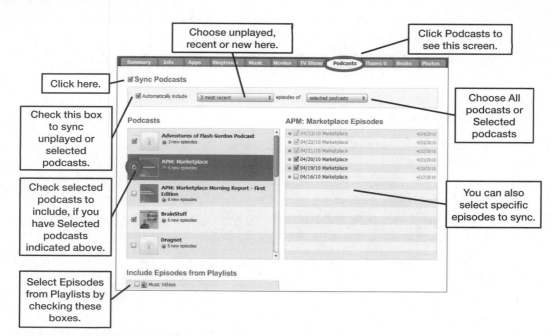

Figure 3–28. *Configuring podcast sync to automatically include selections*

5. Choose **All Podcasts** or **Selected Podcasts** next to **episodes of**.

6. If you choose **Selected Podcasts**, you can choose individual podcasts and even individual episodes in the two sections in the middle of the screen.

7. If you have playlists of podcasts, you can select those for inclusion by checking the boxes in the bottom section of the screen.

8. When you are done choosing podcasts, click the **Apply** button to save your settings and start the sync.

TIP: After you sync these podcasts, you enjoy them in the **Podcasts** section of the iPod app on your device.

Sync iTunes U

When you click the **iTunes U** tab, you can choose to sync specific, recent, or unplayed iTunes U content, or all content.

> **TIP: iTunes U** podcasts are similar to other audio or video podcasts, except that they focus on educational content and are mostly produced by colleges and universities. Most are free to subscribe to in the iTunes store. When you subscribe and set up the auto sync as shown in this section, you'll receive all your favorite **iTunes U** podcasts on your iPhone.
>
> Be sure to check out the **iTunes U** section in the iTunes store. You may find your favorite college or university has shows to teach you biology or astronomy, or a whole lot more. There's even a Stanford University course on how to develop iPhone apps! Many of the top universities broadcast class lectures from famous professors in **iTunes U**. Go ahead and check it out—what you'll find is amazing!

To sync **iTunes U** content from your computer to your iPhone, follow these steps.

1. Connect your iPhone to your computer, start iTunes, and click on your **iPhone** in the left nav bar.

2. Click the **iTunes U** tab on the top of the main window.

3. Check the box next to **Sync iTunes U** (see Figure 3–29).

4. If you'd like to sync recent or unplayed items, check the box next to **Automatically include** and use the pull-down to select **All, 1 newest, All unplayed, 5 newest, 10 most recent unplayed**, etc.

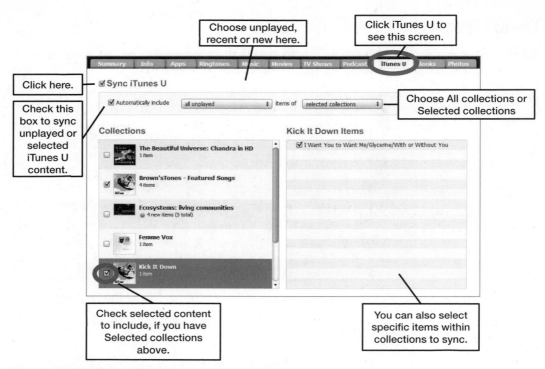

Figure 3–29. *Configuring iTunes U sync to automatically include selections*

5. Choose **All Collections** or **Selected Collections** next to **items of**.

6. If you choose **Selected Collections**, you can choose individual collections and even individual items in the two sections in the middle of the screen.

7. If you have playlists of **iTunes U** podcasts, you can select those for inclusion by checking the boxes in the bottom section of the screen under **Include Items from Playlists**.

8. When you are done choosing individual items, click the Apply button to save your settings and start the sync.

Sync iBooks and Audiobooks

When you click the **Books** tab, you can choose to sync all or selected books and audiobooks.

> **TIP:** Books on the iPhone are electronic versions of their paper cousins. They are in a specific electronic format called *ePub*. You can buy them in the iBookstore on the iPhone or acquire them from other locations and sync them to your iPhone using the steps described here. Books you acquire elsewhere must be unprotected or "DRM-free" in order to sync them to your iPhone. You read these books in the iBooks app or in other book reader apps on your iPhone. See Chapter 14: "iBooks and E-Books" to learn more.

To sync books or audiobooks between your computer and your iPhone, follow these steps.

1. Connect your iPhone to your computer, start iTunes, and click on your **iPhone** in the left nav bar.

2. Click the **Books** tab on the top of the main window.

3. Check the boxes next to **Sync Books** and **Sync Audiobooks** (see Figure 3–30).

4. If you'd like to sync all books, leave the default **All books** selection.

5. Otherwise, choose **Selected books** and make your choices by checking specific books in the window.

> **TIP:** In order to sync iBooks, PDF files and other similar documents to your iPhone, you need to first drag and drop your file from your computer into your iTunes library. Grab the file from any folder on your computer and drag and drop it right on your library in the upper left column in iTunes.

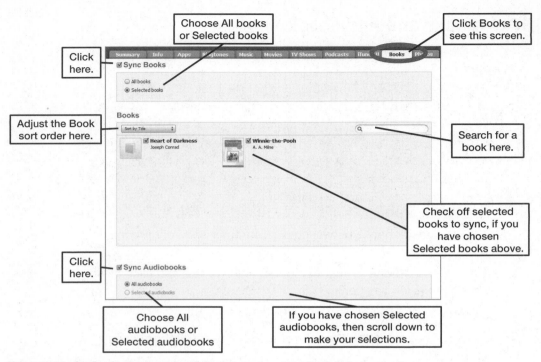

Figure 3–30. *Configuring books and audiobooks sync to automatically include selections*

6. If you would like to sync all audiobooks, leave the default **All audiobooks** selection.

7. Otherwise, choose **Selected audiobooks** and make your choices by checking off specific audiobooks in the window below this selection item.

8. When you are done choosing individual books and audiobooks, click the **Apply** button to save your settings and start the sync.

TIP: After you sync these books, you can enjoy them in the **iBooks** app on your device. You can listen to audiobooks in the **iPod** app, where the **Audiobooks** tab is on the left side.

NOTE: Audiobooks from Audible require that you first authorize your computer with your Audible account before you can sync them to your iPhone from your computer.

Sync Photos

When you click the **Photos** tab, you can choose to sync photos from all folders or selected folders and you can even include videos.

TIP: You can create a beautiful electronic picture frame and share your photos on the stunning iPhone screen (see Chapter: 21 "Working with Photos"). You can even use your photos to set the background wallpaper and screen-lock wallpaper—see Chapter 9: "Personalize and Secure Your iPhone" for more information.

To sync photos from your computer to your iPhone, follow these steps.

1. Connect your iPhone to your computer, start iTunes, and click on your **iPhone** in the left nav bar.

TIP: Mac users can also sync photos using **iPhoto**, including Events (time-based sync), Faces (person-based sync), and Places (location-based sync).

2. Click the **Photos** tab on the top of the main window.

3. Check the box next to **Sync Photos from**. See Figure 3-31.

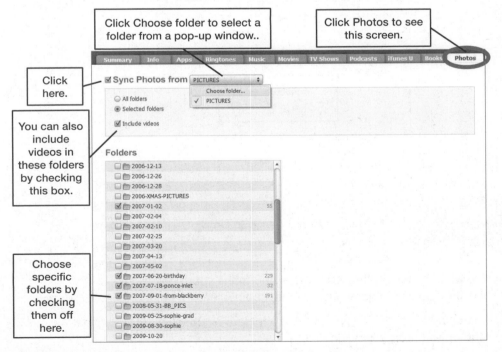

Figure 3–31. *Configuring photo sync to automatically include selections*

4. Click the pull-down menu next to **Sync Photos from** and select a folder from your computer where your photos are stored. If you want to grab all your photos, go to the highest folder level possible (e.g., **C:** on your Windows computer or "**/**" on your Apple Mac). See Figure 3–32.

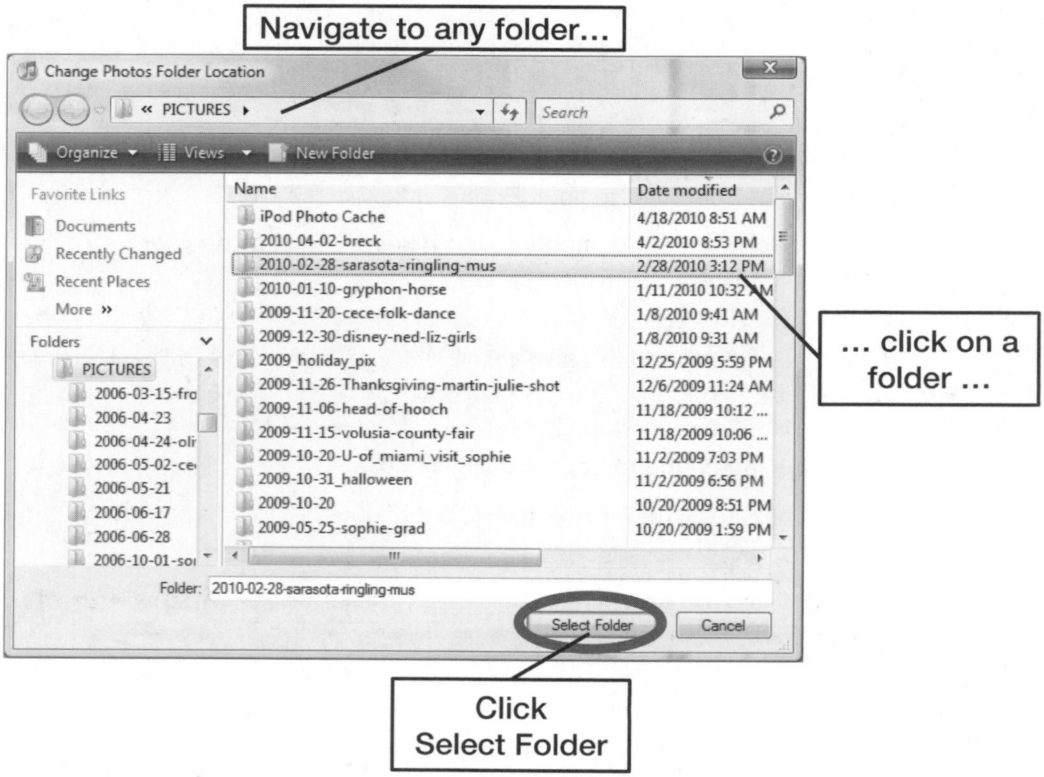

Figure 3–32. *Selecting a folder on your computer to sync your photos*

5. If you'd like to sync all photos from the selected folder on your computer, select **All folders**, shown in Figure 3–31.

CAUTION: Because your photo library on your computer may be too large to fit on your iPhone, be careful about checking **All folders**.

6. Otherwise, choose **Selected folders** and make your choices by checking specific folders in the window below, shown in Figure 3–31.

7. You can also include any videos in the folders by checking the box next to **Include videos,** shown in Figure 3–31.

8. When you are done choosing your photos to sync, click the **Apply** button to save your settings and start the sync.

9. When the sync starts, you'll see the status in the middle-top status window in iTunes.

How to Know What Is New or Unplayed in iTunes

You may notice little numbers next to items in the left nav bar of iTunes. There are similar little blue numbers in the upper-right corner of items in the main window. These numbers show how many items are unplayed, unwatched, or, in the case of apps, require updates. See Figure 3–33.

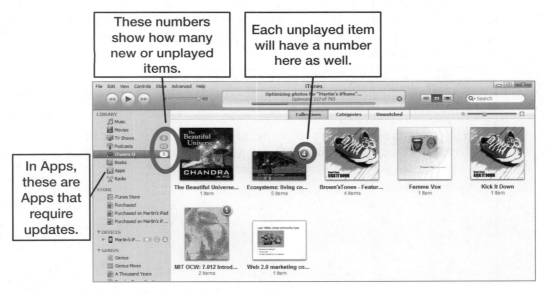

Figure 3–33. *Quickly see the number of unplayed items.*

Manually Transferring Music, Movies, Podcasts, and More on Your iPhone (Drag-and-Drop Method)

The auto sync sections showed you how to automatically sync content to your iPhone. Here you'll learn how to manually transfer songs, videos, books, audiobooks, and more. The process is the same for all types of content, so we'll show you how to do it for just one type.

TIP: Use these same drag-and-drop techniques to add items to a playlist.

To manually transfer content from your computer to your iPhone, follow these steps.

NOTE: Be sure to check **Manually manage music and videos** on the **Summary** tab in iTunes before you try to drag and drop music or videos. If you've chosen to automatically sync content (e.g., music, movies, podcasts, etc.), you won't be able to use this drag-and-drop method to copy items to your iPhone.

1. Connect your iPhone to your computer, and start iTunes.

2. In the left nav bar, click on your **iPhone**. Then click on the **Summary** tab at the top. Near the bottom of the screen, make sure the check box next to **Manually manage music and videos** is checked. You may see a warning message if you have previously synced music or videos to your iPhone, saying that all previously synced music and videos will be replaced with your iTunes library. This is OK.

3. In the left nav bar, under the **LIBRARY** heading, click the type of content (**Music, Movies, TV Shows, Podcasts, iTunes U**, etc.) you'd like to transfer.

4. In the main window you'll see your library of content. It's usually easiest to select **List View** from the top of iTunes, as shown in Figure 3–34. This allows you to see all the content in a list and easily select a single item or group of items.

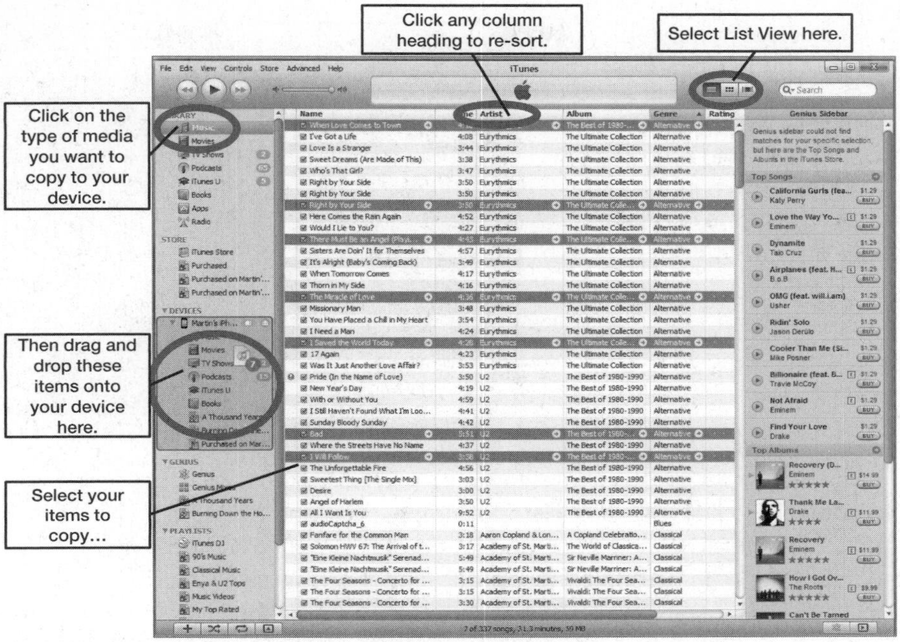

Figure 3–34. *Selecting media to drag and drop onto your device*

5. Start selecting content using any of these methods.

a. To select an individual item, simply click on it to highlight it.

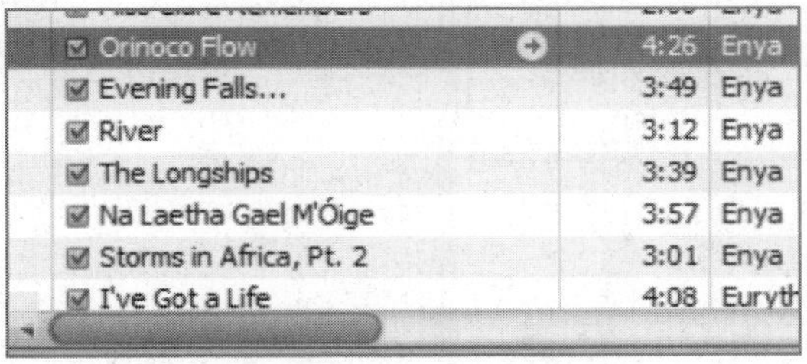

b. To select items that are not in a continuous list, Windows users press and hold the Control key while clicking on items, and Mac users press and hold the Command key while clicking.

c. To select items in a continuous list, press and hold the Shift key while clicking first the top item and then the bottom item in the list. All the items in between will be selected.

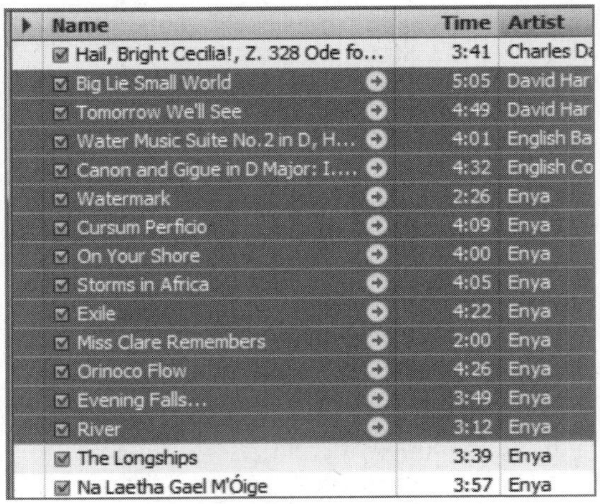

	Name	Time	Artist
	☑ Hail, Bright Cecilia!, Z. 328 Ode fo...	3:41	Charles Da
	☑ Big Lie Small World	➡	5:05	David Har
	☑ Tomorrow We'll See	➡	4:49	David Har
	☑ Water Music Suite No. 2 in D, H...	➡	4:01	English Ba
	☑ Canon and Gigue in D Major: I....	➡	4:32	English Co
	☑ Watermark	➡	2:26	Enya
	☑ Cursum Perficio	➡	4:09	Enya
	☑ On Your Shore	➡	4:00	Enya
	☑ Storms in Africa	➡	4:05	Enya
	☑ Exile	➡	4:22	Enya
	☑ Miss Clare Remembers	➡	2:00	Enya
	☑ Orinoco Flow	➡	4:26	Enya
	☑ Evening Falls...	➡	3:49	Enya
	☑ River	➡	3:12	Enya
	☑ The Longships	3:39	Enya
	☑ Na Laetha Gael M'Óige	3:57	Enya

6. Then, to copy these items to your iPhone, simply click and drag the selected item(s) over to your iPhone and let go of the mouse button. All selected items will then be copied to your iPhone. See Figure 3–35.

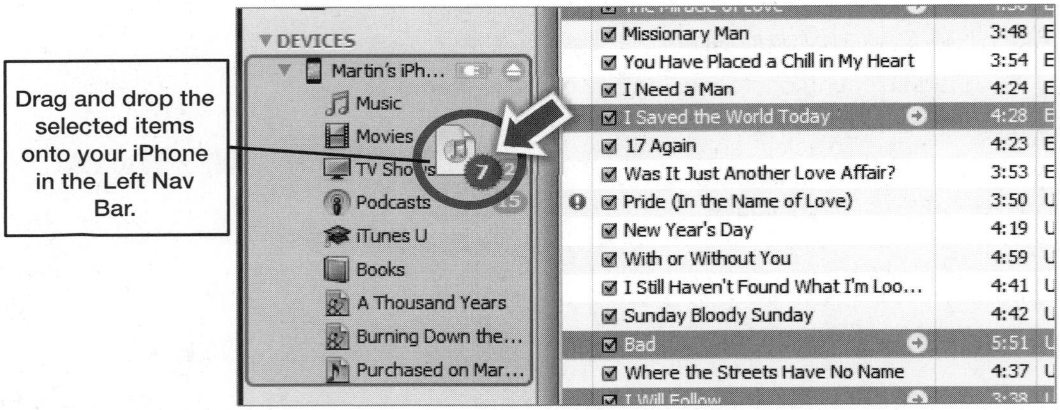

Figure 3–35. *Dragging and dropping selected items onto your device*

Troubleshooting iTunes and the Sync

Sometimes iTunes does not behave exactly as you'd expect it to, so here are a few simple troubleshooting tips.

Check Out the Apple Knowledgebase for Helpful Articles

The first step when you're having a problem is to check out Apple's support pages, where you'll find lots of helpful information. On your iPhone or computer's web browser, go to this web page:

`http://www.apple.com/support/iPhone/`

Then click on a topic in the left nav bar, as shown in Figure 3–36.

Figure 3–36. *Apple knowlegebase for the iPhone*

iTunes Locked Up and Will Not Respond (Windows Computer)

1. Bring up the **Windows Task Manager** by simultaneously pressing **Ctrl** + **Alt** + **Del** keys on your keyboard. The **Task Manager** should look something like Figure 3–37.

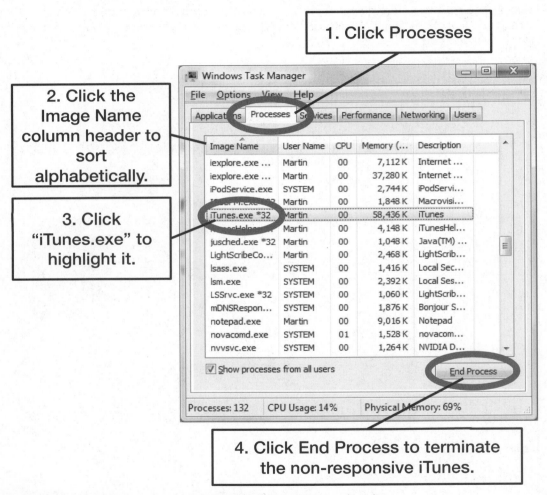

1. Click Processes

2. Click the Image Name column header to sort alphabetically.

3. Click "iTunes.exe" to highlight it.

4. Click End Process to terminate the non-responsive iTunes.

Figure 3–37. Locating iTunes.exe in **Windows Task Manager** to terminate it

2. Then, to end the process, click **End process** from the pop-up window, as shown in Figure 3–38.

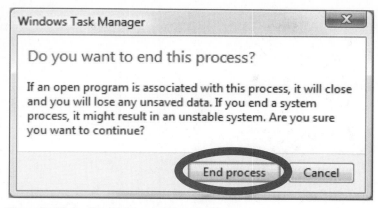

Figure 3–38. Confirming to end process in Windows

3. Now, iTunes should be forced to close.

4. Try restarting iTunes.

5. If iTunes will not start or it locks up again, reboot your computer and try again.

iTunes Locked Up and Will Not Respond (Mac Computer)

TIP: Pressing **Command + Option + Escape** is the shortcut to bring up the **Force Quit Applications** window, shown in Figure 3–39.

1. Go up to the iTunes Menu at the top and click.

2. Click on **Quit iTunes.**

3. If that doesn't work, go to any other program and click on the small "Apple" in the upper left-hand corner.

4. Click on **Force Quit** and the list of running programs will be displayed.

5. Highlight iTunes and click on the **Force Quit** button.

6. If this does not help, try restarting your Mac.

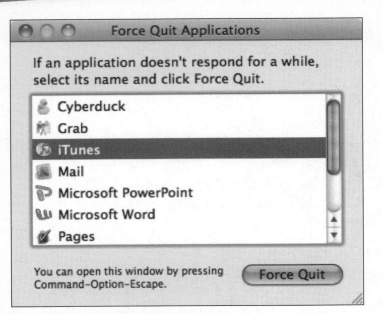

Figure 3–39. Force Quit Applications window on Mac computers

Update Your iPhone Operating System

You can check for updated software and install updated operating system (iOS) software using iTunes.

> **NOTE:** Do this update when you won't mind being without your iPhone for 30 minutes or more depending on the amount of information on your iPhone and the speed of your computer and Internet connection..

Normally, iTunes will automatically check for updates on a set schedule, about every two weeks. If no update is found iTunes will tell you when it will check for another update.

As you can see, iTunes found an update and is showing 4.0.1 is now available in Figure 3–40 .

1. Start iTunes.

2. Connect your iPhone to your computer.

3. Click on your iPhone listed under **DEVICES** in the left nav bar.

4. Click on the **Summary** tab in the top nav bar.

5. Click the **Check for Update** button in the center of the screen in the **Version** section.

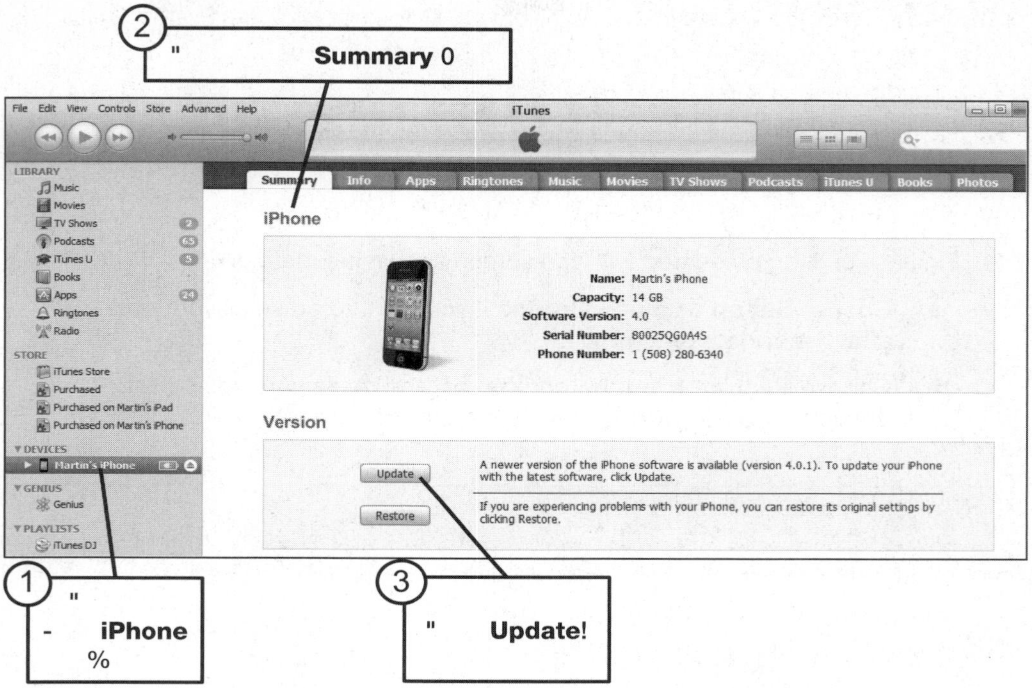

Figure 3–40. *Checking for updated software*

6. If you have the latest version, you'll see a pop-up window saying something like "This version of the iPhone software (4.0.1) is the current version." Click **OK** to close the window. You are done with the update process.

7. If you don't have the latest version, a window will tell you a new version is available and ask if you would like to update. Click **Yes** or **Update**.

8. iTunes will take you through a few screens that describe the update and ask you to agree to the software license. If you agree, click **Next** and **Agree** to download the latest iOS software from Apple. This will take about 5-10 minutes.

TIP: We show you all the screens you might see in this update process in the "Reinstalling the iPhone Operating System" section of Chapter 29: "Troubleshooting."

9. Next, iTunes will backup your iPhone, which might take 10 minutes or more if your iPhone is filled with data.

10. Now the new iOS will be installed and your iPhone erased.

11. Finally, you'll be presented with the screen shown in Figure 3–41.

    a. Choose **Set up as a new iPhone** if you want to erase all your data after the update process.

    b. Choose **Restore from the backup of**, and make sure you select the correct backup file (usually the most recent one).

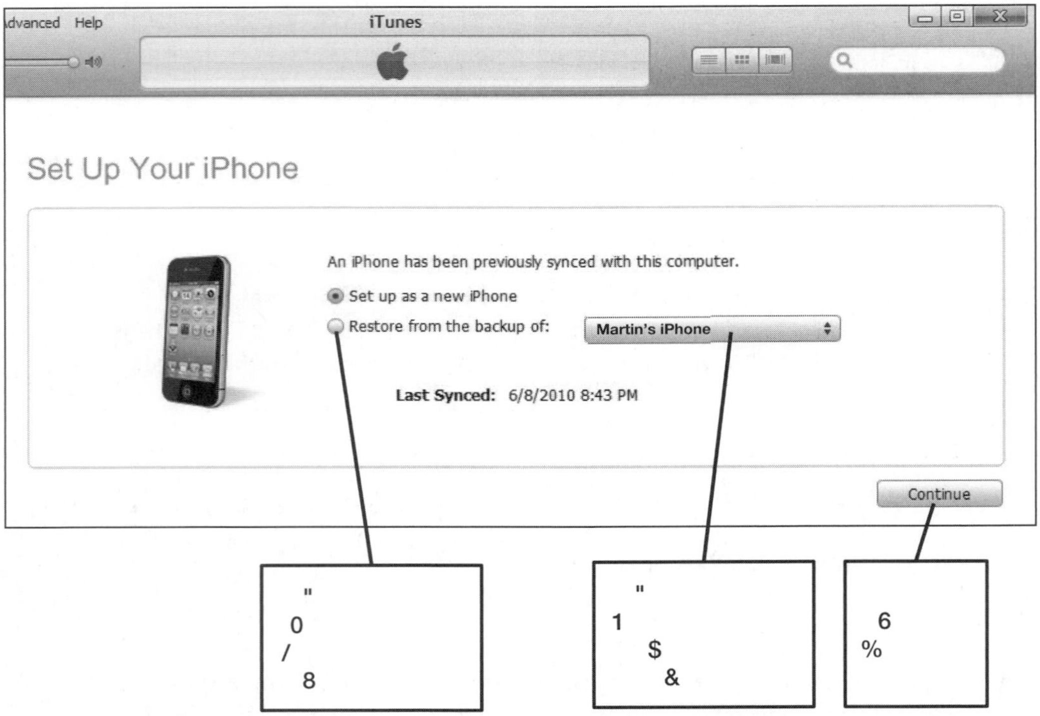

Figure 3–41. *Setting up your iPhone as a new device or restoring from a backup file*

12. Now your iPhone will be restored or set up as you selected.

13. If you have locked your SIM card, then you will need to enter the 4-digit unlock PIN code as shown in Figure 3-42.

CAUTION: If you have locked your SIM card, you will need to enter the unlock 4-digit code after the update is installed. If you forgot the SIM unlock code, then you can use the PUK code to unlock the SIM which you need to get from your wireless carrier. See the "Setting Security on your SIM Card" section of Chapter 10: "iPhone as a Phone."

You only have three attempts.

You will need to enter your SIM PIN if you have previously locked your SIM.

Figure 3–42. *Enter your SIM Unlock PIN Code*

   14. Your iPhone OS update is complete.

Chapter 4

Other Sync Methods

In Chapter 3: "Sync Your iPhone with iTunes," you learned how to connect your iPhone to your computer and use iTunes to sync your personal information, music, videos, and more. In this chapter, we explore some alternative ways to wirelessly synchronize information to your iPhone. The benefit of the wireless methods is that you don't need to connect your iPhone to your computer to have the information updated. Everything happens over the air—automatically. The two methods we cover are Apple's MobileMe Service and Exchange / Google Sync.

NOTE: If you use the Gmail account setting instead of Exchange, as we describe in this chapter, to set up your Gmail, you will be able to wirelessly sync your mail, calendar, and notes, but not your Google contacts. So if you do not need Google Contacts synced, you can use the Gmail setting instead of Exchange.

Wireless Sync of Your Google or Exchange Information

Using the steps we describe here, your iPhone can wirelessly sync your email, contacts, and calendar from a Microsoft Exchange account or a Google Account.

TIP: For the first time ever, you can now wirelessly sync multiple Exchange accounts on your iPhone 4. If you have several Google and Microsoft Exchange accounts, you can wirelessly sync all accounts at the same time to your iPhone. Before the iPhone 4, you had to choose between your accounts. Now you can sync them all!

Why Do We Say Google/Exchange?

We use the words Google and Exchange interchangeably here because you set up your Google sync using the Exchange setting on your iPhone. Google has licensed Microsoft Exchange ActiveSync so you can now set up your Google account just like an Exchange account and enjoy the same push email, contacts, and calendar functionality. We know it is a little confusing, but you set up both your Google and Exchange accounts in the identical manner, using the Exchange settings on your iPhone—so we say Google/Exchange.

If You Want a Google Account, Create One

If you do not have a Microsoft Exchange account, but you still want a wireless sync, then you should set up a free Google account to store your contacts and calendar. The account will allow you to start using Google Mail (Gmail), Contacts, and Calendar.

To set up your Google account, follow these steps:

1. From either your computer's web browser or Safari on your iPhone, type in: www.gmail.com.

2. Press the **Create an account** button.

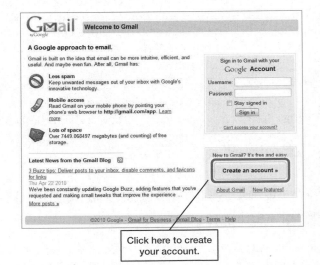

3. On the next screen, enter the information requested and click the button at the bottom of the page that says **I accept. Create my account.**

4. When that's successful, you'll see a screen that says **Congratulations!**

5. Click the **Show me my account>>** button to get started.

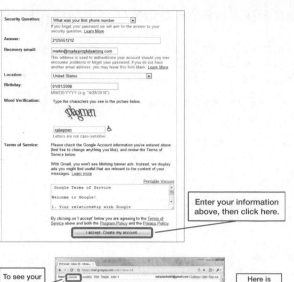

Enter your information above, then click here.

6. To see your Calendar, click the **Calendar** link in the upper left corner.

7. To see your Contacts, click the **Contacts** link in the left side of the Gmail inbox page.

To see your Calendar, click here.

Here is your Gmail inbox.

To see your Contacts, click here.

Note: Contacts are tied to Gmail and must be reached from this inbox screen.

As soon as you set up the sync as shown here, you will begin to see all changes to your contacts and calendar from Google magically appear on your iPhone. The same goes for any changes or additions from your iPhone—they will automatically appear in Google in moments.

TIP: It is extremely easy for your Google Contacts list grow into the thousands because it automatically includes everyone you have ever emailed from your Gmail account. You may want to clean up your list before you set up the sync to your iPhone.

Set Up Your Google or Exchange Account on Your iPhone

Use the following steps to set up the wireless sync for either your Exchange account or your Google contacts and calendar:

1. Touch the **Settings** icon on your iPhone.

2. Touch **Mail, Contacts, and Calendars**.

3. You'll see a list of your email accounts and, below that, the **Add Account** option.

   If you have no accounts set up, you will see only **Add Account**. In either case, tap **Add Account.**

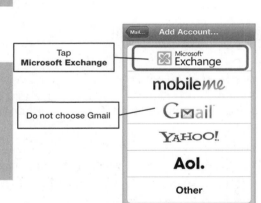

> **TIP:** To edit any account listed, just touch that account.

4. On the next screen, choose **Microsoft Exchange**.

> **NOTE:** You should choose Microsoft Exchange if you want to have the wireless sync with your Google Contacts and Calendar. If you select Gmail, you will not be able to wirelessly sync your Google Contacts.

5. Type your email address.

> **TIP:** To type the **.com** (or .net, .edu, .org, etc.) in the email address, press and hold the period key until you see the **.com** key appear above it. Slide over and press **.com**.
>
>

> **TIP:** Since your email address is usually also your username, save yourself some time by copying and pasting it.

6. Copy and paste your email address into the **Username** field.

   a. Touch and hold the **email address** until you see the black pop-up appear above it.

   b. Tap **Select All**.

   c. Tap **Copy**.

   d. Touch and hold in the **Username** field until you see the pop-up appear. Tap **Paste**.

Touch and hold your Email address. Tap **Select All.**

| Cancel | Select | Select All | Paste |

Email	rtin.trautschold@gmail.com
Domain	Optional
Username	Required
Password	Required

Tap **Copy.**

| Cancel | Cut | Copy | Paste |

| **Email** | rtin.trautschold@gmail.com |
| **Domain** | Optional |

| Cancel | Exchange | Next |

Email	martin.trautschold@gmail...
Domain	Paste	onal
Username	Required
Password	Required

Touch and hold here, then tap **Paste.**

7. Leave the **Domain** blank.
   Type your **Password.**
   If you want, you can adjust the
   Description of the account, which
   defaults to your email address.

8. Tap the **Next** button in the upper right
   corner.

9. You may see an **Unable to Verify
   Certificate** screen as shown. If you
   do see it, click **Accept** to continue.

10. In the **Server** field, type
    m.google.com to sync to Google.
    Otherwise, if you are setting up
    your Exchange Server account,
    enter that server address.

11. Click **Next** in the upper right
    corner.

For Google Sync, type
m.google.com
Otherwise, enter your
Exchange Server
address.

12. On this screen you have the option
    to turn **Mail, Contacts,** and
    Calendars wireless sync **On** or **Off.**
    For each sync you'd like to turn on,
    tap the switch to change it to **On.**

CAUTION: If you already have contacts or calendar items on your iPhone, you may see a warning similar to the one shown here.

Your choices are to **Keep on My iPhone** or **Delete**. If you choose **Cancel** it stops setting up your Exchange account.

Select **Keep on My iPhone** to keep all existing contacts and calendar events on your iPhone. These items will not end up on your Google or Exchange account—they will stay on your iPhone.

You may end up with some duplicate contacts or calendar events on your iPhone if the same ones already exist on your Google or Exchange account.

Select **Delete** if you already have these contacts or calendar items in your Exchange or Google account and do not want to duplicate them.

13. If you turned on the sync for **Mail**, **Contacts**, and **Calendars**, you'll see a screen similar to the one here. Tap **Save** to save your settings.

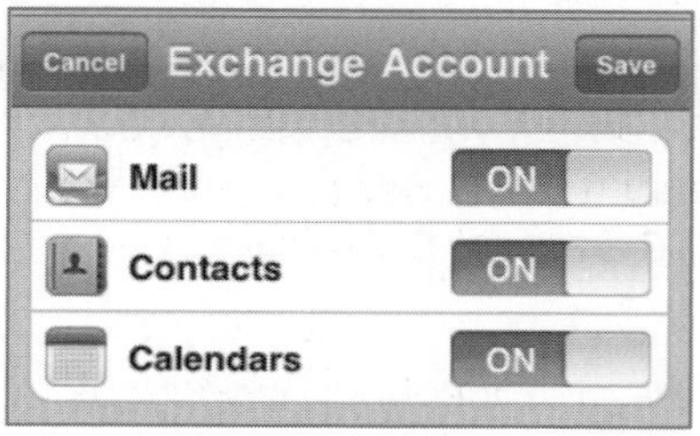

14. You're done with the initial setup of your account. You should see your new account listed under the **Accounts** heading on the **Mail, Contacts, Calendars** screen.

| Settings | Mail, Contacts, Calen... |

Accounts

info@madesimplelearning.com >
Mail

martin@madesimplelearning.com >
Mail

My Gmail >
Mail, Contacts, Calendars

Add Account... >

You're done when you see your new account listed here.

Edit or Delete Your Google or Exchange Account

After you set up your Google or Exchange account on your iPhone, you may want to adjust some of the default settings, such as which mail folders are synced (only the inbox by default), number of days of mail to sync (default is three days), and other settings. You would also use the steps shown here to remove or delete the account.

1. Get into your Mail settings screen as you did when you first set up your account (tap the **Settings** icon, tap **Mail, Contacts, Calendars**).

2. Tap the mail account you wish to adjust or remove.

| Settings | Mail, Contacts, Calen... |

Accounts

info@madesimplelearning.com >
Mail

martin@madesimplelearning.com >
Mail

My Gmail >
Mail, Contacts, Calendars

Add Account... >

Tap the account you wish to adjust.

3. In order to change your account username, account name, and password, tap **Account Info** at the top. You will see the information you saw when you first set up this account.

4. If you want to remove this account from your iPhone, tap **Delete Account** at the bottom and confirm your selection.

5. To enable or disable wireless syncing for **Mail**, **Contacts**, and **Calendar** items, tap the switches to set them **On** or **Off**.

> **NOTE:** If you set any switch to **Off** for these items, they will all be deleted from your iPhone. For example, all synced contacts would immediately be deleted from your **Contacts** app.

6. To adjust how much mail is synced to your iPhone, tap **Mail Days to Sync** and adjust to suit your needs (you can go from **1 Day** to **No Limit** with 3 Days as the default).

   Tap the **Email Account Name** in the upper left corner (shown as **My Gmail** in this image) to save your choices and return to the previous screen.

7. Tap **Mail Folders to Push** to specify which mail folders should sync to your iPhone.

The default is just the **Inbox**, but you can tap to select any number of folders.

> **TIP:** You can only move mail between these folders on your iPhone if you have selected them here to sync.

8. Tap the **Email Account Name** in the upper left corner (shown as **My Gmail** in this image) to save your choices and return to the previous screen.

9. Then press the **Mail...** button in the upper left corner to finish with this account and return to your **Settings**.

10. Press the **Home** button to return to the Home screen.

Working with Google or Exchange Data on Your iPhone

Once you set up the wireless sync, your Google and Exchange Contacts and Calendar information will flow quickly into your iPhone. If you have thousands of contacts, it could take several minutes for the first sync to complete.

You may want to jump ahead and review Chapter 19: "Working with Contacts," and Chapter 20: "Your Calendar," for details about working with both apps.

NOTE: Since the sync with Google or Exchange is wireless, you'll need to make sure you have an active network connection from your iPhone. Check out Chapter 5: "Wi-Fi and 3G Connectivity," to learn more.

New Group for Google/Exchange Contacts

For each Google/Exchange account you add to your iPhone, you will end up with a separate group in your **Contacts** app. If you've added some contacts to your iPhone or synced it at least once with iTunes, you may end up with additional groups of contacts, as shown in Figure 4–1.

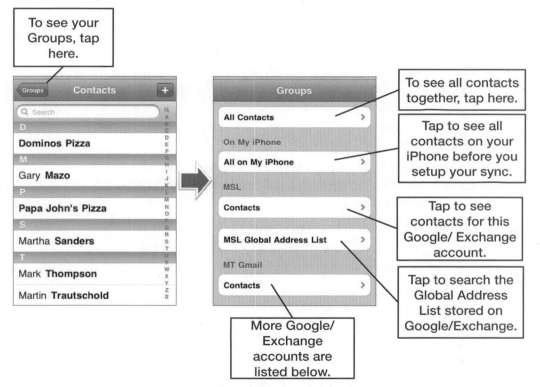

Figure 4–1. *You may see various groups in your Contacts.*

The default view in your **Contacts** list is to see all contacts from all synced accounts. You can selectively view contacts from various accounts. To view your Google or Exchange contacts, follow these steps:

1. Tap the **Contacts** icon.

2. Tap the **Groups** tab in the upper left corner.

3. If you've added new contacts or synced your address book, you'll see a **From My PC** or **From My Mac** group at the top. Under that you will see your Google or Exchange email address or the descriptive name assigned to that account when you set it up. (**MSL** and **MT Gmail** are the two Google/Exchange accounts synced in Figure 4–1.)

4. Tap the **Contacts** listed under your Google or Exchange email address/account name to see all your synced contacts.

Working with Contacts

To add, edit, or delete contacts in your Google or Exchange contacts group, do the following:

1. Follow the steps to view your Google or Exchange contacts group.

2. **To add a contact**: Tap the **+** button in the upper right corner of the **Contacts** list view. Add contact details as we'll show you in Chapter 19: "Working with Contacts." Touch **Done** in the upper right corner.

3. **To edit a contact**: Locate the contact in the list and tap the **Edit** button at the bottom under the contact details. Make any changes and press the **Done** button.

4. **To delete a contact**: Locate the contact you want to remove. Tap the **Edit** button under the contact details. Scroll to the bottom of the details and tap the **Delete Contact** button.

5. **To search for a contact on your iPhone**:

    a. If you don't see the search window at the top, drag your finger all the way up the right-side alphabet to the top.

    b. Tap in the **search** window and type a few letters of someone's first name, last name, or company name to find them.

    c. Your **Contacts** list will immediately be filtered by what you type. If you see the name you want, tap it—otherwise, tap the **Search** button in the lower right corner.

6. **To perform a global address list search**:

    a. Tap the **Groups** button in the upper right corner. See Figure 4–1.

    b. Tap the second button under the Google/Exchange contacts group—that is the **Global Address List** search button. If your email address is long, then you will see only your email address on this button; however, if you have a short email address or have provided a short descriptive name, then you will see something like **MSL Global Address List**, as shown in Figure 4–1.

   c. Tap in the **search** window and type a few letters of someone's
first name, last name, or company name to find them.

   d. Press the **Search** button to start searching.

The great thing is that any changes you make to your Google or Exchange contacts on
your iPhone are wirelessly communicated and appear in your Google or Exchange
account in just a few seconds.

> **NOTE:** To add, edit, or delete contacts in your other group (not the Google or Exchange group),
> first go to that group (**From My PC** or **From My Mac**), then make the changes you want. These
> additions, edits, or deletions will not affect your Google or Exchange contacts—they are kept
> separate.

Working with the Calendar

After you set up the sync with the Google or Exchange calendar on your iPhone, all the
calendar events will appear on your iPhone—no wires or sync cable required. You will
also be able to invite people to meetings and respond to meeting invitations.

Any event you change or update on your iPhone will be wirelessly synced with Google or
Exchange.

Each Calendar Has a Different Color

You will also notice that every new Google
or Exchange account you add to your
iPhone will create a separate calendar with
a new color.

To see the color used for each calendar,
tap the **Calendars** button in the upper left
corner.

Each calendar
has a different
color.

On this screen you can see the color for each calendar.

You can selectively show calendars by tapping on the email address.

To hide a calendar, tap the email address to remove the checkmark.

To show a calendar, tap the email address to add the checkmark.

Calendars	Done
Hide All Calendars	
Exchange	
● msl.training100@gmail.com	✓
My Gmail	
● martin.trautschold@gmail....	✓
Other	
● Birthdays	✓

Invite People to Meetings from Your iPhone

Now you can invite people to your calendar events. Here are the steps to follow:

1. Tap your **Calendar** icon to start your calendar.

2. Touch the + button in the upper right corner to schedule a new event.

3. On the Add Event screen, enter the meeting title and location and adjust the starting and ending time as required.

4. Tap the **Invitees** tab to invite people. (Refer to Figure 4–2.)

5. In order to invite someone, you have a few options.

   a. Type his or her email address (all invitations are sent via email).

   b. Type a few letters of his or her first and last name separated by a space to instantly locate the person if he or she is in your contact list.

   c. Or, tap the **blue plus sign** to find someone by browsing your contact list.

6. Touch the name and email address you want to use. If someone has more than one email address, you'll need to select one.

7. Add more invitees if you desire, then tap **Done** to exit the **Add Invitees** window.

8. Adjust any other items in the Add Event screen and tap **Done** to save.

9. The meeting invitation(s) will be sent via email immediately to everyone you invited.

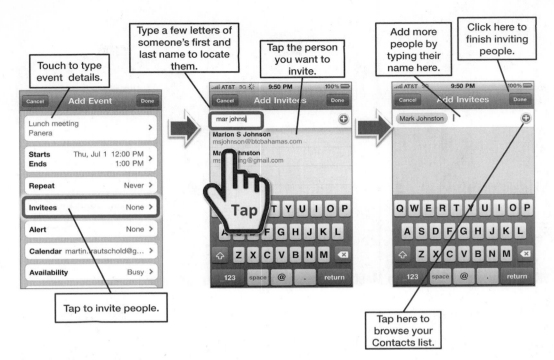

Figure 4–2. *How to invite people to meetings*

Seeing the Status of Invitees on Your Calendar

You can see who has not replied, or who has accepted or rejected your invitations by following these steps. See Figure 4–3.

Tap the meeting in your calendar to view the meeting details.

Tap on the invitees to see everyone who was invited.

You will see the status of each person's reply in square brackets in front of their names.

- * = Not responded
- Check mark = Accepted
- ? = Tentative/Maybe
- X = Declined

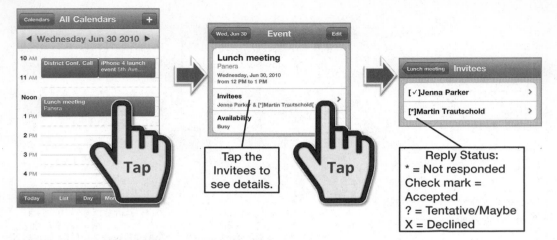

Figure 4–3. *How to see the status of invitations you have sent*

Responding to Exchange Meeting Invitations from Your iPhone

When you are connected to an Exchange email server and the person who invited you to a meeting is also on the same Exchange server, you will be able to use the Invitations inbox inside your Calendar app.

You will receive notifications on your **Calendar** icon as shown here. In this image, there are four new meeting invitations.

Follow these steps to work with Exchange meeting invitations in your Calendar invitations inbox.

1. Start your **Calendar** app.

2. Tap the **Invitations** inbox button in the lower right corner. See Figure 4–4.

3. You will see all your invitations listed. Tap the invitation to which you wish to respond.

4. Then you can review the details of the invitation and type a comment to be included in your response by tapping **Add Comments.**

5. To respond to the invitation, tap one of the three buttons at the bottom of the Event screen: **Accept**, **Maybe**, or **Decline.**

6. If you select **Accept** or **Maybe**, then the calendar event is added to your iPhone calendar.

7. The response is sent immediately via email to the meeting organizer. You're done.

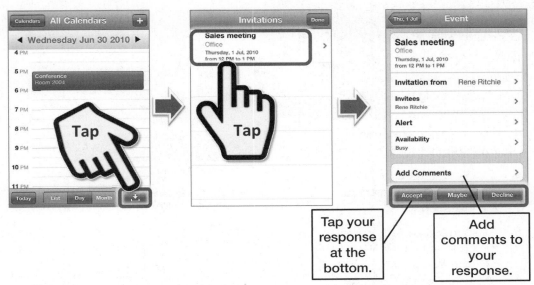

Figure 4–4. *Replying to Exchange meeting invitations using the calendar invitations inbox*

Responding to Google Meeting Invitations from Your iPhone

If you are using Google Calendar with Exchange sync as we described previously, you will be able to reply to meeting invitations in the **Mail** app on your iPhone.

> **NOTE:** As of publishing time, only Exchange invitations (not Google invitations) appeared in your Calendar invitations inbox, so you need to reply to these invitations using your **Mail** app.

1. Tap your **Mail** icon to start the program.

2. Navigate to the **Inbox**, which has the meeting invitation.

3. Locate the invitation.

Most invitations look something like the image shown here. Usually they start with the word **Invitation**.

TIP: To quickly find all meeting invitations in your inbox:

1. Type the word **meet** or **invitation** in the search box.

2. Tap the **Subject** button to search only the message subjects as shown.

4. Tap the Google **Meeting Invitation** to open it.

5. Tap **Yes**, **Maybe**, or **No** next to **Going?** to reply to the invitation.

6. As soon as you tap one of the choices, your reply will be sent. You may be shown a Google Calendar web page to type optional details in your invitation reply.

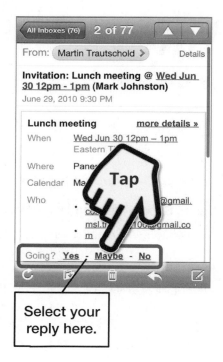

Select your reply here.

Wireless Sync Using the MobileMe Service

Another option if you do not use Google or Exchange and still want to wirelessly sync your information is to use the MobileMe service from Apple. The MobileMe service provides a great service to wirelessly sync your personal information between your computer (PC or Mac) and your iPhone and other mobile devices, such as an iPad.

The MobileMe Cloud: The MobileMe service uses what is sometimes called a cloud to sync all your information. The MobileMe Cloud is a term used to describe the web servers where all your MobileMe information is stored on the Internet. The servers and the associated software you install on your computer (PC or Mac) and your mobile devices (iPhone, iPad, etc.) help keep all your mobile devices in sync with your computer. The idea is that changed information (a new calendar event, a new contact name) gets sent from your iPhone to the cloud. Then the cloud disperses the changed information to all the devices in your MobileMe account. This could be your computer or possibly an iPad or iPod touch.

Once you set up MobileMe from your computer and then set up access from your iPhone, all your personal information (contacts, calendar, even bookmarks) will be shared wirelessly between your computer and your iPhone.

In addition to the wireless sync of personal information, MobileMe lets you do the following:

- Create a web-based photo gallery that you can access and add to from your iPhone.

- Create an **iDisk** that allows you to share documents easily between your iPhone and your computer. You can also use it to share files that are too large to email. Some email systems block files larger than about 5MB.

- Find your lost iPhone using the **Find My iPhone** feature.

- Erase all of the personal data on your lost iPhone remotely using the **Remote Wipe** feature.

- If you have multiple Macs in your home or home and business, MobileMe also allows you to sync **docks**, **settings**, **passwords**, and **other information** between your Macs, and use **Back to my Mac** remote desktop to retrieve files or share screens.

NOTE: As of publishing time, after your 60-day free trial, Apple charges $99/year for individual MobileMe service and $149/year for a family plan.

However, also at publishing time, there was a rumor floating around the web that Apple may make MobileMe a free service. Check with the MobileMe web site (www.mobileme.com) to find out the latest information.

Sign Up for the MobileMe Service (PC or Mac)

Apple makes it easy for you to learn about MobileMe from iTunes after you register your iPhone or the first time you connect your iPhone to your computer. You will most likely see an ad for MobileMe with a **Try It Free** button.

If you use iTunes to sync your iPhone, you will also see a **Learn More** button at the top of the **Info** tab, as shown in Figure 4–5.

1. Connect your iPhone to your computer.

2. Click on your iPhone in the left nav bar of iTunes.

3. Click the **Info** tab at the top.

4. Click the **Learn More** button in the MobileMe section.

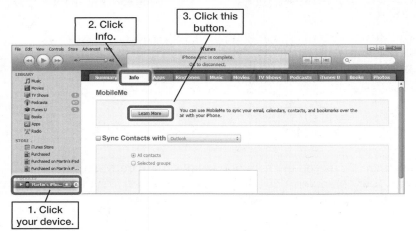

Figure 4–5. *Get started with MobileMe from the iTunes Info tab.*

You can also sign-up for MobileMe directly from their web site.

1. Type your personal information to set up your account and click the **Continue** button.

Enter your information above, then click here.

2. Enter your billing information and click the **Sign Up** button at the bottom.

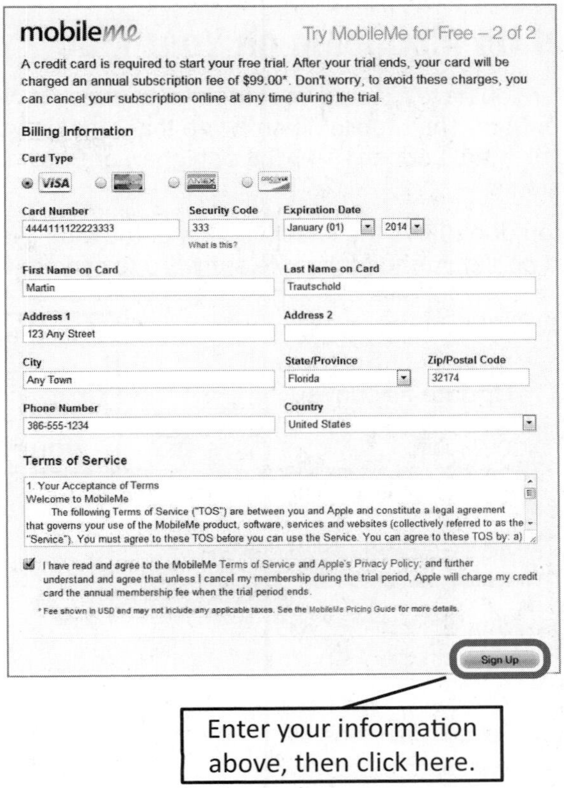

Enter your information above, then click here.

3. If everything was entered correctly, you'll see a **Signup Complete** screen similar to the one shown here.

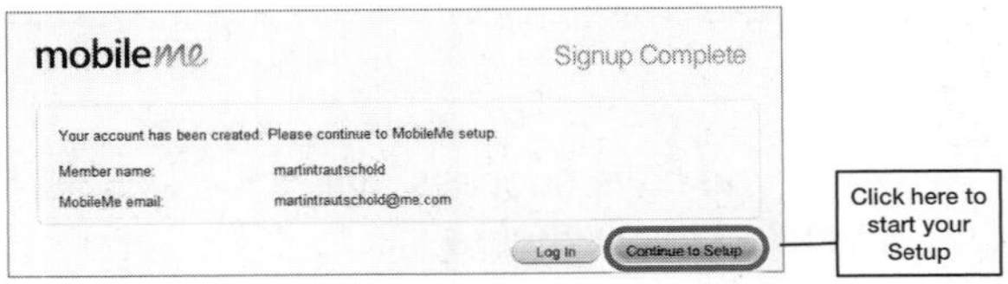

Click here to start your Setup

You have now created your MobileMe account. Now you'll set up MobileMe on your Mac or PC and your iPhone.

If you are a Windows PC user, skip to the "Set Up MobileMe on Your PC" section.

Set Up MobileMe on Your Mac

After you have created your MobileMe account, you are ready to set up the software on your Mac. The MobileMe software that runs on your Mac is included in the latest version of the Mac, Leopard (v10.5.8 or higher) or Snow Leopard (v10.6.3 or higher) operating systems.

If you don't have the latest version of the Mac system software, you'll have to install it and configure the MobileMe software to sync to the MobileMe "cloud" to get started.

1. Click on the Apple menu and select **Software Update** as shown.

   > **TIP:** You'll find extensive step-by-step instructions showing you how to install or upgrade software on your Mac in Chapter 30: "iTunes User Guide."

Click here to get the latest software for your Mac.

2. Follow the steps to complete the software update.

3. After you have successfully installed the software update, click on the Apple menu and select **System Preferences**.

Click here to locate the MobileMe software.

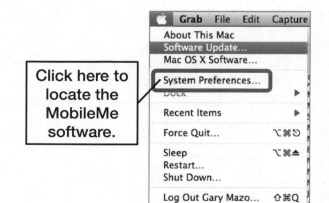

4. Click on the **MobileMe** icon in the Internet & Wireless section of System Preferences.

5. Enter your MobileMe **Member Name** and **Password**.

6. Click **Sign In**.

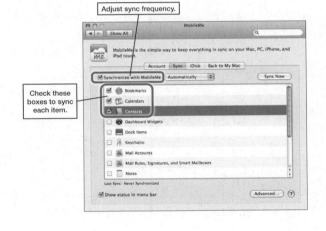

7. Click the **Sync** tab at the top to see the screen shown here.

8. Check the box next to **Synchronize with MobileMe.**

9. Next to this check box there's a drop-down for configuring the sync frequency. The default is **Automatically**, but you can sync every **Hour**, **Day**, **Week**, or **Manually**.

10. To sync bookmarks, check the box next to **Bookmarks** and select your computer's web browser.

11. To sync contacts, check the box next to **Contacts**.

12. To sync calendars, check the box next to **Calendars**.

13. You can also sync various other items by checking them. After you have set up syncing, you can configure your iDisk by clicking the **iDisk** tab and completing the screen shown in Figure 4–6.

14. When you are done, close the **MobileMe** control panel.

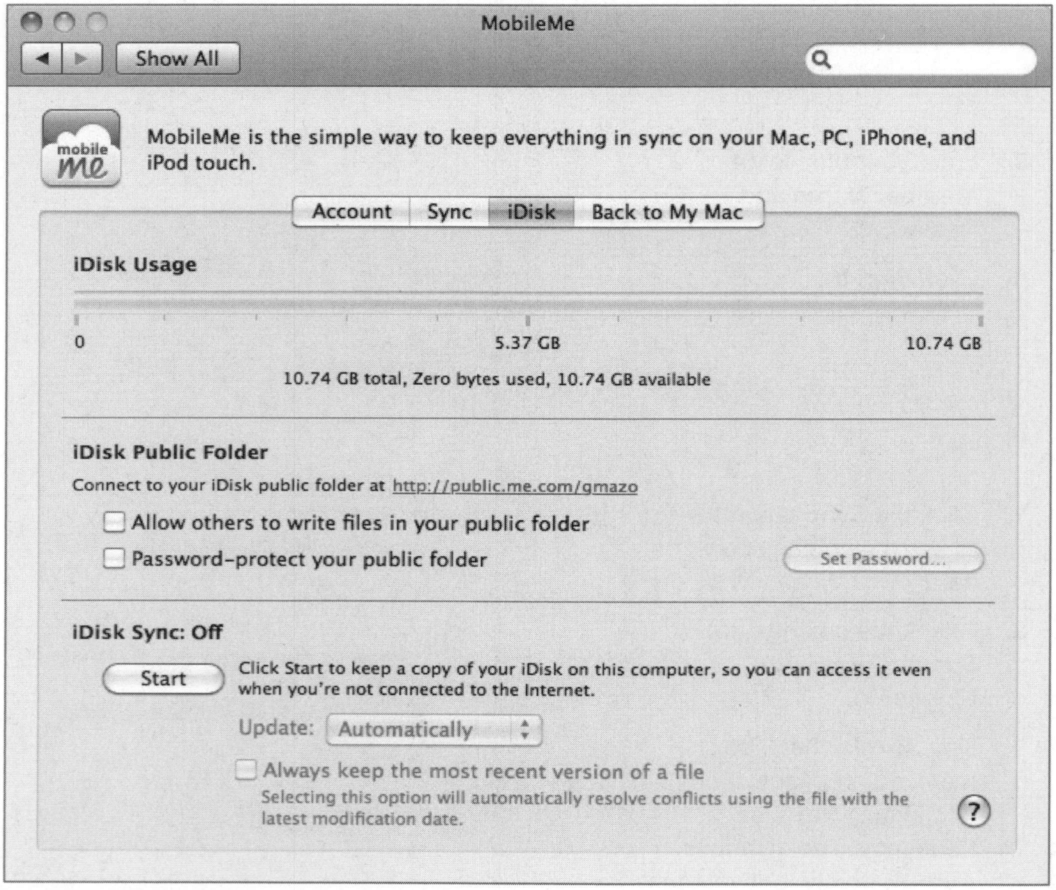

Figure 4–6. *MobileMe control panel showing the iDisk tab*

As soon as you close the MobileMe control panel, MobileMe will start sending your selected items—Contacts, Calendars, and Bookmarks— to the MobileMe web site.

Now you can skip to the "Multiple Ways to Access MobileMe" section while we discuss how Windows users configure MobileMe.

Set Up MobileMe on Your Windows PC

After creating your MobileMe account, you need get the software set up on your PC. You will install the latest version of iTunes and the MobileMe software on your PC and then configure it to sync to the MobileMe "cloud" to get started.

1. On your computer's web browser, go to: www.apple.com/mobileme/setup/pc.html.

2. If you don't have iTunes version 9.2 or later, click the **iTunes** link to download it.

> **TIP:** We give you extensive step-by-step instructions for installing or upgrading iTunes in Chapter 30: "iTunes User Guide."

3. Click the link to download the MobileMe Control Panel for Windows.

1 Get the latest software.

- Download and install the latest version of iTunes (v9.2 or later).
- Download and install the latest version of MobileMe Control Panel for Windows (v1.6 or later).
- Follow onscreen instructions if necessary.

Click these links to download the required software.

4. Click the **Download** button on this screen to download the installation file.

5. Follow the steps on the screen to install the software on your computer.

Click here to download.

MobileMe Control Panel for Windows

6. Once the software is installed, start it up by

■ Clicking on the **MobileMe** icon on your Windows desktop, or by

■ Searching for and starting it from your **Start** button or **Windows** icon in the lower left corner. Type **MobileMe**, and the icon should appear at the top of the Start menu under **Programs**. Click it.

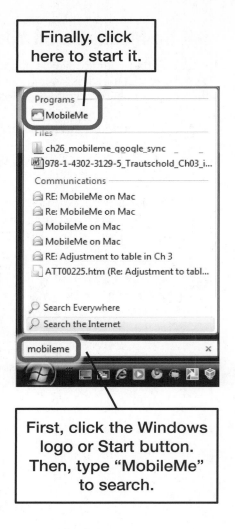

Finally, click here to start it.

First, click the Windows logo or Start button. Then, type "MobileMe" to search.

7. Click the **Sync** tab at the top to see the screen shown here.

8. Check the box next to **Sync with MobileMe.**

9. Next to this check box you'll find a drop-down for the sync frequency. The default is **Automatically**, but you can choose to sync every **Hour**, **Day**, **Week**, or **Manually**.

10. To sync contacts, check the box next to **Contacts** and select where

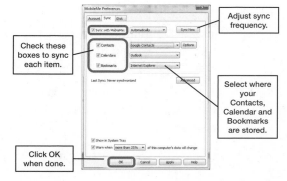

Adjust sync frequency.

Check these boxes to sync each item.

Select where your Contacts, Calendar and Bookmarks are stored.

Click OK when done.

your contacts are stored (such as
Outlook, **Google Contacts**,
Yahoo!, or **Windows Contacts**). For
Google and Yahoo!, you will need to
enter your username and password
by clicking the **Options** button that
appears.

11. To sync calendars, check the box next to **Calendars** and select where
     your Calendars are stored (e.g., **Outlook** or elsewhere).

12. To sync bookmarks, check the box next to **Bookmarks** and select your
     computer's web browser (only Safari and Internet Explorer were supported for
     syncing bookmarks at publishing time).

13. Click **OK** when done.

As soon as you click **OK**, MobileMe will start sending your selected items—Contacts,
Calendars, and Bookmarks—to the MobileMe web site.

Multiple Ways to Access MobileMe

After the first sync, you will have at least three ways to access your synced information:

- The computer where you originally stored your contacts and calendar
- The MobileMe web site
- Your iPhone (or other mobile device)

Since you already know how to get to the information on your computer, we will focus
on how to access information from the MobileMe web site and your iPhone.

A Quick Tour of the MobileMe Web Site

You can do many useful and amazing things from the MobileMe web site from your
computer. You can even locate your iPhone, send messages to it, make it beep loudly,
and remotely lock or erase it. Here we give you a quick tour.

1. Go to the **MobileMe** from a web browser on your computer by typing www.me.com.

2. Type your username and password and click **Log In**.

3. To view your mail, click the **Cloud** icon  in the upper left corner, then click the **Mail** icon.

   This will show your MobileMe inbox for all email going to (membername)@me.com.

4. To view your contacts, click the **Cloud** icon then click the **Contacts** icon.

5. To view your calendar, click the **Cloud** icon  then the **Calendar** icon. Notice there are various buttons at the top for the calendar views: Day, Week, Month and List.

6. To view your photo albums, click the **Cloud** icon  then the **Gallery** icon.

7. To create a new album, click the **+** in the lower left corner.

8. Enter your **Album Name**, and check the **Allow** and **Show** settings you want. Also, for Mac users, decide whether you want to sync with **iPhoto** or **Aperture**.

9. Click the **Create** button to create your new album.

10. Click the **Upload Arrow** to select photos or videos to upload to your MobileMe album.

11. Navigate to the folder on

your computer where your pictures are stored, click the picture or video to select it, and then click the **Open** button.

NOTE: The following image file formats are supported: .png, .gif, .jpg, .jpeg. The following video types are supported: .mov, .m4v, .mp4, .3gp, .3g2, .mpg, .mpeg, .avi.

Click here to upload photos and videos to an album.

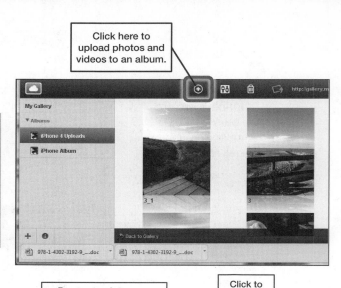

Browse to pictures or videos on your computer.

Click to select an item.

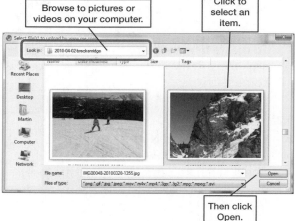

Then click Open.

12. Click the **Cloud** icon then the **iDisk** icon to view the files located on the MobileMe iDisk.

TIP: You can easily store and retrieve files on this iDisk from your computer and your iPhone. You can even share files that are too large to email or that you'd like to print from your iPhone using the **Public** folder.

13. Click the **Cloud** icon  then the **Find My iPhone** icon to locate your iPhone. You will need to re-enter your password for security purposes. This feature assumes you have already logged into MobileMe from the **Settings** app on your iPhone.

14. Click your name in the upper right corner, then select **Account** from the drop down list.

15. In your account page you can adjust the options, see your account type and trial expiration date

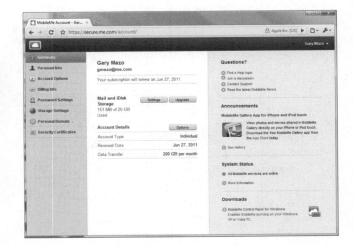

(if you are on a free trial),
get help, or check
whether the MobileMe
service is up and running.

Setting Up Your iPhone to Access Your MobileMe Account

Now that you've set up your MobileMe account, you are ready to sign into it from your iPhone.

1. Tap your **Settings** icon.

2. Tap **Mail, Contacts, Calendars**.

3. Tap **Add Account**.

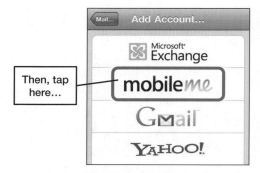

4. Tap **MobileMe** for the account type.

5. Enter your **Name** and your MobileMe email **Address** and **Password,** then tap **Next**.

6. Now you'll see the MobileMe configuration screen showing your sync options.

7. To turn any synced item **On** or **Off**, tap the switch.

8. To turn on **Find My iPhone**, which will show your iPhone on a map on the MobileMe web site, move the switch to **On**.

> **NOTE:** If you have any existing contacts, calendars, or other information on your iPhone, these will be kept separate from your MobileMe contacts and calendars.

9. When you are done, tap **Save.** You should be brought back to the Settings screen and see your MobileMe account listed with the selected items turned **On** for syncing.

Your new MobileMe account. It may show your email address that ends in @me.com.

Using MobileMe After Setup

Using MobileMe is fairly seamless once you get it set up. You update your contacts and calendar on your iPhone and the changes just appear on your computer. And, if you've set up other mobile devices, such as an iPad, on the same account, the changes appear there, too. Everything is kept in sync wirelessly and automatically.

MobileMe has a few very cool features that we will highlight here.

Find My iPhone, Send Message, and Remote Wipe

From any web browser, you can locate your iPhone using the **Find My iPhone** feature in MobileMe. You can send a message and play a loud sound to alert someone on your iPhone, even if it is locked. You can remotely lock your iPhone using a 4–digit code and remotely erase all information on your iPhone.

1. Login to **MobileMe** from any web browser on your computer by going to www.me.com.

2. Type your **username** and **password** and click **Log In**.

3. Click the **Find My iPhone** icon in the top nav bar to display the current location of your iPhone.

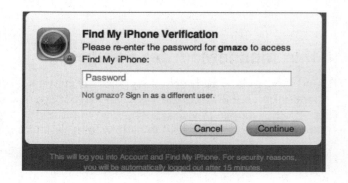

4. Re-enter your password for security purposes.

5. Now you have various options.

    a. You can display a message or play sound on your iPhone.

    b. You can remote lock your iPhone with a passcode.

    c. You can completely erase or wipe your iPhone.

6. Click the **Display a Message** button to display a message on your iPhone and play a loud sound for up to two minutes or until the screen is tapped.

7. You will see a small alert window pop up on the iPhone and the sound will play.

8. If you want to lock your iPhone remotely, tap the **Remote Lock** button on the settings page.

9. Enter a new passcode twice to set it on your iPhone. Your iPhone will immediately be locked with this new passcode.

TIP: Since this overrides your existing passcode, you can also use this feature to unlock your iPhone if you forget your original passcode. Just set a new one using **Remote Lock**.

10. You can also erase all data from your iPhone by pressing the **Remote Wipe** button.

11. Mark the check box and click **Erase All Data**.

CAUTION: This will erase all data on your iPhone and cannot be undone. All your data stored on MobileMe will automatically re-sync when you set up the account again. However, applications and other non-MobileMe information will have to be restored from your iTunes backup or from the App store and iTunes.

Canceling Your MobileMe Account

Should you decide that MobileMe is not for you, you can cancel your account. If you cancel your account within the first 60 days, you can avoid the $99.00 charge.

1. To cancel the service, log in to MobileMe from any web browser on your computer by going to www.me.com.

2. Type your username and password and click **Log In**.

3. Click the **Settings** icon in the top row of icons.

4. Notice on the **Summary** tab the date your trial ends. In this image, the trial ends on June 4, 2010.

5. Click **Account Options** in the left column.

6. From the Account Options screen, click the **Cancel Account** button.

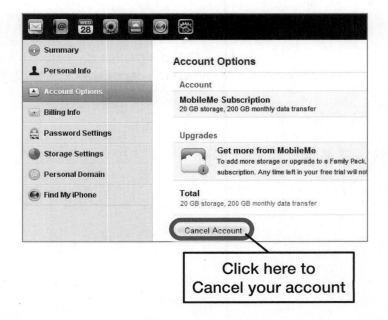

Additional Settings for Google/Exchange or MobileMe

Once you set up the Google/Exchange or MobileMe sync, you may notice a few new options on your Settings screen in addition to the ones shown in Chapter 19: "Working with Contacts," and Chapter 20: "Your Calendar."

1. Tap the **Settings** icon.

2. Tap **Mail, Contacts, Calendars** in the left column.

3. Scroll down the right column to the bottom to see the image shown here.

4. The new option in the Contacts section is the **Default Account**. You can set this to be either your Exchange/Google account or your computer's account.

Settings	Mail, Contacts, Calen...
Contacts	
Sort Order	Last, First >
Display Order	First, Last >
Default Account	My Gmail >

New contacts created outside of a specific account will be added to this account.

Click here to go to the screen to Cancel your account

Calendars	
New Invitation Alerts	ON
Sync	Events 1 Month Back >
Time Zone Support	>
Default Calendar	martin.trauts... >

New events created outside of a specific calendar will default to this calendar.

5. Notice that you can turn your **New Invitation Alerts On** or **Off**.

6. The new option in the Calendars section is **Sync,** which allows you to set how much of your calendar to sync (**2 weeks**, **1 month**, **3 months**, **6 months**, or **All events**).

7. You can also select which is your **Default Calendar** for new events you add to your iPhone. You can change this calendar when you create a new event.

Chapter 5

Wi-Fi and 3G Connectivity

We live in a connected world. Wireless Internet (Wi-Fi) access has become the rule, not the exception—chances are you're already using Wi-Fi at your home or office. Now you can use it to connect your iPhone. And, since your iPhone also has a 3G cellular radio, you can also connect to the Internet anywhere you have cellular data coverage—a much wider area than Wi-Fi networks.

In this chapter we'll talk about the differences between the two types of connections for your iPhone: Wi-Fi (wireless local area network) and 3G (cellular service—the wide area data network used by your mobile phone). We'll show you all the ways to get connected or disconnected from these two types of networks. There will be times you want to disable or turn off your 3G connection and only use Wi-Fi to save money in data connection charges.

We will also show you how to get ready for traveling internationally with your iPhone— what you need to do before, during, and after your trip so you don't get surprised with a very large phone bill when you return home.

We also show you how to use Internet Tethering, the ability that your iPhone has to become a connection to the Internet for your laptop—PC or Mac. This is a great feature to use when you don't have any other way to connect your laptop to the Internet.

Finally, if you work at an organization with a VPN (Virtual Private Network), we show you how to get connected to that network.

What Can I Do When I'm Connected to a Wi-Fi or 3G Network?

Here are some of the things you can do when connected:

- Access and download apps (programs) from the App Store
- Access and download music, videos, podcasts, and more from iTunes on your iPhone
- Browse the web using Safari

- Send and receive email messages

- Use social networking sites that require an Internet connection, like Facebook, Twitter, etc.

- Play games that use a live Internet connection

- Anything else that requires an Internet connection

Wi-Fi Connections

Every iPhone comes with Wi-Fi capability built in, so let's take a look at getting connected to the Wi-Fi network. Things to consider about Wi-Fi connections are the following:

- No additional cost for network access and data downloads (if you are using your iPhone in your home, office, or a free Wi-Fi hotspot)

- Wi-Fi tends to be faster than a cellular data 3G connection.

- More and more places, including some airplanes, provide Wi-Fi access, but you may have to pay a one-time or monthly service fee.

NOTE: iPhone 4 now adds support for the faster, longer range 802.11n standard. However, it only supports 802.11n on the more crowded 2.4Mhz band, not the less crowded 5Mhz band. If you want to use iPhone 4 with your 802.11n Wi-Fi router, make sure to set the router to 2.4Mhz.

Connecting to a Wi-Fi Network

To set up your Wi-Fi connection, follow these steps:

1. Tap the **Settings** icon.

2. Tap **Wi-Fi** near the top.

3. Make sure the **Wi-Fi** switch is set to **On**. If it is currently **Off**, then tap it to turn it **On**.

4. Once Wi-Fi is **On**, the iPhone will automatically start looking for wireless networks.

5. The list of accessible networks is shown below the **Choose a Network...** option. You can see in this screenshot that we have one network available.

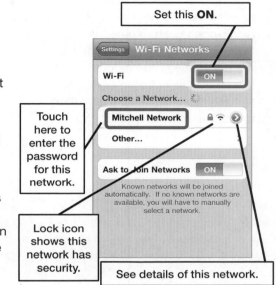

6. To connect to any network listed, just touch the network name. If the network is unsecure (does not have a lock icon), you will be connected automatically.

Connecting at a Public Wi-Fi Hotspot with Web Login

In some locations where they offer free Wi-Fi networks, such as coffee shops, hotels, or restaurants, you will see a pop-up window appear as soon as your iPhone comes into contact with the network. In these cases, simply tap the network name. You may be brought to a Safari browser screen to complete your login to the network.

1. If you see a pop-up window similar to the one shown, tap the network name you wish to join. In this case, we tap the **Panera** network.

2. In some cases, you may see a Safari window pop up, which can be quite confusing because it is so small on your iPhone screen. You need to use the double-tap or pinch-open gesture (see the Quick Start Guide for help) to zoom in on the web page. You are looking for a button that says **Login** or **Agree** or something similar. Tap that button to complete the connection.

NOTE: Some places, like coffee shops, use a web-based login instead of a username/password screen. In those cases, when you click on the network (or try to use Safari), iPhone will open a browser screen and you'll see the web page along with login options.

Secure Wi-Fi Networks—Entering a Password

Some Wi-Fi networks require a password to connect. This is set when the network administrator creates the wireless network. You will have to know the exact password, including whether it is case-sensitive.

If the network does require a password, you will be taken to the password-entry screen. Type the password exactly as given to you and press the enter key on the on-screen keyboard (which is now labeled as **Join**).

On the network screen, you'll see a checkmark showing that you are connected to the network.

TIP: You can paste into the password dialog, so for longer, random passwords, you can transfer them to your iPhone (in an email message) and just copy and paste them. Just remember to delete the email immediately afterwards to keep things secure. Tap and hold the password in the mail message, select it, and then tap **Copy**. In the Wi-Fi network **Password** field, tap and then select **Paste**.

Switching to a Different Wi-Fi Network

At times you may want to change your active Wi-Fi network. This might occur if you are in a hotel, apartment, or other place where the network selected by the iPhone is not the strongest network, or you want to use a secure network instead of an unsecure one.

To switch from the currently selected Wi-Fi network, tap the **Settings** icon, touch **Wi-Fi**, and then touch the name of the Wi-Fi network you want to join. If that network requires a password, you'll need to enter it to join.

Once you type the correct password (or if you touched an open network), your iPhone will join that network.

Verifying Your Wi-Fi Connection

It is easy to see if you are connected to a network (and which one) by looking next to Wi-Fi in your main Settings screen.

1. Tap your **Settings** icon.

2. Look next to Wi-Fi at the top.

   ■ If you see **Not Connected**, you do not have an active Wi-Fi connection.

   ■ If you see some other name, such as **Panera**, then you are connected to that Wi-Fi network.

You do not have an active Wi-Fi connection.

You are connected to this network.

Advanced Wi-Fi Options (Hidden or Undiscoverable Networks)

Sometimes you may not be able to see the network you want to join because the name has been hidden (not broadcasted) by the network administrator. Next, you will learn how to join such networks on your iPhone. Once you have joined such a network, the next time you come in contact with that network it will join automatically without asking. You can also tell your iPhone to ask every time it joins a network; we show you how to do that as well. Sometimes you may want to erase or forget a network. Say you were at a one-time convention and want to get rid of the associated network—you'll learn that here, too.

Why Can't I See the Wi-Fi Network I Want to Join?

Sometimes, for security reasons, people don't make their networks discoverable and you have to manually enter the name and security options to connect.

As you can see in Figure 5-1, your list of available networks includes **Other**. Touch the **Other** button, and you can manually enter the name of a network you would like to join.

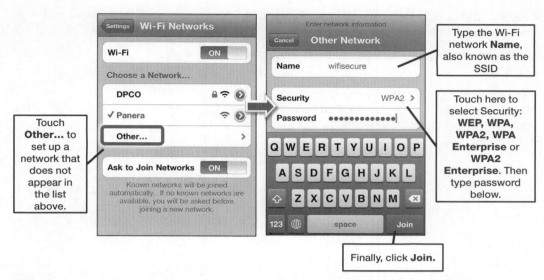

Figure 5-1. *You can manually enter the name of a Wi-Fi network, select the security type, and click **Join**.*

Type in the Wi-Fi network **Name**, touch the **Security** tab, and choose which type of security is being used on that network. If you are unsure, you'll need to find out from the network administrator.

When you have the information you need, enter it along with the proper password and this new network will be saved to your network list for future access.

Reconnecting to Previously Joined Wi-Fi Networks

The nice thing about the iPhone is that when you return to an area with a Wi-Fi network you previously joined (whether it was an open or a secure, password-protected, network) your iPhone will automatically join the network without asking you again. However, you can turn off this automatic-joining feature, as described next.

Ask to Join Networks Main Switch

There is a main **Ask to Join Networks** switch, which is set to **On** by default. Known networks are joined automatically, this only takes effect if no known networks are available. With this switch set to **On**, you will be asked to join visible Wi-Fi networks. If networks are available that are not known to you, you will be asked before being connected.

If the switch is set to **Off**, you will have to manually join unknown networks.

Why might you want to turn off automatically joining a network?

This could be a good security measure if, for example, you don't want your kids to be able to join a wireless network on the iPhone without your knowledge.

Ask to Join and Ask to Login Switch on Each Network

Sometimes, you may find that a particular Wi-Fi network has additional switches that override the main **Ask to Join Networks**

switch. Tap the little blue arrow  next to the network name to see details about this Wi-Fi network. **Auto-Join** and **Auto-Login** are set to **On** by default.

To disable **Auto-Join** or **Auto-Login**, tap each switch to set it to **Off**.

Forget (or Erase) a Network

If you find that you no longer want to connect to a network on your list, you can **Forget it**—i.e., take it off your list of networks.

1. Tap the **Settings** icon.

2. Tap **Wi-Fi** to see your list of networks.

3. Tap the small blue arrow next to the network you want to forget in order to see the screen shown here.

4. Tap **Forget this Network** at the top of the screen.

5. You will be prompted with a warning. Just touch **Forget** and the network will no longer show up on your list.

3G and 2G Cellular Data Connection

Your iPhone can also connect to the cellular data network—the same network you connect to with other mobile phones. Here are things to consider about Cellular Data Connections:

- Wider availability than a Wi-Fi connection—you can connect to 3G in a car or away from a city, whereas Wi-Fi is not typically available in these locations.

- Extra monthly service fees for access to the Cellular Data network

- In the US, AT&T charges about $15 for 200MB per month and about $25 for 2GB of monthly data.

NOTE: Check with your local wireless carrier for iPhone data plan pricing in your country.

Select and Monitor Your Cellular Data Usage

When you purchased your iPhone, you had to select a cellular data plan from your wireless carrier. For the iPhone in the US, this is currently AT&T. If you selected one plan and wish to try another plan, contact your carrier—you may be allowed to switch data plans.

TIP: Saving Money on Data Charges

You might be able to save yourself some money with cellular data plan charges by doing the following:

- Always use Wi-Fi when possible.
- Start with the lower cost cellular data plan ($15 for 200MB).
- Monitor your cellular data usage throughout the month to make sure you are not going to exceed the lower cost data plan.

You may find that you can live with the lower cost plan if you use Wi-Fi for most of your data needs.

To check your current cellular data usage, look in your **Settings** icon.

1. Tap the **Settings** icon.

2. Tap **General**.

3. Tap **Usage**.

4. Swipe up to see the section below **Cellular Data Network** at the bottom.

5. Your total data usage will be the sum of the **Sent** and **Received**. In the image shown here, the total data usage is approximately **346 MB** (19.7 + 326 megabytes).

6. If you want to clear out the statistics, tap the **Reset Statistics** button at the bottom of the screen.

General	Usage
Standby	0 Minutes
Call Time	
Current Period	12 Minutes
Lifetime	12 Minutes
Cellular Network Data	
Sent	19.7 MB
Received	326 MB
Last Reset: Never	
Reset Statistics	

NOTE: The iPhone will notify you when you have 20%, 10%, and 0 left on your monthly data plan and you'll have the option of renewing that plan or upgrading to a higher data plan, if available.

How to Switch Between 3G and 2G Networks

There may be times that you want to turn off your 3G radio and only use the slower 2G connection. One reason might be that you do not need the speed of 3G, and you want to make your battery last longer. Another reason might be that you are in an area that has only 2G connectivity. The 2G connection, which shows up as the letter E next to your wireless carrier in the status bar, uses less battery power than the 3G connection.

1. Tap the **Settings** icon.

2. Tap **General**.

3. Tap **Network**.

4. Set the switch next to **Enable 3G** to **Off**.

5. When you do this, you will see the **3G** in the status bar change to an **E**.

6. To re-enable 3G, simply turn the switch back **On**.

International Travel: Things to Do Before You Go

Depending on which country you are visiting and your current iPhone voice and data plan, you may be well prepared for international travel. However, it is quite likely that your basic iPhone data and phone plan will either not work or cause you to spend a lot extra on data and voice roaming charges.

We always recommend that you call your phone service provider well in advance of a trip to see whether there is an **international** feature you can turn on for your iPhone as you travel.

Avoiding a Shockingly Large Bill

One thing you want to avoid when traveling is returning home to an unusually high voice or data roaming charge phone bill. For example, we have heard of people who returned home after a trip abroad to find a phone bill totaling $1,000 or more in a single month's data and voice roaming charges. Here we show you how to take steps before, during, and after your trip to help avoid surprise charges.

There are a few simple steps you can take before you leave to ensure that your iPhone will successfully and economically connect to the local country's network—no matter where you might be in the world.

Step 1: Call Your Phone Company

You should contact the phone company that supplies your iPhone before you leave home. When you call, you should check a few things:

- Any voice and data roaming charges you might incur when traveling. Be specific about each country to which you plan to travel.

- Check on any temporary international rate plans that you might be able to activate before you leave. Sometimes, these special plans will cost an additional $10 or $20 but save you hundreds in additional charges.

- If you use email, SMS Text, MMS or picture messaging, web browsing, and any other data services, you will also want to specifically ask about whether any of these services are charged separately when traveling abroad. Usually, text and picture messaging are additional charges.

You might be able to find some information on your phone company's web site, but usually you need to call them.

Current AT&T International Plans

While you may not use AT&T, here are a few examples of international plans available at publishing time that can give you a feel for what might be available. Table 5-1.

Table 5-1. *AT&T International Voice, Data and SMS Text Plans*

Plan and Cost	Cost with plan	Cost without plan
Data Roaming $24.99 for 20MB / month $59.99 for 50MB / month More plans available.	Stated number of MB Included $5 per extra MB	$20 / MB data
Voice Roaming $5.99 / month	$1.69 / minute	$2.29 / minute
Text Messaging $10 / month	$0.40 / outgoing message - limit 50 / month Incoming messages - free	$0.50 / outgoing text message $1.30 / picture message

CAUTION: If you watched a 3-minute video on YouTube, then downloaded a 5 megapixel image in email, and finally used **Maps** for a few minutes, you might use about 6 MB of data. If you were roaming internationally without a data plan, you would pay about $120 ($20 per MB) for all these activities together!

Step 2: Check If You Can Use a Foreign SIM Card

In some cases, your iPhone wireless company won't offer special deals on international data roaming plans, or its rates will be unreasonably high. In these cases, you may want to ask your phone company to unlock your iPhone, so you can insert a SIM card purchased in the country you're visiting.

NOTE: Apple sells an unlocked, SIM-free iPhone 4 in many countries outside the US, including Canada and the UK. If you are a frequent traveler, an officially unlocked iPhone might be something to consider.

Inserting a local SIM card will eliminate or greatly reduce data and voice roaming charges. However, you should carefully check the cost of placing and receiving international calls on that foreign SIM card.

Using a foreign SIM card might save you hundreds of dollars, but it's best to do some web research or try to talk to someone who has recently traveled to the same country for advice before settling on that approach.

> **TIP:** If you are going to a country without a good rate plan and your carrier will not unlock your iPhone, you might want to consider renting or purchasing a local cell phone. You may be able to rent a phone for about $30 / week with much lower voice calling rates. Many cell phone rental companies exist such as Travel Cell, Mobal, and Cellular Abroad. (Do a web search for "International Cell Phone Rental" to find more.)

Try some of the iPhone blogs such as www.tipb.com, or do a web search for traveling to country X, Y, and Z with your iPhone.

> **TIP:** Put a paperclip in your luggage—you will need it to remove and replace your SIM card in your iPhone.

Step 3: Do Any Data Intensive Stuff Prior to Leaving

You should do all your data-intensive activities that can be performed before you leave your home country. If you have a lot of apps that need updating, do that before you leave. Look for and add any apps that you might need before your trip. You should also download any large files such as movies, videos or music before you leave.

Flying on an Airplane: Airplane Mode

Often when you are flying on an airplane, the flight crew will ask you to turn off all portable electronic devices for takeoff and landing. Then, when you get to a certain altitude, they will say that "all approved electronic devices" can be turned back on.

If you need to turn off your iPhone completely, then press and hold the **Power** button on the top right edge, then **Slide to Power Off** with your finger.

In order to enable **Airplane Mode**, follow these steps.

1. Tap the **Settings** icon.

2. Set the switch next to **Airplane Mode** in the top of the left column to **On.**

3. Notice that the Wi-Fi is automatically turned **Off** and that the phone will not work.

> **TIP:** Some airlines do have in-flight Wi-Fi networks. In those flights, you may want to turn your Wi-Fi back **On** at the appropriate time.

Tap here to switch **Airplane Mode** to **ON.**

Wi-Fi gets turned **Off** also.

Notice the **Phone** shows **Airplane Mode,** too.

You can turn your Wi-Fi connection **Off** or **On** by following these steps.

1. Tap the **Settings** icon.

2. Tap **Wi-Fi** near the top of the screen.

3. To enable the Wi-Fi connections, set the switch next to **Wi-Fi** in the top of the page to **On.**

4. To disable the Wi-Fi, set the same switch to **Off.**

5. Select the Wi-Fi network and follow the steps given by the flight attendant to get connected.

International Travel: When You Arrive

Once you've completed the steps described so far to prepare for your trip, you will need to address some additional issues when you get to your destination. The next sections explain the things you need to keep in mind after you arrive at your destination.

Step 1: Make Sure the Time Zone Is Correct

When you arrive, you will need to make sure your iPhone is displaying the correct local time. Usually, your iPhone will auto-update your time zone when you arrive at a new destination. However, if it doesn't, you can manually adjust the time zone. See the "Setting Your Date and Time" section in Chapter 1, "Getting Started."

Step 2: Buy and Insert Your Foreign SIM Card

NOTE: This step will only work if the carrier in the foreign country offers an iPhone 4 and also your iPhone 4 has been unlocked. Currently the US carrier AT&T will not unlock iPhone 4 devices. Your fallback plan, especially if you need to make a lot of local in-country calls, is to rent or buy an inexpensive pre-paid mobile phone and reserve your iPhone use for only Wi-Fi connections.

If you have determined that you can use a foreign SIM card, you should purchase and insert it when you arrive. We show you how to remove the SIM card tray in Chapter 1. You need to use a paperclip.

CAUTION: The iPhone uses a MicroSIM and almost all other phones use a MiniSIM. This may make it hard to find an international carrier with a SIM card that will fit. These will also only work if the phone is unlocked.

Step 3: Reset Your Data Usage When You Land

As soon as you land, you should reset your data usage on your iPhone. This will allow you to keep close track of the amount of wireless data you are using overseas. For example, if you purchased a 20 MB plan, you want to make sure you don't go over the amount. A brief test using **Maps** for about 1 minute in the car resulted in almost 1 MB of data usage. So be careful and try not to use extremely data-intensive apps such as **Maps** while roaming.

We show you exactly how to reset your usage earlier in this chapter in the "Select and Monitor Your Cellular Data Usage" section.

TIP: Once you reset your usage, you will want to return to this screen from time to time to see your current usage. You have to add the **Sent** and **Received** to get your total usage. This image shows about the usage shows about 417 MB total. That would cost $8,340 at the $20/MB rate in effect without an international data plan!

	AT&T 4:51 PM 100%
General   **Usage**
Standby   0 Minutes
Call Time
Current Period   31 Minutes
Lifetime   31 Minutes
Cellular Network Data
Sent   32.3 MB
Received   385 MB
Last Reset: Never
Reset Statistics

Step 4: Turn Off Data Roaming If It's Too Expensive

If you were unable to find a foreign SIM card, or if you were unable to find out about the cost of data roaming from your local phone company, you might want to turn off the data charges.

This option will work only if you can survive without your email and web browser while you're away. Follow these steps to do so.

1. Tap the **Settings** icon.

2. Tap **General**.

3. Tap **Network**.

4. Set the switch next to **Data Roaming** to **Off**.

	AT&T 1:01 PM 100%
General   **Network**
Enable 3G   ON
Using 3G loads data faster, but may decrease battery life.
Cellular Data   ON
Data Roaming   OFF
Turn data roaming off when abroad to avoid substantial roaming charges when using email, web browsing, and other data services.

Setting the **Data Roaming** value to **Off** should help you avoid any potentially exorbitant data roaming charges. (You still need to worry about voice roaming charges, but at least you can control those by watching how much you talk on your phone.)

The nice part about setting the **Cellular Data** to **On** and **Data Roaming** to **Off** is that you can still enjoy all your data services until the time you leave your home country and immediately when you return without making any other changes. Of course, you can also use your Wi-Fi network connection any time.

Step 5: Use Wi-Fi When Possible

One good way to save money on cellular data plans is to use local Wi-Fi networks whenever possible, especially when you are going to browse the web, or download large amounts of email or large apps.

> **TIP:** You may be able to find free Wi-Fi networks at Internet cafés, regular coffee shops, public libraries, some hotel lobbies, and Apple retail stores.

International Travel: Returning Home

As you did when you arrived at your travel destination, you will need to make a few changes to your iPhone's settings once you arrive back home before your device will work as expected.

Step 1: Make Sure the Time Zone Is Correct

When you return to your home country, you will need to verify your iPhone is displaying the correct local time. Usually, your iPhone will auto-update your time zone when you arrive back home. However, if it doesn't, you can manually adjust the time zone. See the "Setting Your Date and Time" section in Chapter 1, "Getting Started."

Step 2: Turn Off Your Special International Rate Plan

The final step is optional. If you have activated some sort of special international roaming rate plan with your iPhone wireless company, and you do not need it anymore, contact the company to turn it off to save yourself some money.

Using all the steps we describe before, during, and after your trip should help you be able to use your iPhone successfully and economically while you travel internationally.

Internet Tethering

One of the nice features on your iPhone is that you can use it to connect your laptop—PC or Mac—to the Internet. This is called Internet Tethering. It is very useful if you happen to be traveling away from a Wi-Fi network but are still in wireless cellular data coverage with your iPhone. This greatly expands the places that you can use your laptop to connect to the Internet.

Step 1: Contact your Phone Company

Internet Tethering usually requires a separate rate plan to be purchased and activated from your phone company. Call your phone company or check on their web site to turn on the Tethering plan.

> **TIP:** You may be able to save yourself some money by turning off the Tethering plan when you no longer need it. Check with your phone company to find out if there are any penalties or hidden charges for turning off the Tethering plan at a later date.

Step 2: Enable Internet Tethering on Your iPhone

After you have purchased or activated the Tethering plan from your phone company, you are ready to get it set up on your iPhone.

1. Tap the **Settings** icon.

2. Tap **General**.

3. Tap **Network**.

4. Scroll down and tap **Set Up Internet Tethering**.

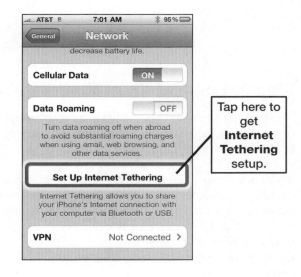

5. If you have not yet set up the plan, or the plan you purchased has not yet been activated on your iPhone, you will see a pop-up message similar to this one. If you did purchase the plan, then you may need to wait a little while for the plan to be correctly activated.

6. If your plan has been correctly activated, you should see this screen. Tap the switch next to **Internet Tethering** to set it to **On**.

Step 3: Connect Your iPhone to Your Computer

You can now connect your iPhone to your computer using the USB cable, or, if you choose, Bluetooth wireless. We show you how to connect Bluetooth devices in Chapter 6, "Bluetooth on Your iPhone."

If you are using Bluetooth, then you will usually see a checkbox at the end of the connection process that asks you if you want to **Use device as a network port** or **Use device as a network connection.** Make sure you check that box.

Select the services you want to use with your mobile phone:

☑ Use device as a network port

Step 4: Set Up Networking on Your Computer

After you have connected your iPhone to your computer, your Windows or Mac computer should recognize your iPhone as a new internet connection and help you set it up automatically. If your computer does not recognize the iPhone immediately, then go into your Network settings on your computer and look for the iPhone as an available connection type.

VPN: Virtual Private Network

Your organization may have what is called a VPN, or Virtual Private Network, to allow you to securely connect your iPhone, laptop, or other device to the corporate network.

Getting Connected

In order to get connected, you need to determine the type of VPN and specific login instructions from your organization's help desk or network administrator. Then, you will type these login details into the VPN area in the **Settings** app on your iPhone.

> **TIP:** Save yourself a call to the help desk if you have already set up your computer to connect to the VPN, because your iPhone will most likely use the same VPN login credentials as your computer. Save yourself some time, skip Step 1, and give those a try first.

Step 1: Contact Your Organization's Help Desk

You need to ask your help desk or VPN administrator for the details about how to log in to the VPN. Your iPhone can currently connect with the following types of VPNs: **L2TP**, **PPTP**, and **IPSec** (Cisco). You also need to know if your VPN uses a **Proxy** and whether the configuration is manual or automatic.

Step 2: Set Up the VPN Connection on Your iPhone

Armed with the login instructions and type of VPN connection, you are ready to connect with your iPhone.

1. Tap the **Settings** icon.

2. Tap **General**.

3. Tap **Network**.

4. Scroll down to the bottom of the screen and tap **VPN**.

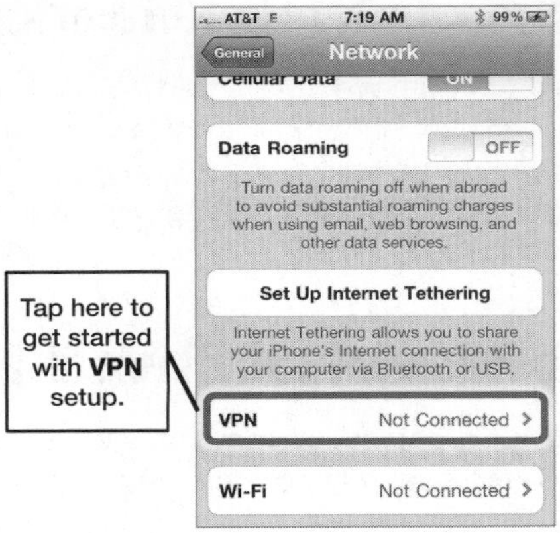

Tap here to get started with **VPN** setup.

5. On the VPN screen, tap the switch next to VPN to set it to **On**. You should then be taken to the Add Configuration screen. If not, then tap **Add VPN Configuration** at the bottom to set up a new VPN connection.

6. The Add Configuration screen is where you set up your VPN login details, using the information from your help desk or VPN administrator.

7. If your VPN is an **L2TP** type, then you would use the screen shown here. Scroll to the bottom and enter the **Proxy** information as required.

8. If your VPN is a **PPTP** type, then you would tap **PPTP** at the top and use the screen shown here. Scroll to the bottom and enter the **Proxy** information as required.

Cancel	Add Configuration	Save

L2TP	**PPTP**	IPSec

Description	Required
Server	Required
Account	Required
RSA SecurID	OFF
Password	Ask Every Time
Encryption Level	Auto ›
Send All Traffic	ON

Proxy

9. If your VPN is an **IPSec** (Cisco) type, then you would tap **IPSec** and use the screen shown here. Scroll to the bottom and enter the **Proxy** information as required.

10. When you are done with your setup, tap the **Save** button in the upper right corner.

11. If you have trouble logging in, make sure you are in a strong wireless coverage area and verify you have typed all your login credentials correctly. It can be difficult when passwords disappear as you type them. You may want to try re-typing passwords and server information before calling the help desk.

Cancel	Add Configuration	Save

L2TP	PPTP	**IPSec**

CISCO

Description	Required
Server	Required
Account	Required
Password	Ask Every Time
Use Certificate	OFF
Group Name	

Knowing When You Are Connected to a VPN Network

You will see a small **VPN** icon [VPN] just to the right of your network connection status display. Only when you see this icon do you know that you are securely connected to the VPN network.

Switching VPN Networks

You may have several VPN networks to which you need to connect. You can select between different VPN configurations on your iPhone.

1. Tap the **Settings** icon.

2. Tap **General**.

3. Tap **Network**.

4. Scroll down to the bottom of the screen and tap **VPN**.

5. On the VPN screen, tap a different **VPN configuration** to connect to it. Don't tap the blue circle with the > symbol, unless you want to change the login settings for that network.

Bluetooth on the iPhone 4

In this chapter we will show you how to pair your iPhone 4 with any Bluetooth device, whether it be another computer, stereo speakers, or a wireless headset. With so many states passing laws requiring motorists to use a "hands-free" method for talking on their phones, using Bluetooth is now more of a necessity than ever.

With initial reports of some reception issues with the iPhone 4 when held in a certain way, using a Bluetooth headset removes that problem as well.

Thanks to the technology known as A2DP, you can also stream your music to a capable Bluetooth stereo.

> **NOTE:** You must have a capable third-party Bluetooth adapter or Bluetooth stereo to stream your music via Bluetooth technology. Also, there is no AVRCP profile support, so many music controls on a Bluetooth device (like Play, Pause, or Skip) won't work quite yet.

Think of Bluetooth as a short-range, wireless technology that allows your iPhone 4 to connect to various peripheral devices without wires. Popular devices are headsets, computers, and vehicle sound systems.

Bluetooth is believed to be named after a Danish Viking and king, Harald Blåtand, whose name has been translated as *Bluetooth*. King Blåtand lived in the tenth century and is famous for uniting Denmark and Norway. Similarly, Bluetooth technology unites computers and telecom. His name, according to legend, is from his very dark hair, which was unusual for Vikings. Blåtand means dark complexion. There does exist a more popular story that the king loved to eat blueberries, so much so that his teeth became stained with the color blue.

Sources:

- http://cp.literature.agilent.com/litweb/pdf/5980-3032EN.pdf
- http://www.cs.utk.edu/~dasgupta/bluetooth/history.htm
- http://www.britannica.com/eb/topic-254809/Harald-I

Understanding Bluetooth

Bluetooth allows your iPhone 4 to communicate with things wirelessly. Bluetooth is a small radio that transmits from each device. Before you can use a peripheral with the iPhone 4, you have to "pair" it with that device to connect it to the peripheral. Many Bluetooth devices can be used up to 30 feet away from the iPhone 4.

Bluetooth Devices That Work with the iPhone 4

Among other things, the iPhone 4 works with Bluetooth headphones, Bluetooth stereo systems and adapters, Bluetooth keyboards, Bluetooth car stereo systems, Bluetooth headsets, and hands-free devices. The iPhone 4 supports A2DP, which is known as Stereo Bluetooth.

Pairing with a Bluetooth Device

Your primary uses for Bluetooth might be with Bluetooth headphones, Bluetooth stereo adapters, or a Bluetooth headset. Any Bluetooth headphones should work well with your iPhone 4. To start using any Bluetooth device, you need to first pair (connect) it with your iPhone 4.

Turning On Bluetooth

The first step to using Bluetooth is to turn the Bluetooth radio **On**.

1. Tap your **Settings** icon.

2. Then, touch **General.**

3. You will see the **Bluetooth** tab in the right-hand column.

4. By default, Bluetooth is initially **Off** on the iPhone 4. Tap the switch to move it to the **On** position.

Settings	General	
About		>
Usage	5h 4m	>
Network		>
Bluetooth	Off	>
Location Services	On	>

TIP: Bluetooth is an added drain on your battery. If you don't plan on using Bluetooth for a period of time, think about turning the switch back to **Off**.

General	Bluetooth
Bluetooth	OFF

Pairing with a Headset or Any Bluetooth Device

As soon as you turn Bluetooth **On**, the iPhone 4 will begin to search for any nearby Bluetooth device—like a Bluetooth headset or stereo adapter (see Figure 6–1). For the iPhone 4 to find your Bluetooth device, you need to put that device into "pairing mode." Read the instructions that came with your headset carefully—usually there is a combination of buttons to push to achieve this.

TIP: Some headsets require you to press and hold a button for five seconds until you see a series of flashing blue or red/blue lights. Some accessories, such as the Apple wireless Bluetooth keyboard, automatically start up in pairing mode.

Once the iPhone 4 detects the Bluetooth device, it will attempt to automatically pair with it. If pairing takes place automatically, there is nothing more for you to do.

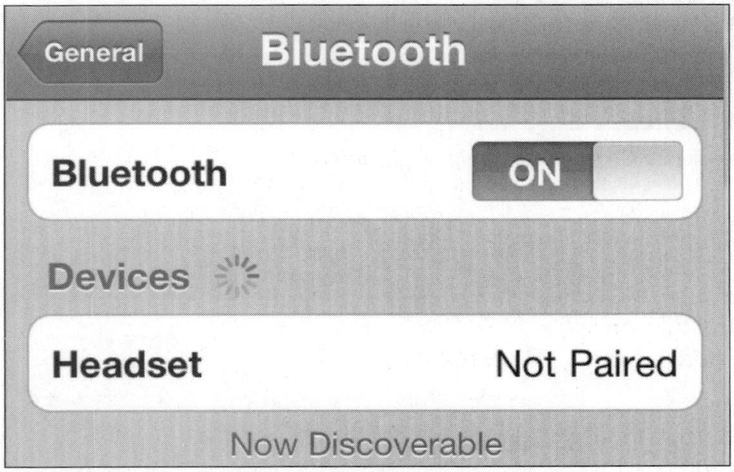

General	Bluetooth
Bluetooth	ON
Devices ⚙	
Headset	Not Paired
Now Discoverable	

Figure 6–1. *Bluetooth device discovered but not yet paired*

NOTE: In the case of a Bluetooth device, such as a headset, you may be asked to enter a series of numbers (passkey) on the keyboard itself. See Figure 6–2.

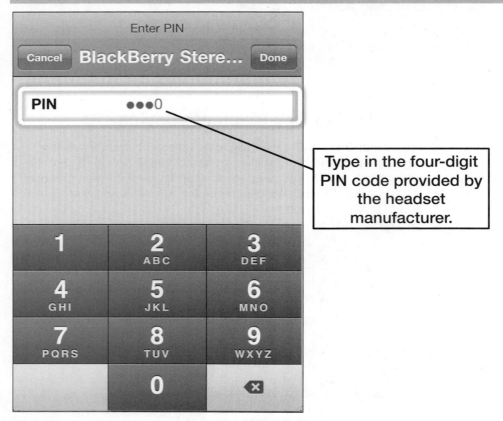

Type in the four-digit PIN code provided by the headset manufacturer.

Figure 6–2. *Type in the four-digit passkey when prompted during the pairing process.*

Newer headsets like the Aliph Jawbone ICON, used here, will automatically pair with your iPhone. Simply put the headset into pairing mode and turn on Bluetooth on the iPhone—that's all you have to do!

Pairing will be automatic and you should never have to re-pair the headset again.

Using the Bluetooth Headset

If your headset is properly paired and on, all incoming calls should be routed to your headset. Usually you can just press the main button on the headset to answer the call or use the **Slide to Answer** function on the iPhone.

Move the phone away from your face (while the iPhone is dialing) and you should see the indicator showing you that the Bluetooth headset is in use. In the image you see that the **Speaker** icon is next to the "Jawbone ICON" Bluetooth headset.

You will also see the options to send the call to your iPhone handset or to the "Speaker" phone. You can change this at any point while you are on the call.

Touch **Hide Sources** and you will see the normal call screen on the iPhone.

Options When on a Call

Once the call is made and you are speaking with your contact, you can still re-route the call to either the iPhone or the speakerphone.

Move the call away from your face (if it is near your face) and you will see

Audio Source  as one of the options for you to touch. Touch that icon and you will have all the options for re-routing the call, as shown previously.

Just choose to send the call to any of the options shown and you will see the small **Speaker** icon move to the current source being used for the call (Figure 6–3).

Figure 6–3. *Changing from Bluetooth headset back to the iPhone while on a call*

Bluetooth Stereo (A2DP)

One of the great features of today's advanced Bluetooth technology is the ability to stream your music without wires via Bluetooth. The fancy name for this technology is A2DP, but it is simply known as Stereo Bluetooth.

Connecting to a Stereo Bluetooth Device

The first step to using Stereo Bluetooth is to connect to a capable Stereo Bluetooth device. This can be a car stereo with this technology built in, a pair of Bluetooth headphones or speakers, or even newer headsets like the Jawbone ICON.

Put the Bluetooth device into pairing mode as per the manufacturer's instructions, and then go to the Bluetooth setting page from the **Settings** icon, as we showed you earlier in the chapter.

Once connected, you will see the new Stereo Bluetooth device listed under your Bluetooth devices. Sometimes it will simply be listed as "Headset." Just touch the device and you will see the name of the actual device next to the **Bluetooth** tab in the next screen, as shown here.

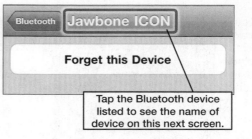

Tap the Bluetooth device listed to see the name of device on this next screen.

Next, tap your **iPod** icon and start up any song, playlist, podcast, or video music library. You will now notice a small **Bluetooth** icon in the lower right-hand corner of the screen. Tap the **Bluetooth** icon to see the available Bluetooth devices for streaming your music (see Figure 6–4).

Figure 6–4. *Selecting a Bluetooth device*

In the previous screens, we selected the **BlackBerry Stereo Gateway** by tapping it. Now, your music will now start to play from the selected Bluetooth device. You can verify this again by touching the **Bluetooth** icon on the screen once more. You should see the **Speaker** icon next to the new Stereo Bluetooth device and you should hear your music coming from that sound source as well.

Disconnecting or Forgetting a Bluetooth Device

Sometimes, you might want to disconnect a Bluetooth device from your iPhone 4.

It is easy to get this done. Get into the Bluetooth settings as you did earlier in this chapter. Touch the device you want to disconnect in order to bring up the next screen, then tap the **Forget this Device** button and confirm your choice.

> **NOTE:** Bluetooth has a range of only about 30 feet, so if you are not nearby or not using a Bluetooth device, turn off **Bluetooth**. You can always turn it back on when you are actually going to be using it.

This will delete the Bluetooth profile from the iPhone 4. (See Figure 6–5.)

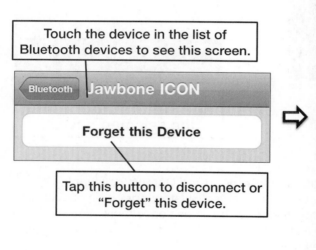

Figure 6–5. *Forgetting or disconnecting a Bluetooth device*

Chapter 7

Organize Your iPhone: Icons and Folders

Your new iPhone is very customizable. In this chapter we will show you how to move icons around and put your favorite icons just where you want them. You've got up to 11 pages of icons to work with, and you can adjust the look and feel of those pages so it suits your tastes.

Like a Mac computer or an iPad, the iPhone has a **Bottom Dock**, where you can put the icons for your favorite apps. iPhones come with four standard icons in the Bottom Dock, but you can replace these with other icons for your favorite apps to always have available at the bottom of your screen. In the new operating system, iOS4, you can even move an entire folder of apps to the Bottom Dock.

> **TIP:** You can also move or delete icons using iTunes on your computer. Check out our "iTunes User Guide" in Chapter 30 for more information.

Moving Icons to the Bottom Dock—Docking Them

When you turn your iPhone on, you'll notice the four icons locked to the Bottom Dock: **Phone**, **Mail**, **Safari**, and **iPod**.

Suppose you decide you want to change one or more of these for apps you use more often. Fortunately, moving icons to and from the Bottom Dock is easy.

Keep up to 4 icons that you want to see all the time. These icons will always remain visible even when you slide the other icon screens left/right.

Bottom Dock

Starting the Move

Press the **Home** button to get to your Home screen. Now, touch and hold any icon on the Home screen for a couple of seconds. You'll notice that all the icons start to shake.

Just try moving a couple of icons around at first. You'll see that when you move an icon down, the other icons in the row move to make space for it.

Once you have the feel for how the icons move, you are ready to replace one of the Bottom Dock icons. While the icons are shaking, take the icon you wish to replace from the Bottom Dock and move it up to an area covered by other icons. If you move it to a large blank area, it will jump back to the dock.

NOTE: You can have up to four icons in the Bottom Dock, so if you already have four there, you will have to remove one to replace it with a new one.

Suppose you want to replace the standard **iPod** icon with your **App Store** icon. The first thing to do is just hold the **iPod** icon and move it up a row—out of the Bottom Dock, as shown in Figure 7-1.

To stop the icons shaking, tap your **Home** button.

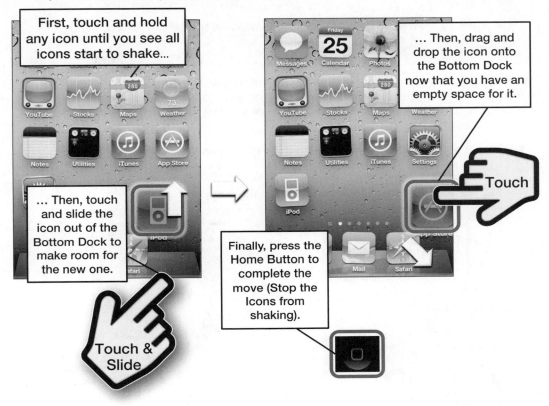

Figure 7–1. *Swapping icons in the Bottom Dock*

Next, locate your **App Store** icon and move it down to the Bottom Dock. As you'll see, the icon becomes sort of transparent until you actually set it into place.

When you are sure that you have the icons just where you want them, simply press the **Home** button once and the icons will lock into place. Now, you have the **App Store** icon in the Bottom Dock, where you want it.

Moving Icons to a Different Icon Page

iPhones can hold 16 icons on a page (not including the dock) and you can find these pages by swiping (right to left) on your Home screen. With all the cool apps available, it is not uncommon to have five, six, or even more pages of icons. You can have up to 11 pages filled with icons if you feel adventurous!

NOTE: You can also swipe from left to right on any screen except the Home screen. On the Home screen, swiping left to right takes you to **Spotlight Search**; see Chapter 2: "Typing Tips, Copy/Paste, and Search" for more information.

You may have an icon you rarely use on your first page, and you want to move it way off to the last page. Or you may want to move an icon you often use from the last of the icons pages to the first page. Both are very easy to do; it's very much like moving icons to the Bottom Dock, as discussed previously.

1. Touch and hold any icon to initiate the moving process.

2. Touch and hold the icon you wish to move. As shown in Figure 7-2, let's say we want to move the **iBooks** icon to the first page.

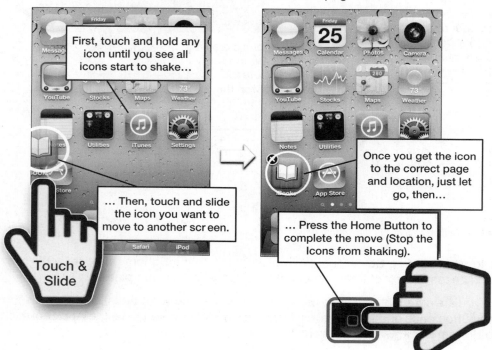

Figure 7-2. *Moving icons from one page to another*

3. Now drag and drop the icon onto another page. To do this, you touch and hold the **iBooks** icon and drag it to the left. You will see all of your pages of icons move by. When you get to the first page, just release the icon, and it is now placed at the very beginning.

4. Press the **Home** key to complete the move and stop the icons from shaking.

Deleting Icons

Be careful—it is as easy to delete an icon as it is to move it, but when you delete an icon on the iPhone, you are actually deleting the program it represents. This means you won't be able to use the program again without reinstalling or re-downloading it.

Depending on your Application Sync settings in iTunes, the program may still reside in your **Applications** folder in iTunes. In that case, you would be able to easily reinstall the deleted app if you wanted to by checking that application in the list of apps to sync in iTunes.

As Figure 7-3 shows, the deleting process is similar to the moving process. Touch and hold any icon to initiate deleting. Just as before, touching and holding makes the icons shake and allows you to move or delete them.

> **NOTE:** You may delete only programs you have downloaded to your iPhone; the preinstalled icons and their associated programs can't be deleted. You can tell which programs can be deleted because the icons contain a small black **x** in the upper left corner.

Just tap the **x** on the icon you'd like to delete. You will be prompted to either delete, or cancel the delete request. If you select **Delete**, the icon and its related app are removed from your iPhone.

First, touch and hold any icon until you see all icons start to shake…

… Then, touch the Black (X) on the corner of the icon you want to delete.

Confirm that you have the correct Icon selected, and touch "Delete"

Delete "NYTimes"

Deleting "NYTimes" will also delete all of its data.

Delete   Cancel

Touch

NYTimes

Touch

Figure 7-3. *Deleting an icon—and its associated program*

Resetting All Your Icon Locations (Factory Defaults)

Occasionally, you might want to go back to the original, factory default icon settings. This might be the case when you've moved too many new icons to your first page and want to see all the basic icons again.

To do this, touch the **Settings** icon. Then touch **General** in the left column and, finally, scroll all the way to the bottom to touch **Reset** in the right column.

Reset	>

NOTE: Built-in apps will get sorted back into the order they were in when Apple shipped the iPhone.

On the Reset screen, touch **Reset Home Screen Layout** near the bottom. Now all your icons will be returned to the original settings.

CAUTION: Be careful you don't touch one of the other **Reset** options, as you can inadvertently erase your entire iPhone if you touch the wrong button. If you do, you'll have to restore data from your iTunes backup.

Reset All Settings
Erase All Content and Settings
Reset Network Settings
Reset Keyboard Dictionary
Reset Home Screen Layout
Reset Location Warnings

Working with Folders

New to iOS4 is the ability to organize your apps into folders. Previously, each app existed in its spot on your Home page, and once you downloaded many apps, it was hard to keep track of what was where.

Using folders will allow you to keep your games, your productivity apps, and other like-functioning apps together in folders. Each folder will be able to hold 12 apps—which can really help you organize your iPhone!

Creating the Folder

Creating folders in iOS4 is intuitive and fun.

1. Hold down an app until all the apps start shaking (as you did before in the "Moving Icons" section).

2. Drag an app onto another like-functioning app.

3. For example, drag one "Game" onto another "Game" or one "Utility" onto another "Utility." The iPhone will initially create a name for the folder.

4. In this example, I dragged one sports-related game onto another and it created a folder called "Sports."

5. Edit the folder name by touching the Name field and typing. I typed **Sports Games** as the name of this new folder. See Figure 7-4.

6. Press the **Home** button to set the new folder name.

7. Press the **Home** button to return to the Home screen and you will now see the new folder with the new name.

NOTE: You can place up to 12 app icons in a given folder. If you try to put more than that, you will see the new icon continually being "pushed" out of the folder, indicating that the folder is full.

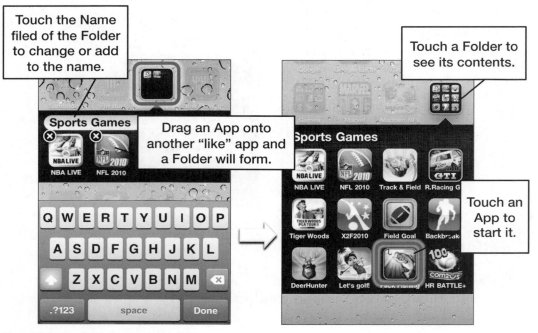

Touch the Name filed of the Folder to change or add to the name.

Drag an App onto another "like" app and a Folder will form.

Touch a Folder to see its contents.

Touch an App to start it.

Figure 7-4. *Moving icons to create a folder*

Moving Folders

Just like apps, folders can also be moved from one Home page to another.

1. Press and hold a folder until the folder and icons on the Home screen start to shake.

2. Touch and hold the folder and drag it to the spot on the screen (or to another Home screen) and then let go.

3. When you have the folder in the spot you desire, just press the **Home** button to complete the move.

TIP: You can even move a folder down to the Bottom Dock if you like. This is a very handy way of having lots of apps right at your fingertips. See Figure 7-5.

Move a Folder down to the Bottom Dock to have access to up to 12 apps at once!

Figure 7-5. *Moving a folder to the Bottom Dock*

Chapter 8

Multitasking and Voice Control

In this chapter, we describe how to multitask or jump between apps on your iPhone and control your iPhone with your voice using the Voice Control feature. Multitasking is a new and very welcome feature on the iPhone, as it was not available with previous versions. You can leave one app running in the background while you do something else. With Voice Control, you can speak basic commands to control your music and phone. We help you get up and running with this feature as well.

Multitasking or App Switching

With multitasking, also called App Switching, you can leave many of your apps running in the background and switch over to another without stopping the first app.

NOTE: Developers have to implement multitasking on their end, and while more and more multitasking-aware apps and updates are appearing every day; many apps still don't do it or don't do it fully.

Why might you want to use multitasking? Here are a few scenarios when you might want to use multitasking on your iPhone:

- Copy and paste from one app (**Mail**) to another (**Calendar**).

- Answer a phone call or reply to an **SMS** message, then jump back into the game you were playing without missing a beat.

- Continue listening to Internet radio (such as **Pandora** or **Slacker**) while checking your e-mail or browsing the Web.

■ You no longer have to wait for photos to upload to **Facebook** or **Flikr**—they can be running in the background while you go and do other things on your iPhone.

■ You use **Skype** to call people—now you can leave it running in the background to receive incoming calls; this was not possible before.

How to Jump Between Apps

In order to multitask, you need to bring up the **App Switcher** bar at the bottom of the screen.

1. From any app or even the **Home** screen, double-click the **Home** button to bring up the **App Switcher** at the bottom of your screen (see Figure 8–1).

2. All open apps will be shown on the **App Switcher** bar.

3. Swipe right or left to find the app you want and tap it.

4. If you don't see the app you want on the **App Switcher** bar, then press the **Home** button and start it from the **Home** screen.

5. Double-click the **Home** button again and tap the app you just left to jump back to it.

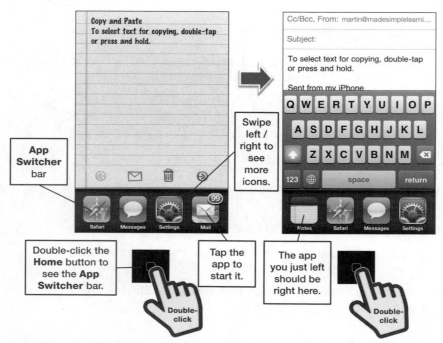

Figure 8–1. *Double-click the Home button to bring up the* App Switcher bar *to multitask.*

How to Close Apps from the App Switcher

If you exit out of an app using a single click of the **Home** button, that app will stay running in the background. There are times when you want to completely close an app. Sometimes, you may find your iPhone running a little slower than you might like, it could be time to close apps completely and free up memory.

1. Double-click the **Home** button to bring up the **App Switcher** bar.

2. Press and hold any icon in the **App Switcher** bar until they all shake. You will notice a **red circle** with a minus sign appears in the upper left corner of each icon.

3. Tap the **red circle** 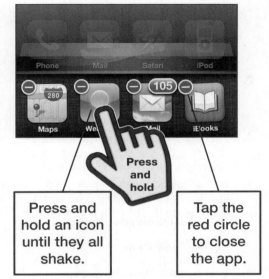 to completely close the app.

4. Keep tapping the red circles to close as many apps as you want.

Press and hold an icon until they all shake.

Tap the red circle to close the app.

iPod Controls and Screen Portrait Orientation Lock

The other thing you can do on the **App Switcher** bar if you swipe from left to right is to see the iPod controls and the screen **Portrait Orientation Lock** icon.

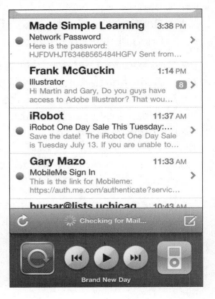

1. From any app or even the **Home** screen, double-tap the **Home** button to bring up the **App Switcher** at the bottom of your screen.

2. Swipe left to right to see the iPod controls and **Portrait Orientation Lock** icon.

3. Tap the **Portrait Orientation Lock** icon to lock the screen in a portrait or vertical orientation, even if you turn the iPhone on its side. You know it is locked when you see a lock inside the button and a lock in the top status bar.

4. You can also use the **previous track**, **play/pause**, and **next track** buttons in the middle. If you hold down **previous** or **next**, they become **rewind** or **fast forward**.

5. Or, tap the **iPod** icon to jump to the iPod.

Voice Control is another feature besides multitasking that makes use of the **Home** button is Voice Control. Voice Control allows you to command some of the features by simply speaking to your iPhone.

Voice Control

With Voice Control on your iPhone, you can do a number of things with your phone, such as play music, call people, and even ask your iPhone the time.

1. Press and hold the **Home** button

   or press the **Center** button attached to the right earbud of your iPhone headset for about two seconds to start **Voice Control**.

2. Speak your command. We show you the various commands you can speak in the next sections.

3. After you speak your command, the iPhone will repeat it briefly and execute the command it thought it heard you say.

TIP: If you are using your headset microphone for Voice Control, just let the microphone dangle from your ear normally, don't pick it up and hold it closer to your mouth. Holding the microphone too close will distort your voice and Voice Control will not understand you correctly.

List of Voice Commands

There are a number of commands you can use with your iPhone to control music, the phone, and more.

TIP: If you have your iPhone inside a protective case and you are having trouble with Voice Control, make sure your case is not interfering with the microphone on the iPhone. Try removing the case and using Voice Control; see if the iPhone without the case works better than with it.

General Commands

There are a few general commands you can use on your iPhone.

Say: "**What time is it?**" to hear the current time.

Say: "**No**, **Nope**, **Cancel**, or **Stop**," or tap the **Cancel** button to exit Voice Command.

Say: "**Help**" to get help about how to use Voice Command.

Phone Voice Commands

It is much safer to use Voice Command while you are driving to dial people from your IPhone.

CAUTION: Voice Command will not always clearly understand you, especially if you are speaking in a noisy environment. Beware that it may end up dialing the wrong person.

ALSO, if Voice Control is set to English, it is more likely to have trouble with French or Italian names that are properly pronounced. Just be ready to press the **End** call button in a hurry if it starts dialing the wrong person.

As one of the Author's daughters' tried on her iPhone: Sophie said, **Play Yo Yo Ma**

The iPhone responded, **Calling Omar** and immediately started the call!

Sophie needed to **End** the call in a hurry!

Say: "**Call Elizabeth**" to call Elizabeth from your **Contacts** list. If you have more than one Elizabeth, you will be asked to clarify.

Say: "**Call Gary Mazo Mobile**" to call Gary Mazo on his mobile phone.

Say: "**Dial 1-800-555-1212**" to call that number.

TIP: For very common names such as John or Susan, you should use both the first and last name for that person. You can also edit contact entries for people you call a lot and add in a unique nickname for those people.

Music and Video Commands

There are quite a few music commands. Because you may be using your headphones to listen to music, you should remember that you can start **Voice Command** by pressing and holding the **Center** button on your right headphone cord.

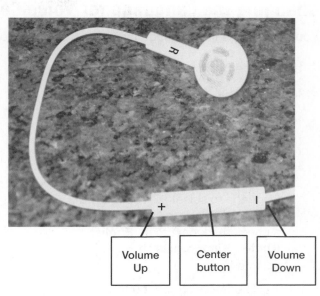

Volume Up | Center button | Volume Down

Say: "**Pause** or **Play**" to pause or play the currently playing song or video.

Say: "**Play songs by U2**" to play all songs by the band U2.

Say: "**Play artist Enya**" to play songs by Enya.

TIP: If a song or artist has the word "the" in the name, be sure to include it when you say the complete name of the song or artist, including the word "the."

Say: "**Next song**" or "**Next track**" to play the next song.

Say: "**Previous song**" or "**Previous track**" to play the next song.

TIP: Remember you can double-click the **Center** button to go to the next song and triple-click it to go to the previous song.

Say: "**Shuffle**" to turn on shuffle.

Say: "**Genius**" or "**Play more like this**" to turn on the Genius feature and play similar songs.

Say: "**Play** (name of album)" to play the entire album.

Say: **Play** (name of playlist)" to play the playlist.

Changing the Language for Voice Control

You can change the language for **Voice Control** in your **Settings** app.

1. Tap the **Settings** icon.

2. Tap **General.**

3. Scroll down and tap **International**.

4. Tap **Voice Control**.

5. On the next screen, you will see a list of languages. Tap any language to select it. You know a language is selected because it has a check mark next to it. **English (United Kingdom)** is shown as selected.

6. Tap the **International** button in the upper left corner to return to your settings.

.ıill AT&T E	2:27 PM	▶ ∦ 100% ▣

International   Voice Control

Danish	
Dutch	
English (Australia)	
English (United Kingdom)	✓
English (United States)	
Finnish	
French (Canada)	
French (France)	
German	

Chapter 9

Personalize and Secure Your iPhone

In this chapter, you will learn several easy ways to personalize your iPhone. You will also learn how to protect your iPhone with passcode security. We'll show you where you can download free wallpaper to change the look of your **Lock** and **Home** screens. We'll also show you how to personalize the sounds your iPhone makes by adjusting when and what sound you hear for various activities. Many aspects of the iPhone can be fine-tuned to meet your needs and tastes—to give your iPhone a more personal look and feel.

Changing Your Lock Screen and Home Screen Wallpapers

There are actually two screens you can personalize on your iPhone by changing the wallpaper.

The **Lock Screen** appears when you first turn on your iPhone or wake it up. The wallpaper for this screen image is shown behind the **Slide to Unlock** slider bar.

The **Home Screen** features all of your icons. You can see the wallpaper behind the icons.

You can use the wallpaper pictures that come with the iPhone or you can use your own images.

> **TIP:** You may want the wallpaper for your **Lock Screen** to be less personal than your **Home Screen** wallpaper. For example, you might choose to put a generic landscape image on your **Lock Screen** and a picture of a loved one on your **Home Screen**. Also, you might want to choose a **Home Screen** wallpaper that is less busy so it does not clash with the icons.

There are a couple of ways to change the wallpaper on the iPhone. The first way is very straightforward.

Changing Wallpaper from Your Settings App

You can adjust your wallpaper from your Settings app.

1. Tap the **Settings** icon.

2. Tap **Wallpaper**.

3. Tap the image of your currently selected wallpapers. The Lock screen is shown on the left and the Home screen is on the right.

4. Choose an album.

   - Tap **Wallpaper** to select a pre-loaded wallpaper.

   - Tap **Camera Roll** to select from images you've saved from the Web, screenshots (which you take by pressing and hold the **Home** button and **Power/Sleep** key), or even from wallpaper apps.

   - Tap **Photo Library** to see images in your library.

   - Tap any of the other albums to view pictures you have synced.

5. Once you tap on an album, you will see all the images within that album. Swipe up or down to view all images. The images you have most recently added will be at the very bottom of the list.

6. Tap any image to select it and view it full screen.

7. Now you can move and scale the image.

   ■ Move the image by touching and dragging your finger.

   ■ Zoom in or out by pinching your fingers open or closed.

   ■ Tap the **Cancel** button to return to the album if you don't like the image.

8. Tap the **Set** button to set the image as a wallpaper.

9. Select where you want this wallpaper to be used.

   ■ Tap the **Set Lock Screen** button to set the image only for your **Lock Screen**.

   ■ Tap the **Set Home Screen** button to set the image only for your **Home Screen**.

   ■ Tap the **Set Both** button to set the image for both your **Lock** and **Home Screens**.

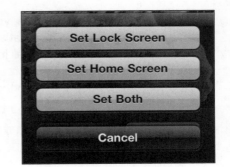

10. Tap the **Home** button to exit out of **Settings** and check out your new wallpapers as shown in Figure 9–1.

Figure 9–1. *Your Lock screen and Home screen. Wallpapers.*

Using any Photo as Wallpaper

The second way to change your wallpaper is to view any picture in your **Photos** collection and select it as your wallpaper.

1. Tap the **Photos** icon to get started. To learn more about working with photos, check out Chapter 21:

"Working with Photos."

2. Touch the photo album you want to look through to find your wallpaper.

3. When you find a photo you want to use, touch it and it will open on your screen.

4. The thumbnail you tap will fill the screen. If this is the image you want to use, tap the **Set as** icon  on the lower left corner of the screen.

5. Tap **Use As Wallpaper.**

6. To move, scale, and set as **Home** or **Lock** screen wallpaper, follow steps 7-9 from the previous section. If you decide you'd rather use a different picture, choose **Cancel** and pick a different one.

Downloading Great Wallpaper from Free Apps

Go to the **App Store** and do a search for **backgrounds** or **wallpapers**. (See Chapter 26: "The Amazing App Store" for help.) You'll find a number of free and low-cost apps designed specifically for your iPhone. In this section we highlight one called **3D Wallpapers** from rise uP! Labs, which has hundreds of beautiful background images you can download for free to your iPhone.

> **NOTE:** With **3D Wallpapers,** as with most wallpaper apps, you will need a live Internet connection—either Wi-Fi or 3G. Because image files tend to be quite large, you should probably stick with Wi-Fi unless you have an unlimited monthly data plan for your 3G cellular data network.

Downloading the Wallpaper from the Free App

After you download **3D Wallpapers**, you can get started.

1. Tap the **3D Wallpapers** icon to start it up.

2. The app has a number of categories of backgrounds to choose from (see Figure 9–2).

3. You can choose to view **Popular**, **Recent,** or **Random** backgrounds using the buttons on the top. After you have indicated that you like a few wallpapers (we show you how below), you can see your picks in the **Favs** category.

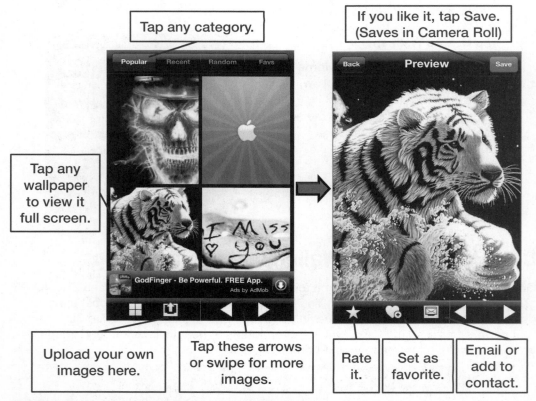

Figure 9–2. *Previewing free wallpaper from the **3D Wallpapers** app.*

4. After touching any wallpaper to bring it to a full-screen preview, tap the **Save** button in the upper right corner to save a copy into your **Camera Roll** album.

5. You can rate the wallpaper by tapping the **star** icon in the lower right corner, mark it as a favorite with the **heart,** or e-mail/add the wallpaper as a contact picture using the **e-mail** icon in the middle of the bottom row.

6. If you don't like the image, click the **Back** button in the upper left corner to get back to the thumbnail images.

> **NOTE:** Like many free apps today, you will see advertisements somewhere in the app; they help the developer pay for the app. In this app, the ads are in the lower bar as you browse the wallpapers.

Using Your Newly Downloaded Wallpaper

Once you've chosen a wallpaper image and saved it to your iPhone, you need to select it using the steps described in the "Changing Wallpaper from your Settings App" section earlier in this chapter.

Remember that the downloaded wallpaper will be in the **Camera Roll** album. After you tap **Camera Roll** to open it, you'll need to flick all the way to the bottom to see your recent entries.

Adjusting Sounds on Your iPhone

You can fine-tune your iPhone so that it does or does not make sounds when certain actions happen, such as an incoming phone call, new mail, or calendar alert. You can also customize what happens when you send mail or type on the keyboard.

To adjust sounds, follow these steps.

1. Tap your **Settings** icon.

2. Tap **General**.

3. Tap **Sounds**.

4. You can adjust whether or not you want your iPhone to vibrate in both **Silent** and **Ring** modes. Set the switches to **On** or **Off** next to **Vibrate**.

5. To adjust the volume of the ringtone and other alerts, move the slider bar just above Ringtone.

6. To change your phone **Ringtone** or sound played when you receive a **New Text Message** tap those items to change them.

7. This is the screen to select a new **Ringtone**. Tap any ringtone to play it and select it. (You can tell it's selected by the checkmark. **Bell Tower** is selected in the image.)

8. When you are done, tap the **Sounds** button in the upper left corner.

9. Use the same steps to change the sound you hear for a **New Text Message**.

TIP: See Chapter 10: "Using Your iPhone as a Phone" to learn about custom ringtones.

10. The only difference for the **New Text Message** is that you can turn it off by selecting the **None** entry a the top of the list.

.ıll AT&T 🤏	10:21 AM	⚹ 100% 🔋
Sounds	**New Text Message**
None	✓
Tri-tone	

11. The rest of the sounds can be adjusted by tapping the switches to set them on or off. You have settings for **New Voicemail**, **New Mail**, **Sent Mail**, **Calendar Alerts**, **Lock Sounds** and **Keyboard Clicks**.

12. When done, press the **Home** button to exit.

New Voicemail	ON
New Mail	OFF
Sent Mail	OFF
Calendar Alerts	OFF
Lock Sounds	ON
Keyboard Clicks	ON

TIP: On a related note, you can lock the maximum volume playable from the iPod app. Go into Settings ➤ iPod ➤ Volume Limit ➤ Lock Volume Limit. We show you how to do this in Chapter 13: "Playing Music."

Keyboard Options

You can fine-tune your keyboard by selecting various languages and changing settings like **Auto-Correction** and **Auto-Capitalization**. You can even have your iPhone speak the Auto-Correction suggestions to you as you type. See Chapter 2: "Typing Tips, Copy/Paste, and Search" for keyboard options and how to use the various features.

How to Secure Your iPhone with a Passcode

Your iPhone can hold a great deal of valuable information. This is especially true if you save information like the Social Security numbers and birth dates of your family members. It's a good idea to make sure that anyone who picks up your iPhone can't access all that information. Also, if your children are like ours, they'll probably pick up your cool iPhone and start surfing the Web or playing a game. You might want to enable some security restrictions to keep them safe.

Setting a Simple 4-Digit Passcode

On your iPhone you have the option of setting a four-digit passcode that prevents unauthorized access to your iPhone and your information. If the wrong passcode is entered, however, even you won't be able to access your information, so it is a good idea to use a code you'll easily remember.

> **TIP:** If you use Apple's MobileMe service described in Chapter 4: "Other Sync Methods," you can use the MobileMe website to set a passcode on your iPhone without even touching the iPhone using the remote-lock feature. You can also remotely erase all data on your iPhone from the MobileMe site using the remote-wipe feature.

To set a passcode to lock your iPhone, follow these steps.

1. Tap the **Settings** icon.

2. Tap **General.**

3. Scroll down and tap **Passcode Lock.**

4. Tap **Turn Passcode On** to set a passcode.

5. The default passcode is a simple four-digit passcode. Use the keyboard to enter a four-digit code. You will then be prompted to enter your code once more.

Setting a More Complex Password

If you prefer to have a password that is more complicated than just four digits, you can do so by turning **OFF** the **Simple Passcode** on the Passcode Lock screen.

You will then be able to enter a new passcode with letters, numbers, and even symbols.

CAUTION: Be careful! If you forget your passcode, you cannot unlock your iPhone.

Passcode Options: Change Time-Out, Disable Picture
Adjusting Passcode Options

Once you have set your passcode, you will be presented with a few options:

- Turn Passcode Off

- Change Passcode

- Require Passcode (Immediately, 1 min., 5 min., 15 min., 1 hour, 4 hours)

- Simple Passcode (On = four digits, Off = any letters, numbers, or symbols)

- Voice Dial (On = Allow voice dialing without entering passcode, Off = Prevent voice dialing until passcode is entered)

- Erase Data (On = Erase all data after 10 incorrect password attempts, Off = Do not erase data)

CAUTION: You may want to set **Erase Data** to **OFF** if you have young children who like to bang away at the security to unlock the keyboard when it comes out of sleep mode and is locked. Otherwise, you may end up with your iPhone being erased frequently.

NOTE: Setting a shorter time for **Require Passcode** is more secure. Setting the time as **Immediately**, the default, is most secure. However, using the setting of 1 minute may save you the headache of retyping your passcode if you accidentally lock your iPhone.

Setting Restrictions

You might decide you don't want your kids listening to explicit lyrics in music on your iPhone. You may also want to block them from visit YouTube or any other web site. Setting these restrictions is quite easy on your iPhone.

Restricting Apps

1. Tap **General** in your **Settings** app.

2. Scroll to down the page and tap **Restrictions.**

3. Tap the **Enable Restrictions** button.

4. You will now be prompted to enter a **Restrictions Passcode**—just pick a four-digit code you will remember.

NOTE: This restrictions passcode is a separate passcode from your main iPhone passcode. You can certainly set it to be the same to help you remember it. However, this could be problematic if you let your family know the main passcode, but do not want them adjusting the restrictions. You will need to enter this passcode to turn off restrictions later.

Notice that you can adjust whether to allow certain apps at all: **Safari**, **YouTube**, **iTunes**, **Installing Apps**, **Camera**, **FaceTime**, or **Location**.

OFF = RESTRICTED

You might think that **ON** means something is restricted, but it is the opposite. In order to disable or restrict something, you need to touch the slider next to it and change it to **OFF**. If you notice the word **Allow** above all the options, then it makes sense.

> **NOTE:** For any apps you restrict, their icons for will disappear. So if you restrict YouTube, the App Store, and FaceTime, for example, the **YouTube** and **App Store** icons would disappear from the Home screen and the **FaceTime** option in the phone would be removed.

Restricting Content

In addition to apps, you can set restrictions for content that is allowed to be downloaded and viewed on the iPhone.   Use this function If you are giving an iPhone to a child and you don't want them to have the ability to download music with explicit lyrics or watch movies with adult content.

1.   Get into the **Restrictions** screen as shown in the previous section.

2.   Scroll down to the bottom to see all of the **Allowed Content** settings.

3.   To restrict content purchased while inside an app, set **In-App Purchases** to **OFF**. This will include music and videos purchased from the **iTunes** app.

4.   Tap **Ratings For** to adjust the ratings based on the country where you live. The set of countries currently supported are: Australia, Austria, Canada, France, Germany, Ireland, Japan, New Zealand, United Kingdom, and the United States.

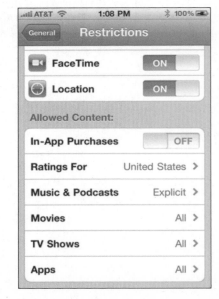

5.   Tap **Music & Podcasts** to restrict access to lyrics to non-explicit content. Make sure **Explicit** is set to **OFF** as shown.

6.   Tap the **Restrictions** button in the upper left corner to return to the list of options.

7.   You can also set the ratings cutoff for **Movies**, **TV Shows,** and **Apps** by tapping each item.

8.   When you tap an item such as Movies, you see a list of allowed ratings. Tap the highest rating level you want to allow. In this image, we tapped **PG-13.** All movies rated above this (**R** and **NC-17)** are not allowed. The red text and lack of checkmark offer visual clues as to which selections are blocked.

9.   Tap **TV Shows** to set those restrictions. Tap the highest rating you want to be allowed. The checkmarks show allowed ratings; the red text is not allowed. In this example, TV-Y, TV-Y7, and TV-G are allowed and higher ratings are not allowed (TV-PG, TV-14, and TV-MA).

Restrictions Music & Podcasts

Allow Music & Podcasts Rated

EXPLICIT   OFF

Allow Playback of Music, Music Videos and Podcasts containing Explicit Content.

Restrictions   Movies

Allow Movies Rated

Don't Allow Movies

G   ✓

PG   ✓

PG-13   ✓

R

NC-17

Allow All Movies

Restrictions   TV Shows

Allow TV Shows Rated

Don't Allow TV Shows

TV-Y   ✓

TV-Y7   ✓

TV-G   ✓

TV-PG

TV-14

TV-MA

Allow All TV Shows

10. Tap **Apps** to set restrictions for Apps.

11. In this screen, we are allowing apps with ratings of 4+, 9+, and 12+ to be played. Apps with ratings of 17+ cannot be played or downloaded.

12. Tap the **Restrictions** button in the upper left corner to return to the list of options.

13. Finally, tap the **Home** button to save your settings.

Restrictions	Apps	
Allow Apps Rated		
Don't Allow Apps		
4+		✓
9+		✓
12+		✓
17+		
Allow All Apps		

Chapter 10

Using Your iPhone as a Phone

The iPhone is capable of so many cool things that it's easy to forget that it's also a very powerful phone. In this chapter, we will explain the many features you would expect from a high-end smartphone. You can dial by name, save time by using your recent call logs, dial by voice, and use voicemail. We'll even show you how to use a free voice dialing app call VoiceBox Dialer.

After we cover the basic phone features, we will explore the more advanced capabilities of the phone on the iPhone. You will learn how to handle multiple callers and set up conference calls. Lastly, we will show you how to create new custom ringtones from your music library and set separate ringtones for individual callers.

Getting Started with the Phone

The iPhone initially places the Phone icon on your bottom dock. You can move it around or off your dock by using the steps shown in Chapter 7: "Organize Your iPhone: Icons and Folders."

Finding Your Phone Number

Maybe you just received your new iPhone and don't yet know the phone number. Don't worry; you can find your number in the Settings app. Tap the **Settings** icon then scroll down and tap **Phone**. Your number is listed at the top.

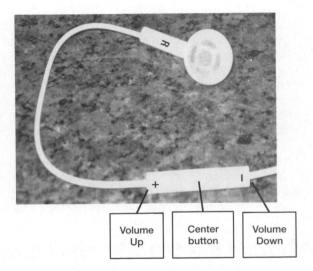

Using the iPhone Headset

If you are in one of the many states or provinces where you cannot legally hold your iPhone while driving a car, you will want to use the headphones or Bluetooth car stereo connection to talk hands-free.

The headset you received with your iPhone works well for phone calls. There is a microphone built into the wire of the headset along with volume controls and a **Center** button that allows you to answer or hang up a phone call. When you have your headset on, the phone will ring in the headset. Click the **Center** button on the headset once to answer, then click again to hang up.

Connecting to a Bluetooth Headset or Car Stereo

You can also connect to a Bluetooth headset or Bluetooth car stereo system to place and receive phone calls. We show you the detailed steps in Chapter 6: "Bluetooth on the iPhone."

Dialing a Number from the Keypad

The simplest way to use your phone is to dial using the keypad. The numbers on the screen are large, so it's easy to dial.

1. Tap the **Phone** icon (see Figure 10–1).

2. If you do not see the keypad to dial, tap the **Keypad** icon at the bottom.

3. Now you can simply start dialing by tapping number keys.

4. If you make a mistake, press the **Backspace** key .

5. If you need to type a plus sign (+) for an international number, press and hold the **zero** (0) key.

6. When you are done dialing, press the **Call** key .

TIP: Dialing pauses in a phone number

Sometimes you have to pause in a phone number then enter another number such as an extension or a password. You can dial a pause by pressing and holding the asterisk key until you see a comma appear next to the phone number. This will be a 2-second pause.

Figure 10–1. *Dialing phone numbers with your iPhone Keypad.*

Different Phone Views

We just used the Keypad soft key. There are icons along the bottom for Favorites, Recents, Contacts, Keypad, and Voicemail.

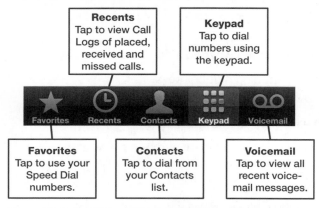

Figure 10–2. *Use these softkeys to see different Phone screens.*

Using Favorites (Speed Dials)

Your **Favorites** are people you frequently call. You can think of **Favorites** as your speed dial list.

> **NOTE:** We understand that Apple is also adding **FaceTime** favorites in future releases of the iPhone operating system. So by the time you read this, you may also be able to add **FaceTime** contacts to **Favorites**.

Adding New Favorites

It is easy to add new favorites to your list from your Contacts.

> **TIP:** You can also add a **Favorite** from your **Recents** call logs. In Recents, tap the ⊙ and on the next screen, scroll to the bottom of the Info page and tap **Add to Favorites**.

1.   If you are not in the Phone, tap the **Phone** icon to start it up.

2.   Touch the **Favorites** icon in the bottom row of soft keys.

3. The first time you start your **Favorites**, you will see a blank screen.

4. Tap the ➕ button in the upper right hand corner to add a new entry. Your contact directory will open.

5. Swipe up or down to locate a contact. Tap any contact entry to select it.

> **TIP:** To search for your Contacts by name, tap the very top of the screen just under the time. This will bring up the search window where you can type a few letters to find people. Remember that you can view different contact groups by tapping the **Groups** button in the upper left corner.

6. If an entry has more than one phone number, you will need to select one of them as your favorite entry.

7. After tapping a number, you will be returned to your list of favorites where you'll see the new person you just added.

8. Repeat steps 4-7 to add more people to your **Favorites**. Each new entry is listed below the previous ones at the bottom of the list.

Organizing Your Favorites

Like other lists on your iPhone, you can re-order it and remove entries.

1. View your **Favorites** list as you did above.

2. Tap the **Edit** button in the upper left corner.

3. To re-order the entries, touch and drag the right edge with the three gray bars up or down the list.

4. To delete an entry, tap the red circle to the left of the entry to make it turn vertical.

5. Then tap the **Delete** button.

6. When you are done re-ordering and deleting entries, tap the **Done** button in the upper left corner.

Calling a Favorite

To call any **Favorite,** just touch the name of the individual. There is no prompt or confirmation. As soon as you touch his or her name, the phone will dial (as shown in Figure 10–3).

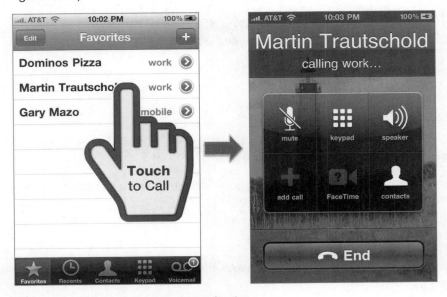

Figure 10–3. *Dialing your Favorites by tapping them.*

Using Recents (Call Logs)

Using your **Recents** is similar to looking at your call log on other smartphones.

When you touch the **Recents** icon, a list of all your recent calls will be listed. You can touch the **All** or **Missed** button at the top to narrow down the list. See Figure 10–4.

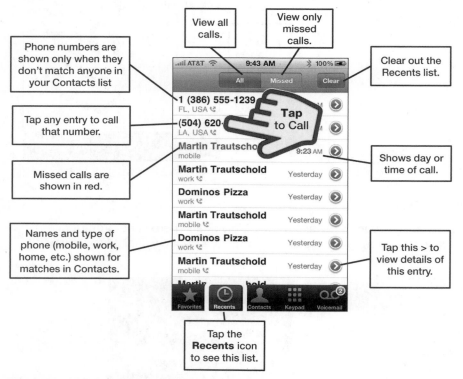

Figure 10–4. *Working with your Recents screen.*

Placing a Call from Recents

Just touch the name or phone number and the iPhone will immediately initiate a phone call to the individual.

Clearing All Recents

To clear or erase all your recent call log entries, press the **Clear** button in the upper right corner.

Details of a Call or Contact Information

Touch the blue arrow next to the name in the Recents list and you will see either the information on the phone number or full contact information for that particular contact if they are in your **Contacts** list.   If there were several calls, you see the history of each call.

Scroll down to the bottom of the contact Info screen to see more options. You can send a **Text Message**, start a **FaceTime** video call, or **Share Contact** by sending the contact information via e-mail or MMS.

Tap **Add to Favorites** to put this person on your Favorites list.

Adding a Phone Number to Contacts from Recents

If the Recents entry is just a phone number, not yet in your Contacts list, then you will see two different buttons on the Info screen.

Tap **Create New Contact** to create a new contact from this phone number.

Tap **Add to Existing Contact** to add this phone number to one of your existing contacts.

Placing Calls from Contacts

One of the great things about having all your contact information in your phone is that it's very easy to place calls from your Contacts list on the iPhone.

1. If you are not in your Phone, tap the **Phone** icon to start it up. Refer to Figure 10–5.

2. Touch the **Contacts** icon in the bottom row of soft keys.

3. Locate a contact to call using one of the following methods:

    a. Swipe up or down through the list.

b. Put your finger on the alphabet along the right side of the screen and scroll up or down.

c. Double-tap the top where it says Contacts to jump to the top. Tap in the search window and type a few letters of the contact's first, last, or company name to search for them.

4. When you find the contact entry you want, tap their name.

5. Touch the phone number you wish to call.

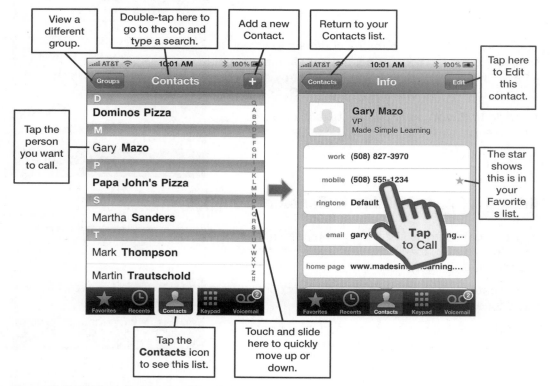

Figure 10–5. *Placing calls from your Contacts list.*

Calling Any Underlined Phone Number (Email, Web, SMS, Anywhere)

You will notice that the iPhone underlines almost every phone number it recognizes on the screen.

This happens in e-mail messages (e-mail signatures), SMS messages, notes, web sites, and more.

To call to any of these underlined phone numbers, tap on it, then tap the **Call** button as shown.

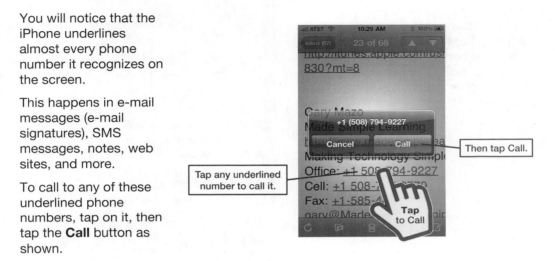

Tap any underlined number to call it.

Then tap Call.

Tap to Call

TIP: Like the underlined phone numbers, your iPhone also recognizes other information on the screen and allows you to act on it by tapping it. This feature is known as a **Data Detector**. You will see underlined addresses (tap to show the address in **Maps**), underlined dates such as **tomorrow at 9am** (tap to schedule a new **Calendar** event), shipping numbers such as a FedEx or UPS tracking number (tap to show the tracking information in **Safari).**

Creating a New Contact from an Underlined Phone Number

Press and hold any underlined phone number for a few seconds until you see a list of buttons appear from the bottom of the screen. Tap Create New Contact to create a new contact from the number or tap Add to Existing Contact if you want to add this number to a person already in your contact list.

Voice Dialing

You can voice dial using the built-in Voice Control feature or you can acquire an app to help you get it done. We'll profile one free voice dialing app in this section.

Voice Control

You can use your voice to place calls using the Voice Control feature on your iPhone. You'll find all the steps in the "Voice Control" section of Chapter 8: "Multitasking and Voice Control."

VoiceBox Dialer App

There are a number of free and paid apps in the App Store if you don't like the way the built-in iPhone dialer works.

We tested one free App called **VoiceBox Dialer** and found that it worked well. Download the app from the App Store by doing a name search first to find it (see Chapter 26: "The Amazing App Store" for more details).

Once you install it, simply tap the VoiceBox icon to get started.

Voice Dial Contacts or Voice Search by Category

The main window has a large button which you hold down while speaking your request. You can call any contact in your Contacts list or simply dial a phone number. Say **Call Gary on his mobile** or Dial **1-800-555-1212**. You can also search for local businesses by tapping the Category button and saying **Find Starbucks** or **Find grocery stores** (see Figure 10–6).

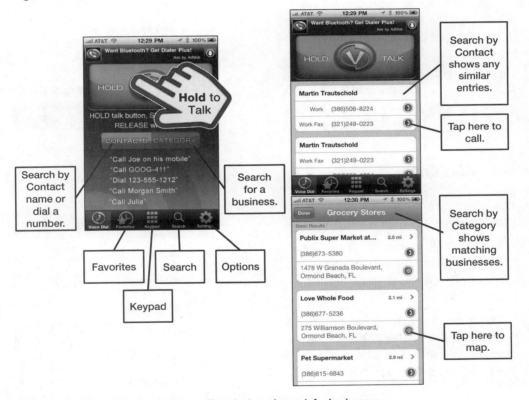

Figure 10–6. *Using VoiceBox Dialer to call contacts and search for businesses.*

Search by Type of Business

You can search for a business of a particular type using the **Search** function.

1. Tap the **Search** soft key at the bottom of the screen.

2. Then tap the **Business** button at the top.

3. Scroll up or down, or type a search.

4. Tap the business type to start the search. The search uses the superpages.com search engine.

> **TIP:** Seeing all the business categories can be helpful if you are not sure of the exact business category name.

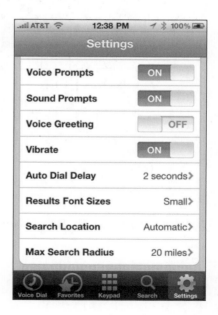

VoiceBox Settings

You can customize the app with the Settings screen.

1. You can adjust whether or not the app gives you **Voice Prompts, Sound Prompts, Voice Greeting,** or **Vibrates**.

2. You may want to lengthen or turn off the **Auto Dial Delay**. This will give you more time if the app misunderstands who you want to call.

3. If your GPS is not working, or you simply want to use another location for the search, you can change it by tapping **Search Location**.

Functions While on a Call

You can do a number of things while your iPhone is dialing and once it is connected to the person you are calling.

All the phone functions available to you are clearly shown with the icons and buttons on the screen.

You can do the following:

- **Mute** yourself

- Dial additional numbers with the **Keypad**

- Turn on the **Speakerphone**

- Create a conference call by tapping **Add Call**

- Start a video call with **FaceTime** (assuming the other caller also has an iPhone 4).

- View your **Contacts** list.

NOTE: Why does the screen go blank when I hold the phone to my ear? When you are talking into the iPhone (holding the phone next to your face), the screen senses this and goes blank so you can't accidentally press a button with your face. As soon as you move the iPhone away from your face, you will see the options.

Using the Keypad

Perhaps the number you're calling requires you to dial an extension. Or maybe you are calling an automated answering service that requires you to input numbers for choices.

In these situations, just touch the **Keypad** icon and the keypad will be displayed. Input numbers as prompted.

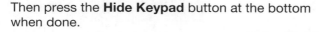

Then press the **Hide Keypad** button at the bottom when done.

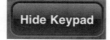

Muting the Call

As the number is dialing, you will see the option in the top left row to mute the call. Just tap the **Mute** button to mute yourself.   Tap it again to turn off the mute.

> **TIP:** When you have **FaceTime** enabled, you can't see a hold button. Use the **Mute** icon to put the call on hold.

Using the Speaker Phone

If you would prefer to use the built-in Speakerphone on the iPhone, tap the **Speaker** icon.

Tap that same icon again to turn off the Speakerphone.

Putting a Caller on Hold

> **NOTE:** You will only see this **Hold** icon if your FaceTime is disabled (which you do in **Settings** > **Phone** > **FaceTime** set to **OFF**). As we said above, if you don't have a **Hold** icon, just tap the **Mute** icon instead – it will accomplish the same result.

Tap the **Hold** icon to put the caller on hold. Tap it again to remove the hold.

Browsing Your Contacts

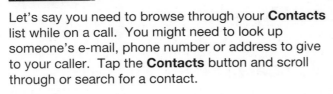

Let's say you need to browse through your **Contacts** list while on a call. You might need to look up someone's e-mail, phone number or address to give to your caller. Tap the **Contacts** button and scroll through or search for a contact.

To return to the call, tap the top green bar where it says **Touch to return to call**.

NOTE: It's a good idea to use the Speakerphone or a Bluetooth Headset while doing this (see Chapter 6: "Bluetooth") so you can continue to talk on the phone while searching for the contact.

FaceTime Video Call

FaceTime

If you are chatting with someone who also has an iPhone 4 and is on Wi-Fi, you can tap the **FaceTime** icon to start a video call. (You may be able to use FaceTime on a 3G cellular connection in the future, but now, it requires a Wi-Fi connection.) You will see your picture in the top left portion of the window and your caller's picture in the main window. You will notice three buttons at the bottom: **Mute**, **End** call and **Switch Camera** to swap between your front-facing and rear-facing cameras.

See Chapter 12: "FaceTime Video Messaging and Skype" for more on using FaceTime.

NOTE: You will only see this **FaceTime** icon if your FaceTime is enabled (which you do in **Settings ➤ Phone ➤ FaceTime** set to **ON**).

Setting Up and Using Voicemail

Your iPhone comes with an enhanced voicemail system called **Visual Voicemail**. This is a nice feature because it allows you to quickly see all voicemails and play them in any order. You don't have to listen to each message in order, just tap the message you want to hear. This image with the number 3 in the red circle shows that there are three unheard voicemail messages.

> **NOTE:** If you live outside the US, your carrier may not have implemented **Visual Voicemail**. If not, then you will need to dial in to retrieve your messages by pressing the **Voicemail** soft key, just as with any other mobile phone.

Setting Up Voicemail

In order to setup voicemail, follow these steps.

1. Tap the **Phone** icon.

2. Tap the **Voicemail** icon in the bottom row of soft keys.

3. Tap the **Set Up Now** button shown in Figure 10–7.

4. Pick a 4-digit password and then re-enter the password.

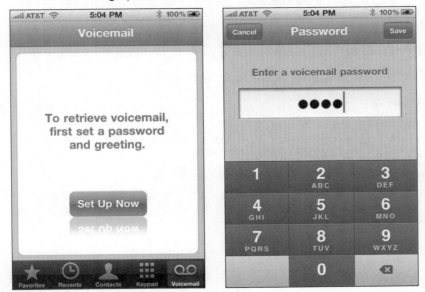

Figure 10–7. *Setting Up Your Voicemail.*

5. Next, you can choose a **Default** or **Custom** greeting. The **Default** greeting will say your phone number in a computer voice and that you are not available.

6. If you chose a Custom greeting, you need to record it by tapping the **Record** button. When done, tap the **Stop** button, which is in the same place as the **Record** button.

7. Once recorded, you can tap the **Play** button to see if you like your Custom greeting.

TIP: If you hold the iPhone too close to your mouth, your voice may sound a little distorted. Just hold the iPhone at a normal distance.

Changing Your Voicemail Password

You may want to change your password. Go to your **Settings** app.

1. Tap the **Settings** icon.

2. Scroll down and tap **Phone.**

3. Scroll down and tap **Change Voicemail Password**

4. Enter your current password, then type your new password twice.

Playing Your Voicemail

The beauty of the Visual Voicemail system is that you never have to call in to check your voicemail. All voicemail messages will reside on your phone. You can save them, scroll through them, or delete them.

You will know how many unheard voicemail messages you have by the little number in the red circle in the top right of the voicemail icon.

Unheard items, like unread e-mail in your inbox, are marked with a little blue dot.

The voicemail icon will show the number of voicemails in your mailbox. Tap the **Play** button next to the message and the message will play through your handset.

> **TIP:** If you cannot look at the screen, you can still dial in to listen to your voicemail hands-free by pressing and holding the 1 key on your keypad.

To Hear the Voicemail Play through the Speaker

If you would like to hear your voicemail through the iPhone's speaker (as opposed to listening through the handset), just touch the **Speaker** button in the upper right hand corner.

To Adjust Your Greeting

Tap **Greeting** button to adjust your voicemail greeting. You can listen to your greeting again, record a new **Custom** greeting, or change the greeting back to the **Default**.

To Call Back the Person Who Left the Voice Mail

Just touch the **Call Back** button and you can immediately return the call of the individual who left you the voicemail.

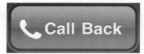

To Delete the Voicemail Message

Your iPhone will store all your voicemails if you want to listen to them at a later date. Sometimes voicemails can get a bit unwieldy if you have too many of them. Just touch the red **Delete** button and the selected message will be removed from your iPhone. See Figure 10–7.

NOTE: You have the option to save a "Deleted" message. Your Voicemail screen will show your "Deleted" messages in its own tab. Touch a "Deleted" message and you can then "Undelete" to restore it.

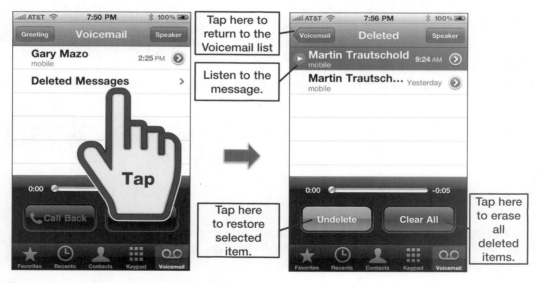

Figure 10–7. *Working with deleted voicemail items.*

If you would like to permanently all deleted voicemails, tap **Clear All.**

Conference Calling

In today's busy world, working with several callers at once has become something that we demand from our phones. Fortunately, conference calling is very intuitive on the iPhone.

Initiating the First Call

As we showed you in the earlier in this chapter, just make a call to any number—a contact, a new number, anyone at all.

You don't have to start a call to create a conference call. You can receive a call from the first caller instead of placing it. Then you conference in the second person.

Move the iPhone away from your face to see the phone functions available to you. Most of these were covered earlier in this chapter.

Tap Add Call to call another person.

Adding a Second Caller

Touch the **+ Add Call** button to add a second caller. This will immediately put the first caller on hold.

Touching the **Add Call** button brings you to your Contacts list. Simply scroll or double-tap the top to search for the contact to add to this call.

You can also add a new caller by choosing from your **Favorites, Recents,** or even dialing their phone number by pressing the **Keypad** soft key on the bottom.

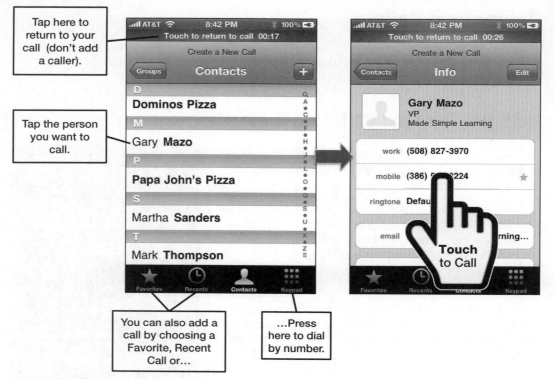

Tap here to return to your call (don't add a caller).

Tap the person you want to call.

You can also add a call by choosing a Favorite, Recent Call or...

...Press here to dial by number.

Figure 10–8. *Adding a second calle.*

If the contact has more than one phone entry, tap the one you would like to call and the call will be initiated.

Merging Calls

Once the call to the second caller has been initiated, you will notice that the **Add Call** button has now been replaced with a **Merge Calls** button. Tap the **Merge Calls** button and both calls will be merged into a three-way conference call. See Figure 10–9.

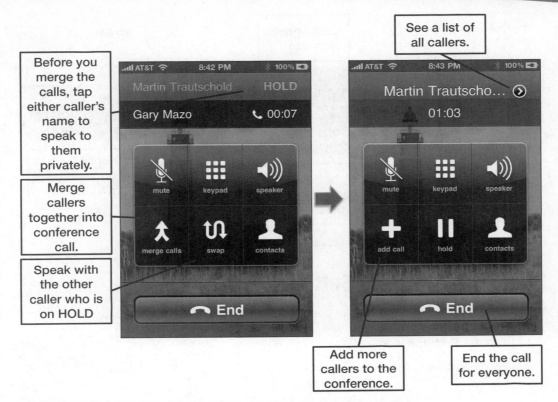

Figure 10–9. *Swapping between callers and merging them into a conference call.*

The top of the screen will now scroll a list of all the callers on the conference call.

Talking Privately with or Disconnecting from Individuals

In order to speak to one caller individually or privately from a conference call, perform these steps.

1. Tap the small black arrow next to the name at the top of the phone screen. See Figure 10–10.

2. Now you will see a list of all callers.

3. Tap the **Private** button next to a person's name to talk privately with that person. Everyone else is put on hold.

4. To hang up with any caller, tap the red phone icon to the left of their name.

See a list of all callers.

Click here to return.

Click here to hang up with this person.

Click here to talk privately with this person.

Notice Gary is on the phone and Martin is on hold.

Figure 10–10. *Talking privately with individual callers or hanging up on them.*

Phone Options and Settings

You can customize many things in your phone by going into the **Settings** app.

1. Tap the **Settings** icon.

2. Scroll down and tap **Phone**.

This section describes all of the phone settings found here.

Call Forwarding

There may be times when you need to forward your calls to another number. Perhaps you are traveling to a friend's house out in the boondocks which has very poor cell reception. You want to forward calls to their land line.

1. In the phone settings screen, tap **Call Forwarding**.

2. Set the **Call Forwarding** switch to **ON.**

3. Tap the **Forward to** row to enter the forwarding number.

4. Once entered, the number will be stored for future reference. All calls will be forwarded from your regular iPhone number to this number until you turn call forwarding **OFF**.

> **CAUTION:** Call forwarding is not always free. Call your phone company to see if you will be charged for enabling call forwarding.

Call Waiting

Another Phone setting is call waiting. Call waiting alerts you to the fact that another call is coming in while you are on the phone.

You then have the option to take the new call, hang up on the first call, or set up a conference call as you did above.

You just need to make sure the **Call Waiting** switch is set to the **ON** position, which is the default setting.

Show or Block (Hide) Your Caller ID

You have the option with the iPhone of blocking
your Caller ID phone number if you choose.

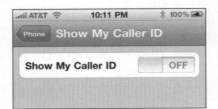

There may be certain situations where you would
prefer that your phone number not show up on the
caller's phone. Set this switch to **OFF** to block your
caller ID.

Setting Security on your SIM card - Assigning a PIN Code

As an added measure of security, you can enable a PIN code to access information
stored on your SIM card. If your iPhone were ever lost or stolen, this would prevent
anyone from accessing the names and numbers stored on your SIM card.

CAUTION: Setting this SIM PIN may lock
your phone so that it is unusable until you
enter a PUK (Personal Unlocking key).
You can get this 8-digit PUK from your
wireless carrier. For AT&T, login to
AT&T's web site, click on My Services at
the top of the page, then click on My
Phone/Device in the middle. Then select
your iPhone and click on the Unblock SIM
Card link. If you do not have AT&T, then
check your carrier's web site or call your
carrier's help desk.

1. Get into the Phone settings menu as before.

2. Scroll down and tap **SIM PIN**.

3. If you try to turn on the SIM PIN on the next screen and you see an error message similar to the one shown to the right, then your iPhone has been locked. You can only unlock it by entering the PUK (Personal Unlocking key). See the caution note above for more details.

4. If you don't see any error message after setting the switch next to **SIM PIN** to **ON**, then you can tap **Change PIN** to enter your new PIN.

TTY for Deaf People

TTY stands for Text Telephone Device. It allows your iPhone to communicate with another phone that is equipped with a TTY device, which lets deaf people type messages that are sent over the phone lines. Set the **TTY** switch to **ON** to use it.

Switching Between Wireless Carriers

If you live in a country where several wireless carriers supply the iPhone, such as Canada, then you will see a **Carriers** tab in your **Settings** app.

Tap **Carrier** to see the screen where you can switch between carriers for your iPhone.

Leave it on **Automatic** to have your iPhone select the best network.

If you want to force your iPhone onto a specific network, such as **ROGERS**, then tap that network name or the number.

> **NOTE:** In this image, since the SIM card is from the ROGERS network, you only see the name of the ROGERS network. The number (302880) is the local Bell/Telus carrier cell tower number.

AT&T (or other carrier) Services

In the United States, as of publishing of this book, AT&T is the still the sole wireless carrier for the iPhone.

If you are not in the U.S., you have another carrier who provides your iPhone service. The button will list your wireless carrier/phone company name.

Tap AT&T Services at the bottom of the phone settings screen to see special numbers related to AT&T. If you use a different carrier, this screen will show the special access numbers for your carrier.

Tap any of the entries on this screen to perform the stated request. For example, if you tap **View My Minutes**, you'll receive a text message response showing details of your minutes remaining in this billing cycle.

Tap the **View** button to see more details.

Ring Tones, Sounds, and Vibration

The iPhone can alert you to incoming calls, voice mails received, and other features with unique sounds or vibrations. These can easily be adjusted using the **Settings** app.

In section "Adjusting Sounds on your iPhone" in Chapter 9: "Personalize and Secure" we show you how to change a ringtone, add vibration to both silent and ring mode, and turn on or off the tone for voicemail messages.

Assigning Unique Ringtones to Contacts

Sometimes, it is both fun and useful to give a unique ringtone to a certain contacts in your address book. This way, you know who is calling without looking at your phone.

You can use ringtones that are already on your iPhone or you have several ways to get new ringtones.

- Purchase ringtones using the **iTunes** app on your iPhone.
- Create and purchase ringtones using your music from iTunes on your computer.
- Create free ringtones using your music from iTunes on your computer.

For example, one of the authors (Gary) sets the ring tone for his son Daniel to the ring tone of Elton John's "Daniel." Later in this chapter we will show you how to make a ring tone from your iTunes music.

Giving a Contact a Unique Ringtone

You need to edit a person's information in Contacts to change their ringtone.

1. Tap the **Contacts** icon (see Figure 10–11).

2. Tap the contact you wish to change (in this case **Daniel**).

3. Tap the **Ringtone** button to see the Ringtones screen.

4. Tap any ringtone from the list. In this case, we wanted the new custom ringtone **Daniel**.

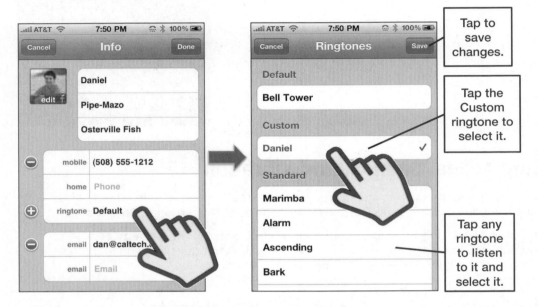

Figure 10–11. *Selecting a Custom Ringtone for a Contact.*

Purchasing a Ringtone from the iTunes App

These steps show how to purchase a ringtone (most are US $1.29). You can then immediately attach it to a contact or set is as your **Default Ringtone** right from the **iTunes** app on your iPhone.

1. Start the **iTunes** app on your iPhone.

2. Tap the **Ringtones** soft key at the bottom and scroll through ring tones. Or you can search for a ringtone by tapping the **Search** soft key at the bottom.

3. You can also browse ringtones by using the buttons at the top— **Featured**, **Top Tens,** and **Genres**.

4. We selected **Top Tens** and then **Alternative** to see the image to the right.

5. Tap any name or album cover to preview the ringtone. If you like it, tap the price to buy it, and tap **Buy Now**.

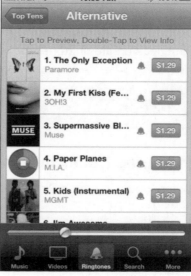

6. Once you select the ringtone to purchase, iTunes will prompt you to either **Set as Default Ringtone** (your main phone ringtone) or **Assign to a Contact**.

7. If you choose **Assign to a Contact**, your **Contacts** list will launch. Scroll through or search for the contact. You will now hear the new ringtone each time that contact calls.

Creating Custom Ringtones

Your iTunes library is filled with all your favorite songs. Wouldn't it be great if you could turn your own songs into ringtones for your iPhone? The good news is that you can turn most of your music into a ringtone. There is an easy way to do this (it costs about $1 per ringtone) and a more challenging but free way to do this. We will show you both.

The Easy Way to Create Ringtones Using iTunes

First, let's create ringtones in iTunes using songs you have purchased from iTunes.

NOTE: You cannot use this method unless you have purchased the song from iTunes and the song itself allows ringtones to be created. Some artists prevent this feature.

Preparing iTunes to Create Ringtones

Before you can create Ringtones from the iTunes Store, you need to adjust a few settings in iTunes itself.

1. From your iTunes menu, select **Edit** from the menu and then choose **Preferences** to see the screen shown to the right.

2. Make sure **Ringtones** is checked and click **OK.**

3. Now you will notice a new **Ringtones** category appear under **Apps** in your library in the left column.

4. From your iTunes menu, select **View** from the menu and then choose **View Options** to see the screen shown to the right.

Make sure Ringtones is checked.

Now, you will see a new Ringtones category in your library.

Make sure Ringtones is checked.

5. When you click OK, you may be asked if you would like iTunes to check which songs can be converted to ringtones. Select **Check Songs** from the pop-up window.

6. After iTunes checks your music library, you will notice a new column with a bell icon at the top. Only songs with a bell icon next to them can be converted into a ringtone with iTunes normal method.   These are songs that have been purchased from the iTunes store.

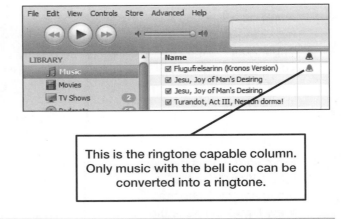

This is the ringtone capable column. Only music with the bell icon can be converted into a ringtone.

CAUTION: There is a charge for ringtone creation.

As of press time, iTunes charges for this service, usually US $0.99 for each Ringtone created.

Creating the Ringtone in iTunes

Now you are ready to choose a song from which you will make a Ringtone.

1. Select a song that iTunes will allow you to use. These are songs that have a bell 🔔 icon in the new Ringtone column.

2. Highlight the song, then select **Store ➤ Create Ringtone** from the menu.

3. Sign in to iTunes using the account that was used to originally purchase the song.

4. iTunes will show you the Create Ringtone page (Figure 10–12).

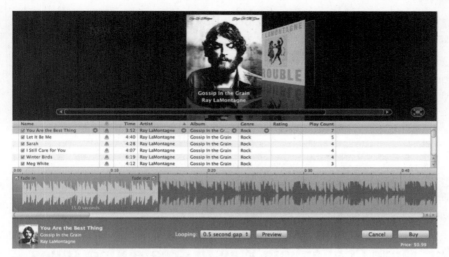

Figure 10–12. *iTunes Create New Ringtone page.*

5. The song is displayed as a sound wave along the bottom with the first 15 seconds highlighted in blue.

6. You can grab the blue highlighted section in the middle and drag it to any section of the song. You can also drag either of the corners to extend the ringtone beyond the initial 15 seconds.

7. Figure 10–13 shows a highlighted section of a particular song that is almost 30 seconds long.

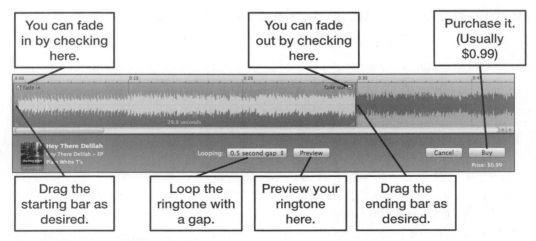

Figure 10–13. *Creating a Ringtone in iTunes.*

8. To listen to the highlighted section, click **Preview.**

9. When you are satisfied with the selection, click **Buy** and input your iTunes password, if prompted.

10. Once your purchase the ringtone, it will appear in the ringtone list. Click on **Ringtones** in the left hand column of iTunes (Figure 10–14).

Figure 10–14. *Viewing Ringtones in iTunes.*

The Free, But More Challenging Way to Create Ring Tones

The second method for creating a Ringtone is a little trickier. It certainly helps to be technically inclined if you are going to try this method. One very good reason to give this method a try is that it is totally free. The second reason is that it will work on many more songs than the iTunes method described above.

This method will work on any music in iTunes that is not protected with DRM (Digital Rights Management) copy protection. Older iTunes purchases might contain DRM. Any music you loaded into iTunes from a CD or other non-DRM music (including newer non-DRM music from iTunes) will work.

Locating the Song to Turn into Your Custom Ringtone

First, locate the song in your iTunes library.

1. Select and highlight a song in iTunes to use as a basis for your custom ringtone.

   In the iTunes menu, select **File > Get info.** You can also right-click the song with your mouse and choose **Get info**.

2. Click on the **Options** tab and put a check mark in the **Start time** and **Stop Time** boxes.

CAUTION: Make sure the total duration is less than 40 seconds; otherwise the ringtone will be too large.

3. Click **OK** to close the **Get Info** dialog box.

4. In iTunes, click on the **Advanced** menu and select **Create AAC Version**.

5. You should now see a new version of the song that is only a few seconds long appear in your iTunes list. Our new version of **Daniel** is only **0:30** long.

6. Once you have your new 30-second version, make sure you go back into the original song and uncheck the Start and Stop times via the **Get Info ➤ Options** tab.

7. Once the new, shorter ringtone ACC version of the song is created, just drag it from iTunes to your desktop or copy and paste it onto the desktop.

8.

9. Change the extension of the file from **m4a** to **m4r** so it will be recognized as a ringtone. Click on it to highlight the name and change it or right-click on the file and choose **Get Info** and then change the extension.

10. You will see a warning message that the file may be unusable. Just accept the change.

11. You must now delete the 30-second version that still is in iTunes in order to move to the next step.

12. Drag the new file with the new **m4r** extension back into your iTunes library and drop it there.

13. If everything went well, you should now see your ringtone listed when you click on **Ringtones** in the left column.

Syncing the Ringtone to Your iPhone

See the "Sync Ringtones" section of Chapter 3: "Sync with iTunes" to learn how to get the new ringtone onto your iPhone.

Using Your New Custom Ringtone

If you want to tie your ringtone to a particular person in your **Contacts** list, you will need to edit that contact. Follow the steps in the "Giving a Contact a Unique Ringtone" section in this chapter.

If you want to use your new ringtone for your main phone ringtone, follow the steps in the "Sounds" section of Chapter 9: "Personalize and Secure Your iPhone."

Chapter 11

SMS and MMS Messaging

SMS stands for Short Messaging Service and it is commonly referred to as "Text Messaging." Text messages are usually limited to 160 characters and are a great way to quickly touch base with someone without interrupting them with a voice call. Sometimes you can text someone and receive a text reply when it would be impossible or difficult to do a voice call.

In this chapter, we will cover how to send and receive SMS text messages and MMS–Multi-Media Messages (picture/video messages) on your iPhone.

You will learn how to send a text message from your **Contacts** app and how to send a picture as an MMS from your **Photos** app.

SMS Text Messaging on your iPhone

Text messaging has become one of the most popular services on cell phones today. While it is still used more extensively in Europe and Asia, it is growing in popularity in North America.

The concept is very simple; instead of placing a phone call, send a short message to someone's handset. It is much less disruptive than a phone call and you may have friends, colleagues, or co-workers who do not own an iPhone–so e-mail may not be an option.

One of the authors uses text messaging with his children all the time–this is how their generation communicates. "R u coming home 4 dinner?" "Yup." There you have it–meaningful dialogue with an eighteen-year-old–short, instant, and easy.

Composing SMS Text Messages

Composing an SMS message is much like sending an e-mail. The beauty of an SMS message is that it arrives on virtually any handset and is quite simple to reply to.

Composing an SMS Message from the Messages App

There are a couple of ways to start your **Messages** app. The easiest is to just touch the **Messages** icon on the **Home** screen.

When you first start the **Messages** app, you most likely won't have any messages, so the screen will be blank. Once you get started with SMS messaging, you will have a list of messages and current "open" discussions with your contacts.

1. Touch the **Compose** icon in the top right-hand corner of the screen.

2. The cursor will immediately go to the **To:** line. You can either start typing in the name of your contact or just touch the **+** button and search or scroll through your contacts.

3. If you want to just type someone's mobile phone number, then press the **123** button and dial the number.

4. When you find the contact you wish to use, just touch the name and now their name will appear in the **To:** line (Figure 11–1).

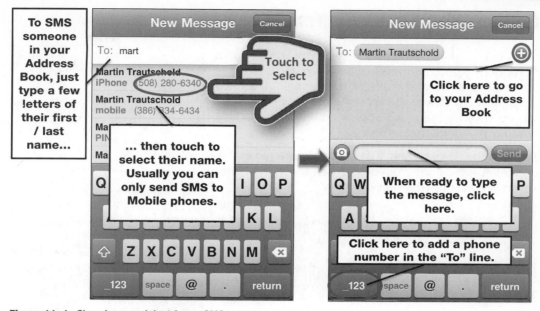

Figure 11–1. *Choosing a recipient for an SMS message*

5. When you are ready to type the SMS message, touch anywhere in the box in the middle of the screen (next to the **Send** button).

6. The keyboard will be displayed. Just type in your message and then touch **Send** when you are done.

> **NOTE**: New in iOS 4, a character counter will appear after you've been typing for a while.

> **TIP**: If you prefer, you can use the larger landscape keyboard for sending Text Messages. It can be easier to type with the larger keys, especially when your fingers are a little larger, or it is hard to see the smaller keys.

Options After Sending a Text

Once the text has been sent, the window changes to a "threaded" discussion window between you and the contact. Your text that you sent is in a green bubble on the right-hand side of the screen. When your contact replies, their message will appear on the opposite side of the screen in a gray bubble.

To leave the SMS screen, just touch **Messages** in the upper left-hand corner or you can just touch the **Home** key to go back to your home screen.

> **NOTE:** If the message fails to send, you'll get an exclamation mark beside it. New in iOS 4, you'll also get an "! "on the **Messages** app icon.

You can send another text just as you did before or you can also "Call" the contact or view their "Contact Info."

To initiate a call to the contact with whom you are "texting," just touch the **Call** button. To look at their contact info, just touch the **Contact Info** button.

Composing an SMS Message from "Contacts"

You also have the ability to start the **SMS** app and compose an SMS message from any contact in your iPhone.

1. Find the contact you wish to "text" by searching or scrolling through **Contacts**.

2. At the very bottom of the contact info, there will be a box that says **Text Message** (Figure 11–2). Just touch that box and you will be prompted to choose which number to use (if you have more than one number listed for the contact.)

3. Choose the number and follow the steps listed previously.

NOTE: Remember that you can only send SMS messages to a mobile number.

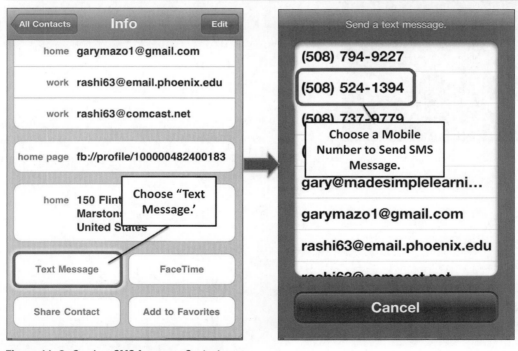

Figure 11–2. *Send an SMS from your Contacts app.*

Replying to a Text Message

When a text message is received, your iPhone will play an indicator tone or vibrate or both—depending on your settings. An indicator will appear on the screen giving you the option of replying right away.

When you see and/or hear the indicator, just touch **Reply** to go directly to the messaging screen and type your response, as shown previously.

> **NOTE**: If your screen is locked, you will see the message, but you won't have a **Reply** button. You will see a **slide to view** button. Just slide the **Lock** tab and you will see the message.

Viewing Stored Messages

Once you begin a few threaded messages, they will be
stored in the **Messages** app. Just touch the **Messages** icon
and you can scroll through your message threads.

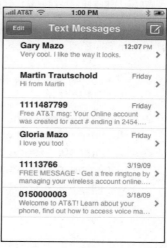

To continue a conversation with someone, just touch on
that thread and it will open up showing you all the past
messages back and forth. Just touch the text box, type in
your message, and touch the **Send** button to continue the
conversation.

SMS Notification Options

There are a couple of options available to you with regards to how your iPhone reacts when an SMS message comes in.

1. Start your **Settings** app, scroll to **Sounds**, and touch the tab.

2. In the **Sounds** menu, if you choose to have the **Vibrate**feature **ON** when the phone rings (see Chapter 10: "Your iPhone as a Phone"), you will also receive a vibration when an SMS message comes in.

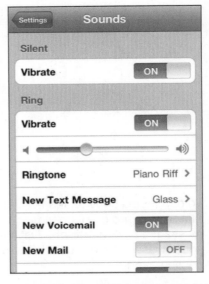

3. Scroll down a bit further and you will see a tab that says **New Text Message**. Touch this and you can choose the tone for the SMS message. You are limited to the choices offered (usually six) or you can choose **None**.

4. Just choose the sound for SMS message notification and then touch the **Sounds** button in the top left-hand corner to "set" your selection.

MMS—Multi-Media Messaging

With the **Messages** app, iPhone users have the tools to send and receive MMS–including picture messages and video messages. MMS messages appear right in the messaging window like your SMS text messages.

> **NOTE**: You can send images, videos, location (from maps), audio (from Voice Memo), and vCard (from Contacts) all via the **MMS** app.

The Messages Icon

To send an MMS message:

1. Touch the **Messages** icon to start messaging–just like you did with SMS.

2. The Text enter screen is the same as in the SMS program covered earlier.

3. You will notice that next to the Text input bubble is a small "camera" image. Just touch the camera and you will be prompted to **Take a Photo/Video** or **Choose   Existing.**

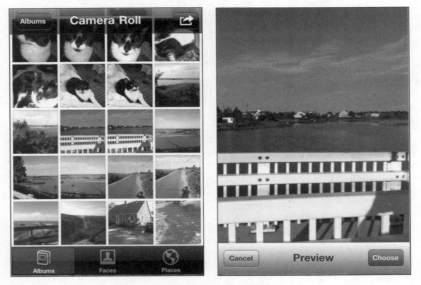

4. To take a photo, follow the instructions in Chapter 21: "Working with Photos." If you **Choose Existing**, just navigate through your pictures/videos and find the item you would like to add to your message (Figure 11–3).

Figure 11–3. *Choose an existing photo to send as MMS.*

5. Touch the blue **Choose** button in the lower right-hand corner and you will see the picture load into the small window.

6. Select a recipient as we showed you earlier and type in a short note if you like. Then, touch the blue **Send** button.

If you already have a threaded discussion with that particular contact, the picture will show up in the midst of the threaded discussion.

> **NOTE**: You can continue to interchange images and text in the midst of a threaded discussion. You can then always scroll through to see the entire discussion—pictures and all!

Choosing a Picture from "Photos" to Send via MMS

The second way to send an MMS message is to just go straight to your **Photos** app and choose a picture.

1. Start your **Photos** app and navigate your pictures as we show you in Chapter 21: "Working with Photos."

2. To only send just one picture, touch the picture you wish to send and then touch the **Send** icon in the lower left-hand corner.

3. You will now see MMS as the second option.

4. Choose MMS and the photo will load into the bubble, just as it did previously.

Sending Multiple Pictures

Start up your **Photos** app as you did in the previous section. Instead of touching one picture, touch the **Send** icon in the lower left-hand corner. Now, just tap as many pictures as you want. You will see them lighten in color and then a red check mark appears in the box (Figure 11–4).

Figure 11–4. *Select multiple photos to send in an MMS message.*

Once you have chosen all the picture you want to send, just touch the **Share** button in the lower left-hand corner. Choose **MMS** and the pictures will appear in the message bubble (Figure 11–5).

Figure 11–5. *Choose MMS and all selected pictures go inside the message bubble.*

Chapter 12

FaceTime Video Messaging and Skype

Your iPhone 4 brings many new capabilities to your life, some of which seemed like science fiction just a few years ago. For example, video calling is now not only possible, but extremely easy to use with the new **FaceTime** feature. As long as you and your caller are on iPhone 4s and you're both on a Wi-Fi network, you can have unlimited video calls. In this chapter, we will show you how to enable and use **FaceTime**, as well as how to start having fun with this great new feature.

New services that provide similar functionality are sprouting up almost daily. In this chapter, we will take a look at **Fring**, a new, cross-platform video chat app that works very similarly to **FaceTime**.

Making calls over Wi-Fi is also possible with Skype, the popular video calling and chat program that many of us use on our computers. We will also show you how you can use the **Skype** app.

Speaking of video, your iPhone 4 is a very capable video recorder. You can record and export HD video up to 720p. You can then publish that video straight to YouTube or MobileMe or even send it to an email recipient. We will also show you how to shoot and quickly "trim" your videos, as well as upload them.

New to the iPhone 4 this year is the **iMovie** app that Mac users have been using for some time. With iMovie, you can actually create movies by joining movie clips, adding pictures and transitions, and then adding your own audio track. When you're finished, you can upload the movie to the Web.

Video Calling

For many years, we have watched TV episodes and movies debut future technology like this. For example, many of these episodes and movies show people talking on small, portable phones and having video conversations. Even *The Jetsons* cartoon in the 1970s had this as a future concept.

The iPhone 4 makes that future thinking a reality today. There are a few apps that enable you to make video calls on your iPhone using the front-facing camera. At this time, only one app allows you to use both the front-facing camera and the rear camera: **FaceTime**.

Video Calling with FaceTime

FaceTime is the proprietary feature app highlighted in many of Apple's iPhone 4 commercials. Essentially, **FaceTime** is free over Wi-Fi calling that allows you to see the caller on the other end of the conversation through the phone's front-facing camera.

> **NOTE**: For now **FaceTime** is only available for iPhone 4 to iPhone 4 calls, and it's only available over a Wi-Fi network. Apple says it is exploring expanding this service, so it works over standard 3G networks in the near future; however, this will also depend on carriers.

Enabling FaceTime calling on your iPhone

When you first use your iPhone, **FaceTime** is not yet enabled. To enable the iPhone to receive and make **FaceTime** calls, follow these steps:

1. Go to your **Settings** icon and touch it.

2. Scroll down to the **Phone** option tab.

3. Toggle the **FaceTime** switch to the **ON** position.

Using FaceTime

Once **FaceTime** is enabled, you will see it as an option with every call you place from the iPhone. The **FaceTime** icon will be part of the option display on all phone calls. **FaceTime** will only work, however, if the other caller is on an iPhone 4, and the **FaceTime** feature is enabled on both phones.

To initiate a FaceTime call, follow these steps:

1. Make a call just as you normally would on your iPhone 4.

2. Touch the **FaceTime** button (where the **Hold** button usually is), and the app will ask the caller on the other end to Accept the **FaceTime** call.

3. Or, you can simply Accept the **FaceTime** call from the other caller (see Figure 12–1).

Figure 12–1. *Accepting a FaceTime call.*

Once a **FaceTime** call is initiated, follow these steps to conduct a video conference:

1. Hold the phone away from you a bit.

2. Make sure you are "framed" properly in the window.

3. You can move the small image of yourself around the screen to a convenient spot.

4. Touch the **Switch Camera** button to show the **FaceTime** caller you are looking at. The **Switch Camera** button will now use the standard camera on the back of the iPhone. In Figure 12–2, I get to see the beautiful vistas of Colorado from Martin's vacation with his family, and he gets to see my dog on the couch!

5. Touch the **End** button to end the **FaceTime** call.

6. Touch the **Mute** button to temporarily mute the call.

Touch "Switch Camera"
Button to Show What
you See using the Main
Camera

Figure 12–2. *Switching camera views on a FaceTime call.*

Video Calling with Fring

FaceTime is not the only way to make video calls on the iPhone 4. For example, you can also use **Fring**, an app that has already been in use on Android phones.

Fring is a bit different from **FaceTime** because it can be used to make video calls through existing accounts, such as the **Facebook chat** program.

We do believe that Fring will be able to make video calls through other programs in time.

Here is an explanation from its application's maker from its web site at
`www.fring.com/fring_is/what_is_fring/`:

Fring is a free mobile application that lets users communicate with friends on popular
networks over their mobile phone's internet connection.fring users make **free mobile
calls, video calls, live chat** & more, from their mobile phone with all their friends on
fring & other internet services like Skype®, MSN Messenger®, GoogleTalk™, AIM®,
ICQ®, Facebook® & Twitter, all through one central, integrated phone book. **fring is
completely free**. It's free to download and free to use to make calls, video calls, instant
messages and more, all via your mobile phone's internet connection (over 'IP').

There is a special **Fring** app for your
iPhone that you can get for free in the App
store. Just go to the App store (see
Chapter 26: "The Amazing App Store" for
more information on how to do this) and
search for Fring.

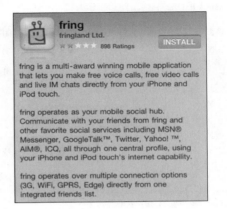

Once the app is downloaded and installed, you will be prompted to create a new Fring
account or log in in to your existing account.

Fring calls are made to people on your Buddy List. Follow these steps to add people to
your **Fring** Buddy List:

1. Touch the **More** button in the lower right corner.

2. Touch **Add New Buddy**.

3. Choose whether to add a buddy **By phone contact** or **by a Fring User ID**.

4. The Buddy will now show in your contacts with a unique **Buddy** icon.

> **TIP**: It is much easier to add contacts to **Fring** if you know a person's unique Fring User ID. All
> you need to do is ask a person for that information, and then add it to your **Contact** information
> for that individual. When you select to add a contact **By phone contact**, **Fring** will search the
> **Fring** database for that individual.

Placing a Call Using Fring

Placing a call using **Fring** is easy. Follow these steps to do so:

1. Start the **Fring** app.

2. Search for buddies with **Fring** in the Buddy List or touch the **Stream** button to see recent Fring activity with Buddies.

3. Once you find a **Fring** Buddy, touch the **Video** icon to make a **Fring** video call (see Figure 12–3.)

4. To end the call, just touch the **End Call** button.

> **NOTE**: You can also initiate a **Fring** chat session by touching the **Fring Chat** icon or by placing an audio only call to someone's cell phone. **Fring** can also be used to call other devices such as Android and Nokia phones that are running the Fring software.

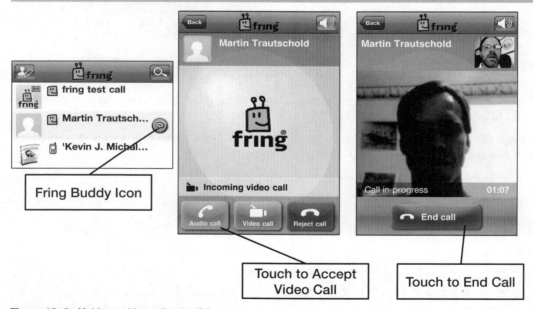

Figure 12–3. *Making a video call using Fring.*

Making Phone Calls and More with Skype

Social Networking is all about keeping in touch with our friends, colleagues, and family. Passive communication through sites such as www.facebook.com and www.myspace.com is nice, but sometimes there is just no substitute for hearing someone's voice.

Amazingly, you can make phone calls using the **Skype** app from any iPhone 4. Calls to other Skype users anywhere in the world are free. A nice thing about Skype is that it works on computers and many mobile devices, including iPhone 4s, iPhones, some BlackBerry smartphones, and other mobile devices. You will be charged for calls to mobile phones and land lines, but the rates are reasonable

NOTE: As of an update in July, Skype now does currently support iOS 4 multitasking or **FaceTime**. You can also now place Skype calls over a 3G network.

Downloading Skype to Your iPhone 4

You can download the free **Skype** app from the **App Store** by searching for Skype and installing it. If you need help getting this done, please check out Chapter 26: "The Amazing App Store."

Creating Your Skype Account on Your iPhone 4

If you need to set up your Skype account and have not already done so from your computer (see the "Using Skype on your Computer" section later in this chapter), then follow these steps to set up **Skype** on your iPhone 4:

1. Tap the **Skype** icon from your **Home** screen.

2. Tap the **Create Account** button.

3. Tap **Accept** if you accept the **No Emergency Calls** pop-up warning window.

4. Enter your **Full Name**, **Skype Name**, **Password**, and **Email**, and then decide whether you want to **Get News and Offers** by setting the switch at the bottom.

5. Tap the **Done** button to create your account.

Log in to the Skype App

After you create your account, you're ready to log in to **Skype** on your iPhone 4. To do so, follow these steps:

1. If you are not already in **Skype**, tap the **Skype** icon from your **Home** screen.

2. Type your Skype Name and Password.

3. Tap the **Sign In** button in the upper right corner.

4. You should not have to enter this log in information again; it is saved in **Skype**. The next time you tap **Skype**, it will automatically log you in.

Finding and Adding Skype Contacts

Once you have logged into the **Skype** app, you will want to start communicating with people. To do so, you will have to find them and add then to your **Skype** contacts list:

1. If you are not already in **Skype**, tap the **Skype** icon from your **Home** screen and log in, if asked.

2. Tap the **Contacts** soft key at the bottom.

3. Tap the **Search** window at the top, and then type someone's first and last name or **Skype** name. Tap **Search** to locate that person.

4. Once you see the person you want to add, tap his name.

Tap here and type a name to search.

Then, tap the name to select it.

Tap here to add this person.

Tap here to learn more about this person.

5. If you are not sure whether this is the correct person, tap the **View Full Profile** button.

6. Tap **Add Contact** at the bottom.

7. Adjust the invitation message appropriately.

8. Tap the **Send** button to send this person an invitation to become one of your **Skype** contacts.

9. Repeat the procedure to add more contacts.

10. When you are done, tap the **Contacts** soft key at the bottom.

11. Tap **All Contacts** from the **Groups** screen to see all new contacts you have added.

12. Once this person accepts you as a contact, you will see him listed as a contact in your **All Contacts** screen.

TIP: Sometimes you want to get rid of **Skype** a contact. You can remove or block a contact by tapping her name from the contact list. Tap the **Settings** icon (upper right corner) and select either **Remove from Contacts** or **Block**.

Tap the Settings icon.

Then, tap to Remove or Block this contact.

Making Calls with Skype on Your iPhone 4

So far you have created your account and added your contacts. Now you are ready to finally make that first call with **Skype** on your iPhone 4:

1. If you are not already in **Skype**, tap the **Skype** icon from your **Home** screen and log in, if asked.

2. Tap the **Contacts** soft key at the bottom.

3. Tap **All Contacts** to see your contacts.

4. Tap the contact name you wish to call (see Figure 12–4).

5. Tap the **Call** button.

6. You may see a **Skype** button and a **Mobile** or other phone button. Press the **Skype** button to make the free call. Making any other call requires that you pay for it with Skype Credits.

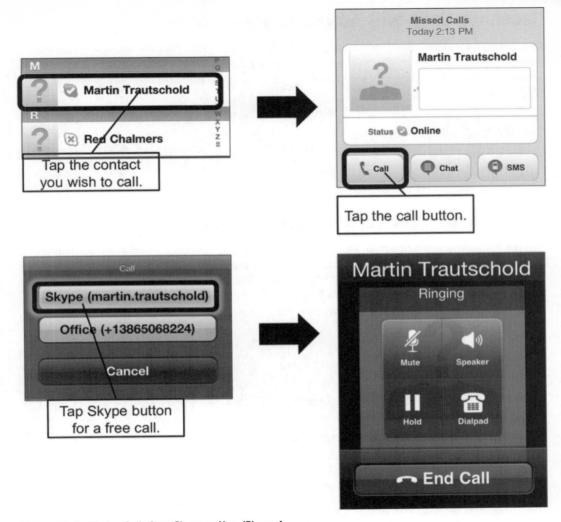

Figure 12–4. *Placing Calls from Skype on Your iPhone 4.*

NOTE: You can call toll free numbers for free using **Skype Out** on your iPhone 4. The following notice comes from the Skype web site at www.skype.com:

"The following countries and number ranges are supported and are free of charge to all users. We're working on the rest of the world. France: +33 800, +33 805, +33 809 Poland: +48 800 UK: +44 500, +44 800, +44 808 USA: +1 800, +1 866, +1 877, +1 888 Taiwan: +886 80"

Receiving Calls with Skype on your iPhone 4

Apple's iOS4 innately supports background VoIP calls. With the new version of **Skype**, you can have **Skype** running in the background and still be able to receive a **Skype** call when it comes in. You can even, in theory, be on a voice call and then answer your **Skype** call!

> **TIP:** If you want to call someone whom you know uses **Skype** on her iPhone 4, just send her a quick email or give her a quick call to alert her to the fact you would like to talk to her using the **Skype** app.

Buying Skype Credits or a Monthly Subscription

Skype-to-**Skype** calls are free. However, if you want to call people on their land lines or mobile phones from **Skype**, then you will need to purchase Skype Credits or purchase a monthly subscription plan. If you try to purchase the credits or subscription from within the **Skype** app, it will take you to the Skype web site. For this reason, we recommend using **Safari** on your iPhone 4 or using your computer's web browser to purchase these credits.

> **TIP:** You may want to start with a limited amount of Skype Credits to try out the service before you sign up for a subscription plan. Subscription plans are the way to go if you plan on using Skype a lot for non-Skype callers (e.g., regular landlines and mobile phones).

Follow these steps to use **Safari** to buy Skype Credits:

1. Tap the **Safari** icon.

2. Type www.skype.com in the top address bar and tap **Go**.

3. Tap the **Sign In** link at the top of the page.

4. Enter your Skype Name and Password, and then tap **Sign me in**.

5. If you are not already on your **Account** screen, tap the **Account** tab in the right end of the Top Nav Bar.

6. At this point, you can choose to buy credits or a subscription:

   a. Tap the **Buy pre-pay credit** button to purchase a fixed amount of credits.

   b. Tap the **Get a subscription** button to buy a monthly subscription account.

7. Finally, complete the payment instructions for either type of purchase.

Chatting with Skype

In addition to making phone calls, you can also chat via text with other **Skype** users from your iPhone 4. Starting a chat is very similar to starting a call; follow these steps to do so:

1. If you are not already in **Skype**, tap the **Skype** icon from your **Home** screen and log in if asked.

2. Tap the **Contacts** soft key at the bottom.

3. Tap **All Contacts** to see your contacts.

4. Tap the name of the contact you wish to chat with (see Figure 12–5).

5. Tap the **Chat** button.

6. Type your chat text and press the **Send** button. Your chat will appear in the top of the screen.

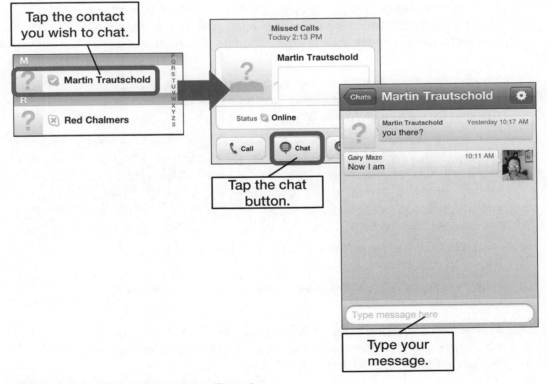

Figure 12–5. *Chatting with Skype on Your iPhone 4.*

Adding Skype to Your Computer

You can use the **Skype** app on your computer, as well. We will show you how this works next. You can also use **Skype** to make video calls on your computer if you also have a web cam hooked up.

NOTE: When you call from your computer to an iPhone 4, you will not be able to do a video call.

To create a Skype account and download **Skype** software for your computer, follow these steps:

1. Open a web browser on your computer.

2. Go to: www.skype.com.

3. Click the **Join** link at the top of the page.

4. Create your account by completing all required information and clicking the **Continue** button. Notice that you only have to enter information in the required fields, which are denoted with an asterisk. For example, you do not need to enter your gender, birthdate, and mobile phone number.

5. You are now done with the account setup process. Next, you are presented with the option of buying Skype Credits; however, this is not required for the free **Skype**-to-**Skype** phone calls, video calls, or chats.

TIP: You only need to pay for **Skype** if you want to call someone who is not using **Skype**. For example, calls to phones on land lines or mobile phones (not using **Skype**) will cost you. At publishing time, pay-as-you-go rates were about US 2.1 cents; monthly subscriptions ranged from about US $3 - $14 for various calling plans.

6. Next, click the Get Skype link in the Top Nav Bar of the site to download **Skype** to your computer.

7. Click the **Get Skype for Windows** button or the **Get Skype for Mac** button.

8. Follow the instructions to install the software. For more information on downloading and installing software, see the "Getting iTunes Software" section in Chapter 30: "iTunes User Guide.'

9. Once the software is installed, launch it and log in using your Skype account.

10. You are ready to initiate (or receive) phone calls, video calls, and chats to anyone else using **Skype**, including all your friends with **Skype** on their iPhones.

Video Recording

In addition to letting you make video calls and chat, the iPhone lets you make full-featured videos using the built-in video recorder. You can use your iPhone 4 to shoot HD video in 720p and then upload this video to Facebook, YouTube, or MobileMe. You can also send your videos via MMS or email.

> **NOTE:** When you share a video, it will be compressed, so the quality will no longer be 720p.

Next, we will show you how to record video and trim your video right on your iPhone. We will also discuss an amazing piece of software: Apple's **iMovie** software. In the next section, you will learn how to add video clips, audio, pictures, and transitions. You will also learn how to produce a high quality, high definition video right on your iPhone 4.

Starting the Video Recorder

The software for the video recorder is actually part of the **Camera** app (see Figure 12–6). Follow these steps to use the built-in video recorder.

1. Start up the **Camera** app (see Chapter 21: "Working with Photos" for more information on how to do this).

2. Move the slider in the lower right corner from the **Camera** icon to the **Video Recorder** icon.

3. Try to keep the iPhone 4 steady as you record your scene.

4. Touch the **Stop** button when you are done recording.

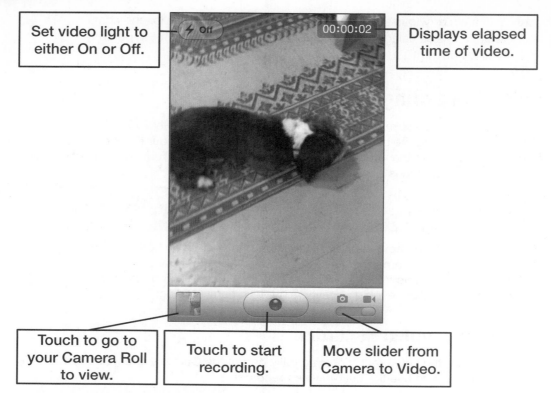

Set video light to either On or Off.

00:00:02

Displays elapsed time of video.

Touch to go to your Camera Roll to view.

Touch to start recording.

Move slider from Camera to Video.

Figure 12–6. *Layout and controls of the video recorder.*

Focusing the Video

The iPhone 4 can adjust the focus of the video based on the subject. Follow these steps to take advantage of this feature:

1. To focus on something in the foreground of the video, touch the screen in the foreground. This brings up a small box appears to show the area of focus.

2. To switch the focus to a subject in the background, touch another part of the screen. The box will temporarily display the new area of focus.

Trimming the Video

The iPhone 4 allows you to perform edits on your video right on the phone. Once the video has been recorded and you press the **Stop** button, the video immediately goes into your **Camera Roll**.

Touch the small image of the video in the lower left hand corner to bring up the video. At the top of the screen, you will see a timeline with all the frames of your video at the top of the screen (see Figure 12–7). Follow these steps to edit your just-recorded video.

1. Drag either end of the timeline and you will see that the video goes into **Trim** mode.

2. Drag the ends of the video on either end until it is the length you desire.

3. When the video is the correct length, touch the **Trim** button in the upper right corner.

4. Next, select either **Trim Original** or **Save as New Clip**. The latter option saves another version of the newly trimmed video.

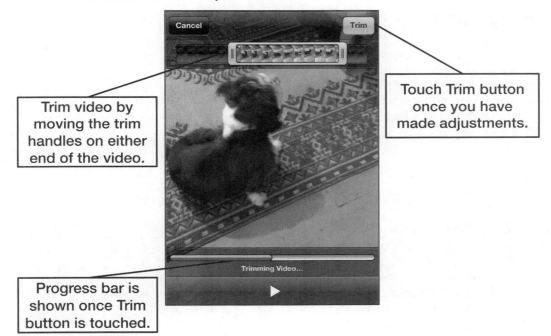

Trim video by moving the trim handles on either end of the video.

Touch Trim button once you have made adjustments.

Progress bar is shown once Trim button is touched.

Figure 12–7. *Trimming a video.*

Sending the Video

As with photos, you have several options for using your iPhone 4 to send recorded video to others. Follow these steps to send a video from your iPhone 4:

1. Touch the **Send** icon in the lower left corner.

2. Choose your preferred option for sending the video: **Email**, **MMS**, **MobileMe**, or **YouTube**.

3. The next screen you see will depend on the choice you made in Step 2. If you selected **Email**, your **Email** app will launch. If you selected **MMS**, your **Messaging** app will launch. And so on.

NOTE: To upload a video to MobileMe or YouTube, you need to have an account with the site you want to upload to. See Chapter 4: "Other Sync Methods" to learn more about MobileMe.

Using iMovie

Mac users have been enjoying the **iMovie** app for years. This app lets you combine movie clips with pictures and music, enabling you to add fancy transitions between scenes to make a professional-looking movie.

For the first time, iPhone4 lets users enjoy the power of **iMovie** right on their iPhone. The **iMovie** app is a US $4.99 download from the App store. It is usually listed under either the **Featured** apps or the **Awesome iOS4** apps sections. You can also just search the App store for "iMovie" to go straight to the download page (see Chapter 26: "The Amazing App Store" for more information on searching the App store for content).

Getting Started with iMovie

The **iMovie** app works with *projects*. If you have stored projects, they appear on the **Projects** page. This will most likely be your first time using the app, so you won't have any projects. Follow these steps to start an **iMovie** project:

1. Tap the **Plus sign** icon to start a new project.

2. Select a theme for the project. Current themes include **Modern**, **Bright**, **Travel**, **Playful**, and **News**.

3. Select **Theme Music ON** if you want to use specific music designed for that theme.

4. Tap the **Insert Media** icon to choose media for your movie. To choose a video, touch the **Video** soft key at the bottom. To choose photos, touch the **Photos** soft key. Finally, to choose a sound track from your own music files, touch the **Audio** soft key and navigate to the song desired (see Figure 12–8).

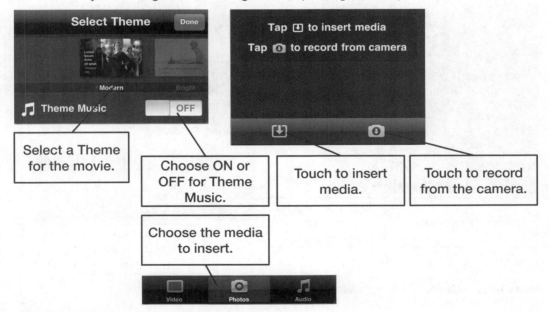

Figure 12–8. *Choosing media to add to your iMovie project.*

Constructing Your Movie

Creating a movie in **iMovie** is as simple as adding new content, transitions, and audio. Follow these steps to build your movie:

1. Tap the **Insert Media** button again and choose another movie clip or photo from your **Photos** app.

2. There is now a small **Double Arrow** icon between the different media in the project. This is the **Transition** icon. Double-tap the **Transition** icon to bring up the **Transitions Settings** menu (see Figure 12–9).

3. Choose a transition (currently there are only three choices: **None**, **Cross Dissolve**, and **Theme**).

4. Choose a transition length. These can range from .5 seconds to 2.0 seconds.

5. Touch the **Done** button.

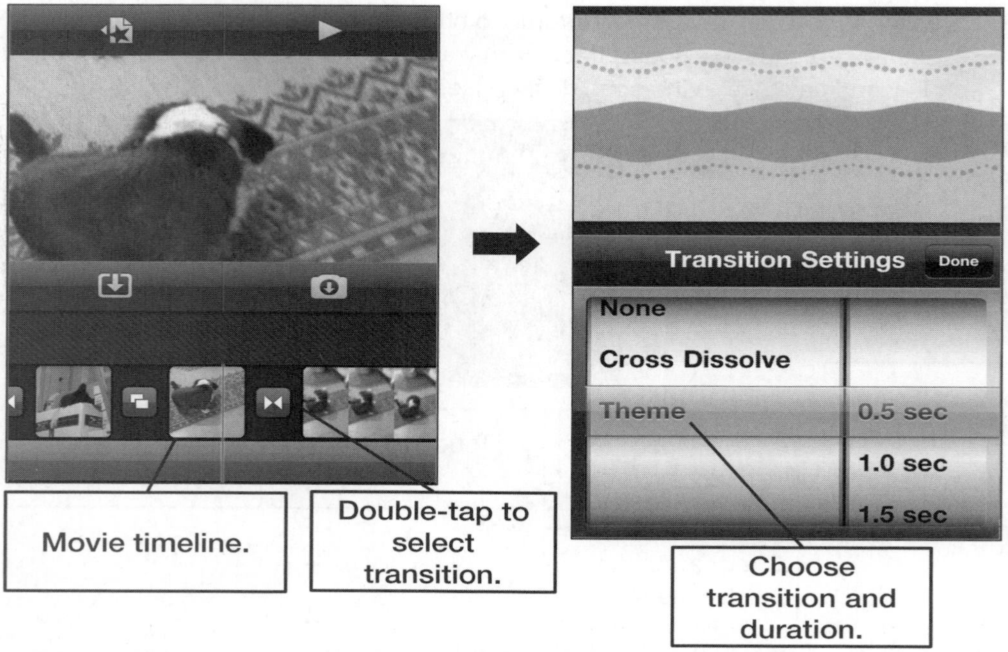

Figure 12–9. *Adding transitions to the* ***iMovie*** *project.*

Follow these steps to preview the movie:

1. Slide the timeline at the bottom to the beginning, and then touch the **Play**

 button.

2. When you are done, touch the **Projects** button in the top left of your screen. This will return you to the **Projects** screen.

Sharing Your Movie

Touch the **Share** button and **iMovie** gives you an option screen that lets you choose the export size of the movie. You can choose to export your movie as an HD (720p), large (540p), or medium (360p) movie file.

> Choose an export size
>
> **Medium - 360p**
>
> **Large - 540p**
>
> **HD - 720p**
>
> **Cancel**

> **NOTE**: HD -720p movies have the best quality; however, these can be quite large, depending on the length of the movie. Obviously, it will take longer to email or upload an HD movie than an equivalent large- or medium-sized movie.

The **Export** screen marks the progress of the movie export. The iPhone tells you that the movie was exported to the **Camera Roll** feature of your **Photo** app. Follow these steps to share a project from your **Camera Roll**:

1. Go to your **Camera Roll** (see Chapter 21: "Working with Photos" for more information on how to do this).

2. Find the new movie in the **Camera Roll**. You will see a **Video** icon at the bottom of the picture; the image will also show the length of the video).

3. Touch the video from the **Camera Roll**.

4. Choose **Share** from the soft keys at the bottom

5. Choose to send your project through one of the following methods: **Email**, **MMS**, **MobileMe**, or **YouTube**.

NOTE: To maintain your high quality 720p video, you should sync it back to your computer. Manual uploads over Wi-Fi or Ethernet will almost certainly let you share your movie at the highest quality. 3G uploads will reduce the resolution of your movie most severely.

Chapter 13

Playing Music

In this chapter we show you how to turn your iPhone into a terrific music player. Since the iPhone comes from Apple—which popularized electronic music players—you'd expect it to have some great capabilities, and it does. We'll show you how to play and organize the music you buy from iTunes or sync from your computer, how to view playlists in a variety of ways, and how to quickly find songs. You'll learn how to use the Genius feature to have the iPhone locate and group similar songs in your library—sort of like a radio station that plays only music you like.

> **TIP:** Learn how to buy music right on your iPhone in Chapter 25: "iTunes on Your iPhone 4." And take a look the "iTunes Guide" in Part 4 to find out how to buy music using iTunes on your computer or load your music CDs onto iTunes so you can sync them with your iPhone.

And you'll see how to stream music using an app called Pandora. With Pandora, you can select from a number of Internet radio stations, or create your own by typing in your favorite artist's name, and it's all free.

Your iPhone as a Music Player

Your iPhone is probably one of the best music players on the market today. The touch screen makes it easy to interact with and manage your music, playlists, cover art, and the organization of your music library. You can even connect your iPhone to your home or car stereo via Bluetooth, so you can listen to beautiful stereo sound from your iPhone!

> **TIP:** Check out Chapter 6: "Bluetooth on the iPhone 4" to learn how to hook up your iPhone to your Bluetooth stereo speakers or car stereo.

Whether you use the built-in **iPod** music app or an Internet radio app like **Pandora**, you'll find you have unprecedented control over your music on the iPhone.

The iPod App

Most music is handled through the **iPod** app—the icon is on the **Home** screen, usually in the bottom dock of icons, the last one on the right.

Touch the **iPod** icon and, as Figure 13–1 shows, you'll see five soft keys across the bottom:

- **Playlists** lets you see synced playlists from your computer, as well as playlists created on the iPhone.

- **Artists** lets you see an alphabetical list of artists (searchable like your Address Book).

- **Songs** lets you see an alphabetical list of songs (also searchable).

- **Videos** lets you see a   list of videos (also searchable).

- **More** lets you see audiobooks, compilations, composers, genres, iTunes U, and podcasts.

Editing the Soft Keys

One very cool feature on the iPhone is that you can edit the soft keys at the bottom of the **iPod** app and really customize it to fit your needs and tastes. To do so, first touch the **More** button.

Then touch the **Edit** button at the top left of the screen.

The screen changes to show the various icons that can be dragged down to the bottom dock.

Figure 13–1. *iPod soft keys*

Let's say you want to replace the **Videos** icon with the one for **Albums**. Just touch and hold the **Albums** icon and drag it to where the **Videos** icon is on the bottom dock (see Figure 13–2). When you get there, release the icon and the **Albums** icon will now reside where the **Videos** icon used to be. You can do this with any of the icons on this **Configure** screen. When you are finished, touch the **Done** button at the top right of the screen.

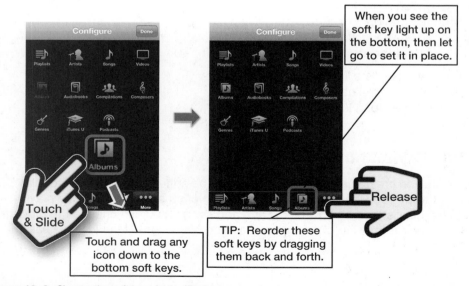

Figure 13–2. *Change the soft keys in the iPod app.*

TIP: You can also reorder the icons across the bottom by dragging and dropping them back and forth along the soft key row.

Playlists View

NOTE: A playlist is a list of songs you create and can include any genre, artist, year of recording, or collection of songs that interest you.

Add a new playlist here.

Your playlists are listed here.

Many people group together music of a particular genre, like classical or rock. Others may create playlists with fast beat music and call it workout or running music. You can use playlists to organize your music just about any way you want.

You can create playlists in iTunes on your computer and then sync to your iPhone (see the iTunes Guide), or you can create a playlist right on your iPhone as we describe in the next section.

NOTE: You can edit the contents of some of your playlists on your iPhone. However, you can't edit Genius playlists on the iPhone itself.

Once you've synced a playlist to your iPhone or created one on your iPhone, it shows up on the left-hand side of the **iPod** screen, under **Library**.

If you have several playlists listed along the left side, just touch the name of the one you want to listen to.

Creating Playlists on the iPhone

The iPhone lets you create unique playlists that can be edited and synced with your computer. Let's say you want to add a new selection of music to your iPhone playlist. Just create the playlist as we show below and add songs. You can change the playlist whenever you want, removing old songs and adding new ones—it couldn't be easier!

To create a new playlist on the iPhone, touch the **Add Playlist** tab under **Genius Playlist**.

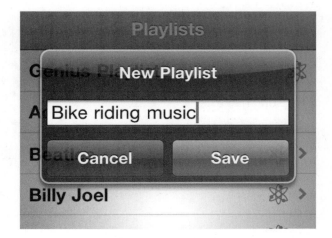

Give your playlist a unique name (we'll call this one "Bike-riding music"), then touch **Save**.

Now you'll see the **Songs** screen. Touch the name of any song you want to add to the new playlist.

You know a song is selected and will be added to the playlist when it turns gray.

> **NOTE:** Don't get frustrated trying to remove or deselect a song you tapped by mistake. You can't remove or deselect songs on this screen; you have to click **Done**, then remove them on the next screen, as we describe.

Select **Done** at the top right and the playlist contents will be displayed.

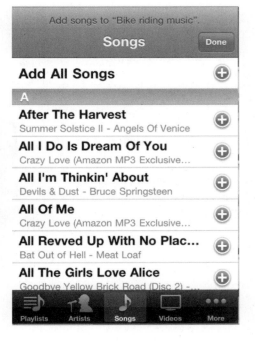

If you tapped a song by mistake or change your mind, after you click **Done** you can remove songs on the next screen.

To delete a song:

1. Touch the **Edit** button at the top (it will disappear once it is touched).

2. Tap the red circle next to the song name.

3. Tap the **Delete** button to the right of the song.

4. Touch the **Done** button.

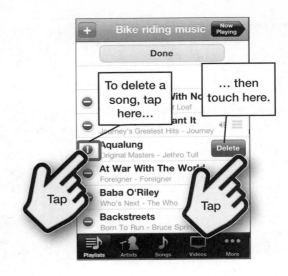

To move a song up or down in a playlist:

1. Touch the **Edit** button as you did above.

2. Touch and hold the three gray bars to the right of the song.

3. Drag the song up or down and then let go.

4. When you're all finished, just touch the **Done** button and your playlist will be set.

To change the playlist later, touch the **Edit** button and follow the steps above.

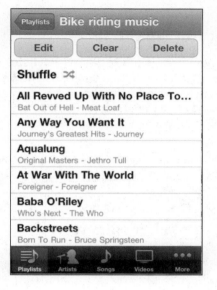

Searching for Music

Almost every view from your **iPod** app (**Playlists**, **Artists**, **Videos**, **Songs**, etc.) has a search window at the top of the screen, as shown in Figure 13–3. Tap once in the search window and type a few letters of the name of an artist, album, playlist, video, or song to instantly see a list of all matching items. This is the best way to quickly find something to listen to or watch on your iPhone.

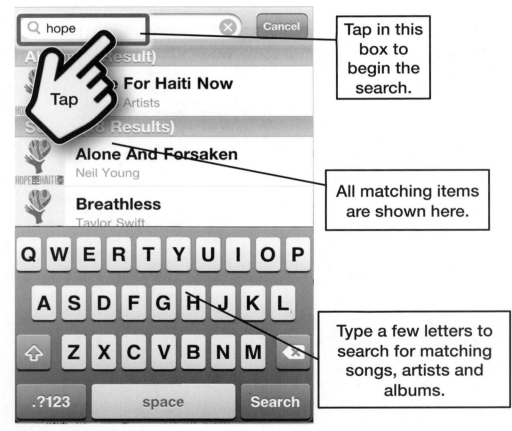

Figure 13–3. *Finding music*

Changing the View in the iPod App

The **iPod** app is very flexible when it comes to ways of displaying and categorizing your music. Sometimes, you might want to look at your songs listed by the artist. At other times, you might prefer seeing a particular album or song. The iPhone lets you easily change the view to help manage and play just the music you want at a given moment.

Artists View

The **Artists** view lists all the artists on your iPhone, or, if you are in a playlist, it lists the artists in that playlist.

Flick through the list to move to the first letter of the artist's name you're looking for.

When you find the artist's name, touch it and all the songs and albums by that artist will be listed, with a picture of the album art to the left.

> **TIP:** Use the same navigation and search features as you do with the **Contacts** app (the address book).

Songs View

Touching the **Songs** button displays a list of every song on your iPhone.

If you know the name of the song, flick through the list or touch the first letter of the song in the alphabetical list to the right.

Albums View

The music on your iPhone is also organized by albums, which you'll see when you touch the **More** button (bottom right) and then the **Albums** icon.

Again, you can scroll through the album covers or touch the first letter of the album name in the alphabetical list and then make your selection.

When you choose an album, all the songs on that album will be listed.

To go back, just touch the **More** button in the upper left corner.

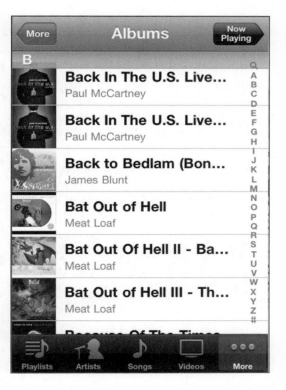

Genres

The **Genres** tab arranges your music into music types. This can be an easier approach to finding music, as well as a way to have more of a "themed" listening experience.

Thus, if you wanted to hear a rock or jazz mix, you could select those particular genres and start playing some or all of the songs.

> **NOTE**: The **Genres** tab is usually available in the **More** section, as you can see in Figure 13–1.

In this image, we touched **Rock**, and the iPhone shows us the list of albums and songs we have in this genre.

Composers

𝄞 Composers

As with the other views, touching the **Composers** icon (in the **More** section) lists your music in a specific way.

Suppose you forget the title of the song but you know the composer. Browsing by **Composers** on your iPhone can help you find just what you are looking for.

Similar to other views, **Composers** shows you how many albums and songs are by each composer.

Composers
B. Crewe, E. Johnson, J....
B. Joel
-B. Springsteen-
Baha Men
Benjy & Heather Werthei...
Benny Gallagher, Graham...
Bernie Taupin

Playlists   Artists   Songs   Videos   More

Viewing Songs in an Album

When you're in **Albums** view, just touch an album cover or name and the screen will slide, showing you the songs on that album (see Figure 13–4).

TIP: When you start playing an album, the album cover may expand to fill the screen. Tap the screen once to bring up (or hide) the controls at the top and bottom. You can use these controls to manage the song and screen as we describe below.

To see the songs on an album that is playing, tap the **List** button and the album cover and the cover will turn over, revealing all the songs on that album. The song that is playing will have a small blue arrow next to it.

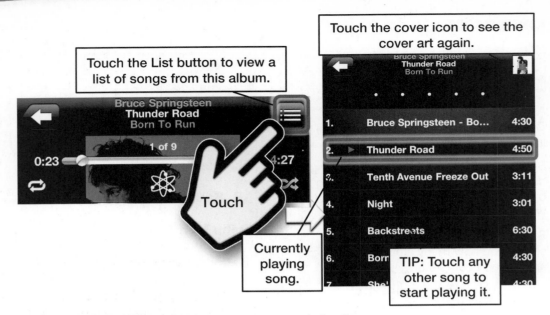

Figure 13–4. *Touch the **List** button to see the songs on a particular album.*

Tap the title bar above the list of songs to return to the album cover view.

Navigating with Cover Flow

Cover Flow is a proprietary and very cool way of looking at your music by album covers. If you're playing a song in the **iPod** music app and turn your iPhone horizontal—into landscape mode— your iPhone will automatically change to **Cover Flow** view.

Viewing Songs in Cover Flow

Just touch an album cover and the cover will flip, showing you all the songs on that album.

To see the song that is playing now (in Cover Flow view), tap the album cover and it will turn over, revealing the songs on that album (Figure 13–5). The song that is currently playing will have a small blue arrow next to it.

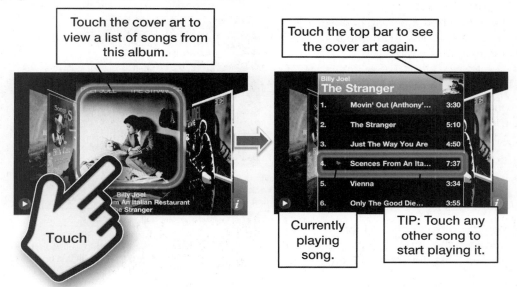

Figure 13–5. *You can look at an album's contents using* ***Cover Flow***.

Tap the title bar (above the list of songs) and the album cover will be displayed once more. You can then keep swiping through your music until you find what you are searching for.

> **NOTE**: You can also touch the small "*i*" in the lower right corner and the album cover will flip, showing you the songs, just as if you touched the cover.

Playing Your Music

Now that you know how to find your music, it's time to play it! Find a song or browse to a playlist using any of the methods mentioned above. Simply tap the song name and it will begin to play.

This screen shows a picture of the album that the song I chose comes from, with the name of the song at the top.

Along the bottom of the screen you'll find the **Volume** slider bar, and the **Previous Song**, **Play/Pause**, and **Next Song** buttons.

To see other songs on the album, just double-tap the album cover and the screen will flip, showing all of the other songs.

You can also touch the **List** button in the upper right corner to view a list of songs on the album.

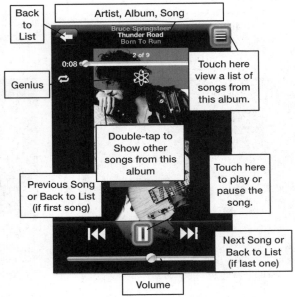

Pausing and Playing

Tap the pause symbol (if your song is playing) or the play arrow (if the music is paused) to stop or resume your song.

To Play the Previous or Next Song

If you are in a playlist, touching the **Next Song** arrow (to the right of the **Play/Pause** button) advances you to the next song in the list. If you are searching through your music by album, touching **Next** moves you to the next song on the album. Touching the **Previous Song** button does the reverse.

> **NOTE:** If you're at the beginning of a song, **Previous** takes you to the preceding song. If the song is already playing, **Previous** goes to the beginning of the current song (and a second tap would take you to the previous song).

Adjusting the Volume

There are two ways to adjust the volume on your iPhone: using the external **Volume** buttons or using the **Volume Slider** control on the screen.

The external **Volume** buttons are on the upper left side of the device. Press the **Volume Up** key (the top button) or the **Volume Down** key to raise or lower the volume. You'll see the **Volume Slider** control move as you adjust the volume. You can also just touch and hold the **Volume Slider** key to adjust the volume.

> **TIP:** To quickly mute the sound, press and hold the **Volume Down** key and the volume eventually reduces to zero .

Volume Slider

Double-Click the Home Button for iPod Controls

You can play your music while you are doing other things on your iPhone, like reading and responding to e-mail, browsing the Web, or playing a game. With the iPhone's new multitasking function, a quick double-tap to the **Home** button on the bottom, followed by a swipe to the right, will bring up the "now playing" **iPod** controls in the multitasking window, as shown in Figure 13–6.

> **NOTE:** The widgets show whatever app last played music, so if Pandora was last, you'll see that instead of **iPod,** and the widgets will control Pandora instead.

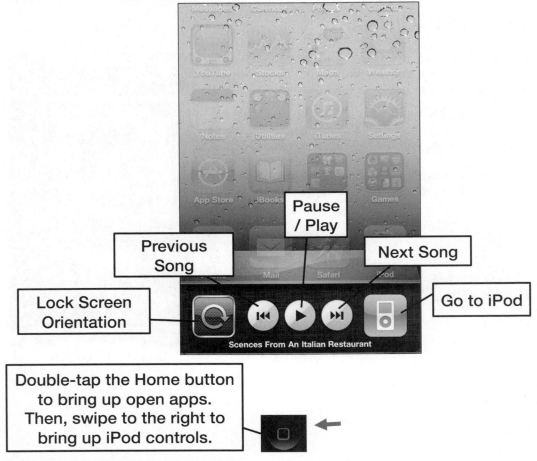

Figure 13–6. *Bringing up the **iPod** music controls*

TIP: If you hold down the **Previous Song** control, the song will rewind; if you hold down the **Next Song** control, it will fast forward.

Repeating, Shuffling, Moving around in a Song

In play mode, you can activate additional controls by tapping the screen anywhere on the album cover. You'll then see an additional slider (the scrubber bar) at the top, along with the symbols for **Repeat**, **Shuffle,** and **Genius**.

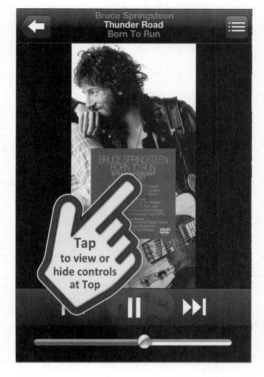

Moving to Another Part of a Song

Slide the scrubber bar to the right and you'll see the elapsed time of the song (displayed to the far right) change accordingly. If you are looking for a specific section of the song, drag the slider, then let go and listen to see if you're in the right place.

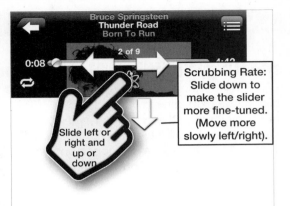

Repeat One Song or All Songs

To repeat the song you're listening to, touch the **Repeat** symbol at the left of the top controls twice until you see it turn blue and display a 1.

To repeat all songs in the playlist, song list, or album, touch the **Repeat** icon until it turns blue (and does not display a 1).

To turn off the **Repeat** feature, press the icon until it turns white again.

Shuffle

If you are listening to a playlist or album or any other category or list of music, you might decide you don't want to listen to the songs in order. You can touch the **Shuffle** symbol so the music will play in random order. You know **Shuffle** is turned on when the icon is blue, and off when it is white.

Shake to Shuffle

The **Shake to Shuffle** feature was introduced in the last iPhone. So, to turn on **Shuffle** mode, all you have to do to change songs is simply give your iPhone a shake, then shake it again. Every time you shake your iPhone, you'll skip to the next randomly selected song in the list.

Shake to ⤧

> **TIP**: If you plan on dancing to your tunes, turn off **Shake to Shuffle**!

Settings	iPod	
Music		
Shake to Shuffle	ON	
Sound Check	OFF	
EQ	Rock >	
Volume Limit	Off >	
Lyrics & Podcast Info	ON	
Video		
Start Playing	Where Left Off >	
Closed Captioning	OFF	

You can turn on **Shake to Shuffle** in your **Settings** menu.

1. Tap the **Settings** icon.

2. Scroll down and touch the **iPod** icon.

3. Move the **Shake to Shuffle** switch to **ON** or **OFF**.

Genius

Apple has a new feature for iTunes called **Genius**. If the **Genius** feature is activated in iTunes, it will show up on your iPhone with the symbol you see here.

Genius Playlist: Tap here to create a new playlist based on this song.

Tap

NOTE: You must enable **Genius Playlists** using iTunes on your computer. Check out Chapter 30; "Your iTunes User Guide" to learn how.

Genius Playlists

Genius playlists are not enabled. Use iTunes to enable Genius Playlists.

OK

What the **Genius** feature does is create a playlist by associating songs similar to the one you're listening to. Unlike a random "shuffle" of music, **Genius** scours your music library and then creates a new playlist of 25, 50, or 100 songs (you set the **Genius** features in iTunes on your computer).

TIP: If you get tired of your **Genius** playlist, just touch **Refresh** and the list will reset with new songs.

Genius is a great way to mix up your music and keep it fresh—playing the type of music you like but also finding some buried songs that may not be part of your established playlists.

TIP: To create permanent **Genius** playlists, just create them in iTunes on your computer and sync them to your iPhone. The **Genius** playlists you sync from iTunes can't be edited or changed on the iPhone itself, but you can save, refresh, or delete any **Genius** playlists created on the iPhone.

Now Playing

Sometimes you're having so much fun exploring your options for playlists or albums that you get deeply buried in a menu—then find yourself just wanting to get back to the song you're listening to. Fortunately, this is always very easy to do—you can just touch the **Now Playing** icon at the top right of most of the music screens.

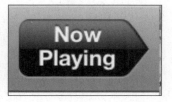

Viewing Other Songs on the Album

You may decide you want to listen to another song from the same album rather than going to the next song in the playlist or genre list.

In the upper-right corner of the **Now Playing** screen, you'll see a small button with three lines on it.

Tap that button and the view switches to a small image of the album cover. The screen now displays all the songs on that album.

Touch another song on the list and that song will begin to play.

NOTE: If you were in the middle of a playlist or a **Genius Playlist** and you jump to another song from an album, you won't be taken back to that playlist. To return to that playlist, you'll need to either go back to your playlist library or tap **Genius** to make a new **Genius Playlist**.

Adjusting Music Settings

There are several settings you can adjust to tweak music-playing on your iPhone. You'll find these in the **Settings** menu. Just touch the **Settings** icon on your **Home s**creen.

In the middle of the **Settings** screen, touch the **iPod** tab to go to the settings screen for **Music**. You'll find five settings you can adjust on this screen: **Shake to Shuffle**, **Sound Check**, **EQ**, **Volume Limit**, and **Lyrics & Podcast Info**.

Using Sound Check (Auto Volume Adjust)

Because songs are recorded at different volumes, sometimes during playback a particular song may sound quite loud compared to another. **Sound Check** can eliminate this. If **Sound Check** is set to **ON**, all your songs will play at roughly the same volume.

Music

Shake to Shuffle   ON

Sound Check   ON

EQ (Sound Equalizer Setting)

Sound equalization is very personal and subjective. Some people like to hear more bass in their music, some like more treble, and some like more of an exaggerated mid-range. Whatever your music tastes, there is an **EQ** setting for you.

NOTE: Using the **EQ** setting can diminish battery capacity somewhat.

Just touch the **EQ** tab and then select either the type of music you most often listen to or a specific option to boost treble or bass. Experiment, have fun, and find the setting that's perfect for you.

iPod	EQ	
Loudness		
Lounge		
Piano		
Pop		
R & B		
Rock		✓
Small Speakers		
Spoken Word		
Treble Booster		

Volume Limit (Safely Listen to Music at a Reasonable Level)

This is a great way for parents to control the volume on their kids' iPhones. It is also a good way to make sure you don't listen too loudly through headphones so you don't damage your ears. You just move the slider to a volume limit and then lock that limit.

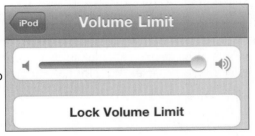

To lock the volume limit, touch the **Lock Volume Limit** button and enter a 4-digit passcode. You will be prompted to enter your passcode once more and the volume limit will then be locked.

Showing Music Controls When Your iPhone is Locked

You may want to get to your music controls even if your iPhone is locked. Here's how: Just double-click the **Home** button and the controls for adjusting the music show up on the top of the locked screen. There's no reason to unlock the screen and then go to the Music program to find the controls.

In the image to the right, notice that the screen is still locked—yet the music controls are now visible along the top. You can pause, skip, go to a previous song, or adjust the volume without actually unlocking the iPhone.

NOTE: You'll only see these controls if there is music playing.

Listening to Free Internet Radio (Pandora)

While your iPhone gives you unprecedented control over your personal music library, there may be times when you want to just "mix it up" and listen to some other music.

TIP: A basic **Pandora** account is free and can save you considerable money compared with buying lots of new songs from iTunes.

Pandora grew out of the Music Genome Project. This was a huge undertaking. A large team of musical analysts looked at just about every song ever recorded and then developed a complex algorithm of attributes to associate with each song.

NOTE: Pandora may have some competition by the time you read this book. Right now there's one other competitor called **Slacker Personal Radio**, but there will probably be more. If you want to find more options, try searching the App Store for "iPhone Internet Radio." Please also note that Pandora is a US-only application and Slacker available is only in the US and Canada. Spotfly is a similar app for Europe. Hopefully, more options will begin to pop up for international users.

Getting Started with Pandora

With Pandora you can design your own unique radio stations built around artists you like. Best of all, it is completely free!

Start by downloading the Pandora app from the App Store. Just go to the App Store and search for Pandora.

Now just touch the Pandora icon to start.

The first time you start Pandora, you'll be asked to either create an account or to sign in if you already have an account. Just fill in the appropriate information—an email address and a password are required—and you can start designing your own music listening experience.

Pandora is also available for your Windows or Mac computer and for most smartphone platforms. If you already have a Pandora account, all you have to do is sign in.

TIP: Remember that you can move apps into folders in iOS4. As you can see in Figure 13–7, we've put three Music apps, including Pandora, into one folder named Music. See more about using folders in Chapter 7: "Working with Icons and Folders."

Figure 13–7. Put like Music apps, such as Pandora, into one folder for easy retrieval.

Pandora's Main Screen

Your stations are listed along the left-hand side. Just touch one and it will begin to play. Usually, the first song will be from the actual artist chosen and the next songs will be from similar artists.

Once you select a station, the music begins to play. You'll see the current song displayed, along with album art—very much like when you play a song using the **iPod** app.

You'll also see a small **Now Playing** icon in the upper right corner—very much like the **Now Playing** icon in the iPod music app.

Touch the **Information** icon, just like the one you find in the **iPod** app, and you'll see a nice bio of the artist, which changes with each new song.

Thumbs Up or Thumbs Down in Pandora

If you like a particular song, touch the thumbs-up icon and you'll hear more from that artist.

Conversely, if you don't like an artist on this station, touch the thumbs-down icon and you won't hear that artist again.

If you like, you can pause a song and come back later, or skip to the next selection in your station.

NOTE: With a free Pandora account, you are limited in the number of skips per hour you can make. Also, you'll occasionally hear advertising. To get rid of these annoyances, you can upgrade to a paid "Pandora One" account as we show you below.

Pandora's Menu

Between the two thumbs is a **Menu** button. Touch this and you can bookmark the artist or song, go to iTunes to buy music from this artist, or email the station to someone in your **Contacts**.

Creating a New Station in Pandora

Creating a new station couldn't be easier.

Just touch the **New Station** button along the bottom row. Type in the name of an artist, song, or composer.

When you find what you are looking for, touch the selection and Pandora will immediately start to build a station around your choice.

You can also touch **Genre** and build a station around a particular genre of music.

You'll then see the new station listed with your other stations.

You can build up to 100 stations in Pandora.

> **TIP:** You can organize your stations by pressing the **By Date** or **ABC** buttons at the top of the screen.

Adjusting Pandora's Settings—Your Account, Upgrading, and More

You can sign out of your Pandora account, adjust the audio quality, and even upgrade to Pandora One (which removes advertising) by tapping the settings icon in the lower right corner of the screen. (See Figure 13–8.)

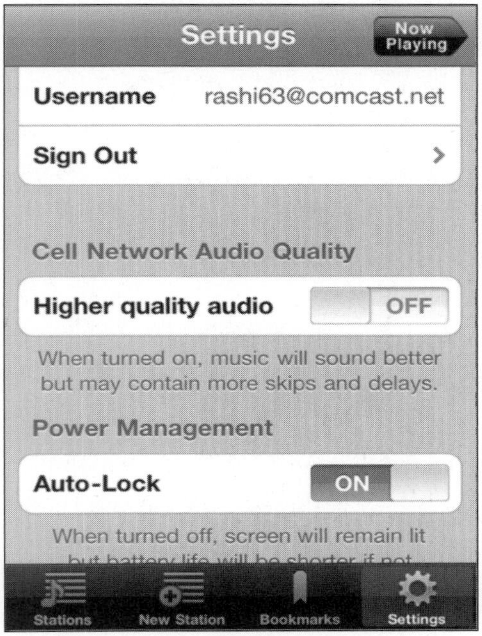

Figure 13–8. *Setting options in Pandora*

To sign out, tap your account name.

To adjust the sound quality, move the switch under **Cell Network Audio Quality** either **ON** or **OFF**. When you are on a cellular network, setting this off is probably better, otherwise you may hear more skips and pauses in the playback.

When you are on a strong Wi-Fi connection, you can set this to **ON** for better quality. See our "Wi-Fi and 3G Connections" chapter to learn more about the various connections.

To save your battery life, you should set the **Auto-Lock** to **ON**, which is the default. If you want the force the screen to stay lit, then switch this to **OFF**.

To remove all advertising, tap the **Upgrade to Pandora One** button. A web browser window will open and you'll be take to Pandora's web site to enter your credit card information. As of publishing time, the annual account cost is $36.00, but that may be different by the time you read this book.

Chapter 14

iBooks and E-Books

Ever since the new iPhone was announced, one of the features touted has been its ability as an e-book reader. In this chapter we will show you that what emerged was an unparalleled book-reading experience. We will cover iBooks, how to buy and download books, and how to find some great free classic books. We will show you other e-book reading options using the third-party Kindle and Kobo (formerly Shortcovers) readers on your iPhone.

The iPhone uses Apple's proprietary e-book reader, iBooks. In this chapter, we will show you how to download the iBooks app, how to shop for books in the iBooks store, and how to take advantage of all the iBooks features.

With iBooks, you can interact with a book like never before. Pages turn like a real book, and you can adjust font sizes, look up words in the built-in dictionary, and search through your text.

In the App store, you can also find apps for Amazon's Kindle reader, a Barnes and Noble reader, the Stanza reader, and the Kobo reader. Both the Kindle reader and the Kobo reader offer a great reading experience on the iPhone.

Downloading iBooks

Search the App store for "iBooks" or
"Apple." Among the selections available
for download will be iBooks.

> **NOTE**: On a brand new iPhone, you should
> get a notice asking you "do you want to
> download iBooks now?"

Select the **iBooks** app and touch the **Free**
button to download.

Select **Install** and iBooks will be
downloaded and installed on the iPhone.

The iBooks Store

Before you can start enjoying your reading experience, you need to load up your iBooks
library with titles. Fortunately, many books can be found for free in the iBooks store,
including the near complete Gutenberg Collection of classics and public domain titles.

> **NOTE**: Paid iBooks content is not available in all countries. Free content, however, is.

Just touch the **Store** button in the upper
right-hand corner of your bookshelf, and
you will be taken to the iBooks store.

The iBooks store is arranged much like the App store. There is a **Categories** button in the top left, opposite from the **Library** button. Touch this to see all the available categories from which you can choose your books.

Featured books are highlighted on the front page of the store, with **New** and **Notable** titles displayed for browsing.

At the bottom of the store are five soft keys: **Featured**, **Charts**, **Browse**, **Search**, and **Purchases**.

Touch the **Charts** button to see all the top charts and New York Times bestselling books. Touch the **Purchases**

 button to see all the books you have purchased or downloaded for your library.

Purchasing a book is much like purchasing an app. Touch the book title in which you are interested and browse the description and customer reviews. When you are ready to purchase the title, touch the price button.

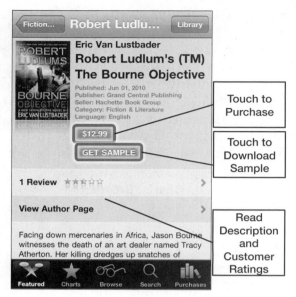

Touch to Purchase

Touch to Download Sample

Read Description and Customer Ratings

NOTE: Many titles have a sample download. This is a great idea if you are not sure that you want to purchase the book. Just download a sample, and you can always purchase the full book from within the sample.

Once you decide to download a sample or purchase a title, the view shifts to your bookshelf and you can see the book being deposited onto your bookshelf. Your book is now available for reading.

Using the Search Button

Just like iTunes and the App store, iBooks gives you a search window in which you can type virtually any phrase. You can search for an author, title, or series. Just touch **Search** at the bottom of the screen, and the on-screen keyboard pops up. Type in an author, title, series, or genre of book.

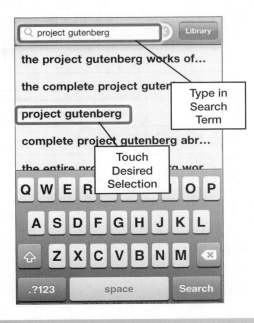

TIP: To search for lots of free books, do a search for "Project Gutenberg" to see thousands of free public domain titles.

You will see suggestions pop up that match your search; just touch the appropriate suggestion to go to that title.

Reading iBooks

Touch any title in your library to open it for reading. The book will open to the very first page, which is often the title page or other "front matter" in the book.

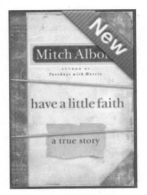

In the upper left-hand corner, next to the **Library** button, is a **Table of Contents** button, as you can see in Figure 14–1. To jump to the table of contents, either touch the **Table of Contents** button or simply turn the pages to advance to the table of contents.

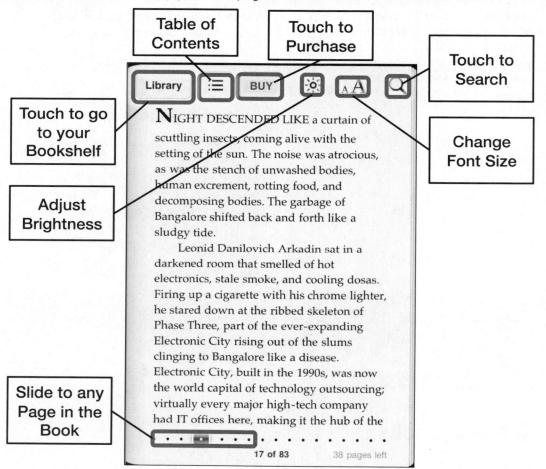

Figure 14–1. *iBooks page layout*

Pages can be turned in one of three ways. You can either touch the right-hand side of the page to turn to the next page, or slowly touch and hold the screen on the right-hand edge of the page, and, while continuing to touch the screen, gently and slowly move your finger to the left.

Robert Ludlum's (TM) The Bourne Objective

with his chrom... nature it had down at the... terest of his. At Phase Th... evening— expanding... utsourcing of the slums c... and large like a disease. Ele... acity—the in the 1990s, was now... s quiet capital of technology out... they virtually every major high-te... M. The company had IT offices here,... to making it the hub of the technical s... support industry spawned by technologies that morphed e... months.

Gold from con... thought, dazzle... on the history of al...

Touch and
"Turn"

Touch the right-hand side of the Page and "Turn," just like a Book

TIP: If you move your finger very slowly you can actually see the words on the back of the page as you "turn" it—a very cool visual effect.

The last way to turn pages is to use the slider at the bottom of the page. As you slowly slide from left to right you will see the page number on top of the slider. Release the slider and you can advance to that particular page number.

444 of 843

Customizing Your Reading Experience: Brightness, Fonts, and Font Sizes

In the upper center of the book, there are three icons available (brightness, size, and search) to help make your reading experience that much more immersive (see Figure 14–2).

Touch the **Brightness** icon and you can adjust the brightness of the book.

If you are reading in bed in a very dark room, you might want to slide it all the way down to the left. If you are out in the sunlight, you may need to slide it all the way up to the right. However, remember that the screen brightness consumes more battery power than most other features, so turn it back down when you don't need it so bright anymore.

NOTE: This adjusts the brightness only within iBooks. To adjust the global brightness of the iPhone, use the control in the Settings app. (Go to the **Settings** icon -> **Brightness & Wallpaper**.)

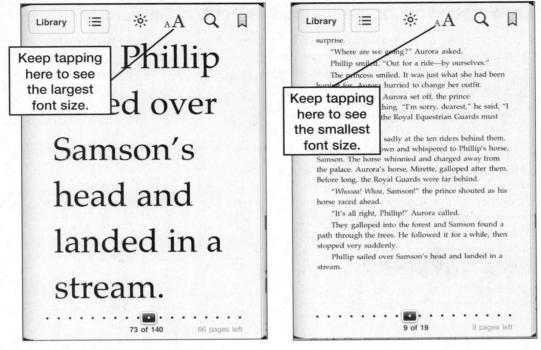

Figure 14–2. *iBooks adjusting font sizes*

The next icon is the **Font Size and Type** adjustment.

To Increase the Font Size:

Tap the large "A" multiple times.

To Decrease the Font Size:

Tap the small "A" multiple times.

There are six available font styles. (There may well be more fonts when you read this book.)

Have fun and try out some of the various fonts. The default selection is the Palatino font, but all of the fonts look great, and the larger font size can make a difference for some. The goal is to make this as comfortable and as enjoyable a reading experience as possible.

Grow Your Vocabulary Using the Built-In Dictionary

iBooks contains a very powerful built-in dictionary, which can be quite helpful when you run across a word that is new or unfamiliar.

NOTE: The first time you attempt to use the dictionary, the iPhone will need to download it. Follow the on-screen prompts to download the dictionary.

Accessing the dictionary could not be easier. Just touch and hold any word in the book. A pop-up will appear with the options of using the dictionary, highlighting a word, creating a note, or searching for other occurrences of this particular word.

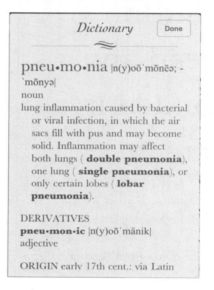

Touch **Dictionary**, and a pronunciation and definition of the word will be displayed. Touch **Done** to leave the dictionary and go back to the book.

Setting an In-Page Bookmark

There may be times when you wish to set an in-text bookmark for future reference.

In the upper right-hand corner is a **Bookmark** icon. Touch the **Bookmark** icon and it will change to a red bookmark on the page.

To view your bookmarks, just touch the **Table of Contents** icon at the top left of the screen (next t the **Library** icon) and then touch **Bookmarks**. Touch the bookmark highlighted and you will jump to that section in the book.

Library	Resume	Have a Little Faith

TABLE OF CONTENTS	BOOKMARKS

BOOKMARKS

The End of Spring   146
Today, June 25, 2010

The Things We Lose...   171
Today, June 25, 2010

> **TIP:** You do not need to set a bookmark every time you leave iBooks. iBooks will automatically remember where you left off in your book. Even if you jump to another book, when you return to the book you were just reading, you will return to exactly where you left off. iBooks will now also sync with your iPad iBooks so you can move back and forth between devices and keep your place

Using Highlighting and Notes

There are some very nice "added touches" to the iBooks app. There may be times that you want to highlight a particular word to come back to at another time. There may be other times you want to leave yourself a note in the margin.

Both of these are very easy to do in iBooks.

Highlighting Text

To highlight text, do the following:

1. Touch and hold any word to bring up the menu options.

2. Choose **Highlight** from the menu options.

3. To remove the highlight, just touch and hold, and then select **Remove Highlight**.

To change the color of the highlight, do the following:

1. Touch and hold the highlighted word.

2. Choose **Colors** from the menu.

3. Choose a new color (see Figure 14–3).

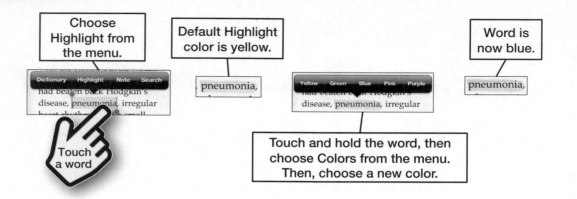

Figure 14–3. *Using the highlighting feature in iBooks*

Adding Notes

To add a note in the margin just do the following:

1. Touch and hold any word, as you did previously.

2. Choose **Note** from the menu.

3. Type in your note and then touch **Done**.

4. The note now appears on the side of the page in the margin (see Figure 14–4).

> **TIP**: Your notes will also appear under your bookmarks on the title page. Just touch the **Title Page** button and then touch **Bookmarks**. The notes you write will be at the bottom of the page.

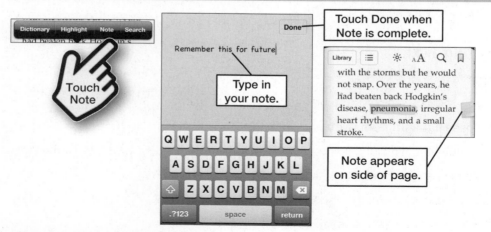

Figure 14–4. *Using the **Notes** feature in iBooks*

Using Search

iBooks contains a powerful search feature built right in. Just touch the **Search** icon and then (as in other programs on the iPhone) the built-in keyboard will pop up. Type in the word or phrase for which you are searching, and a list of chapters is shown where that word occurs.

Just touch the selection desired and you will jump to that section in the book. You also have the option of jumping right to Google or Wikipedia by touching the appropriate buttons at the bottom of the search window.

> **NOTE:** Using the Wikipedia or Google search will take you out of iBooks and launch Safari.

Deleting Books

Deleting books from your iBooks library is very similar to deleting applications from the iPhone.

In the "Library" view, just touch **Edit** in the top right-hand corner.

Once you touch the **Edit** button, you will notice a small black "x" in the upper left-hand corner of each book.

Just touch the "x" and you will be prompted to delete the book. Once you touch **Delete**, the book will disappear from the shelf.

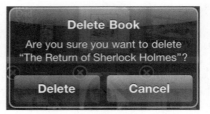

Other E-Book Readers: Kindle and Kobo

iBooks, as we have shared, offers an unparalleled e-book reading experience. There are, however, other e-book reader apps available for the iPhone that are worth checking out.

Many users already have a Kindle and have invested in their Kindle library. Others use Kobo e-reader software (formerly Shortcovers) and have invested in a library of books for that platform.

Fortunately, both e-book platforms have apps in the iPhone App store. When either program is downloaded and installed, you can sign in and read your complete library on your iPhone.

> **NOTE:** No matter which of these other e-readers you choose, you can always just "sign in," see your complete library, and pick up just where you left off in your last book—even if you started reading on a different device.

Download E-Reader Apps

Go to the App store, touch **Categories,** and, from there, touch **Books**. There you will find the Kindle app and the Kobo app. Both are free apps, so just touch the **Free** button and the downloads will initiate.

> **TIP:** It is usually faster to just "search" by the name of the app if you know which one you are looking for.

Once the e-reader software is installed, just touch the icon to start the app.

Kindle Reader

Amazon's Kindle reader is the world's most popular e-reader. Millions of people have Kindle books, so the Kindle app allows you to read your Kindle books on your iPhone.

The Kindle app has just been updated to support audio/video on iPhone and iPad, making it even more advanced than on Kindle hardware itself.

> **TIP:** If you use a Kindle device, don't worry about signing in from your iPhone. You can have several devices tied to your single account. You will be able to enjoy all the books you purchased for your Kindle right on the Kindle app on the iPhone.

Just touch the Kindle app and either sign in to your Kindle account or create a new account with a user name and password.

Once you sign in, you will see your Kindle books on the home page. You can either touch a book to start reading, or touch **Get Books** to start shopping in the Kindle store.

NOTE: Touching **Get Books** will start up your Safari browser. From there you can purchase Kindle books. Once you are done, you will need to exit Safari and start up the Kindle app once again.

To read a Kindle book, touch on the book cover. The book will open.

To see the options for reading, just touch the screen, and they will be along the bottom row of icons.

You can add a bookmark by touching the plus (+) button. Once the bookmark is set, the plus (+) turns to a minus (-).

You can go to the cover, table of contents, or beginning of the book (or specify any location in the book) by touching the **Book** button.

The font, as well as the color of the page, can be adjusted. One very interesting feature is the ability to change the page to "**Black**," which is great when reading at night.

To advance pages, either swipe from right to left, or touch the right-hand side of the page. To go back a page, just swipe from left to right or touch the left-hand side of the page.

Tap the screen and a slider appears at the bottom, which you can move to advance to any page in the book.

To return to your list of books, just touch the **Home** button.

Kobo Reader

Like the Kindle reader, the Kobo
reader asks you first to sign in to
your existing Kobo Books account.
All of your existing Kobo Books will
then be available for reading.

Kobo uses a "bookshelf" approach,
similar to iBooks. Tap the book
cover for whichever book you wish
to open.

Or, touch the **List** tab to see your
books organized in a list format.

You can also directly go to the Kobo
store to purchase books by
touching the **Discover** or **Browse**
buttons at the bottom.

Open any book, and along the top
of the Kobo reader are two buttons:
I'm Reading and **Settings**.

Touch the **I'm Reading** button and
a bookmark is placed where you left
off in the book and the screen goes
back to your bookshelf.

Touch the **Settings** button, and along the bottom will be buttons for viewing bookmarks, seeing information about the book, and adjusting the page transition style and font. Under those buttons are four icons: **Font**, **Brightness**, **Screen Lock**, and **Nighttime Reading**. Touch any of the buttons to make adjustments to your viewing.

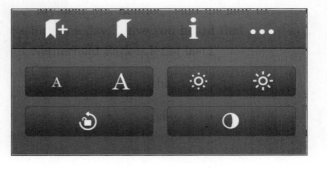

To advance pages in the Kobo reader, touch the right-hand side of the page. To go back a page, just touch the left-hand side of the page. You can also use the slider at the bottom to advance through the pages.

Chapter 15

New Media: Reading Newspapers, Magazines, and More

In last chapter, we spoke about how the iPhone 4 has revolutionized the world of reading. Not only is the iPhone 4 unparalleled for reading e-books, it's also unequaled in dealing with new media such as online newspapers and magazines, PDF files, and more. The iPhone 4 is even set to revitalize the comic book industry with comic books that look beautiful and are amazingly interactive.

In this chapter, we'll explore how to enjoy new media using the iPhone 4's vivid screen and terrific touch interface.

Newspapers on the iPhone 4

Remember the days when newspapers were delivered to the house? Invariably, if there was one puddle in the sidewalk, that was where the newspaper landed! You took it out of that plastic bag, shook it off, and tried to make out what was in section two – the section that got soaked.

Well, those days may be gone forever. You now have the opportunity to interact with the news and even get your paper delivered every day—but to your iPhone 4 instead of your driveway.

Many newspapers and news sites are developing apps for the iPhone 4, with new apps seeming to appear every day. Let's take a quick look at three apps from the largest newspapers in the country (see Figure 15–1), and see how they revolutionize reading the news on the iPhone 4.

Figure 15–1. *The front pages of various newspaper apps*

Popular Choices: The New York Times, The Wall Street Journal, and USA Today

Each of these three papers has a circulation of millions of readers, and each has taken a different approach to bringing you the news on the iPhone 4.

NOTE: You can always go and visit the dedicated web site for any news source. Some are optimized for the iPhone 4, while others offer you a full web experience. Some require registration or a paid subscription to view the paper's full content.

The common denominator with all three is that you must first find, download, and install a news app on the iPhone 4. Here are the steps:

1. Locate your desired news app in the App Store. You may find one or more news apps in the **Featured** section, and there's also a direct link to **News** under **Quick Links** at the bottom of the App Store home page.

2. Next, touch the **Categories** button at the bottom of the page and then touch the **News** icon. This will take you to all the news apps in the App Store. Browse or search for your desired news app, just as you would for any other app.

3. Once you locate the desired news app, download it as you would any other app.

> **NOTE:** Many news apps are free. Some are free to try, but require you to buy them to continue receiving them. Others offer limited free content, but you need to subscribe to gain access to their full content.

4. Once the app is downloaded, touch its icon to start it.

The New York Times app

The New York Times offers a slimmed-down version of the paper in its free iPhone 4 app.

There are five soft keys at the bottom of the page for **Latest**, **Popular**, **Saved**, **Search**, and **More**. Each section carries a sampling of stories from those sections in the current day's paper.

Touching **More** shows you tabs for all sections of the *New York Times*.

Navigating **The New York Times** app is as simple as touching an article and scrolling through. While reading a story, just touch the center of the screen and the soft keys on top and bottom appear.

To go back to the **Home** page, touch the **Latest News** button in the upper left-hand corner.

NOTE: If you are in another section—say *Technology*—the button in the upper left corner would

Latest News

say **Technology**.

To email an article, just touch the **Email** icon in the lower left-hand corner. This button is only available when you are inside an article, not on the **Home** page.

Touch the icon and you can send the article via email, text message, or Twitter.

The Wall Street Journal app

The Wall Street Journal app takes a different approach to delivering the news. When the app launches, you'll be prompted to create an online account.

Once you've created the account, you have access to a subset of content from *The Wall Street Journal*.

Material that is unavailable to free-account users is marked

with a small key icon, indicating that the material is locked.

If you fully subscribe to The Wall Street Journal app, all articles and tools become available.

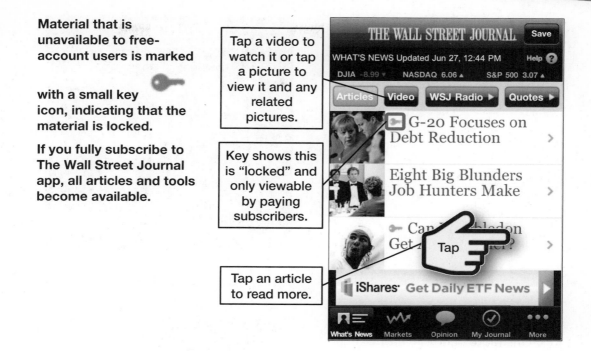

Tap a video to watch it or tap a picture to view it and any related pictures.

Key shows this is "locked" and only viewable by paying subscribers.

Tap an article to read more.

To order the full subscription to the *Wall Street Journal* for the iPhone 4, touch a "locked" article and then the **Subscribe Now** button that appears on the next page. At the time of writing, subscription for weekly access was about US $4 a week or about US $17 a month.

The articles without the key are available to read. Touch an article, and it loads onto the iPhone 4.

Similar to **The New York Times** app, **The Wall Street Journal** app lets you simply scroll through to continue reading.

You'll notice that the **The Wall Street Journal** app's home page has a **Video** button next to the **Articles** button. Touch **Video** to look at the video menu. Touch a video and it will start playing in the iPhone video player.

To access other sections of the paper, touch the **More** button in the lower right-hand corner.

USA Today app

While not as full featured as the iPad equivalent, the USA Today is still a great source to get your iPhone news. The app is available in the News category of the App Store.

Download the app as you did the other News apps.

When you first start the app you will be asked to input your location so your local weather and news can be configured.

The "sections" of the paper are at the top of the home screen. Just slide from right to left and then touch the section of the paper you want to read.

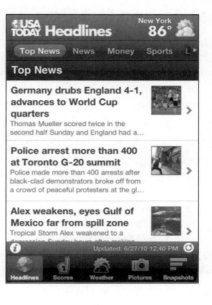

Moving Through and Enjoying Content

After you play for a while with all these news sites, you'll begin to realize that there is no real standard for moving around. This means you'll need to become familiar with each app's own way of navigating articles, as well as how to return to the main screen. Here's a short guide for generally navigating these types of apps; specifically features common to **The New York Times**, **The Wall Street Journal** and **USA Today**:

- **Showing or Hiding Control buttons or Captions:** Tapping the screen once usually shows hidden controls or picture captions. You can tap them again to rehide them.

- **Getting to the Details of an Article:** Usually, you just scroll through the articles, as you'd read a web page.

- **Viewing a Video:** Tap a video to start playing it. Usually, this plays the video in the same manner as any other video. See Chapter 16: "Viewing Videos, TV Shows and More" to learn how to navigate videos on the iPhone.

- **Expanding a Video or Image Size:** You can try pinching open in the video or image and then double-tapping it. Look for an **Expand** button, and you can also try rotating to landscape mode.

- **Reducing a Video or Image Size:** You can try pinching closed inside the video or image. Look for a **Close** or **Minimize** button, and you can also try rotating back to portrait mode.

Adjusting Options: Font Sizes, and Share, Email, or Save an Article

The various apps for reading newspapers and other content usually include a button or icon for changing the font size. That same button or another one near it may also allow you to share, save, or email an article to a friend. Some apps allow you to share the article with a social networking site, such as Facebook or Twitter.

> **TIP:** Almost all newspaper or magazine apps let you change font sizes and email or otherwise share an article. Look for a button or icon that says **Tools**, **Options**, **Settings**, or something similar. In some apps, the font-size adjustment option shows as small **A** and large **A** icons.

In the **Wall Street Journal** app, touch the **More** button in the lower right-hand corner and then touch the **Options** tab on the next page to adjust options such font sizes, saving, or emailing an article:

If you choose **Save Article,** the article ends up in the **Saved Articles** section on the **Start** screen.

If you choose **Email Article,** the article is sent in an email.

If you want to change the font size, in the Options menu choose font size and just tap the larger or smaller letter to make the font bigger or smaller.

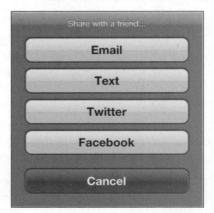

In the **USA Today** app, the font size and share options are separate.

Touch the **Share Article** icon to email an article or share it with a social networking site.

You can also touch the **info** button

to launch the **Settings & Info** menu.

Doing so brings up a page that lets you choose the font size, link the app to your **Facebook** and **Twitter** accounts, and set your default weather location.

Tap **Done** to return to the **Home** page.

The **New York Times Editor's Choice** app has one button in the lower left-hand corner of the article screen for sharing the article.

You adjust the font size is using the **T-** and **T+** buttons at the bottom.

Magazines on the iPhone 4

It is no secret that both newspapers and magazines have suffered declines in readership over the last few years. The iPhone 4 offers a totally new way of reading magazines that might just give the industry the boost it needs.

Pictures are incredibly clear and brilliant in magazines on the iPhone 4. Navigation is usually easy, and stories seem to come to life, much more so than in their print counterparts. Add video and sound integration right into the magazine, and you can see how the iPhone 4 truly enhances the magazine reading experience.

Some magazines, such as *TIME Magazine*, include links to live or frequently updated content. These might be called **Newsfeeds**, **Live Edition**, or **Updates**. Check for them in any magazine you purchase—they will give you the most up-to-date information.

> **TIP:** Make sure to check the user ratings for a magazine or other app before you purchase it. Doing so may save you some money and some grief!

The App Store is filled with both individual magazines you can purchase (or possibly view limited content for free), and with magazine readers that provide samples of many magazines and allow you to subscribe to weekly or monthly delivery of a given magazine.

Unlike newspapers, only a few magazines are available for free.

One magazine with strong reviews is **GQ Magazine** for the iPhone 4, which retails for US $4.99 per issue at the time of writing.

Zinio Magazine App—A Sampler

The **Zinio** app takes a unique approach. This app is free in the App Store, and it gives you the ability to subscribe to hundreds of magazine titles. Reading an article in **Zinio** requires a few simple steps.

1. Login into the **Zinio** app.

2. You automatically go the **My Library** section that has some free magazines you can download.

3. Download any free samples or choose the **Shop** button to purchase magazines.

4. Some magazines may be giving away full, free issues. Just look in the **My Library** section to see what is available.

To subscribe to any of the magazines featured in **Zinio**, touch the **Shop** button at the bottom of the screen.

You can navigate magazines by category along the left-hand side, or you can slide the icons at the bottom to see available magazines.

There are many popular magazines you can choose. The categories cover everything from art to sports and more. Prices vary, but often you can buy either a single issue or a yearly subscription.

For example, the latest issue of *Popular Mechanics* was $1.99 on **Zinio**, and a yearly subscription was $7.99.

Some of the subscriptions make great sense. A single issue of *Bike Magazine* (one of my favorites) was $4.99 at the time of this writing, while a yearly subscription was only $9.00.

A closer look showed me that there were more than 16 cycling magazines I could subscribe to.

Comic Books on the iPhone 4

One genre of "new media" poised for a comeback with the advent of the iPhone 4 is the comic book. The iPhone 4, with its high-definition screen and powerful processor, makes the pages of comic books come alive.

There are already a few comic book apps available, including one from the famous Marvel Comics. DC Comics has just launched its app as well, which was created by the same people who make the Marvel app, Comixology (who also make the more generic Comics app)

To locate the **Marvel Comic** app in the App Store, go to **Categories** and then **Books**. The app is free, and you can purchase comic books from inside the app.

At the bottom of the **Home** screen you'll see five buttons: **My Comics**, **Featured**, **Free, Top 25,** and **Browse**. Purchases you make will be under the **My Comics** heading.

The App Store gives you the opportunity to download both free comics and individual issues for sale. Most sell for $1.99 per issue.

Each tab takes you to a new list of comics to browse, much like the iTunes store.

Touch the **Browse** button to browse by **Genre**, **Creator**, **Storylines**, or **Series**. Or you can type in a search to find a particular comic.

You can read a comic book in one of two ways. First, you can swipe through the pages and read one after the other. Second, you can double-tap a frame to **Zoom** in, then tap the screen to advance to the next frame in the comic strip. From there, you can just swipe from right to left to advance a frame; or, if you want to go back, swipe from left to right.

To return to the **Home** screen or to see the onscreen options, just tap the center of the screen. You'll see a **Settings** button in the top left-hand corner. Touch this and you can **Jump to the First Page**, **Browse to a Page**, or go to the **Settings** menu.

NOTE: The makers of this app, **COMIXOLOGY**, also make the **COMICS** app that contains the Marvel comics, as well as a bunch of others, including Archie, Image, and Top Cow.

The iPhone 4 as a PDF Reader

In the Chapter 18 discussion of email, we showed you how to open up attachments, including PDF files. You can now read PDF files in iBooks, but another great PDF reader is called GoodReader. And the added benefit of GoodReader is that you can use Wi-Fi to transfer large PDF files.

Fortunately, there are some programs available that turn the iPhone 4 into a very capable PDF viewing program. One such program with multiple uses is **GoodReader**.

You'll find the **GoodReader** app in the **Productivity** section of the App Store. At the time of writing, this app costs only US $0.99.

> NOTE: **iBooks** can also read PDF files that are emailed as attachments. If **iBooks** is installed, just choose **Open in iBooks** when opening a PDF.

Transferring Files to your iPhone 4

One of the great things about the **GoodReader** app is that you can use it to wirelessly transfer large files from your Mac or PC to the iPhone 4 for viewing in the **GoodReader** app. You can also use **GoodReader** for document sharing in iTunes, as we discussed in Chapter 3. Follow these steps to transfer a file with **GoodReader**.

1. Touch the small **Wi-Fi** icon at the bottom left of the screen, and the **Wi-Fi Transfer Utility** pops up. You are prompted to type in either an IP address into your browser or a Bonjour address if you use the **Bonjour** service (see Figure 15-2).

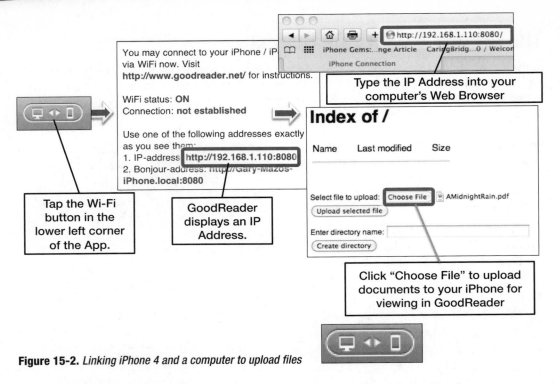

Figure 15-2. *Linking iPhone 4 and a computer to upload files*

2. Type the address shown in the pop-up window from the **GoodReader** into a web browser on your computer. Now you can make your computer act as a server. You'll see that your computer and iPhone 4 are now connected.

3. Click the **Choose File** button in the web browser on your computer to locate a file to upload to your iPhone 4.

4. Once you've selected the file, click **Upload Selected File** and the file will be automatically transferred to your iPhone 4 inside **GoodReader** (see Figure 15-3).

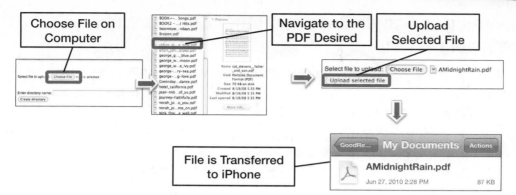

Figure 15–3. Uploading a file to iPhone 4

How is this useful? Well, for one of the authors (Gary), the iPhone 4 has become a repository for more than 100 pieces of piano sheet music. This means no more downloading PDF files, printing them out, putting them into binders, and then trying to remember which song is in which binder. Now, all his music is catalogued on the iPhone 4. All he has to do is put the iPhone 4 on the piano, and he has access to all his music in one place.

NOTE: You can also transfer **Word, Excel**, and **PowerPoint** files in the same manner. However, using the document transfer utility in iTunes, described in Chapter 3, might be a bit easier for this.

Navigating the **GoodReader** PDF viewer is quite easy. This app is more sensitive than others, so tap the center of the screen quickly to bring up the onscreen controls. You can then go to your library or touch the **Turn Page** icon to turn the page.

The easiest way to move through pages is to touch the lower right-hand side of the screen to advance a page, or touch the upper left-hand side of the screen to go back a page. This becomes quite natural after a while.

You can also flick up or down to turn pages.

To go to another PDF file or another piece of sheet music, just touch the center of the iPhone 4 quickly and touch the **My Documents** button in the upper left-hand corner.

Connecting to Google Docs and other Servers with GoodReader

You can also connect to **Google Docs** and other servers with **GoodReader**. Follow these steps to do so.

1. In the **Web Downloads** tab, choose **Connect to Servers**.

2. Select **Google Docs.** (You can select a number of different servers: mail servers, MobileMe iDisk, Public iDisk, Dropbox, box.net, FilesAnywhere.com, MyDisk.se, WebDAV Server, and FTP Servers.)

3. Enter your **Google Docs** username and password to log in.

4. Once you've made the connection, a new **Google Docs Server** icon will appear under the **Connect to Server** tab on the right-hand side of the page.

5. Tap the new **Google** tab to connect to the server (an Internet connection is required).

6. Now you'll see a list of all the documents you have stored on **Google Docs**. Tap any document and select the file type to download it. Usually PDF works well for this. (Google docs will do a save as and PDF files are easier to work with.)

7. Once the file is downloaded, it will appear on the left-hand side of GoodDocs, and you can simply touch it to open it.

Chapter 16

Viewing Videos, TV Shows, and More

The iPhone 4 is an amazing "media consumption" device. Nowhere is this more apparent than in the various video-viewing applications available.

In this chapter, we will show you how you can watch movies, TV shows, podcasts, and music videos on your iPhone 4. You can buy or download many videos for free from the iTunes store or iTunes University. Beginning in late summer, 2010, you can also link your iPhone 4 to your Netflix account (and most likely other video rental services soon), allowing you to watch streaming TV shows and movies.

With your iPhone 4, you can also watch YouTube videos and videos from the Web on your Safari browser and through various apps such as the **Hulu Plus** app from the App store.

NOTE: As of publishing, Hulu Plus and Netflix are U.S.-only apps. We hope similar apps will make their way to the international market.

Your iPhone 4 as a Video Player

The iPhone 4 is not only a capable music player; it is a fantastic portable video playing system. The widescreen, fast processor, incredible pixel density and great operating system make watching anything from music videos to TV shows and full-length motion pictures a real joy. The size of the iPhone 4 is perfect for sitting back in a chair or watching on an airplane. It is also great for the kids in the back seat of long car trips. The near ten-hour battery life means you can even go on a coast-to-coast flight and not run out of power! You can buy a "power inverter" for your car to keep the iPhone 4 charged even longer (see the "Charging Your iPhone 4 and Battery Tips" section in Chapter 1).

Loading Videos onto Your iPhone 4

You can load videos on your iPhone 4 just like your music, through iTunes from your computer or right from the iTunes app on your iPhone 4.

If you purchase or rent videos and TV shows from iTunes on your computer, then you will manually or automatically sync them to your iPhone 4.

Watching Videos on the iPhone 4

To watch videos, touch your **Videos** icon, which is a soft key along the bottom row of the **iPod** app.

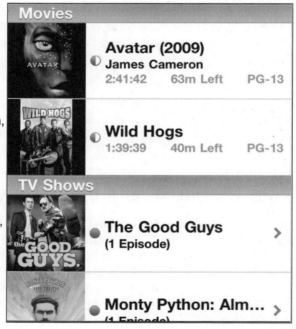

NOTE: You can also watch videos from the **YouTube** icon, the **Safari** icon, and other video-related apps you load from the App store.

Video Categories

Each section of the **Videos** screen is under the **Video** tab in the **iPod** app separated by horizontal bars: **Movies, TV Shows**, **Podcasts**, and **Music Videos**.

The first category is the **Movies** section, so if you have movies loaded on the iPhone 4, they will be visible.

You may see more or fewer categories depending on the types of videos you have loaded on your iPhone 4. If you have only **Movies** and **iTunes U** videos, then you would see only those two category buttons. Just touch any of the other categories to show the corresponding videos in each category.

Playing a Movie

Just touch the movie you wish to watch and it will begin to play (see Figure 16–1). Most videos take advantage of the relatively large screen real estate of the iPhone 4 and they play in widescreen or landscape mode. Just turn your iPhone 4 to watch.

Most videos will play in landscape mode. Turn your iPhone sideways to watch them.

Figure 16–1. *Playing a video.*

When the video first starts, there are no menus, no controls, and nothing on the screen except for the video.

To Pause or Access Controls

Touch anywhere on the screen and the control bars and options will become visible (see Figure 16–2). Most are very similar to those in the Music player. Tap the **Pause** button and the video will pause.

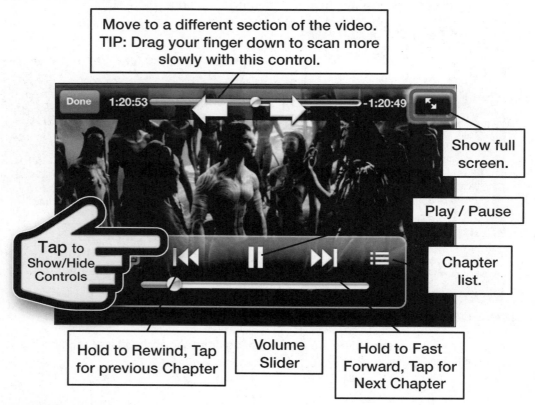

Move to a different section of the video. TIP: Drag your finger down to scan more slowly with this control.

Show full screen.

Play / Pause

Tap to Show/Hide Controls

Chapter list.

Hold to Rewind, Tap for previous Chapter

Volume Slider

Hold to Fast Forward, Tap for Next Chapter

Figure 16–2. *Video controls.*

Fast-Forward or Rewind the Video

On either side of the **Play/Pause** button are typical **Fast-Forward** and **Rewind** buttons. To jump to the next chapter-specific part of the video, just touch and hold the **Fast-Forward** button (to the right of **Play/Pause**). When you get to the desired spot, release the button and the video will begin playing normally.

To rewind to the beginning on the video, tap the **Rewind** button. To rewind to a specific part or location, touch and hold like you did while you were fast forwarding the video.

NOTE: If this is a full-length movie with several chapters, tapping either **Reverse** or **Fast-Forward** will move either back or ahead one chapter.

Using the Time Slider Bar

At the top of the video screen is a slider that shows you the elapsed time of the video. If you know exactly (or approximately) which point in the video you wish to watch, just hold and drag the slide to that location. Some people find this to be a little more exact than holding down the **Fast-Forward** or **Rewind** Buttons.

TIP: Drag your finger down to move the slide more slowly. In other words, start by touching the slider control, then drag your finger down the screen—notice that the further down the screen your finger is, the slower the slider moves left or right. The screen may say "Scrubbing"—this just means to lower the sensitivity of how fast the slider moves.

Changing the Size of the Video (Widescreen vs. Full Screen)

Most of your videos will play in widescreen format. However, if you have a video that was not converted for your iPhone 4 or is not optimized for the screen resolution, you can touch the expand button, which is to the right of the upper Status bar.

You will notice that there are two arrows. If you are in full-screen mode, the arrows are pointing in toward each other. If you are in widescreen mode, the arrows are pointing outward.

Viewing Full-Screen Mode   **Viewing Widescreen Mode**

Zoom Out To Widescreen   **Zoom In** To Full-Screen

In a widescreen movie that is not taking up the full screen of the iPhone 4, touching this button will zoom in a bit. Touching it again will zoom out.

NOTE: You can also simply "double-tap" the screen to zoom in and fill the screen as well. Be aware that, just like on your widescreen TV, when you try to force a non-widescreen video into widescreen mode, sometimes you will lose part of the picture.

Using the Chapters Feature

Most full-length movies purchased from the iTunes store, and some that are converted for the iPhone 4, will give you a Chapters feature—very much like you were watching a DVD on your home TV.

Just bring up the controls for the video by tapping the screen, and then select **Chapters**.

This will bring you back to the main page for the movie.

Touch the **Chapters** button in the upper right corner, and then scroll through to and touch the chapter you wish to watch.

Viewing the Chapters

You can scroll through or flick through quickly to locate the scene or chapter that you wish to watch.

You will also notice that to the far right of each chapter is the exact time (relative to the start of the movie) that the chapter begins.

Touch any chapter
to jump there.

In addition to the chapter menu, mentioned previously, you can also quickly advance to the previous or next chapter in a movie by tapping the **Rewind** or **Fast-Forward** buttons. One tap moves you one chapter in either direction.

NOTE: The Chapters feature usually works only with movies that are purchased from the iTunes store. Movies that are converted and loaded on usually will not have chapters.

Watching a TV Show

The iPhone 4 is great for watching your favorite TV shows. You can purchase TV shows from the iTunes store, and you can download sample shows from some iPhone 4 apps, such as the **Hulu Plus** app.

Just scroll down to the **TV Shows** category separator   to see the shows you have downloaded on your iPhone 4. Scroll through your available shows and touch **Play**. The video controls work just like the controls when you watch a movie.

Watching Podcasts

We normally think of podcasts as being audio-only broadcasts that you can download using iTunes. Video podcasts are now quite prevalent and can be found on any number of sites, including many public broadcasting web sites and on iTunes U, a listing of university podcasts and information found within iTunes.

iTunes U Story from Gary Mazo:

> "Recently, I was browsing the **iTunes U** section inside the **iTunes** app on the iPhone 4 with my son, who was just accepted to CalTech. We were wondering about the housing situation and, lo and behold, we found a video podcast showing a tour of the CalTech dorms. We downloaded it and the podcast went right into the **podcast** directory for future viewing. We were able to do a complete virtual tour of the housing without flying out there from the East Coast."

Watching Music Videos

Music videos are available for your iPhone 4 from a number of sources. Often, if you buy a "Deluxe" album from iTunes, it might include a music video or two. You can also purchase music videos from the iTunes store, and many record companies and recording artists make them available for free on their web sites.

Music videos will automatically get sorted into the **Music Videos** section of your **Videos** app.

The **Music Videos** are usually right under **TV Shows** in the **Videos** list. The controls work just as they do in all other video applications.

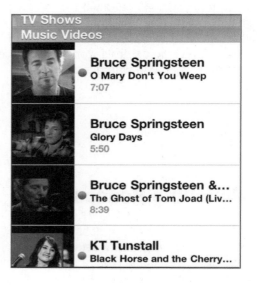

Video Options

As in your music player, there are a few options that you can adjust for the video player. These options are accessed through the **Settings** icon from your **Home** screen.

Touch the **Settings** icon and then scroll down to touch **iPhone 4** and then to the **Video** options.

Start Playing Option

Sometimes, you will have to stop watching a particular video. This option lets you decide what to do the next time you want to watch. Your options are to either watch the video from the beginning or from where you left off. Just select the option that you desire and that will be the action from now on.

Closed Captioned

If your video has closed captioned capabilities, when this switch is turned to **ON**, closed captioning will be shown on your screen.

TV-Out: Widescreen

There are many third-party gadgets out there that allow you to watch the video from your iPhone 4 on some external source, either a TV or computer screen, or even an array of video glasses that simulate watching on a very large screen monitor. Most of these require that your TV widescreen setting be set to **ON**. By default, it is set to **OFF**.

TIP: You can purchase a VGA adapter to plug your iPhone 4 into a VGA computer monitor to watch movies.

VGA supports video only, requires that the app supports it, and isn't usually compatible with DRM. Apple also makes component video cables that are DRM-compliant and work with most TVs.

See our "Accessories" section of our Quick Start Guide for more information.

TV Signal

There are some advanced ways of taking content from your iPhone 4 and playing them on your TV or DVR with the right cable. You also need to have the right TV signal setting. This is typically changed only if you use your iPhone 4 in another country. If you live in the U.S., your TV works with the NTSC standard.

Most European countries use PAL. If you are not sure which you use, contact your TV, cable, or satellite company.

Deleting Videos

To delete a video (to save space on your iPhone 4), just choose the category from which you wish to delete the video—as you did at the start of this chapter (see Figure 16–3).

> **NOTE:** If you're syncing videos from iTunes, make sure to uncheck it there as well, or iTunes just might sync it right back to the iPhone 4 on the next sync!

Just touch and swipe to the right on a video you wish to delete. Just like deleting an email, a red **Delete** button will appear in the top left-hand corner. Touch the **Delete** button and you will be prompted to delete the video.

Touch the **Delete** button and the video will be deleted from your system.

> **NOTE:** This deletes the video only from your iPhone 4—a copy will still remain in your video library in iTunes assuming that you have synced with your computer after purchasing the video and you can once again load it back onto your iPhone 4. However, if you delete a rented movie from the iPhone 4, it will be deleted permanently!

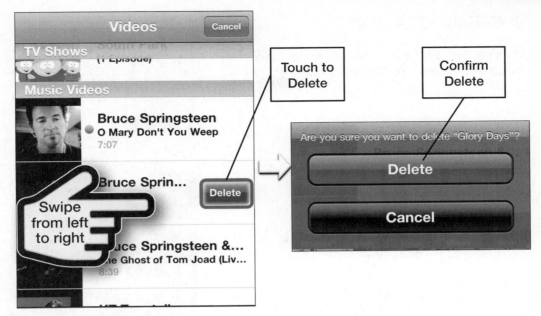

Figure 16–3. *Delete video.*

YouTube on your iPhone 4

Watching YouTube videos is certainly one of the most popular things for people to do on their computers these days. YouTube is as close to you as your iPhone 4.

Right on your **Home** screen is a **YouTube** icon. Just touch the **YouTube** icon and you will be taken to the **YouTube** app.

Searching for Videos

When you first start **YouTube**, you usually see the **Featured** videos on YouTube that day.

Just scroll through the video choices as you do in other apps.

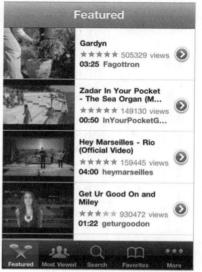

Using the Bottom Icons

Along the bottom of the **YouTube** app are five icons; **Featured**, **Most Viewed**, **Search**, **Favorites** and **More**. Each is fairly self-explanatory.

To see the videos that YouTube is featuring that day, just touch the **Featured** icon. To see those videos that are most-viewed online, just touch the **Most Viewed** icon.

After you watch a particular video, you will have the option to set it as a favorite on **YouTube** for easy retrieval later on. If you have set bookmarks, they will appear when you touch the **Favorite** icon.

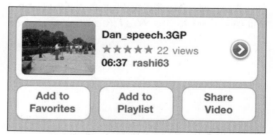

You can search the huge library of YouTube videos. Touch the **Search** box as in previous apps, and the keyboard will pop up. Type in a phrase, topic, or even the name of a video.

In this example, I am looking for the newest Made Simple Learning video tutorial—so I just type in "Made Simple Learning" and I see the list of videos to watch.

When I find the video I want to watch, I can touch on it to see more information. I can even rate the video by touching on the video during playback and selecting a rating.

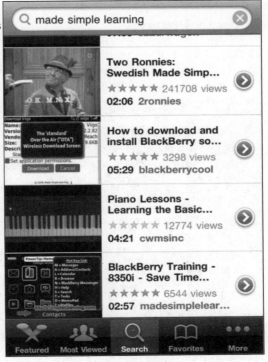

Playing Videos

Once you have made your choice, touch the video you want to watch. Your iPhone 4 will begin playing the YouTube video in portrait or landscape mode. To force portrait mode, just turn the iPhone so that the screen orientation is vertical (see Figure 16–4).

Figure 16–4. *Video playing in portrait mode.*

Video Controls

Once the video begins to play, the on-screen controls disappear, so you see only the video. To stop, pause, or activate any other options while the video is playing, just tap the screen (see Figure 16–5).

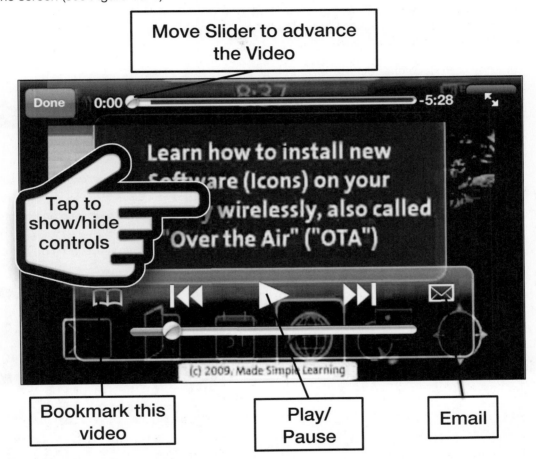

Figure 16–5. *Options within YouTube.*

The on-screen options are very similar to watching any other video. Along the bottom is the slider, showing your place in the video. To move to another part in the video, just drag the slider.

To fast-forward through the video (in landscape mode,) just touch and hold the **Fast-Forward** arrow. To quickly move in reverse, just touch and hold the **Reverse** arrow. To advance to the next video in the YouTube list, just tap the **Fast-Forward/Next** arrow. To watch the previous video in the list, just tap the **Reverse/Back** arrow.

To set a favorite, touch the **Favorite** icon farthest to the left.

To email the video, just touch the **Share** icon and your email will start with the link to the video in the body of the email. Type the recipient as we show you in Chapter 21 when you send a picture via email.

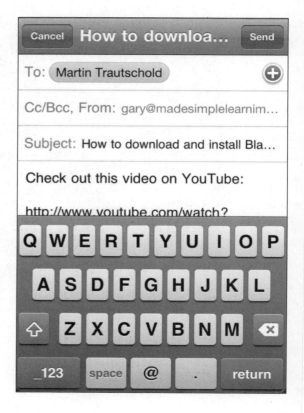

Checking and Clearing your History

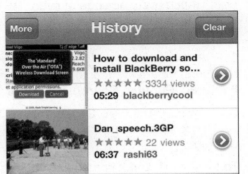

Touch **More** and then **History** and your recently viewed videos appear.

If you want to clear your history, just touch the **Clear** button in the upper right corner.

To watch a video from your history, just touch it and it will start to play.

Hulu on the iPhone 4

In recent years, Hulu has grown to become a leading source of video "streaming" of content delivered wirelessly to computers and other set-top boxes for your TV.

Just after launch of the iPhone 4, the **Hulu Plus** app was released in the App Store. Hulu Plus is a subscription-based service of $10.00 a month, but there is also free content available.

Essentially, with the full subscription, pretty much every episode of every TV show you watch or have ever watched is now available to stream to your iPhone.

Launch the app and you will see at the bottom there are five icons; **Free Gallery**, **Featured**, **Popular**, **Search**, and **More**.

Scroll through the **Free Gallery** to see which shows are available now for free viewing.

Touch a show and it immediately begins playing. Hold the iPhone in landscape mode to have the video fill up the screen.

Searching for Videos

Touch the **Search** icon at the bottom and type in the name of a particular TV show. You can also just browse the **Featured** or **Popular** categories. When you find your show, all the videos available will be available to watch.

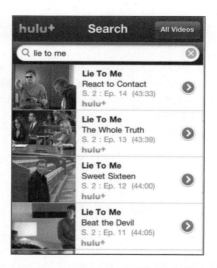

NOTE: if you do not have a Hulu Plus subscription, you will not be able to view the videos.

Watching Movies and Viewing Queue and History

Touch the **More** button and you will be taken to a screen that allows you to see available **TV** shows, **Movies**, **Recently Added** content, your **Queue**, your **History**, and your **Subscriptions** to **Hulu Plus**.

Just touch the appropriate tab to go to a particular section of the app.

Video Controls in Hulu Plus

The video controls are a bit different in the **Hulu Plus** app. Touch the screen, as in any other video and the video controls appear.

There is a **Play/Pause** button at the left and then a timeline for the video. Simply drag your finger along the timeline to advance to another part of the video.

Figure 16-6. Video controls in the Hulu Plus app.

NOTE: You cannot advance through commercials in **Hulu Plus**. During a commercial, an icon will appear in the upper right-hand corner that resembles the **Share** icon, but if you touch it you will go to the web site of the advertiser.

CAUTION: Hulu Plus and **Netflix** use a great deal of data, so make sure you have a strong Wi-Fi signal if you are streaming over Wi-Fi or, if you are using 3G cellular data, make sure you have an adequate data plan.

Chapter 17

Surfing the Web with Safari

Now, we'll take you through one of the most fun things to do on your iPhone: surfing the Web. You may have heard web surfing on the iPhone is a more intimate experience than ever before—we agree! We'll show you how to touch, zoom around, and interact with the Web like never before with Safari on your iPhone. You'll learn how to set and use bookmarks, quickly find things with the search engine, open and switch between multiple browser windows, and even easily copy text and graphics from web pages.

Web Browsing on the iPhone

You can browse the web to your heart's content via Wi-Fi or with your iPhone's 3G connection. Like it's larger cousin the iPad, your iPhone has what many feel is the most capable mobile browsing experience available today. Web pages look very much like web pages on your computer. With the iPhone's ability to zoom in, you don't even have to worry about the smaller screen size inhibiting your web browsing experience. In short, web browsing is a much more personal experience on the iPhone.

Choose to browse in portrait or landscape mode, whichever you prefer. Quickly zoom into a video by double-tapping it or pinching open on it, which is natural to you because those are the motions to zoom in text and graphics.

Why Do Some Videos and Sites Not Appear? (Flash Player Required)

⚠This content requires Flash

To view this content, JavaScript must be enabled, and you need the latest version of the Adobe Flash Player.

Download the free Flash Player now!

Get ADOBE®
FLASH PLAYER

Live video and data delivery across platforms
DIRECTV uses the Adobe® Flash® Platform to power its NFL SUNDAY TICKET™ SUPERCAST™ service, which enables subscribers using a wide variety of browsers, desktops, and operating systems to view live video streams of games, as well as the latest statistics and video highlights.

WHY THE FLASH PLATFORM WORKED

• DIRECTV is able to deliver rich content to a diverse, cross-platform audience.

SEE MORE CUSTOMER EXAMPLES

Demandbase ›
Finetune ›
Model Metrics ›

Some web sites are designed with Adobe Flash Player, and at the time of this writing, the iPhone does not support Adobe Flash. Apple has made a decision to not support the Flash Player. If you tap a video and the video does not play, or you see something like "Flash Plugin Required," "Download the Latest Flash Plugin to view this video," or "Adobe Flash Required to view this site," you will not be able to view the video or web page.

The only way to see these Flash videos is to view them from a computer that does support Adobe Flash. Remember, you can send the web address to yourself in an e-mail message (see our section on e-mailing links to web pages for instructions).

More and more sites are now starting to use HTML5 video instead of Flash, including YouTube, Vimeo, TED, the *New York Times*, and *Time* magazine, which will play on your iPhone.

An Internet Connection Is Required

You do need a live Internet connection on your iPhone, either Wi-Fi or 3G, to browse the web. Check out the Chapter 5, "Wi-Fi and 3G Connectivity" to learn more.

Launching the Web Browser

You should find the Safari (web browser) icon on your **Home** screen. Usually, the **Safari** icon is in the **Bottom Dock**.

Touch the **Safari** icon, and you will be taken to the browser's home page. Most likely, this will be Apple's iPhone page.

Just turn your iPhone on its side to see the same page in wider landscape mode. As you find web sites you like, you can set bookmarks to easily jump to these sites. We will show you how to do that later in this chapter.

Layout of Safari Web Browser Screen

Figure 17–1 shows how a web page looks in Safari and the different actions you can take in the browser.

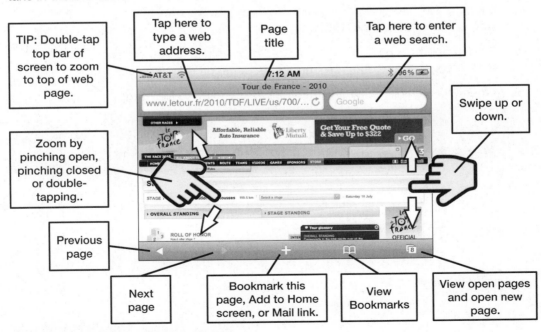

Figure 17–1. *Safari web browser page layout.*

As you look at your screen, notice that the **Address Bar** is in the upper left side of the screen. This displays the current web address. To the right is the **Search** window. By default, this is set to Google search, but you can change that if you want.

At the bottom of the screen are five icons: **Back**, **Forward**, **Add Bookmark**, **Bookmarks**, and **Pages view**.

Typing a Web Address

The first thing you'll want to learn is how to get to your favorite web pages. Just like on your computer, you type in the web address (URL) into the browser.

1. To start, tap the **Address Bar** at the top of the browser as shown in Figure 17–2. You'll then see the keyboard appear and the window for the address bar expand.

2. If there is already an address in the window and you want to erase it, press the ⊗ at the right end of the bar.

3. Start typing your web address (you don't need the **www.**).

4. When you start typing, you may see suggestions appear below, just tap any of those to go to that page. The suggestions are very complete because they are pulled from your browsing history, bookmarks, the web address (URL), and web page titles.

5. Remember the **.com** key at the bottom of the page. If you press and hold it, you will see **.edu**, **.org**, and other common domain types.

6. When you are finished typing, tap the **Go** key to go to that page.

> **TIP:** Don't type the **www.** because it's not necessary. Remember to use the **colon, forward slash**, **underscore**, **dot**, and **.com** keys at the bottom to save time.

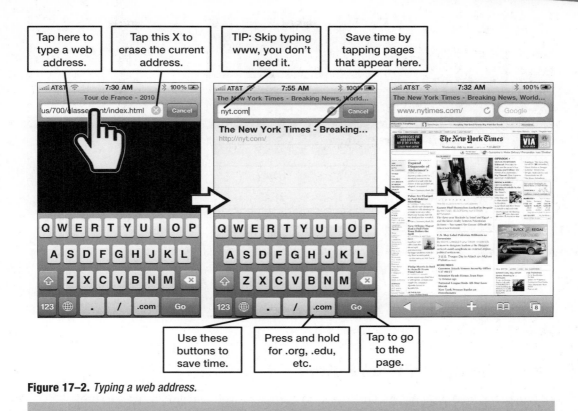

Figure 17–2. *Typing a web address.*

TIP: Press and hold the **.com** key to see all the options: **.org**, **.edu**, **.net**, **.de**, and so on.

Moving Backward or Forward Through Open Web Pages

Now that you know how to enter web addresses, you'll probably be jumping to various web sites. The **Forward** and **Back** arrows make it very easy to go to recently visited pages in either direction, as Figure 17–3 shows. If the **Back** arrow is grayed out, the "Using the **Open Pages** Button" section can help.

Let's say you were looking at the news on the *New York Times* web site, and you jumped to ESPN to check sports scores. To go back to the *New York Times* page, just tap the **Back** arrow. To return to the ESPN site again, touch the **Forward** arrow.

Tap here to return to the previous web page (**nytimes.com**).

This would take you back to **espn.com.**

Figure 17–3. *Returning to a previously viewed web page*

Using the Open Pages Button

Sometimes, when you click a link, the web page you were viewing moves to the background and a new window pops up with new content (another web page, a video, etc.). You will see the page you were on move to the background and a new page being opened. In such cases, the **Back** arrow in the new browser window will not work.

Instead, you have to tap the **Open Pages** icon in the lower right corner to see a list of open web pages and then tap the one you want. In the example shown in Figure 17–4, we touched a link that opened a new browser window. The only way to get back to the old one was to tap the **Open Pages** icon and select the desired page.

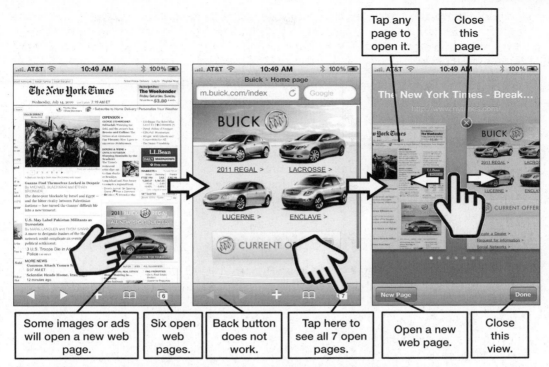

Figure 17–4. *Jumping between open web pages when the **Back** button doesn't work.*

Zooming In and Out in Web Pages

Zooming in and out of web pages is very easy on the iPhone. There are two primary ways of zooming—double-tapping and pinching.

Double-tapping

If you tap twice on a column of a web page, the page will zoom in on that particular column. This lets you home in on exactly the right place on the web page, which is very helpful for pages that aren't formatted for a mobile screen.

To zoom out, just double-tap once more. See graphically how this looks in the "Quick Start Guide" earlier in this book.

Pinching

This technique lets you zoom in on a particular section of a page. It takes a little bit of practice but will soon become second nature. Take a look in the "Quick Start Guide" to see graphically how it looks.

Place your thumb and forefinger close together at the section of the web page you wish to zoom into. Slowly pinch out, separating your fingers. You will see the web page zoom in. It takes a couple of seconds for the web page to focus, but it will zoom in and be very clear in a short while.

To zoom out to where you were before, just start with your fingers apart and move them slowly together; the page will zoom out to its original size.

Activating Links from Web Pages

When you're surfing the Web, often you'll come across a link that will take you to another web site. Because Safari is a full-function browser, you simply touch the link and you will jump to a new page.

Working with Safari Bookmarks

As soon as you start browsing a bit on your iPhone, you will want to quickly access your favorite web sites. One good way to do this is to add bookmarks for one-tap access to web sites.

> **TIP:** You can sync your Bookmarks from your computer's web browser (Safari or Internet Explorer only) using iTunes on your computer. Check out Chapter 3: "Sync Your iPhone with iTunes" for more details.

Adding a New Bookmark

Adding new bookmarks on your iPhone is just a few taps away.

1. To add a new bookmark for the web page you are currently viewing, tap the **plus sign** ⊞ at the bottom of the screen.

2. Choose **Add Bookmark**.

3. We recommend that you edit the bookmark name to something short and recognizable.

4. Tap **Bookmarks** if you want to change the folder where your bookmark is stored.

5. When you're finished, tap the **Save** button.

Tap to change the bookmark name.

Tap to change the bookmark folder.

Using Bookmarks and History

Once you have set a few bookmarks, it is easy to view and work with them. In the same area, you can also see and use your web browsing history. A very useful tool on your iPhone is the ability to browse the web from your **History**, just as you would on a computer.

1. Tap the **Bookmarks** icon at the bottom of the page.

2. Swipe up or down to view all your bookmarks.

3. Tap any bookmark to jump to that web page.

4. Tap the **History** folder to view your recent history of visited web pages.

5. Notice that, at the bottom of the list, you see additional folders for **Earlier Today** and previous days.

6. Tap any history item to go to that web page.

> **TIP:** To clear your history, tap the Clear button in the lower left corner. You can also clear your history, cookies, and cache in the **Settings** app. Tap **Settings**, tap **Safari**, scroll to the bottom and tap **Clear History, Clear Cookies,** or **Clear Cache.**

Managing Your Bookmarks

It is very easy to accumulate quite a collection of bookmarks, since setting them up is so easy. You may find you no longer need a particular bookmark, or you may want to organize them by adding new folders.

If you have organized your **Phone Favorites** list, you already know how to organize your bookmarks; you use the same steps.

Like other lists on your iPhone you can reorder your bookmarks' list and remove entries.

1. View your **Bookmarks** list as you did previously.

2. Tap the **Edit** button in the lower left corner.

3. To reorder the entries, touch and drag the right edge with the three gray bars up or down the list. In this case we are dragging the bookmark to the **iPad Made Simple** book page on amazon.com up to the top.

4. To create a new folder for bookmarks, tap the **New Folder** button in the lower right corner.

5. To delete a bookmark, tap the red circle to the left of the entry to make it turn vertical.

6. Then tap the **Delete** button.

7. When you are finished reordering and deleting entries, tap the **Done** button in the upper left corner.

8. To edit a bookmark name, folder, or web address, tap the bookmark name itself.

9. To edit a bookmark name, folder, or web address, tap the bookmark name itself.

10. Then, you can make any adjustments to the name, web address, or folder.

11. To change the folder where the bookmark is stored, tap the button below the web address. In this image, it says **Bookmarks**, but in your iPhone, it may be different. This bookmark points to the iPad Made Simple page on amazon.com.

12. Tap **Done** when you're finished.

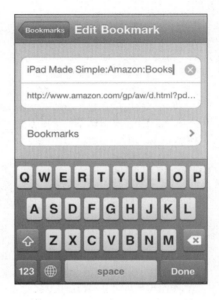

Safari Browsing Tips and Tricks

Now that you know the basics of how to get around, we will cover a few useful tips and tricks to make web browsing more enjoyable and fast on your iPhone.

Jumping to the Top of the Web Page

Sometimes, web pages can be quite long, which can make scrolling back to the top of the page a bit laborious. One easy trick is to just tap the gray title bar of the web page; you'll automatically jump to the top of the page, as shown in Figure 17–5.

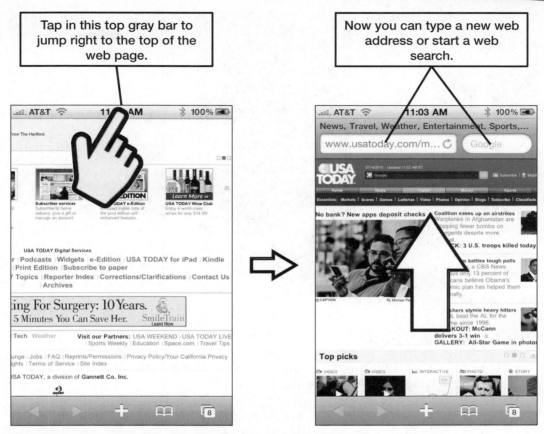

Figure 17–5. *Jump quickly to the top of a web page by tapping at the top.*

E-mailing a Web Page

Sometimes while browsing, you find a page so compelling you just have to send it to a friend or colleague. Touch the **plus sign** in the middle of the bottom bar, and select **Mail Link to this Page** (see Figure 17–6). This creates an e-mail message with the link that you can send.

Figure 17–6. *Email a link to a web page.*

Printing a Web Page

The iPhone (at the time of this writing) does not have a built-in **Print** command. You have a couple of options, but neither is very simple.

- *Option 1:* Email yourself or a colleague the web page link and print it from a computer. If you are traveling and staying at a hotel with a business center, you may be able to send it to someone at the business center or front desk to print the page.

- *Option 2:* Buy a network printing app from the **App Store** that allows you to print to a networked printer. Of course, this only works if you have access to a networked printer. It's usually best if you do this from your home or office network and can get help setting up, as doing so can be challenging.

Watching Videos in Safari

You will find videos in web sites. You will be able to play many but not all videos. Those formatted with Adobe Flash will not be playable on your iPhone (see our note at the beginning of this chapter).

When you tap the play button, you will be taken out of Safari into the iPod video player.

You can then turn your iPhone on its side to view the video in landscape, or wide-screen, mode.

Tap the screen to bring up the player controls if they have disappeared.

When you are finished watching the video and want to return to the web page, tap the **Done** button in the upper left corner.

> **TIP:** Check out all the video player tips and tricks in Chapter 16, "Viewing Videos, TV Shows and More."

Saving or Copying Text and Graphics

From time to time, you may see text or a graphic you want to copy from a web site. We tell you briefly how to do this in this section, but to see graphically how to get it done, including using the **Cut** and **Paste** functions, please see the "Copy and Paste" section in Chapter 2: "Typing Tips, Copy/Pate and Search." Here's a quick look:

To copy a single word, touch and hold the word until you see it highlighted and the **Copy** button appears. Then tap **Copy.**

To copy a few words or entire paragraph, touch and hold a word until it is highlighted. Then drag the blue dots left or right to select more text. You can flick up or down to select an entire paragraph. Then tap **Copy**.

> **TIP:** Selecting a single word puts the copy feature in word-selection mode, where you can drag to increase or decrease the number of words selected. If you go past a single paragraph, it will typically switch to element-selection mode where, instead of corners, you get edges that you can drag out to select multiple paragraphs, images, and so on.

To **Save** or **Copy** a graphic, touch and hold the picture or image until you see the pop-up asking if you would like to **Save** or **Copy** the image.

Saving Time with AutoFill

AutoFill is a great way to save time typing your personal information including usernames and passwords on web sites. The AutoFill tool can remember and fill in information required in web forms. You will save a lot of time by enabling AutoFill.

Check out the steps we show you later in this chapter in the "Enabling AutoFill" section to set up AutoFill to work on your iPhone.

Once **AutoFill** is enabled, just go to any web page that has a field to fill out. As soon as you touch the field, the keyboard will come up at the bottom of the screen. At the top of the keyboard, you will see a small button that says **AutoFill**. Touch it, and the web form should be filled out automatically.

> **CAUTION:** Having your name and password entered automatically means that anyone who picks up your iPhone will be able to access your personal sites and information. You may want to use passcode security as we show you in Chapter 9: "Personalize and Secure Your iPhone."

For Usernames and Passwords

The first time you go to a web site where you have to enter a username and password, you type them and press **Submit** or **Enter**. At that time, AutoFill will ask if you want to remember them.

Tap **Yes** if you want them to be remembered and next time automatically entered.

The next time you visit this login page, your username and password will be automatically filled in.

For Personal Information

There are many times on the web where you have to enter your name, e-mail address, home address, and more. With AutoFill set up and tied to your contact record on the iPhone, filling in these forms just takes a single tap of your finger.

You will go to many sites with web forms that need to be completed. Take this example of a web form on www.madesimplelearning.com for free iPhone tips. It would take a while to manually type your e-mail address, first, and last name.

As soon as you tap the first field to type, in this case **Email**, you see the AutoFill bar appear just above your keyboard.

Tap the **AutoFill** button, and your e-mail address and name are immediately filled in from your contact record.

Adding a Web Page Icon to Your Home Screen

If you love a web site or page, it's very easy to add it as an icon to your **Home Screen**. That way, you can instantly access the web page without going through the **Safari ➤ Bookmarks** bookmark selection process. You'll save lots of steps by putting the icon on your **Home Screen** (see Figure 17–7). This is especially good for quickly launching web apps, like Gmail or Buzz from Google, or web app games.

Here's how to add the icon:

1. Touch the **plus sign** ➕ at the bottom of the browser.

2. Touch **Add to Home Screen**.

3. Adjust the name to shorten it to about 10 or fewer characters, because there's not much room for the name of the icon on your Home screen.

4. Tap the **Add** button in the upper right corner.

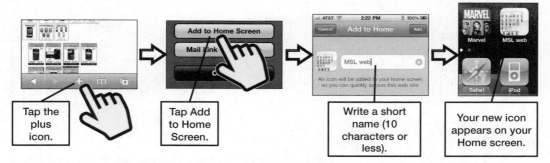

Figure 17–7. *How to add an icon for a web page to your Home Screen.*

Adjusting the Safari Browser Settings

As with other settings we've adjusted so far, the settings for Safari are found in the **Settings** app.

1. To access settings for **Safari**, tap the **Settings** icon.

2. Tap **Safari**.

Changing the Search Engine

By default, the search engine for the Safari browser is **Google**. To change this to **Yahoo** or **Bing**, just touch the **Search Engine** button and then choose the new search engine.

Adjusting Security Options

Under the **Security** heading, **Fraud Warning, JavaScript**, and **Block Pop-ups** should, by default, be set to **ON**. You can modify either of these by just sliding the switch to **OFF**.

> **NOTE:** Many popular sites like Facebook require JavaScript to be ON.

Tap the **Accept Cookies** button to adjust to accept cookies **Always, Never,** or **From visited**. We recommend keeping it as **From visited**. If you make it **Never**, some web sites will not work properly.

Speeding Up Your Browser by Clearing History and Cookies

On the bottom of the Safari settings screen, you can see the **Clear History, Clear Cookies,** and **Clear Cache** buttons.

If you notice your web browsing getting sluggish, it's probably a good time to clear out all three of these by tapping them and confirming your choices.

> **TIP:** Clearing the history, cookies, and cache is also a good privacy measure, as it prevents others from seeing where you've been browsing.

Enabling AutoFill

As we showed you earlier in this chapter, AutoFill is a convenient way to have Safari automatically fill out web page forms that ask for your name, address, phone number, or even username and password. It can save you a tremendous amount of time typing and retyping your name and other information.

To enable **AutoFill**, follow these steps:

1. From the **Safari** menu in the **Settings** app, tap **AutoFill**.

Settings	Safari	
General		
Search Engine		Bing >
AutoFill		Off >

2. Set the switch next to **Names & Passwords** to **ON**.

3. Set the switch next to **Use Contact Info** to **ON**.

Safari	AutoFill	
Use Contact Info		ON
My Info		Martin Trautschold >
Names & Passwords		ON
	Clear All	
Automatically fill out web forms using your contact info or previous names and passwords.		

4. After setting **Use Contact Info** to **ON**, you will be brought to your **Contacts** list to select a contact to use.

5. Swipe up and down to find someone, or double-tap the top bar that says **Contacts** to bring up the search window.

6. Once you find the contact you want to use, tap it to be returned to the Safari settings screen.

Chapter 18

Email on Your iPhone

In this chapter, we will help you explore the world of email in the **Mail** app on your iPhone. You will learn how to set up multiple email accounts, check out all the various reading options, open attachments, and clean up your Inbox.

If you had an earlier version of the iPhone before your new iPhone 4, you will be pleased with the new Unified Inbox feature that lets you see all your email in a single inbox. You will also enjoy the new threaded message feature where all messages related to a single topic (replies, forwards, and so on) are kept together in a single group.

And for cases when your email is not working quite right, you will learn some good troubleshooting tips to help you get back up and running.

Getting Started with Mail

Setting up email on your iPhone is fairly simple. You can sync email account settings from **iTunes** (see the "Sync Email Account Settings" section in Chapter 3: "Sync Your iPhone with iTunes"), or you can set up email accounts directly on your iPhone. You do need a network connection to get email up and running.

A Network Connection Is Required

Mobile email is certainly all the rage today. You can view, read, and compose replies to emails already synced to your iPhone without a network connection; however, you will need to have network connectivity (either Wi-Fi or 3G/cellular) to send and/or receive email from your iPhone. Check out Chapter 5: "Wi-Fi and 3G Connectivity" to learn more. Also check out the "Reading the Top Connectivity Status Icons" section in the Quick Start Guide in Part 1.

> **TIP:** If you are taking a trip, simply download all your email before you get on the airplane; this lets you read, reply, and compose your messages while offline. All emails will be sent after you land and re-establish your connection to the Internet.

Setting up Email on the iPhone

As mentioned a moment ago, you have two options for setting up your email accounts on the iPhone:

1. Use iTunes to sync email account settings.

2. Set up your email accounts directly on the iPhone.

If you have a number of email accounts that you access from an email program on your computer (e.g., **Microsoft Outlook**, **Entourage**, and so on), then the easiest approach is to use **iTunes** to sync your accounts. See the "Sync Email Account Settings" section in Chapter 3: "Sync Your iPhone with iTunes" for help.

If you only have a few accounts, or you do not use an email program on your computer that **iTunes** can sync with, then you will need to set up your email accounts directly on the iPhone.

Entering Passwords for Email Accounts Synced from iTunes

In the "Sync Email Account Settings" section of Chapter 3, we showed you how to sync your email account settings to your iPhone. After this sync completes, you should be able to view all of the email accounts your iPhone by opening the **Settings** app. All you will need to do is enter the password for each account.

To enter your password for each synced email account, follow these steps (see Figure 12–1):

1. Tap the **Settings** icon.

2. Tap the **Mail, Contacts, and Calendars** option.

3. Under **Accounts**, you should see all your synced email accounts listed.

4. Tap any listed email account, type its password, and click **Done**.

5. Repeat for all listed email accounts.

Figure 18–1. *Entering passwords for each email account synced from iTunes.*

Adding a New Email Account on the iPhone

To add a new email account on your iPhone, follow these steps:

1. Tap the **Settings** icon.

2. Tap the **Mail, Contacts, and Calendars** option.

3. Tap **Add Account** below your email accounts.

   If you have no accounts set up, you will only see the **Add Account** option.

> **TIP:** To edit any email account, just touch that account.

4. Choose which type of email account to
   add on this screen.

   ■ Choose **Microsoft Exchange** if you use
     a Microsoft Exchange email server.

   ■ You should also choose **Microsoft
     Exchange** if you use Google Calendar
     and Google Contacts to store your
     personal information, and you want to
     wirelessly sync them to your iPhone.

   ■ Choose **MobileMe** if you use this
     service.

> **NOTE:** We will show you how to set up both
> **Google/Microsoft Exchange** and **MobileMe** in Chapter 4:
> "Other Sync Methods."

   ■ Choose **Gmail** if you use Google for only
     your email, but you do *not* (or do *not* want
     to) wirelessly sync email with your **Google
     Contacts**.

   ■ Choose **Yahoo!** if you use Yahoo!

   ■ Choose **AOL** if you use AOL.

   ■ Choose **Other** if none of the above apply,
     and you want to sync a standard POP or
     IMAP email account. Then choose **Add
     Mail Account** from the next screen.

5. Type your name as you would like others to see
   it when they receive mail from you into the
   Name field.

6. Next, add the appropriate information into the
   Address, **Password**, and **Description** fields.

7. Tap the **Next** button in the upper right corner.

Specifying Incoming and Outgoing Servers

Sometimes, the iPhone will not be able to automatically set up your email account. In these cases, you will need to type in a few more settings manually to enable your email account.

> **TIP:** You may be able to find the settings for your email provider by doing a web search for your email provider's name and "email settings." For example, if you use **Windows Live Hotmail** (formerly known as Hotmail), then you might search for "POP or IMAP email settings for Hotmail." If you cannot find these settings, then contact your email provider for assistance.

If the iPhone is unable to log in to your server with only your email address and password, then you see a screen similar to this one.

Under **Incoming Mail Server**, type the appropriate information into the **Host Name**, **User Name**, and **Password** fields. Usually, your incoming mail server is something like mail.*name_of_your_isp*.com.

To adjust the name of your outgoing server, tap **Outgoing Mail Server.** You can adjust the outgoing mail server on the following screen. These server names usually look like either smtp.*name_of_your_isp*.com or mail.*name_of_your_isp*.com.

You can try to leave the **Server Name** and **Password** fields blank. If that doesn't work, you can always go back and change them.

You may be asked if you want to use SSL (secure socket layer), a type of outgoing mail security that may be required by your email provider. If you don't know whether you need it or not, just check the mail settings with your email provider.

> **TIP:** The authors recommend that you use SSL security whenever possible. If you do not use SSL, then your login credentials, messages, and any private information is sent in plain text (unencrypted), leaving it open to snoopers.

Verifying that Your Account Is Set Up

Once all the information is entered, the iPhone will attempt to configure your email account. You may get an error message; if that happens, you need to review the information you input.

If you are taken to the screen that shows all your email accounts, look for the new account name.

If you see it, your account was set up correctly.

Fixing the Cannot Get Mail Error

If you tap **Mail** icon and you receive an error that says "Cannot Get Mail – No password provided for (your account)," you will need to enter your password.

Review this chapter's "Enter Passwords for Email Accounts Synced from iTunes" section for help

A Tour of Your Mail Screens

Now that you have set up your email accounts on your iPhone, it's time to take a brief tour of the **Mail** app. To better understand how to get around your **Mail** program, it helps to have a picture of how all the screens fit together (see Figure 18-2).

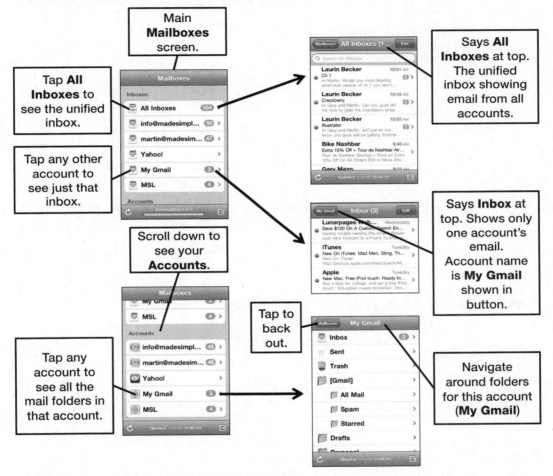

Figure 18–2. *How all the Screens in the Mail app fit together.*

Mailboxes Screen - Inboxes and Accounts

The top level screen is your **Mailboxes** screen. You can always get to it by tapping the button in the upper left corner. Keep tapping this upper left button until you see no more buttons. When that happens, you are in the **Mailboxes** screen.

From the **Mailboxes** screen you can access the following items:

- *The unified inbox*: Do so by tapping **All inboxes**.

- *The inbox for each individual account*: Do this by tapping that email account name in the Inboxes section.

- The folders for each email account in the **Accounts** section: Do so by tapping the account name to see all folders.

Inbox and Threaded Messages Views

You will notice that any unread messages are marked with a blue dot ● to the left of the message (see Figure 18-3).

You will also notice that some messages show a number and a right-facing arrow (>) to the right of the message, like this: **2** > This shows that there are two related messages (replies and forwards) to the message shown.

Tap any message to open it. The only time it will not open is if there are related messages. In that case, you will first see a screen with all the related messages. Tap any of those messages to open and view them.

To leave the **Inbox** view, tap the button in the upper left corner.

You can tell which email account you are viewing by looking at the button in the upper left corner.

- If the button says **Mailboxes**, you know you are looking at all your inboxes together.

- If the button says an account name, such as **martin@madesimplelearning.com**, then you know you are only looking at the inbox for that account.

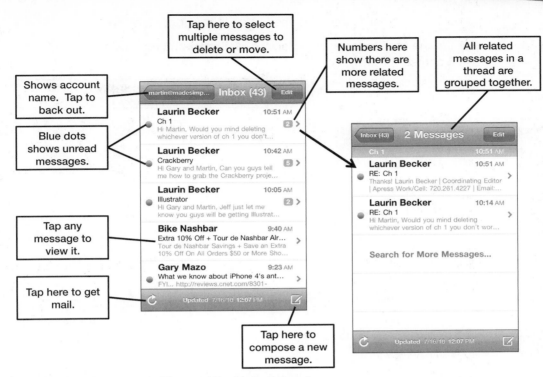

Figure 18–3. *Inboxes on your iPhone and threaded message views.*

Moving Around in Mail Folders

You can get around your mail folders for each individual account by starting from the **Mailboxes** screen shown In Figure 18-4:

1. Swipe down to the bottom of the **Mailboxes** screen to see your accounts.

2. Tap any account to view all folders synced in that account.

> **NOTE:** You will only see those mail folders you have chosen to sync during the mail set up process. For example, you might have 20 mail folders on your main mail account, but you might only see a few folders on your iPhone. The default synced mail folders are **Inbox**, **Sent**, **Draft**, and **Deleted Items**.

3. You may need to swipe to the bottom to see all your synced email folders.

4. Tap any folder to view the mail items in that folder.

5. To get back to the mail folders, tap the button in the upper left corner.

6. To return to the **Mailboxes** screen, tap the **Mailboxes** button in the upper left corner.

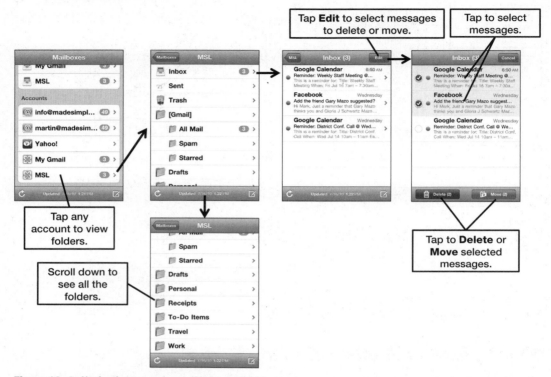

Figure 18–4. *Navigating around your iPhone mail folders.*

Move or Delete Multiple Messages

If you want to move or delete several messages at once, you can do so from the **Inbox** screen (see the right-most two images in Figure 18-4). Follow these steps to delete multiple messages at once:

1. Tap the **Edit** button in the upper right corner while you are viewing an **Inbox** screen.

2. Tap to select the desired messages; a red check mark next to a message indicates it is selected.

3. To delete the messages, tap the **Delete** button at the bottom.

4. To move the messages to another folder, tap the **Move** button and select the folder.

Viewing an Individual Message

When you tap a message from the **Inbox** screen, you see the **Main** message view.

Portrait View

Holding your iPhone in **Portrait** (vertical) orientation gives you the image shown in Figure 18-5. We will describe the various buttons and functions shown on this screen later in this chapter.

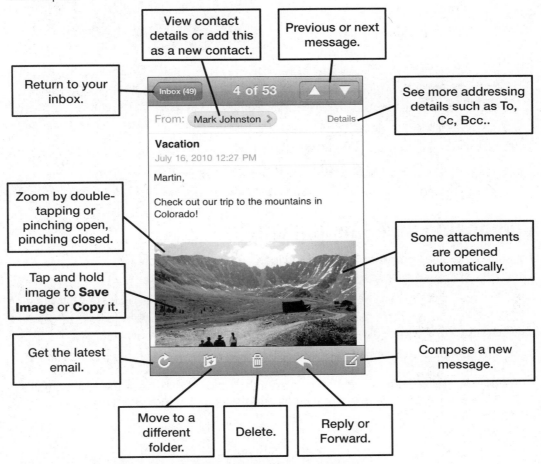

View contact details or add this as a new contact.

Previous or next message.

Return to your inbox.

See more addressing details such as To, Cc, Bcc..

Zoom by double-tapping or pinching open, pinching closed.

Some attachments are opened automatically.

Tap and hold image to **Save Image** or **Copy** it.

Get the latest email.

Compose a new message.

Move to a different folder.

Delete.

Reply or Forward.

Figure 18–5. *Buttons and actions available while viewing an email message.*

Landscape View

You may prefer to use the wider screen view, especially when enjoying pictures. To do this, just turn your iPhone on its side to get the **Landscape** orientation.

TIP: If you are setting your iPhone down on a desk or holding it in your lap, then you may want to use the **Portrait Lock** icon to lock your view in **Portrait** (vertical) mode. This will prevent the image from flipping around unnecessarily. To lock the view, follow these steps:

1. Double-tap the **Home** button and swipe left to right.

2. Tap the **Portrait Lock** button to lock the screen in **Portrait** mode.

Composing and Sending Emails

To launch the email program, tap the **Mail** icon on your **Home** screen.

TIP: If you left the **Mail** app while viewing a particular email, list of folders, or an account, then you will be returned directly to that same location when you return to the **Mail** app.

If you are going into your email for the first time, you may see an empty **Inbox**. Hit the **Refresh** button in the lower left corner of the window to retrieve the latest email. The iPhone will begin to check for new mail and then display the number of new messages for each account.

Composing a New Email Message

When you start the **Mail** program, your first screen should be your **Accounts** screen. At the bottom right corner of the screen, you will see the **Compose** icon. Touch the **Compose** icon to get started creating a new message.

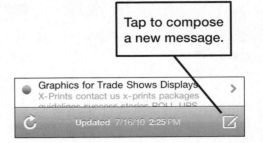

Tap to compose a new message.

Addressing Your Message - Choose the Recipients

You have a few options for selecting recipients, depending on whether the person is in your **Contact List** on your iPhone:

Option 1: Type a few letters of someone's first name; hit the **Space** key, and then type a few letters of that person's last name. The person's name should appear in the list; tap that person's name to select that contact.

Option 2: Type an email address. Notice the **@** and **Period (.)** keys on the bottom, which help your typing.

> **TIP:** Press and hold the **period** key to see **.com**, **.edu**, **.org**, and other email domain name suffixes.

Option 3: Hit the **+** sign to view your entire **Contact List** and search or select a name from it.

If you want to use a different contact group, tap the **Groups** button in the upper left screen.

Double-tap **Contacts** at the top of the screen to see the **Search** window. Next, type a few letters to search for your contact.

Deleting a Recipient

If you need to delete a name from the recipient list (**To:**, **Cc:**, or **Bcc:**), tap the name to select it   To: martha@abcco.com   and hit the **Backspace** key   .

> **TIP:** If you want to delete the last recipient you typed (and the cursor is sitting next to that name), hit the **Delete** key once to highlight the name and hit it a second time to delete it.

Adding a CC or BCC Recipient

To add a carbon copy (**Cc:**) or blind carbon copy (**Bcc:**) recipient, you need to tap the **Cc:/Bcc:** just under the **To:** field at the top of the email message. Doing so opens up the tapped field.

Changing the Email Account to Send From

If you have more than one email account set up, the iPhone will use whichever account is set as the default account. (This is set in **Settings** > **Mail, Contacts, Calendars** > **Default Account** at the bottom of the **Mail** section.)

Follow these steps to change the email account you send from:

1. Tap an email's **From:** field to highlight it.

2. Tap the **From:** field again to see a list of your accounts in a scroll wheel at the bottom of the screen.

3. Scroll up or down, and then tap a new email account to select it.

4. Tap the **Subject** field to finish changing the sending email address.

Type Your Subject

Now you need to enter a subject for your email. Follow these steps to do so:

1. Touch the **Subject:** line and enter text for the **Subject:** field of the email.

2. Press the **Return** key or tap the **Body** section of the email to move the cursor to the **Body** section.

Typing Your Message

Now that the cursor is in the body of the email (under the subject line), you can start typing your email message.

Email Signatures

The default email signature is shown in the image to the right: **Sent from my iPhone**.

> **TIP:** You can change this signature to be anything you want; see the "Changing Your Email Signature" section later in this chapter to learn how to change your email signature.

Keyboard Options

While you are typing, remember you have two keyboard options: the smaller **Portrait** (vertical) keyboard and the larger **Landscape** (horizontal) keyboard (see Figure 18–6).

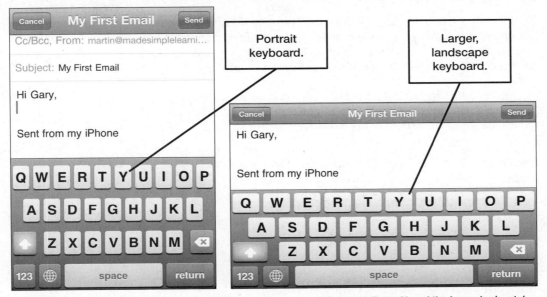

Figure 18–6. *You have two built-in keyboards: the smaller vertical keyboard (Portrait) and the larger horizontal one (Landscape).*

> **TIP:** If you have larger hands, it might be easier to type when the keyboard is larger. Once you get the hang of typing on the larger keyboard with two hands, you will find that it is much faster than typing with one finger. See Chapter 2: "Typing Tips, Copy/Paste, and Search" for more typing tips.

Auto Correction, Auto Capitalization, Period Trick, Spell Checking, and More

As you type, you will notice that some words will be auto-capitalized and automatically corrected. Red underlined words are flagged as misspelled by the spelling checker. See Chapter 2: "Typing Tips, Copy/Paste, and Search" to learn how these all functions work, as well as for some additional typing tips.

Send Your Email

Once you have typed your message, tap the blue **Send** button in the top right corner.

Your email will be sent, and you should hear the iPhone's sent mail sound, which confirms that your email was sent. You can learn how to enable or disable this sound in the "Adjusting Sounds on your iPhone" section of Chapter 9: "Personalize and Secure your iPhone."

Save As Draft to Send Later

If you are not ready to send your message, but want to save it as a draft message to send later, follow these steps:

1. Compose your message, as described earlier.

2. Press the **Cancel** button in the upper left corner.

3. Select the **Save Draft** button at the bottom of the screen.

Later, when you want to locate and send your draft message, follow these steps:

1. Open the **Drafts** folder in the email account from which you composed this message. See the "Moving Around in Mail Folders" section earlier in this chapter for help getting into the **Drafts** folder.

2. Tap the email message in the **Drafts** folder to open it.

3. Tap anywhere in the message to edit it.

4. Tap the **Send** button.

Checking Sent Messages

Follow these steps to confirm that the email was sent correctly:

1. Tap the **Email account name** button in the upper left corner to see the mail folders for the account you just used to send your message.

2. Tap the **Sent** folder.

3. Verify that that the top email you see in the list is the one you just composed and sent.

> **NOTE:** You will only see the **Sent** and **Trash** folders if you have actually sent or deleted email from that account on the iPhone. If your email account is an IMAP account, you may see many folders other than those described in this chapter.

Reading and Replying to Mail

Follow these steps to read your email:

1. Navigate to the **Inbox** of the email account you want to view using the steps described earlier in this chapter.

2. To read any message, just touch it from your **Inbox**.

3. New, unread messages are shown with a small blue dot to the left of the message.

4. Flick your finger up or down in the **Inbox** to scroll through your messages.

5. When you are reading a message, swipe up or down to scroll through it.

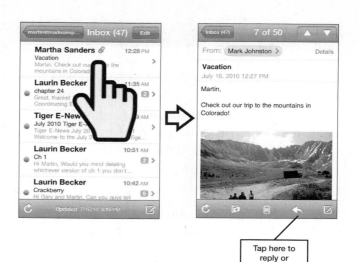

Tap here to reply or forward.

Zooming In or Out

As when browsing the Web, you can zoom in to see your email in larger text. You can also double-tap, just as you do on the Web; and you can also **Pinch** to zoom in or out (see the "Zooming" section in our Quick Started Guide in Part 1 of this book for more information on these features.)

Email Attachments

Some email attachments are opened automatically by the iPhone, so you don't even notice that they were attachments. Examples of these include Adobe's portable document format (**PDF**) files (used by **Adobe Acrobat** and **Adobe Reader**, among other apps) and some types of image, video, and audio files. You may also receive documents such as Apple **Pages**, **Numbers**, **Keynote**, Microsoft **Word**, **Excel**, and **PowerPoint** files as attachments. You will need to open these.

Knowing When You Have an Attachment

Any email with an attachment will have a little **Paperclip** icon next to the sender's name, as shown to the right. When you see that icon, you know you have anattachment.

This paperclip shows the message has an attachment.

Receiving an Auto-open Attachment

Now assume you received a one-page **PDF** file or an image. (Multipage **PDF** files require that you tap to open them.) Once you open the mail message with this kind of attachment, you will see it directly below the message (see Figure 18–7).

This attachment was opened automatically.

These two attachment need to be tapped in order to view them.

Figure 18–7. *Some attachments will open automatically, while others will need to be tapped to be opened.*

TIP: If you want to save or copy an auto-opened attachment, simply press and hold it until you see the popup window. At this point, you can select **Copy** or **Save Image**. When you save an image, it will be placed in your **Photos** app in the **Camera Roll** album.

Opening Email Attachments

Instead of immediately opening in the body of the email as we just described, other types of attachments, such as spreadsheets, word processing documents, and presentation files, will need to be opened manually.

Tap for Quick Look Mode

Follow these steps to open attachments in **Quick Look** mode:

1. Open the message with an attachment (see Figure 18–8).

2. Quickly tap the attachment to instantly open it in **Quick Look** mode.

3. You can navigate around the document. Remember you can zoom in or out and swipe up or down.

4. If you open a spreadsheet with multiple tabs or spreadsheets, you will see tabs across the top. Touch another tab to open that spreadsheet.

5. When you are done looking at the attachment, tap the document once to bring up the controls, and then tap **Done** in the upper left corner.

6. If you have apps installed that can open the type of attachment you are viewing (in this case a spreadsheet), then you will see an **Open In** button in the upper right corner. Tap the **Open In** button to open this file in another app.

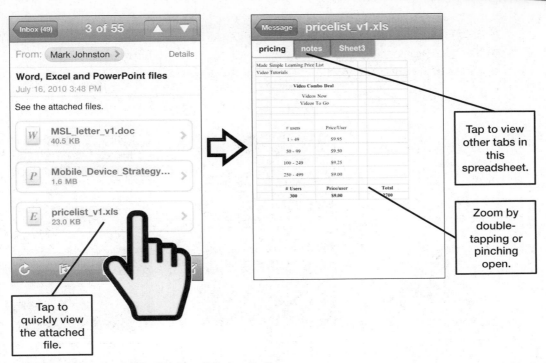

Figure 18–8. *Quickly viewing attachments by tapping them.*

Opening Docs in Other Apps

You may want to open the attachment in another application. For example, you might want to open a **PDF** file in **iBooks, Stanza** or **GoodReader.** Follow these steps to do so:

1. Open the email message.

2. Press and hold the attachment until you see the popup window.

3. Select the **Open In** option.

4. Select the application you would like to use from the list (Figure 18–9 shows the user choosing **Stanza**).

5. Finally, you can edit the document, save it, and email it back to the sender.

TIP: We have heard rumors that the Apple word processor, spreadsheet and presentation software (**Pages**, **Numbers**, and **Keynote**) is coming soon to the iPhone. Our *iPad Made Simple* book (Apress, 2010) includes descriptions of these apps because they are already available for the iPad.

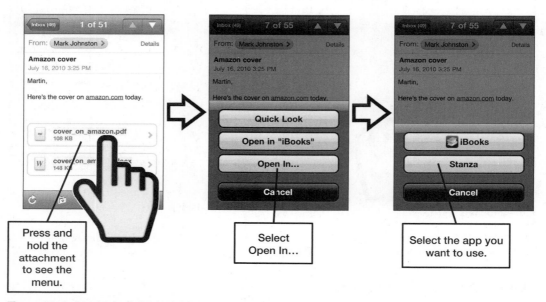

Figure 18–9. *Opening and viewing attachments in other apps*

Viewing a Video Attachment

You may receive a video as an attachment to an email. Certain types of videos can be viewed on your iPhone (see the "Supported Email Attachment Types" section later in this chapter for a list of supported video formats). Follow these steps to open a video attachment:

1. Tap the video attachment to open it and view it in the video player.

2. When you are done viewing the video, tap the screen to bring up the player controls.

3. Tap the **Done** button in the upper left corner to return to the email message.

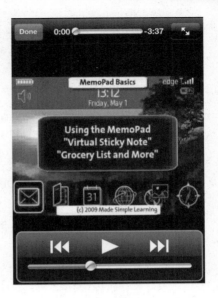

Opening and Viewing Compressed .zip Files

Your iPhone will not be able to open and view a compressed file of .zip format unless you install an app such as GoodReader. At publishing time, GoodReader was still a free app and well worth installing.

> **TIP:** Learn how to install and use GoodReader it in Chapter 15: "New Media: Reading Newspapers, Magazines, and More."

1. Install the free **GoodReader** from the **App Store**.

2. Open up the email message with the **.zip** file attachment.

3. Touch and hold the .zip attachment until you see a pop-up at the bottom with a button that says **Open in "GoodReader".** Tap that button to open the .zip in **GoodReader**.

CAUTION: Do not just quickly tap the attachment to open it. At publishing time, this resulted in a blank white or black screen with nothing happening. Make sure to touch and hold the attachment until you see the button pop-up.

4. **GoodReader** should now open and your .zip file should be at the top of the list of files. To open or uncompress the .zip file, tap the file and select the **Unzip** button.

5. Now you should see the uncompressed file, in this case an Adobe **.pdf** file in the list of files above the **.zip** file.

6. **Tap that uncompressed file to view it.

7. When you are done reading the attachment, double-click your **Home** button and tap the **Mail** icon to return to your reading your email.

Issues When Opening Email Attachments

When you try to open an attachment, you may get an error message similar to the one shown to the right. In this example, we tried to click an attachment of the type **winmail.dat**, which failed.

Attachments with a ? icon are not able to be opened on your iPhone.

Supported Email Attachment Types

Your iPhone supports the following file types as attachments:

- **.doc** and **.docx** (**Microsoft Word** documents)
- **.htm** and **.html** (web pages)
- **.key** (a **Keynote** presentation document)
- **.numbers** (an **Apple Numbers** spreadsheet document)
- **.pages** (an **Apple Pages** document)
- **.pdf** (Adobe's portable document format, used by programs such as **Adobe Acrobat** and **Adobe Reader**)
- **.ppt** and **.pptx** (**Microsoft PowerPoint** presentation documents)
- **.txt** (a text file)
- **.vcf** (a contact file)
- **.xls** and **.xlsx** (Microsoft Excel spreadsheet documents)
- **.mp3** and **.mov** (audio and video formats)
- **.zip** (compressed files) these are only readable if you have an app installed that can read them such as **GoodReader** - see the "Opening and Viewing Compressed .zip Files" section in this chapter.
- Audio formats supported:
  - HE-AAC (V1)
  - AAC (16 to 320 Kbps)

- Protected AAC (from iTunes Store)
- MP3 (16 to 320 Kbps)
- MP3 VBR
- Audible (formats 2, 3, and 4)
- Apple Lossless
- AIFF
- WAV
- Video formats supported:
    - H.264 video up to 720p at 30 frames per second
    - Main Profile level 3.1 with AAC-LC audio up to 160 Kbps, 48kHz
    - Stereo audio in **.m4v**, **.mp4**, and **.mov** file formats
    - MPEG-4 video, up to 2.5 Mbps, 640 by 480 pixels, and at 30 frames per second
    - Simple Profile with AAC-LC audio up to 160 Kbps, 48kHz, stereo audio in **.m4v**, **.mp4**, and **.mov** file formats
    - Motion JPEG (M-JPEG) up to 35 Mbps, 1280 by 720 pixels, 30 frames per second, and audio in ulaw
    - PCM stereo audio in **.avi** file format

Replying, Forwarding, or Deleting a Message

At the bottom of your email-reading pane is a toolbar.

From this toolbar, you can move the message to a different mailbox or folder; delete it; or reply, reply all, or forward it.

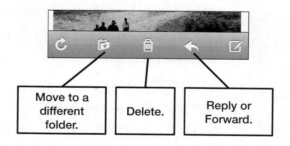

Move to a different folder.

Delete.

Reply or Forward.

Touch the small arrow to see these option buttons appear: **Reply**, **Reply All**, and **Forward**.

> **NOTE:** The **Reply All** button appears only if there was more than one recipient for the email message.

Replying to an Email

You will probably use the **Reply** command most frequently. Follow these steps to respond to an email on your iPhone:

1. Touch the **Reply** button.

   You will see that the original sender is now listed as the recipient in the **To:** line of the email. The subject will automatically state: "Re: *(Original subject line).*"

2. Type your response.

3. When you are done, just touch the blue **Send** button at the top right corner of the screen.

Using Reply All

Using the **Reply All** option is just like using the **Reply** function, except that all of the original recipients of the email and the original sender are placed in the address lines. The original sender will be in the **To:** line, while all other recipients of the original email will be listed on the **Cc:** line. You will only see the **Reply All** option if more than one person received the original email.

CAUTION: Be careful when you use **REPLY ALL**. This can be dangerous if some of the recipients are not shown on the original email because they stretch off the edge of the screen. If you do use **REPLY ALL**, then make sure your check the **To:** and **Cc:** lists to make sure everyone should be receiving your reply.

Using the Forward Button

Sometimes, you get an email that you want to send to someone else. The **Forward** command will let you do that (see the "Email Attachments" section in this chapter for more about working with attachments.)

NOTE: You need to forward attachments to send them to others. If you want to send someone an attachment from an email you receive, you must choose the **Forward** option. (Note that choosing the **Reply** and **Reply All** options will not include the original email attachment(s) in your outgoing message.)

When you touch the **Forward** button, you may be prompted to address whether you want to include attachments (if there were any) from the original message.

At this point, you follow the same steps described previously to type your message, add addressees, and send it.

Cleaning up and Organizing Your Inbox

As you get more comfortable with your iPhone as an email device, you will increasingly find yourself using the **Mail** program. It will eventually become necessary to occasionally do some email housecleaning. You can delete or move email messages easily on your iPhone.

Deleting a Single Message

To delete a single message from your **Inbox**, follow these steps:

1. Swipe right or left on a message in the **Inbox** to bring up the **Delete** button.

2. Tap **Delete** to remove the message.

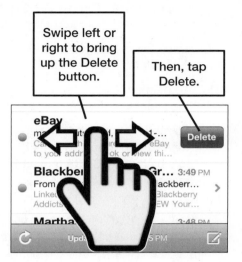

Deleting or Moving Several Messages

It's easy to delete several messages on the iPhone. Follow these steps to do so.

1. View any mail folder on your iPhone.

2. Tap the **Edit** button.

3. Select one or more messages by tapping them. You will see a red check mark for each selected message.

4. Once the messages are selected, you can delete or move them.

5. To delete the selected messages, tap the **Delete** button at the bottom.

6. To move the selected messages, tap the **Move** button and select the folder to which you want to move the messages.

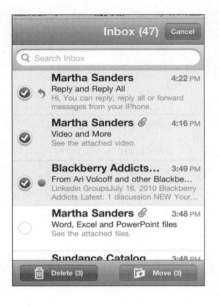

TIP: You do not get another prompt before the messages are moved to the **Trash** or **Archived** folder. If you need to restore any of these messages, navigate to your **Trash** folder and move the messages back to your Inbox folder. Exchange and IMAP email accounts will sync these folder moves to your email server, POP3 accounts will not.

Deleting from the Message Screen

The **Message** screen includes another way to delete messages. Follow these steps to do so:

1. Open any message to read it.

2. Tap the **Trash Can** icon in the middle of the bottom of the screen.

   You will see the email shrink and fly into the **Trash Can**, so it can be deleted.

TIP: You can use the **Settings** app to make your iPhone ask you before deleting email. To do so, tap **Mail, Contacts, Calendars** and set the switch next to **Ask Before Deleting** to **Yes**.

You can organize your mail by moving it into other folders. Email messages can be moved out of your **Inbox** for storage or for reading at another time.

NOTE: To create folders in addition to the default **Inbox** and **Trash** folders, you need to set them up in your main email account and sync them to your iPhone. We will show you how to do this in this chapter's "Fine Tune Your Email Settings" section.

Moving an Email to a Folder While Viewing It

Sometimes, you may want to organize your email for easy retrieval later. For example, you might receive an email about an upcoming trip and want to move it to the **Travel** folder. Sometimes you receive emails that require attention later, in which case you can move them to the **Requires Attention** folder. This can help you remember to work on such emails later.

Follow these steps to move an email message:

1. Open the email message.

2. Tap the **Move** icon in the upper right corner.

3. Choose a new folder, and the message will be moved out of the **Inbox**.

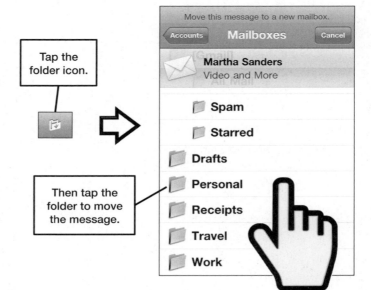

Tap the folder icon.

Then tap the folder to move the message.

Move this message to a new mailbox.

Accounts   **Mailboxes**   Cancel

Martha Sanders
Video and More

Spam

Starred

Drafts

Personal

Receipts

Travel

Work

Copy-and-Paste from an Email

Here are a few tips to select text or pictures and copy them from an email message:

- Double-tap text to select a word, then drag the blue handles up or down to adjust the selection.

  Next, select **Copy**.

- Press and hold text, and then choose **Select** or **Select All**.

- Press and hold an image, and then select **Save Image** or **Copy**.

For a more complete description, please check out the "Copy and Paste" section in Chapter 2: "Typing Tips, Copy/Paste and Search."

Searching for Email Messages

The iPhone has some good built-in search functionality to help you find your emails. You can search your **Inbox** by the **From:**, **To:**, **Subject**, or **All** fields. This helps you filter your **Inbox**, so you can find exactly what you are searching for.

Activating Email Search

Get to the **Inbox** of the account you wish to search. If you scroll up to the top, you will now see the familiar **Search** bar at the top of your **Inbox** (see Figure 18–10).

If your email account supports the feature, you can also search the server for email messages. At the time of writing, a few of the supported types of searchable email accounts include **Exchange**, **MobileMe**, and **Gmail IMAP**. Follow these steps to search through your email on a server:

1. Touch the **Search** bar to see a new menu of soft keys under the **Search** bar.

2. Type the text you wish to search for.

3. Touch one of the soft keys under the search window:

    a. **From**: Searches only the sender's email addresses.

    b. **To**: Searches only the recipients' email addresses.

    c. **Subject**: Searches only message **Subject** fields.

    d. **All**: Searches every part of the message.

For example, assume I want to search my **Inbox** for an email I received from Martin. I would type Martin's name into the **Search** box and then touch **From**. My **Inbox** would then be filtered to show only the emails from Martin.

> **NOTE:** If you have multiple email accounts, you will not be able to search all of your inboxes at the same time because your iPhone only lets you search one inbox at a time. For a more global search on your iPhone, use the **Spotlight Search** feature shown in the "Finding Things with Spotlight Search" section of Chapter 2: "Typing Tips, Copy/Paste, and Search."

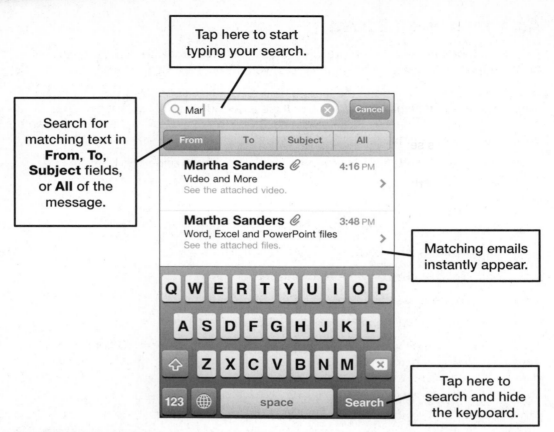

Tap here to start typing your search.

Search for matching text in **From, To, Subject** fields, or **All** of the message.

Matching emails instantly appear.

Tap here to search and hide the keyboard.

Figure 18–10. *Searching for email using the From, To, Subject, or all text fields.*

Fine Tuning Your Email Settings

You can fine tune your email accounts on your iPhone with the myriad options available in the **Settings** app.

Follow these steps to change these settings:

1. Tap the **Settings** icon.

2. Tap **Mail, Contacts, Calendars**.

The sections that follow explain the adjustments you can make.

Automatically Retrieve Email (Fetch New Data)

In addition to the options under **Advanced**, you can use the **Email** settings to configure how often your email is fetched or pulled to your iPhone. By default, your iPhone automatically receives mail or other contact or calendar updates when they are "pushed" from the server.

You can adjust this setting by taking the following steps:

1. Touch the **Settings** icon.

2. Touch **Mail, Contacts, Calendars**.

3. Touch **Fetch New Data** under the email accounts listed.

4. Set **Push** to **ON** (default) to automatically have the server push data. Turn It **OFF** to conserve your battery life.

5. Adjust the timing schedule to pull data from the server. This is how frequently applications should pull new data from the server.

> **NOTE:** If you set this option to **Every 15 Minutes**, you will receive more frequent updates, but sacrifice battery life compared to a setting of **Hourly**.

Having automatic retrieval is very handy if you just want to turn on your iPhone and see that you have messages; otherwise, you need to remember to check.

Advanced Push Options

At the bottom of the **Fetch New Data** screen, below the **Hourly** and **Manually** settings, you can touch the **Advanced** button to see a new screen with all your email accounts listed.

Tap any email account to adjust its settings.

Most accounts can be **Fetched** on the schedule you set or set to **Manual**. The Manual option requires that you retrieve data using the **Update** button. This screen gives you the ability to adjust **Fetch**, **Manual**, or in some cases **Push** settings for each account you have set up.

Adjusting Your Mail Settings

Under the **Accounts** section, you can see all the email settings listed under **Mail**. The **Default** settings may work well for you; but if you need to adjust any of these, you can follow these steps.

Show: This sets how many emails are pulled from the server. You can specify anywhere from 25 to 200 messages (the default is 50 recent messages).

Preview: This option lets you set how many lines of text in addition to the **Subject** are shown in the **Inbox** preview. You can adjust this value from **None** to **5 Lines** (the default is **2 Lines**).

Minimum Font Size: This is the default font size shown when opening an email the first time. It is also smallest font size that you are allowed to zoom out to when viewing an email. Your options are **Small**, **Medium**, **Large**, **Extra Large**, and **Giant** (the default is **Medium**).

Show To/Cc Label: With this option **ON**, you will see a small **To** or **Cc** label in your **Inbox** before the subject. This label shows which field your address was placed in (the default state of this option is **OFF**).

Ask Before Deleting: Turn this option **ON** to be asked every time you try to delete a message (the default is **OFF**).

Load Remote Images: This option allows your iPhone to load all the graphics (remote images) that are placed in some email messages (the default value for this option is **ON**).

Organize by Thread: This option groups related emails together. It shows only one message, with a number next to it. That number indicates how many related emails exist. This feature gives you a good way to keep all discussions together in one place (the default value of this option is **ON**).

Always Bcc Myself: This option sends a blind carbon copy (**Bcc:**) of every email you send from your iPhone to your email account (the default value of this option is **OFF**).

Changing Your Email Signature

By default, emails you send will say "Sent from my iPhone." Follow these steps to change the **Signature** line of the email:

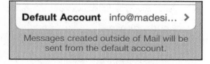

1. Tap the **Signature** tab and type in the new email signature you want at the bottom of emails sent from your iPhone.

2. When you are done editing the **Signature** field, tap the **Mail, Contacts...** button in the upper left corner. This will return you to the **Mail** settings screen.

Changing Your Default Mail Account (Sent From)

If you have multiple email accounts set up on your iPhone, you should set one of them – usually, the one you use most – as your **Default Account**. When you select **Compose** from the **Email** screen, the default account is always chosen. Follow these steps to change the email account you send from by default:

Default Account   info@madesi... >

Messages created outside of Mail will be sent from the default account.

1. Tap the **Default Account** option, and you will see a list of all your email accounts.

2. Tap the one you wish to use as your **Default Account** choice.

3. When you are done, touch the **Mail, Contacts...** button to return to the **Mail** settings menu.

Mail...	Default Account
info@madesimplelearning.com	
martin@madesimplelearning.com ✓	
Yahoo!	
My Gmail	
MSL	

Toggling Sounds for Receiving and Sending Email

You may notice a little sound effect every time you send or receive email. What you hear is the default setting on your iPhone.

If you want to disable this or change it, you do so in the **Settings** program:

1. Tap your **Settings** icon.

2. Tap **General**.

3. Tap **Sounds**.

4. You will see various switches to turn sound effects on or off. Tap **New Mail** and **Sent Mail** to adjust the **ON** or **OFF** options.

Advanced Email Options

NOTE: Email accounts set up as **Exchange**, **IMAP**, or **MobileMe** will not have this **Advanced** email settings screen. This only applies to POP3 email accounts.

To get to the **Advanced** options for each email account, follow these steps:

1. Touch the **Settings** icon.

2. Touch **Mail, Contacts, Calendars**.

3. Touch an email address listed under **Accounts**.

4. At the bottom of the mail settings popup window, tap the **Advanced** button to bring up the **Advanced** dialog.

Removing Email Messages from iPhone After Deletion

You can select how frequently you want email removed completely from your iPhone once it is deleted.

Touch the **Remove** tab and select the option that is best for you; the default setting is **Never**.

Using SSL/Authentication

These features were discussed previously, but this option supplies another location to access these features for a particular email account.

Deleting from Server

You can configure your iPhone to handle the deletion of messages from your email server. Usually, this setting is left at **Never**, and this function is handled on your main computer. If you use your iPhone as your main email device, however, you might want to handle that feature from the phone itself. Follow these steps to remove deleted emails on the server from your iPhone.

1. Touch the **Delete from Server** tab to select the feature that best suits your needs: **Never**, **Seven Days**, or **When removed from Inbox**.

2. The default setting is **Never**. If you want to choose **Seven Days**; that option should give you enough time to check email on your computer, as well as your iPhone, and then decide what to keep and what to get rid of.

Changing the Incoming Server Port

As you did with the **Outgoing Server Port** earlier, you can change the **Incoming Server Port** if you are having trouble receiving email. It is very rare that your troubles will be related to the port you receive mail on, which means that you will rarely need to change this number. If your email service provider gives you a different number, just touch the numbers and input a new port. The value for an **Incoming Server Port** is usually 995, 993, or 110; however, the port value could also be another number.

Troubleshooting Email Problems

Usually, your email works flawlessly on your iPhone. Sometimes, whether it is a server issue, a network connectivity issue, or an email service provider requirement; email may not work as flawless as you would hope.

More often than not, there is a simple setting that needs to be adjusted or a password that needs to be re-entered.

If you try out some of the troubleshooting tips that follow and your email is still not working, then your email server may just be down temporarily. Check with your email service provider to make sure your mail server is up and running; you might also check whether your provider has made any recent changes that would affect your settings.

> **TIP:** If these tips that follow do not solve the problem, please check out Chapter 29: "Troubleshooting" for more helpful tips and resources.

Email Isn't Being Received or Sent

If you can't send or receive email, your first step should be to verify you are connected to the Internet. Look for Wi-Fi or 3G connectivity in the upper left corner of your **Home** screen (see the "How Do I Know When I'm Connected?" section of "Quick Start Guide" for details).

Sometimes, you need to adjust the outgoing port for email to be sent properly. Do so by following these steps.

1. Tap **Settings**.

2. Touch **Mail, Contacts and Calendars**.

3. Touch your email account that is having trouble sending messages under **Accounts**.

4. Touch **SMTP** and verify that your outgoing mail server is set correctly; also check that it is set to **On**.

5. Touch **Outgoing Mail Server** at the top and verify all the settings, such as **Host Name**, **User Name**, **Password**, **SSL**, **Authentication**, and **Server Port**. You might also try 587, 995, or 110 for the **Server Port** value; sometimes that helps.

6. Click **Done** and the email account name in the upper left corner to return to the **Email** settings screen for this account.

7. Scroll down to the bottom and touch **Advanced**.

8. You can also try a different port setting for the server port on this screen, such as 587, 995, or 110. If those values don't work, contact your email service provider to get a different port number and verify your settings.

Verifying Your Mail Account Settings

Follow these steps to verify your account settings:

1. Tap the **Settings** icon.

2. Tap **Mail, Contacts, Calendars**.

3. If you received an error message from a particular email account, touch that that account.

4. Verify that the **Account** is set to **ON**.

5. Verify that your email **Address** is correct in the **POP Account Information** section.

6. Verify that the information in the **Host Name**, **User Name**, and **Password** fields is all correct.

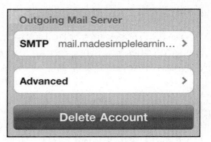

7. If you received an error message while trying to send an email, the issue will be most likely in the **SMTP** settings in your **Outgoing Mail Server** area.

8. Tap **SMTP** to adjust more settings.

9. Touch the **Primary Server** tab and make sure that it is set to **On**.

10. Underneath the **Primary Server** tab, you will see other SMTP servers that are used for your other email accounts. One option is to use one of the other SMTP servers that you know is working. In that case, just touch the tab for that server and turn that switch to **On**.

11. Tap the **Primary Server** address to view and adjust more settings.

12. Verify that the **Primary Server** is **ON**.

13. Contact your email service provider to verify other settings, such as **Host Name**, **User Name**, **Password**, **SSL**, **Authentication**, and **Server Port**. We will share more details and some tips about these settings in the sections that follow.

14. Tap the **Done** button when finished and then tap the button with your email account listed in the upper left corner to return to previous screens. Or, you can tap the **Home** button to exit to your **Home** screen.

Using SSL

Some SMTP servers require the use of Secure Socket Layer ("SSL") security. If you are having trouble sending email and the **Use SSL** switch is set to **OFF**, try setting it to **ON** to see if that helps.

Changing the Method of Authentication

Under the SSL switch is an **Authentication** tab. Usually, **Password** is the correct setting for this switch. We don't recommend that you change this setting unless you have specific directions from your email service provider to make a change.

Changing the Server Port

Most often, when you configure your email account, the server port is set for you. Sometimes, there are tweaks that need to be made that are specific to your ISP.

If you have been given specific settings from your ISP, you can change the server port to try to alleviate any errors you might be seeing. Follow these steps to change the **Server Port** settings:

1. Go back to the specific **SMTP** settings for your account.

2. Touch the tab for the **Primary Server**, as you did in the "Verify Mail Account Settings" section.

3. Scroll down to **Server Port** and touch the screen on the number indicated.

4. This causes a keyboard to pop up, which you can use to input a new port number (the one given you by your ISP). Most often, the number provided by your ISP will be 995, 993, 587, or 110; however, if you're given a different number, just input it.

5. When you are done, touch the **SMTP** tab in the upper left corner to return to the previous screen.

Chapter 19

Working with Contacts

Your iPhone 4 gives you immediate access to all your important information. Just like your computer, your iPhone 4 can store thousands of contacts for easy retrieval. In this chapter we'll show you how to add new contacts (including from an email address), customize your contacts by adding new fields, organize your contacts with groups, quickly search or scroll through contacts, and even show a contact's location with the iPhone 4 **Maps** app. We will also show you how to customize the **Contacts** view so it is sorted and displayed just the way you like it. Finally, you will learn a few troubleshooting tips that will save you some time when you run into difficulties.

The beauty of the iPhone 4 is how it integrates all of the apps so you can email and map your contacts right from the contact entry.

Loading Your Contacts onto the iPhone 4

In Chapter 3, "Sync Your iPhone 4 with iTunes," we show you how to load your contacts onto the iPhone 4 using iTunes on your Mac or Windows computer. You can also use the Google Sync or MobileMe services described in the Chapter 4, "Other Sync Methods."

> **TIP:** You can add new contact entries from email messages you receive. Learn how in Chapter 18: "Email on Your iPhone."

When Is Your Contact List Most Useful?

The **Contacts** app is most useful when two things are true:

1. You have many names and addresses in it.

2. You can easily find what you need.

Two Simple Rules to Improve Your Contact List

We have a couple of basic rules to help make your contact list on your iPhone 4 more useful.

Rule 1: Add anything and everything to your contacts.

You never know when you might need that obscure restaurant name, or that plumber's number, etc.

Rule 2: As you add entries, make sure you think about how to find them in the future (First, Last, Company).

We have many tips and tricks in this chapter to help you enter names so that they can be instantly located when you need them.

TIP: Here's a good way to find restaurants. Whenever you enter a restaurant into your contacts list, make sure to put the word "restaurant" into the company name field, even if it's not part of the name. Then when you type the letters "rest," you should instantly find all your restaurants!

Adding a New Contact Right on Your iPhone 4

You can always add your contacts right on your iPhone 4. This is handy when you're away from your computer—but have your iPhone 4—and need to add someone to your contacts. It's very easy to do. Here's how.

Start the Contacts App

From your Home screen, touch the **Contacts** icon
and you'll see the **All Contacts** list. Tap the **+** in the
upper right corner to add a new contact, as shown in
Figure 19–1.

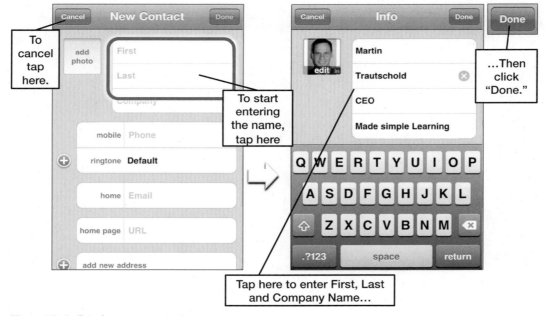

Figure 19–1. *Entering a new contact name*

Touch the **First Last** button and enter the new contact's first and last names. You can
also add a company name.

TIP: Keep in mind that the contacts search feature uses first, last, and company names. When you add or edit contacts, adding a special word to the company name can help you find a particular contact later. For example, adding the words "Cece friend" to the **Company** field can help you find all of Cece's friends quickly using the search feature.

Under the **First Last** button are five more buttons, as shown in Figure 19–2. Each is activated by touching either the green **+** to the left of the button (when available) or the button itself.

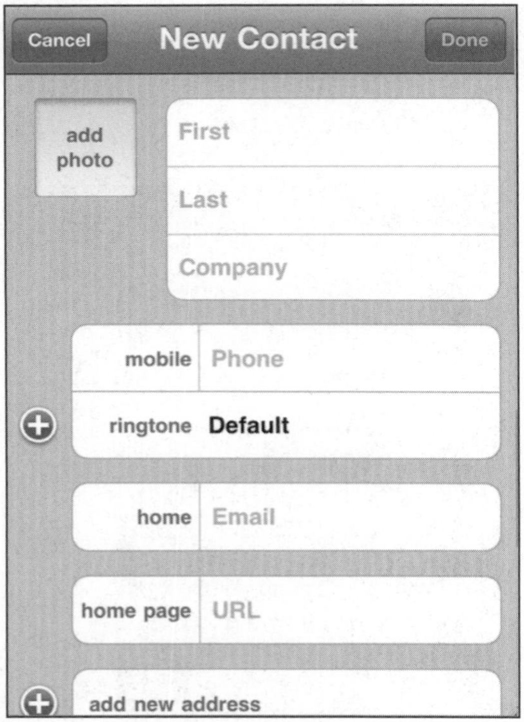

Figure 19–2. *Available contact fields*

Adding a New Phone Number

mobile	Phone

Touch the **Phone** button and use the number keyboard to input the phone number.

> **TIP:** Don't worry about parentheses, dashes, or dots—the iPhone 4 will put the number into the correct format. Just type the digits of the area code and number. If you know the country code, it's a good idea to put that in as well.

Next, choose which type of phone number this is—mobile, home, work, or other type. There are nine fields you can choose from, and there's also a **Custom** field if you find none of the built-in fields apply.

> **TIP:** Sometimes you need to add a pause to a phone number—for example, when the phone number is for someone at an organization where you have to dial the main number and then an extension. This is easy to do on the iPhone 4. You just add a comma between the main number and the extension like this: 386-555-7687, 19323. When you dial this number, say from your iPhone, the phone would dial the main number, pause for two seconds, and then dial the extension. If you need more of a pause, simply add more commas.

Adding an Email Address and Web Site

other	Email

Touch the **Email** tab and enter the email address for your contact. You can also touch the tab to the left of the email address and select whether this is a home, work, or other email address.

⊖	home page	fb://profile/1256299769
⊖	home	www.madesimplelearn…
	work	URL

Under the **Email** field you'll also find a **home page** field in which you can enter the address of your contact's web site.

> **NOTE**: If you used MobileMe to sync your contacts, MobileMe will automatically look for a Facebook homepage to integrate into the contact info.

⊕	add field

The iPhone 4 gives you the option to include only the fields that are relevant for a particular contact. Just touch the **add field** tab and select any of the suggested fields to add to that particular contact.

For example, to add a **Birthday** field to this contact, just touch **Birthday**.

Cancel	Add Field
Prefix	
Phonetic First Name	
Phonetic Last Name	
Middle	
Suffix	
Nickname	
Department	
Instant Message	

When you touch **Birthday**, you're presented with a wheel. You can turn the wheel to the corresponding date to add the birthday to the contact information.

> **TIP:** Suppose you met someone at the bus stop—someone you wanted to remember. Of course, you should enter your new friend's first and last names (if you know it), but also enter the words "bus stop" in the **Company name** field. Then when you type the letters "bus" or "stop," you should instantly find everyone you met at the bus stop, even if you can't remember their names!

Adding the Address

Below the **home** field are the fields for adding the address. Input the **Street**, **City**, **State** and **Zip Code**. You can also specify the **Country** and whether this is a home or work address.

When you are done, just touch the **Done** button in the upper right corner of the **New Contact** form.

Adding a Photo to Contacts

From the New Contact screen we've been working in, just touch the **Add Photo** button next to the **First Last** tab.

If you are changing a photo, when you are in "edit contact" mode, you'll see **edit** at the bottom of the existing photo.

After you touch the **add photo** button, you'll see that you can

- Take a Photo
- Choose a Photo

If there's a photo already in place, you can

- Edit a Photo
- Delete a Photo

To choose an existing photo, select the photo album where the picture is located and touch the corresponding tab. When you see the picture you want to use, just touch it.

You'll notice that the top and bottom of the photo become grayed out and that you can manipulate the picture by moving it, pinching to zoom in or out, and then arranging it in the picture window.

Once the picture is sitting where you want it, just touch the **Choose** button in the lower right corner and that picture will be set for the contact.

TIP: If you just moved into a new neighborhood, it can be quite daunting to remember everyone's name. A good practice to follow is to add the word "neighbor" into the **Company name** field for every neighbor you meet. Then, to instantly call up all your neighbors, simply type the letters "neigh" to find everyone you've met!

Searching Your Contacts

Let's say you need to find a specific phone number or email address. Just touch your **Contacts** icon as we did previously and you'll see a search box at the top of your **All Contacts** list, as in Figure 19–3.

Figure 19–3. *The contacts search box*

Enter the first few letters of any of these three searchable fields:

- First Name
- Last Name
- Company Name

The iPhone 4 begins to filter immediately and displays only those contacts that match the letters typed.

> **TIP:** To further narrow the search, hit the space key and type a few more letters.

Q Mart	⊗ Cancel
Chris **Martello**	>
Eric **Marthinsen**	>
Martin & Roz **Rodman**	>
Martin **Trautschold**	>

When you see the correct name, just touch it and that individual's contact information will appear.

Quickly Jump to a Letter by Tapping and Sliding on the Alphabet

If you hold your finger on the alphabet on the left edge of the screen and drag it up or down, you can jump to that letter.

Search by Flicking

If you don't want to manually input letters, you can just move your finger and flick from the bottom up, and you'll see your contacts move quickly on the screen. Just continue to flick or scroll until you see the name you want. Tap the name and the contact information will appear.

Search Using Groups

If you have your contacts sorted by groups on your PC or Mac and you sync your iPhone 4 with the computer or over the air using MobileMe, those groups will be synced to your iPhone 4. When you start your **Contacts** app you will see **Groups** at the top. Under the Groups heading, you will see **All Contacts**.

Choose **All Contacts** to search all the available contact information on the iPhone.

If you have multiple accounts synced, you will see a tab for each individual account and one for **All Contacts** at the top.

This example shows two groups—one is from a Microsoft Exchange account (i.e., a company email account), and one from my **MobileMe** contacts.

If you have an Exchange ActiveSync account and your company has enabled it, your Exchange Global Address List shows up here, under Groups, as well. You can search to find anyone in your company there.

> **NOTE:** You can't create groups in the **Contacts** app on the iPhone 4— they must be created on your computer or synced when you add contact accounts to your iPhone 4.

Adding Contacts from Email Messages

Often you'll receive an email message and realize that the contact is not in your address book. Adding a new contact from an email message is easy.

Open the email message from the contact you'd like to add to your contacts list. Then, in the email message's **From** field, just touch the name of the sender next to the **From:** tag.

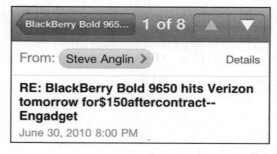

If the sender is not in your address book, you'll be taken to a screen that lets you choose whether to add that email address to an existing contact or to create a new one.

If you select **Create a New Contact**, you'll be taken to the same New Contact screen we saw earlier (Figure 19–1).

But suppose this is someone's personal email address and you already have an entry for that person with a work email address. In that case, you would select **Add to Existing Contact** and choose the correct person. Then you'd give this email address a new tag—"personal," in this case.

Linking Contact to Another App

You might have contact information for the sender of the email message in another app on the phone. With the iPhone it is easy to link these contacts together.

In this example, Steve, the sender of the email message, is one of my LinkedIn contacts, but not a contact on my iPhone, for some reason. Here is how I can link his contact information in my iPhone to the information I have in LinkedIn.

1. I add him to my contacts as shown previously.

2. I start up my LinkedIn app—see Chapter 28: "Social Networking," for more information on the topic.

3. I find my contact information for Steve to verify that he is in my LinkedIn app.

4. I go to the **Connections** icon.

5. I choose **Download All** in the top right-hand corner.

6. The LinkedIn app then informs me that this will add the photo, current company and title, email addresses, and web sites associated with this contact (see Figure 19–4).

7. This is exactly what I want in my iPhone contacts, so I choose **Download All New Connections**.

8. Steve's picture and updated information are then brought into his contact information on my iPhone.

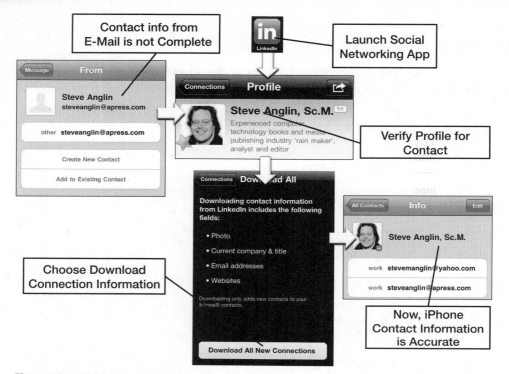

Figure 19–4. *Linking new contact from an email message to an existing social networking contact profile*

TIP: Learning the names of parents of your school-age children's friends can be fairly challenging. In the **First** field, however, you can add not just your child's friend's name but the parents' names as well (e.g., **First: Samantha (Mom: Susan, Dad: Ron)**). Then in the **Company** field, add in the name of your child and "school friend" (e.g., **Cece school friend**). Now, just typing your child's name in your **All Contacts** list's search box, you'll instantly find every person you ever met at your child's school. Now you can say, "Hello, Susan, great to see you again!" without missing a beat. *Try your best to covertly look up the name.*

Sending a Picture to a Contact

If you want to send a picture to a contact, you will need to do that from the **Photos** app. (See Chapter 21, "Working with Photos.")

Sending an Email Message from Contacts

Since many of the core apps (**Contacts**, **Mail**, and **Messages**) are fully integrated, one app can easily trigger another. So, if you want to send an email message to one of your contacts, open the contact and tap the email address. The **Mail** app will launch, and you can compose and send an email message to this person.

Start your contacts by touching the **Contacts** icon. Either search or flick through your contacts until you find the contact you need.

> home **martin@madesimplelearni...**

In the contact information, touch the email address of the contact you'd like to use.

You'll see that the **Mail** program launches automatically with the contact's name in the **To:** field of the email message. Type and send the message.

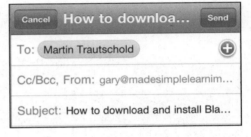

Showing Your Contacts Addresses on the Map

One of the great things about the iPhone 4 is its integration with Google Maps. This is very evident in the **Contacts** app. Let's say you want to map the home or work address of any contact in your address book. In the old days (pre-iPhone 4), you'd have to use Google, MapQuest, or some other program and laboriously retype or copy and paste the address information. This is very time-consuming—but you don't have to do this on the iPhone 4.

Simply open the contact as you did earlier. This time, touch the address at the bottom of the contact information.

> work **25 Forest View Way**

Your **Maps** app (which is powered by Google Maps) immediately loads and drops a push-pin at the exact location of the contact. The contact name will appear above the push-pin.

Touch the tab on the top of the push-pin to get to the info screen.

Now you can select **Directions To Here** or **Directions From Here**.

Then type the correct start or end address and touch the **Route** button in the lower right corner. If you decide you don't want the directions, just tap the **Clear** button in the top left.

What if you had just typed the address in your **Maps** app, instead of clicking from your contact list? In that case, you might want to touch **Add to Contacts** to add this address.

TIP: To return to your contact information, tap the **Map** button, and then exit **Maps** and start up **Contacts**. You can also use multi-tasking (see Chapter 8: "Multitasking and Voice Control") and double-click the **Home** button and choose the **Contacts** app.

Changing Your Contact Sort Order and Display Order

Like other settings, the Contacts options are accessible via the **Settings** icon.

Touch the **Settings** icon, scroll down to **Mail, Contacts, Calendars**, and touch the tab.

Scroll down and you'll see **Contacts**, with two options underneath. To change the sort order, touch the **Sort Order** tab and select whether you want your contacts sorted by first name or last name.

> **Mail...** Sort Order
>
> **First, Last**
>
> **Last, First** ✓

You may want to change how your contacts are displayed. Here's where you get it done; you can choose **First, Last** or **Last, First**. Tap the **Display Order** tab and choose whether you want your contact displayed in first-name or last-name order. Tap the **Mail, Contacts...** button in the upper left corner to save your settings changes.

> **Mail...** Display Order
>
> **First, Last** ✓
>
> **Last, First**

Searching for Global Address List (GAL) Contacts

If you have an Exchange account configured, you should have an option for a Global Address List. This gives you access to your Global Address List if you are connected to your organization's server.

> Exchange
>
> Contacts >
>
> Exchange Global Address List >

Open your **Contacts** app and look under Exchange for a tab that says **Exchange Global Address List**.

Contacts Troubleshooting

Sometimes, your **Contacts** app might not work the way you expect. If you don't see all your contacts, review the steps in the Chapter 3, "Sync Your iPhone 4 with iTunes," or Chapter 4, "Other Sync Methods," on how to sync with your address book application. Make sure you have selected **All Groups** in the settings in iTunes.

TIP: If you are syncing with another contact application, such as **Contacts** in Gmail, make sure you select the option closest to **All Contacts** rather than a subset like a particular group.

When Global Address List Contacts Don't Show Up (For Microsoft Exchange Users)

First, make sure you are connected to a Wi-Fi or 3G cellular data network.

Next, check your Exchange settings and verify you have the correct server and login information. To do so, tap the **Settings** button, and then scroll to and touch **Mail, Contacts and Calendar**. Find your Exchange account on the list and touch it to look at the settings. You may need to contact technical support at your organization to make sure your Exchange settings are correct.

Chapter 20

Your Calendar

The iPhone makes the old calendar that used to hang on the fridge obsolete. In this chapter, we will show you how to utilize the **Calendar** app of the iPhone to its full potential. We will show you how to schedule appointments, how to manage multiple calendars, how to change views on your calendar, and even how to deal with meeting invitations.

> **NOTE:** For most of this chapter, we will talk about syncing your iPhone calendar with another calendar because it is nice to have your calendar accessible on your iPhone and other places. If you choose, you can also use your iPhone in a *standalone* mode, where you do not sync to any other calendar. In the latter case, all the steps we describe for events, viewing, and managing events still apply equally to you. It is critical, however, that you use the **iTunes** automatic backup feature to save a copy of your calendar, just in case something happens to your iPhone.

Manage Your Busy Life on Your iPhone

The **Calendar** app is a powerful and easy-to-use application that helps you manage your appointments, keep track of what you have to do, set reminder alarms, and even create and respond to meeting invitations (for Exchange users).

Today's Day and Date Shown on Calendar Icon

The **Calendar** icon is usually right on your iPhone **Home** screen. You will quickly notice that your **Calendar** icon changes to show today's date and the day of the week. The icon to the right shows that it is a Friday, the 16th day of the month.

TIP: If you use your iPhone's **Calendar** app often, you might want to think about pinning or moving it to the **Bottom** dock; you learned how to do this in the section on docking icons in Chapter 7: "Organize Your iPhone: Icons and Folders."

Syncing or Sharing Your Calendar(s) with Your iPhone

If you maintain a calendar on your computer or on a web site such as **Google Calendar**, you can synchronize or share that calendar with your iPhone either by using **iTunes** and your sync cable or by setting up a wireless synchronization (see Chapter 3: "Sync Your iPhone with iTunes" and Chapter 4: "Other Sync Methods" for more information on syncing).

After you set up the calendar sync, all of your computer calendar appointments will be synced with your iPhone calendar automatically, based on your sync settings (see Figure 20–1).

If you use **iTunes** to sync with your calendar (e.g., **Microsoft Outlook**, **Entourage**, or Apple's **iCal**), your appointments will be transferred or synced every time you connect your iPhone to your computer.

If you use another method to sync (e.g., **MobileMe**, **Exchange**, or similar), this sync is wireless and automatic, and it will most likely happen without you having to do anything after the initial setup process.

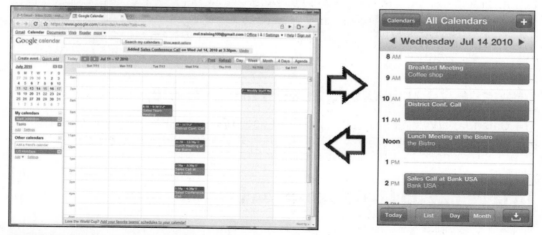

Figure 20–1. *Syncing a PC or Mac Calendar to an iPhone.*

Viewing Your Schedule and Getting Around

The default view for the **Calendar** app shows your **Day** view. This view shows you at a glance any upcoming appointments for your day. Appointments are shown in your calendar (see Figure 20–2). If you happen to have multiple calendars set up on your computer, such as **Work** and **Home**, then appointments from the different calendars will display as different colors on your iPhone calendar.

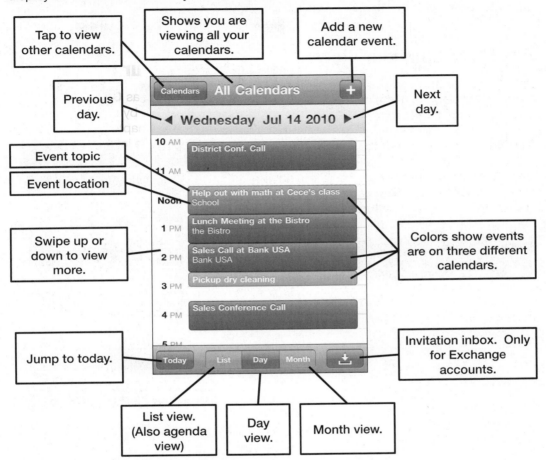

Figure 20–2. *The Calendar Day view layout.*

You can manipulate the calendar in various ways:

Move a day at a time: If you tap the triangles next to today's date at the top, you move forward or backward a day.

TIP: Touch and hold the triangles next to the date to advance quickly through days.

Change views: Use the **List**, **Day**, and **Month** buttons at the bottom to change the view.

Jump to today: Use the **Today** button at the bottom left corner.

The Three Calendar Views

Your **Calendar** app comes with three views: **Day**, **Month**, and **List**. You can switch views by tapping the name of the view at the bottom of the screen. Here's a quick overview of the three views.

Day view: When you start the iPhone's **Calendar** app, the default view is usually the **Day** view. This allows you to quickly see everything you have scheduled for the day. You can find buttons to change the view at the bottom of the **Calendar** app.

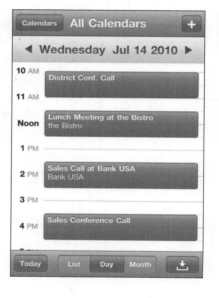

List view (also known as **Agenda** view): Touch the **List** button at the bottom, and you can see a list of your appointments.

Depending on how much you have scheduled, you could see the next day or even the next week's worth of scheduled events.

Swipe up or down to see more events.

Month view: Touch the **Month** button at the bottom, and you can see a layout of the full month. Days with appointments have a small dot in them. Dots for the current day will show up highlighted in blue.

TIP: To return to the **Today** view, just touch the **Today** button at the bottom left.

Go to the next month: Tap the triangle to the right of the month shown at the top.

Go to the previous month: Tap the triangle to the left of the month.

NOTE: While you can scroll in the **Calendar** app, you cannot swipe through your days, which runs counter to what you might expect.

Working with Several Calendars

The **Calendar** app can view and work with more than one calendar. The number of calendars you see depends on how you set up your synchronization using the **iTunes** program or other sync methods. In the example that follows, we have categorized personal appointments in our **Home** calendar and categorized work appointments in a separate **Work** calendar.

In the appointments in our **Calendar** app, we have our **Home** calendar appointments displayed in red and our **Work** appointments displayed in orange or green.

When you set up your **Sync** settings, you were able to specify which calendars you wanted to sync with your iPhone. You can customize your calendar further by following these instructions:

Changing the colors: You will need to change the color of the calendar in the program on your computer that is synced to your iPhone; this will change the colors on your iPhone. Sometimes you cannot change colors. For example, such as when syncing a Google calendar using the Exchange setting.

Adding a new calendar: It's a two-step process to add a new calendar to sync with your iPhone:

1. Set up that new calendar on your computer's **Calendar** program.

2. Adjust your Sync settings to make sure this new calendar syncs to your iPhone.

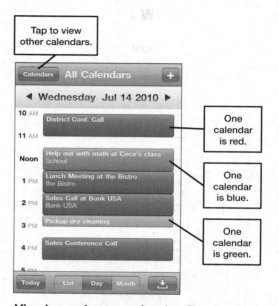

Viewing only one calendar: To view just one calendar at a time, tap the **Calendars** button at the top and select only the calendar you wish to see.

Adding New Calendar Events

You can easily add new events or appointments right on your iPhone. These new events and appointments will be synced (or shared with) your computer the next time the sync takes place.

Adding a New Appointment

Your instinct will most likely be to try to touch the screen at a particular time to set an appointment; unfortunately, this is not how you set appointments.

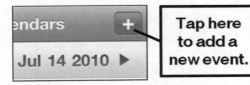

Tap here to add a new event.

To add a new calendar event from any **Calendar** view, follow these steps.

1. Tap the + icon at the upper right corner of the screen to see the **Add Event** screen.

2. Next, touch the box marked **Title & Location**.

> Title
> Location   >

Type in a title for the event and the location (optional). For example, you might type "Meet with Martin" as the title and input the location as "Office." Or, you might choose to type "Lunch with Martin" and then choose a very expensive restaurant in New York City.

3. Touch the blue **Done** button in the upper right corner to return to the **Add Event** screen.

> **Starts**   Tue, Jul 20 11:00 PM >
> **Ends**   Wed, Jul 21 12:00 AM

4. Touch the **Starts** or **Ends** tab to adjust the event timing. To change the start time, touch the **Starts** field to highlight it in blue. Next, move the rotating dials at the bottom to reflect the correct date and start time of the appointment.

5. Alternatively, you can set an all-day event by touching the switch next to **All-day** to set it to **ON**.

NOTE: You will see a tab labeled **Invitees** before the **Repeat** tab only if your event is set up on an Exchange/Google or MobileMe calendar. We show you how to invite people to meeting and reply to invitations in Chapter 4: "Other Sync Methods."

Recurring Events

Some of your appointments happen every day, week, or month at the same time. Follow these steps if you are scheduling a repeating or recurring appointment:

1. Touch the **Repeat** tab and then select the amount of time for the repeat from the list.

2. Touch **Done** to return to the main Event screen.

3. If you set a **Repeat** meeting, then you will also have to say when the repeat ends. Tap the **End Repeat** button to set this.

4. You can select **Repeat Forever** or set a date.

5. Tap **Done** when finished.

Calendar Alerts

You can have your iPhone 4 give you an audible reminder, or *alert*, about an upcoming appointment. Alerts can help you keep from forgetting an important event. Follow these steps to create an alert:

1. Touch the **Alert** tab and then select the option for a reminder alarm. You can have no alarm at all or set a reminder anytime from five minutes before the event all the way to two days before, depending on what works best for you.

2. Touch **Done** to get back to the main **Event** screen.

Second Alert

> **NOTE:** You will see a **Second Alert** if the calendar you are using is synced using iTunes or MobileMe. However, you will not see a second alert if your event is tied to a Google Calendar synced using the Exchange setting.

Alert	5 minutes before	>
Second Alert	30 minutes before	>

After you have set your first alert, in most cases you will then see a tab for a **Second Alert**. This is another alert that you can set to another time before or after the first alert. Some people find a second alert very helpful for remembering critical events or appointments.

> **TIP:** Here's a practical example that illustrates when you might want to set up two calendar alerts.
>
> If your child has a doctor or dentist appointment, then you might want to set the first event to go off the night before. This will remind you to write a note to the school and give it to your child.
>
> You can then set the second event for 45 minutes prior to the appointment time. This will leave you enough time to pick up your child from school and get to the appointment.

Choosing Which Calendar to Use

Calendar	martin.trautschold@g...	>

If you use more than one calendar in **Outlook**, **Entourage**, **iCal** or some other program, then you will have various calendars available to you when you sync your iPhone with that program.

> **NOTE:** If you create an event and choose an **Exchange** or **MobileMe** calendar, you'll see an option to invite other users to the event.

Touch the **Calendar** button in the upper left corner to see all your calendars.

Cancel	**Calendar**	Done
From My PC		
● Calendar		
● From My PC		✓
MSL		
● msl.training100@gmail.com		
My Gmail		
● martin.trautschold@gmail.com		

Tap the calendar you want to use for this particular event. Usually, the calendar selected by default is the one you selected the last time you used your iPhone to schedule an event.

Availability

Availability	Busy >

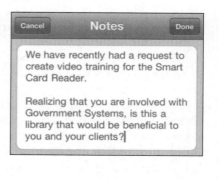

You can also let others know about your availability during the scheduled event. You can choose your availability from the following options: **Busy** (default), **Free**, **Tentative**, or **Out of Office**.

NOTE: You will only see the **Availability** field if the calendar you are using for this event is synced with the **MobileMe**, **Exchange**, or **Exchange/Google** settings.

Adding Notes to Calendar Events

Notes	>

Follow these steps if you want to add some notes to this calendar event.

1. Tap **Notes** and type or copy-and-paste a few notes.

2. Tap **Done** to finish adding notes.

3. Tap **Done** again to save your new calendar event.

TIP: If this is a meeting somewhere new, you might want to type or copy-and-paste some driving directions.

Using Copy-and-Paste Between the Email and Calendar Apps

The iPhone software's new **App Switcher** program means you can now easily jump between your **Email** and your **Calendar** programs to copy-and-paste information. This information could be anything, ranging from critical notes you need at your fingertips for a meeting to driving directions. Follow these steps to copy-and-paste information between your **Email** and **Calendar** programs:

1. Create a new calendar event or edit one, as explained previously in this chapter.

2. Scroll down to the **Notes** field and tap it to open it up.

3. Double-tap the **Home** button to bring up the **App Switcher.**

4. If you see the **Mail** icon, tap it. If you don't see **Mail** icon, swipe left or right to look for it. Once you find it, tap it to open the **Mail** app.

5. Double-tap a word, then use your fingers to drag the blue handles to select the text you want to copy.

6. Tap the **Copy** button.

7. Double-tap the **Home** button to bring up the **App Switcher.**

8. Tap the **Calendar** icon. It should be the first icon on the left, since you just jumped out of it.

9. Now tap and hold in the **Notes** field. When you let go, you should see the **Paste** pop-up field. If you don't see it, then hold your finger down a bit longer until you do see it.

10. Tap **Paste**.

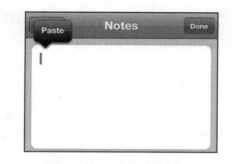

11. Now you should see the text you copied pasted into the **Notes** field.

12. Tap **Done** to save your changes.

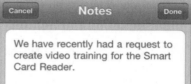

Editing Appointments

Sometimes, the details of an appointment may change and need to be adjusted (see Figure 20–3). Fortunately, it's easy to revise an appointment on your iPhone:

1. Tap the appointment that you want to change.

2. Tap the **Edit** button in the upper right corner to see the **Edit** screen showing the appointment details.

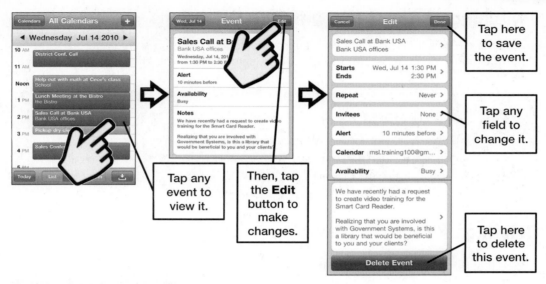

Figure 20–3. *Editing an Appointment.*

Just touch the tab in the field you need to adjust. For example, you can change the time of this appointment by touching the **Starts** or **Ends** tab, and then adjusting the time for the event's starting or ending time.

Editing a Repeating Event

You edit a recurring or repeating event in exactly the same manner as any other event. The only difference is that you will be asked a question after you finish editing the event. You need to answer this question and tap the **Done** button.

Tap **Save for this event only** if you want to make changes to only this instance of the repeating event.

Tap **Save for future events** if you want to make changes to all instances of this repeating event.

Switching an Event to a Different Calendar

If you mistakenly set up an event on the wrong calendar, then go ahead and tap the **Calendar** button to change the calendar. Next, select one of the different calendars you have synced to your iPhone.

> **NOTE:** Different fields may appear or disappear depending on the calendar you choose to use.
>
> If you change your event from a calendar synced using **iTunes** to one synced with **Exchange**, you will see the **Second Alert** field disappear. Also, you will see two new fields appear with an **Exchange**, **Google**, or **MobileMe** calendar: **Invitees** and **Availability**.

Deleting an Event

Notice that, at the bottom of the **Edit** screen, you also have the option to delete this event. Simply touch **Delete Event** at the bottom of the screen to do so.

Delete Event

Meeting Invitations

For those who use **Microsoft Exchange**, **Microsoft Outlook**, or **Entourage** regularly, meeting invitations become a way of life. You receive a meeting invitation in your email, you accept the invitation, and then the appointment gets automatically placed in your calendar.

On your iPhone, you will see that invitations you accept placed into your calendar immediately.

> **NOTE:** If you use an **Exchange** calendar or a **Google** calendar, you can invite people and reply to meeting invitations on your iPhone. See the "Working with the Google or Exchange Calendar" section of Chapter 4 to learn more about this subject.

If you touch the meeting invitation in your calendar, you can see all the details that you need: the dial in number, the meeting ID, and any other details that might be included in the invitation.

Sales Call at Bank USA | **Invitees**

? [?]Gary Mazo	>
? [*]Martha Sanders	>
? [✓]Martin Trautschold	>

NOTE: As the time of writing, you can accept meeting invitations on your iPhone from your **Exchange** account. You can create meetings for your **Exchange** account, as you choose the **Exchange** calendar. Invitations will also transfer automatically from **Entourage**, **iCal**, or **Outlook** if you have **iTunes** set to sync with those programs.

Calendar Options

There are only a few options to adjust in your **Calendar** app; you can find these in the **Settings** app. Follow these steps to adjust these options:

1. Tap the **Settings** from your **Home** screen.

2. Scroll down to the **Mail, Contacts, Calendars** and tap it.

3. Scroll down to **Calendars** (it's at the very bottom!) to see a few options.

Calendars	
New Invitation Alerts	ON
Sync	Events 1 Month Back >
Time Zone Support	>
Default Calendar	martin.trauts... >
New events created outside of a specific calendar will default to this calendar.	

4. The first option is a simple switch that notifies you about **New Invitation Alerts**. If you receive any meeting invites, it is good to keep this option set in the default **ON** position.

5. Next, you may see the **Sync** option if you sync your **Calendar** program using **Exchange** or **MobileMe**. You can adjust the setting to sync events to **2 weeks back, 1 month, 3 months, 6 months**, or **All Events**.

6. Next, you can choose your time zone. This setting should reflect your **Home** settings from when you set up your iPhone. If you are traveling, however, and want to adjust your appointments for a different time zone, you can change the **Time Zone** value to whatever city you prefer.

Mail...	Time Zone Support
Time Zone Support	ON
Time Zone	New York >

Time Zone Support always shows event dates and times in the time zone selected for calendars.

When off, events will display according to the time zone of your current location.

Changing the Default Calendar

We mentioned earlier that you can have multiple calendars displayed on your iPhone. This option allows you to choose which calendar will be your **Default** calendar.

Specifying a calendar as the default means that when you go to schedule every new appointment, this calendar will be selected by default.

If you wish to use a different calendar – say, your **Work** calendar – then you can change that when you actually set the appointment, as shown earlier in this chapter.

Mail...	Default Calendar
From My PC	
● **Calendar**	✓
● **From My PC**	
MSL	
● msl.training100@gmail.com	
My Gmail	
● martin.trautschold@gmail.com	

iPhone Photography

While previous versions of the iPhone have included a camera, the camera on the iPhone 4 is truly incredible. The iPhone 4 comes with not one, but two cameras: a 5.0-megapixel camera on the back with an LED flash and a 0.3-megapixel VGA camera on the front for video chats and self-portraits. Learn more about using the front-facing camera in the new **FaceTime** app in Chapter 12: "FaceTime Video Messaging and Skype."

Viewing and sharing your pictures on the iPhone 4 is truly a joy, due in large part to the beautiful high-resolution screen. In this chapter, we discuss the many ways to get pictures onto your iPhone 4. We also show you how you to use the touch screen to navigate through your pictures, and how to zoom in and out, and manipulate your photos.

> **TIP:** Did you know you can take a picture of the entire screen of your iPhone 4 by pressing two keys simultaneously? This is great to show someone a cool app or to prove that you got the high score on Tetris!
>
> Here's how to get it done: press both the **Home** button and the **On/Off/Sleep** key on the top right edge (you can press one, hold it, and then press the other). If you have done this correctly, the screen should flash and you'll hear a camera sound. The screen capture you have taken will be in your Camera Roll album in the **Photos** app.

Using the Camera App

The **Camera** app should be on your home page—usually on the first screen at the top. If you don't see it, then swipe left or right until you find it.

Touch the **Camera** icon and the shutter of the camera opens with an animation on your screen.

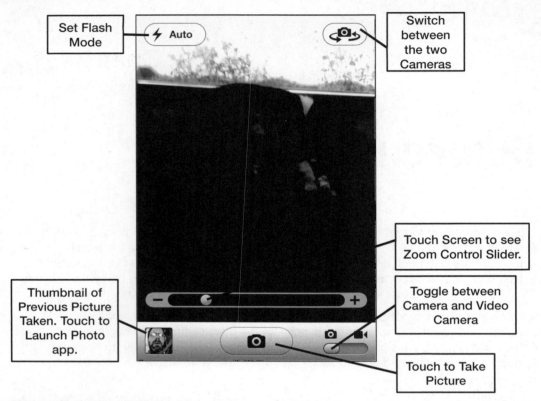

Set Flash Mode

Switch between the two Cameras

Touch Screen to see Zoom Control Slider.

Thumbnail of Previous Picture Taken. Touch to Launch Photo app.

Toggle between Camera and Video Camera

Touch to Take Picture

Figure 21–1. *Layout of Camera app.*

Geo-Tagging

Geo-tagging is a feature that puts your GPS (geographic positioning system) coordinates into the picture file. If you upload your pictures to programs like Flickr, the coordinates of your picture can be used for your friends to locate you and locate the site of where the picture was taken.

NOTE: For Mac users, iPhoto uses geo-tagging to put photos into the Places category of iPhoto.

If you have "Location Services" turned on (see Chapter 1: "Getting Started") when you start the camera, you will be asked if it is OK to use your current location.

To double-check, do the following:

1. Start your **Settings**.

2. Go to **General**.

3. Then touch **Location Services**. You will see a screen like the one here.

4. Make sure the switch next to **Camera** is toggled to **ON**.

Taking a Picture

Taking a picture is as simple as pointing and shooting, yet there are some adjustments that you can make if you choose.

Once your camera is on, center your subject in the screen of your iPhone.

When you are ready to take a picture, just touch the **Camera** button along the bottom. You will hear a shutter sound, and the screen will show an animation indicating that the picture is being taken.

Once the picture is taken, it will drop down into the window in the lower left-hand corner. Touch that small thumbnail, and the Camera Roll album of your **Photos** app will load.

Using the Zoom

Unlike previous versions of the iPhone, the iPhone 4 does include a zoom. The particular zoom included is a 5x digital zoom.

> **NOTE**: A digital zoom is never as clear as an analog zoom, so be aware that picture quality is usually degraded slightly when using the zoom.

To use the zoom, just touch the screen and move the Zoom slider, as shown in Figure 21-1.

Using the Flash

Also new to the iPhone 4 is a built-in LED flash. The default flash setting is automatic, but you can also manually turn it **On** or **Off**.

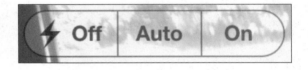

1. Touch the **Flash** icon in the upper left-hand corner.

2. Touch either **On**, **Off**, or **Auto**.

> **TIP**: We recommend keeping the Flash setting on **Auto**, but if you notice that a photo looks over-exposed, just touch the **Flash** icon and turn the flash **Off**.

Switching Cameras

As mentioned, the iPhone 4 comes with two cameras: a 5-megapixel camera for most photography and a VGA camera for self-portraits or for use in **FaceTime** video calls (see Chapter 12: "FaceTime Video Messaging and Skype.").

To switch between the cameras, do the following:

1. Touch the **Switch Camera** icon from the **Camera** app.

2. Wait for the camera to switch to the front-facing camera and line up the shot.

3. Touch the **Switch Camera** icon again to switch back to the standard camera.

TIP: Because of the placement of the front-facing camera, faces can look somewhat distorted. Try moving your face back a bit and adjusting the camera angle to get a better image.

Viewing Pictures You Have Taken

Your iPhone will store pictures you take on the iPhone in what is called your Camera Roll. You can access the Camera Roll from inside both the **Camera** and **Photos** apps. In the Camera app, touch the "pictures" icon in the bottom left corner of the camera screen.

Once you touch a picture to view, you can "swipe" through your pictures to see all the pictures in the Camera Roll.

To get back to the Camera Roll, press the **Camera Roll** button in the upper left corner.

To take another picture, touch the **Done** button in the upper right corner.

Getting Photos onto Your iPhone 4

You have many options for loading photos onto your device:

Sync using iTunes: Probably the simplest way is to use iTunes to sync photos from your computer. We describe this in detail in Chapter 3: "Sync with iTunes."

Receive as email attachments: While this is not useful for large numbers of pictures, it works well for one or a few photos. Check out Chapter 18: "Email on your iPhone 4," for more details about how to save attachments. (Once saved, these images show up in the Camera Roll album.)

Save images from the Web: Sometimes you'll see a great image on a web site. Press and hold it to see the pop-up menu and then select **Save Image**. (Like other saved images, these end up in the Camera Roll album.)

Download images from within an app: A good example of this is the Wallpaper image shown in Chapter 9: "Personalize & Secure your iPhone 4."

Sync with iPhoto (for Mac users): If you use a Mac computer, your iPhone 4 will most likely sync automatically with iPhoto.

Here are a few steps to get iPhoto sync up and running:

1. Connect your iPhone 4 and start **iTunes**.

2. Go to the **Photo** tab along the top row of Sync Options.

3. Choose the **Albums**, **Events**, **Faces**, or **Places** you want to keep in sync with the iPhone 4.

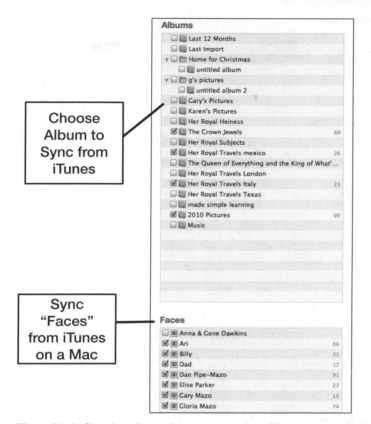

Choose Album to Sync from iTunes

Sync "Faces" from iTunes on a Mac

Figure 21–2. *Choosing albums, faces, or events from iTunes to sync with the iPhone.*

Drag and drop (for Windows users): Once you connect your iPhone 4 to your Windows computer, it will appear in Windows Explorer as a Portable Device, as shown in Figure 21–3. Here are the steps to follow to drag and drop photos between your iPhone 4 and computer.

Figure 21–3. *Windows Explorer showing the iPhone 4 as a portable device (connected with USB cable).*

1. Double-click on the iPhone 4 image under Portable Devices to open it.

2. Double-click on **Internal Storage** to open it.

3. Double-click on **DCIM** to open it.

4. Double-click on **100APPLE** to open it.

5. You will see all the images in the Saved Photos album on your iPhone 4.

6. To copy images to your iPhone 4, select and then drag and drop images from your computer into this folder.

7. To copy images from your iPhone 4, select and drag and drop images out of this folder onto your computer.

> **TIP:** Here's how to select multiple images in Windows.
>
> Draw a box around the images, or click on one image and then press Ctrl+A to select them all. Hold down the **Ctrl** key and click on individual pictures to select them. Right-click on one of the selected pictures and choose **Cut** (to move) or **Copy** (to copy) all of the selected images. To paste the images, press and click on any other disk or folder, such as **My Documents**, and navigate to where you want to move or copy the files. Then right-click again and select **Paste**.

Viewing Your Photos

Now that your photos are on your iPhone 4, you have a few very cool ways to look through them and show them to others.

Launching from the Photos Icon

If you like using your **Photos** icon, you might want to place it in your Bottom Dock for easy access if it's not already there (see Chapter 7: "Organize your iPhone: Icons and Folders.")

To get started with photos, touch the **Photos** icon.

The first screen shows your photo albums, which were created when you set up your iPhone 4 and synced with iTunes. In Chapter 3: "Sync your iPhone with iTunes" we showed you how to choose which photos to sync with your iPhone 4. As you make changes to the library on your computer, they will be automatically updated on your iPhone 4.

Choosing a Library

From the Photo Albums page, touch one of the library buttons to show the photos in that album. We touched a photo library and immediately the screen changed to show us thumbnails of the pictures in this library.

Tap and drag your finger up and down to view all the pictures. You can flick up or down to quickly move throughout the album.

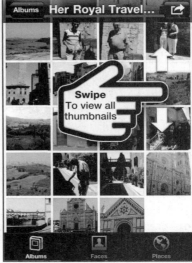

Working with Individual Pictures

Once you locate the picture you want to view, just tap on it. The picture then loads into the screen.

NOTE: Usually, your pictures will not take up the full screen on your iPhone 4 if they were shot in landscape mode.

TIP: The picture here was shot in landscape mode, so to see it in a full screen, you'll have to turn your iPhone 4 on its side or just double-tap it to fill the screen.

Moving Between Pictures

The swipe gesture is used to move from one picture to the next. Just swipe your finger left or right across the screen, and you can move through your pictures.

> **TIP:** Drag your finger slowly to move more gradually through the picture library.

When you reach the end of an album, just tap the screen once and you'll see a tab in the upper left corner that has the name of the photo album. Touch that tab and you'll return to the thumbnail page of that particular album.

To get back to your main photo album page, just touch the button that says **Albums** in the top left corner.

Zooming In and Out of Pictures

As described in the "Getting Started" section of the book, there are two ways to zoom in and out of pictures on your iPhone 4: double-tapping and pinching.

Double-Tapping

As the name describes, this is a quick double-tap on the screen to zoom in on the picture, as shown in Figure 21–4. You will be zoomed in to the spot where you double-tap. To zoom out, just double-tap once more.

See Chapter 1: "Getting Started" for more help on double-tapping.

Figure 21–4. *Double-tapping on a picture to zoom.*

Pinching

Also described in Chapter 1: "Getting Started," pinching is a much more precise form of zooming in. While double-tapping zooms in or out only to one set level, pinching really allows you to zoom in or out just a little bit or quite a lot.

To pinch, hold your thumb and forefinger close together and then slowly (while touching the screen) separate them, making the picture larger. To zoom out, start with your thumb and forefinger apart and move them together.

> **NOTE:** Once you have activated the zoom using either method, you will not be able to easily swipe through your pictures until you return the picture to its standard size.

Viewing a Slideshow

You can view the pictures in your photo album as a slideshow if you'd like. Just tap the screen once to bring up the on-screen soft keys. In the center is a **Slideshow Play** button—just touch once to start the slideshow. You can start the slideshow from any picture you are viewing.

Slideshow Options let you adjust how long each picture remains on the screen, as well as choose transitions and other settings, as shown in Figure 21–5. To end the slideshow, just tap the screen.

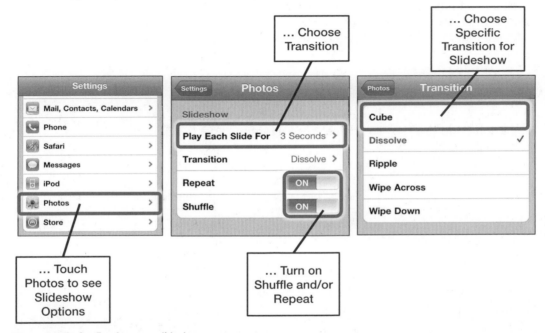

Figure 21–5. *Configuring your slideshow.*

Adjusting Slideshow Options

To configure a slideshow, you will need to change your settings. To do so, touch the **Settings** icon on the Home screen.

Scroll down to the **Photos** tab and touch the screen. You will then see the various options you can use, including four options you can adjust for slideshows.

To specify how long to play each slide, touch the **Play Each Slide For** tab. You can choose a range between 2 and 20 seconds.

If you want pictures to repeat in a slideshow, just move the **Repeat** switch to **ON**.

If you want the pictures to move in an order different from the way they are listed, choose **Shuffle**, and, just like the Shuffle command on the music player, the pictures will play in a random order.

Using a Picture as Your iPhone 4 Wallpaper

We show you how to select and use a picture as your iPhone 4 wallpaper (and more wallpaper options) in Chapter 9: "Personalize & Secure your iPhone 4."

NOTE: You can have different pictures for your Home screen and Lock screen or use the same picture for both.

Emailing a Picture

As long as you have an active Internet connection (Wi-Fi or 3G; see Chapter 5: "Wi-Fi and 3G Connectivity"), you can send any picture in your photo collection via email. Tap the **Options** button on the thumbnail bar—the one furthest to the left of the bottom row of soft keys. If you don't see the icons, tap the screen once.

Choose the **Email Photo** option and the **Mail** app will automatically launch (Figure 21–6).

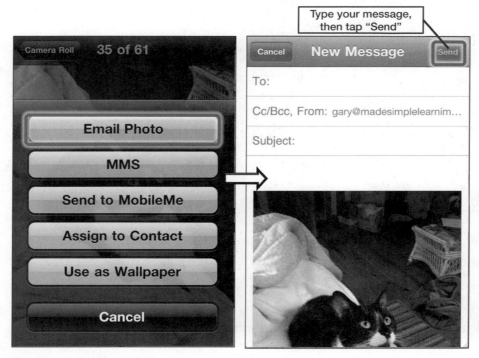

Figure 21–6. *Emailing a photo.*

Touch the **To** field as you did in Chapter 18: "Email on your iPhone 4," and select the contact to receive the picture. Tap the blue **+** button to add a contact.

Type in a subject and a message, and then touch **Send** in the upper right corner—that's all there is to it.

Email, Copy, or Delete Several Pictures At Once

If you have several pictures you want to email, copy, or delete at the same time, you can do it from the thumbnail view, as shown in Figure 21–7.

> **NOTE:** The **copy** function allows you to copy and paste multiple pictures into an email message or other app. **Share** renames the image to photo.png; **copy**-and-**paste** leaves it with the DCIM folder file name.png. **Share** also reduces the pixel size of large photos while **copy** retains the original pixel size. When you select **Share**, a pop-up will ask you if you want to send them in small, medium, large, or original size.
>
> At publishing time, you could share or email only a maximum of five pictures. This may change with future software.

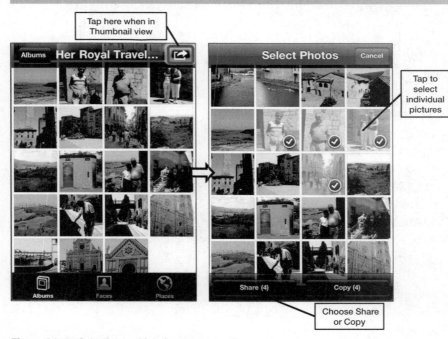

Figure 21–7. *Selecting multiple images to email.*

Assigning a Picture to a Contact

In Chapter 19: "Working with Contacts," we show you how to add a picture when editing a contact. You can also find a picture you like and assign it to a contact. First, find the photo you want to use.

As we did with wallpaper, and emailing a photo, tap the **Options** button— the one furthest to the right of the upper row of soft keys. If you don't see the icons, tap the screen once.

When you touch the **Options** button, you'll see a drop-down of choices: **Email Photo**, **Assign to Contact**, **Use as Wallpaper**, and **Copy Photo**.

Touch the **Assign to Contact** button.

Select a Picture, then choose Assign to Contact

You will see your contacts on the screen. You can either perform a search using the search bar at the top or just scroll through your contacts.

Once you find the contact to which you would like to add the picture, touch the name.

You will then see the Move and Scale screen. Tap and drag the picture to move it; use pinch to zoom in or out.

When you have it just as you want, touch the **Set Photo** button to assign the picture to that contact.

NOTE: You will return to your Photo Library, not to the contact. If you want to check that the picture did get set to your contact, exit the **Photo** app, start the **Contact** app, and then search for that contact.

Deleting a Picture

Why are there some pictures you can't delete from your iPhone 4 (the **Trash Can** icon is missing)?

You'll notice that the **Trash Can** icon is not visible for any photo that is synced from iTunes. You can delete such pictures only from your computer library. Then, the next time you sync your iPhone 4, they will be deleted.

Trash Can Icon is **Only** Visible in "Camera Roll."

When you are looking through pictures in your Saved Photos (which is not synced with iTunes, but is comprised of pictures you save from an email message or download from the Web), you'll see the **Trash Can** icon in the bottom icon bar. This **Trash Can** icon does not appear when you are viewing pictures from your Photos Library or other synced albums.

If you don't see the bottom row of icons, tap the photo once to activate them. Then tap the **Trash Can** icon. You will be prompted with the option to delete the picture.

Touch **Delete Photo** and the picture will be deleted from your iPhone 4.

Downloading Pictures from Web Sites

We have shown you how you can transfer pictures from your computer to your iPhone 4 and save them from email messages. You can also download and save pictures right from the Web onto your iPhone 4.

> **CAUTION:** We strongly encourage you to respect image copyright laws as you download and save images from the Web. Unless the web site indicates an image is free, you should check with the web site owner before downloading and saving any pictures.

Finding a Picture to Download

The iPhone 4 makes it easy to copy and save images from web sites. This can be handy when you are looking for a new image to use as wallpaper on your iPhone 4.

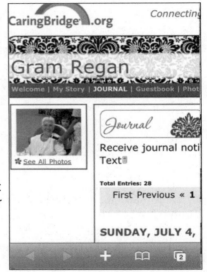

First, tap the **Safari** web browser icon and type a search for iPhone 4 wallpaper to locate a few sites that might have some interesting possibilities. (See Chapter 17 "Surf the Web with Safari" for help.)

Once you find a picture you want to download and save, tap and hold it to bring up a new menu of options that includes **Save Image** (among others), as shown in Figure 21–8. Choose this option to save the picture in your Saved Photos album.

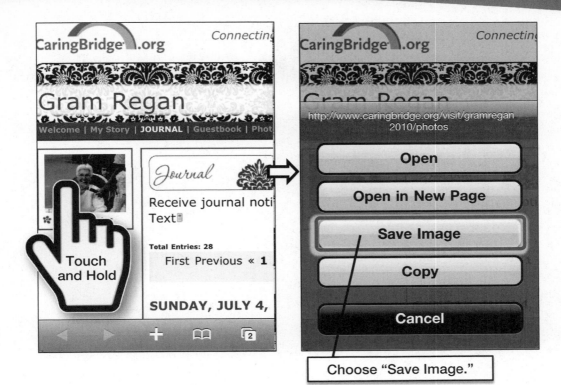

Figure 21–8. *Saving an image from a web site.*

Now touch your **Photo** icon and you should see the picture in the Camera Roll album.

The **Saved** Photo is now in your Saved Photos Directory

Chapter 22

Maps

Mapping on your iPhone 4 is very convenient and pretty amazing. As we explore the power of the **Maps** app in this chapter, you'll see how to find your location on the map and get directions to just about anywhere. You'll learn how to change views between classic Map, Satellite, and Hybrid. You'll also see how, if you need to find out the best route, you can check out the traffic and construction view using **Maps**. If you want to find the closest pizza restaurant, golf course, or hotel to your destination, that's easy, too. And you can use Google's Street View right from your iPhone 4 to help you get to your destination. It is easy to add an address you have mapped to your contacts. There's also a digital compass feature that is fun to play with.

Getting Started with Maps

The beauty of the iPhone 4 is that the programs are designed to work with one another. You've already seen how your contacts are linked to the **Maps** app; just look back at Chapter 19: "Working with Contacts."

The **Maps** app is powered by Google Maps—the leader in mobile mapping technology. With **Maps** you can locate your position, get directions, search for things nearby, see traffic, and much more.

Simply touch the **Maps** icon to get started.

Determining Your Location (the Blue Dot)

When you start the **Maps** program, you can have it begin at your current location.

1. Tap the small blue **arrow** icon at the lower-left corner.

Find my Current Location

The "Blue Dot" = Your Location

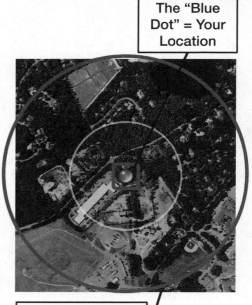

2. **Maps** will ask to use your current location—touch **OK** or **Don't Allow**.

   We suggest choosing **OK**, which makes it much easier to find directions from or to your current location.

If you see a circle around the dot, then your location is approximate.

Changing Your Map Views

The default view for **Maps** is Map view, a basic map with a generic background and streets shown with their names. Maps can also show you a Satellite view or a combination of Satellite and Map called Hybrid. Finally, another view called List view appears only when you perform a search that generates a list of turn-by-turn directions. You can switch among all the views using the following steps.

To change from one map view to another:

1. Touch the turned-up edge of the map in the lower-right corner.

2. The corner of the map turns up to reveal buttons for views, traffic, pins, and more. (See Figure 22–1.)

3. Tap the view you'd like to switch to:

   ■ **Map** is a regular map with street names (Figure 22–2).

   ■ **Satellite** is a satellite picture with no street names (Figure 22–1).

   ■ **Hybrid** is a combination of satellite and classic, that is, a satellite view with street names (Figure 22–2).

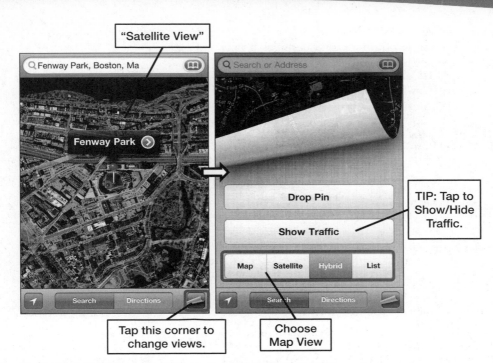

Figure 22–1. *Satellite view and how to change to another map view.*

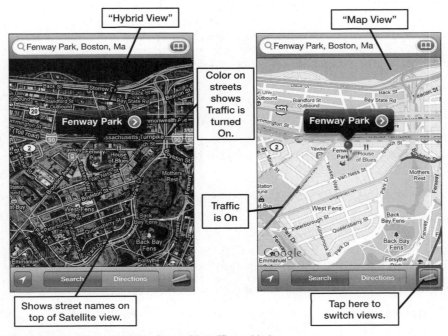

Figure 22–2. *Hybrid and Map views with traffic enabled.*

As noted, List view is available only when your search produces multiple results (like "pizza 32174") or you've asked for directions, as shown in Figure 22–3.

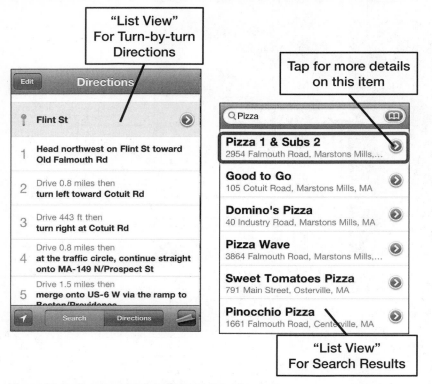

Figure 22–3. *List views for directions and search results*

Checking Traffic

Not only does your **Maps** program tell you how to get somewhere, but it can also check traffic along the way. This feature is supported only in the United States for now.

1.   Tap the lower-right corner of the map to see the options.

2.   Touch **Show Traffic**.

On a highway, if there is a traffic situation, you usually see yellow lights instead of green, and sometimes, the yellow might be flashing to alert you to traffic delays.

You may even see construction worker icons to indicate construction zones.

Maps uses color on major streets and highways to indicate the speed that traffic is moving:

Green = 50 MPH or more

Yellow = 25–50 MPH

Red = Less than 25 MPH

Gray (or no color) = No traffic data currently available

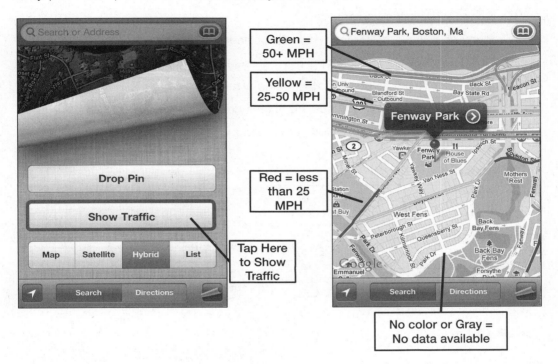

Searching for Anything

Because **Maps** is tied to Google Maps, you can search for and find just about anything: a specific address, type of business, city, or other point of interest, as shown in Figure 22–4.

1. Touch the **Search** bar in the top-right corner of the screen.

2. Type in your address, point of interest, or town and state you would like to map on your iPhone 4.

Google Maps Search Tips

Enter just about anything in the search:

- First name, last name, or company name (to match your Contacts list)

- 123 Main Street, City (some or all of a street address)

- Orlando Airport (to find an airport)

- Plumber, painter, roofer (any part of a business name or trade)

- Golf courses + city (to find local golf courses)

- Movies + city or ZIP/postal code (to find local movie theaters)

- Pizza 32174 (to search for local pizza restaurants in ZIP Code 32174)

- 95014 (ZIP code for Apple Computer headquarters in California, United States)

- Apress

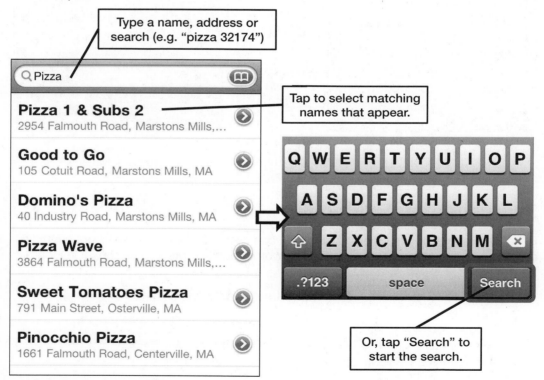

Figure 22–4. *Searching in the **Maps** app.*

To use numbers, tap the **123** key on the keyboard. For letters, tap the **ABC** key to switch back to a letter keyboard.

Mapping Options

Now that your address is on the **Maps** screen, a number of options are available to you.

1. Touch the blue **arrow** icon ⊙ next to the address to see some of these.

2. If you have mapped one of your contacts, you'll see the contact details, as shown in Figure 22–5. **Maps** will also pull up contact information for specific searches. You can also get directions, share a location, or add as a bookmark.

NOTE: You can also tap and hold the address to get the Copy pop-up menu.

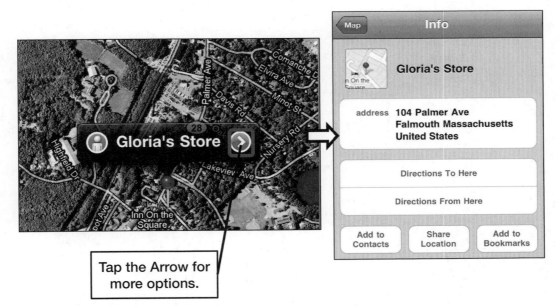

Tap the Arrow for more options.

Figure 22–5. *Touching the information button to see the mapped contact details.*

Working with Bookmarks

Bookmarks work in **Maps** very much as they do in the web app. A bookmark simply sets a record of places you've visited or mapped and want to remember in the future. It is always easier to look at a bookmark than have to do a new search.

Adding a New Bookmark

Bookmarking a location is a great way to make it easy to find that place again.

1. Map a location, as shown in Figure 22–6.

2. Touch the blue **information** icon next to the address.

3. Touch **Add to Bookmarks**.

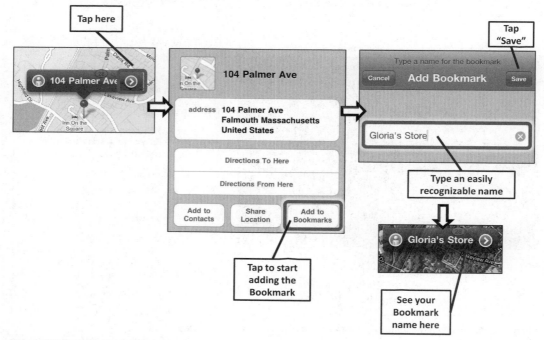

Figure 22–6. *Adding a bookmark.*

4. Edit the bookmark name to make is short and recognizable—in this case, we edit the address to simply say **Gloria's Store**.

5. When you are done, just touch **Save** in the top-right corner.

> **TIP:** You can search for bookmark names just as you search for names in Contacts.

Accessing and Editing Your Bookmarks

To view your bookmarks, follow these steps:

1. Tap the **Bookmarks** icon next to the search window in the top row.

2. Tap any bookmark to immediately jump to it.

3. Tap the **Edit** button at the top of the bookmarks to edit or delete bookmarks.

   a. To reorder the bookmarks, touch and drag the right edge of each bookmark up or down.

   b. To edit the name of a bookmark, touch it and retype the name. After editing the name, touch the **Bookmarks** button in the top left to get back to your list of bookmarks.

   c. To delete a bookmark, swipe to the left or right on the bookmark, and tap the **Delete** button.

4. Tap the **Done** button when you are finished editing your bookmarks.

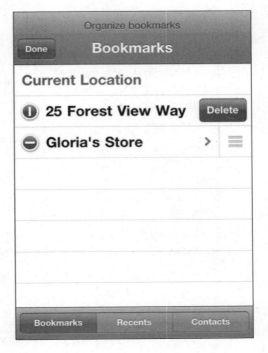

Adding a Mapped Location to Contacts

It is easy to add a location you mapped to your contact list.

1. Map an address.

2. Tap the **arrow/information** icon.

3. Tap Add to Contacts .

4. Tap either **Create a New Contact** or **Add to Existing Contact**.

5. If you choose **Add to Existing Contact**, you then scroll through or search your contacts and select a name. The address will automatically be added to that contact.

Searching for Establishments Around Your Location

1. Map a location on the map, or use the blue dot for your current location.

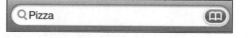

2. Tap the search window. Let's say you want to search for the closest pizza restaurants, so you type **pizza**.

All local pizza restaurants will be mapped.

3. Notice that each mapped location may have a **Street View** icon on the left and the **information** icon on the right.

4. If you want to zoom in or out, you can pinch the screen open or closed, or you can double-tap the screen.

5. Just as with any mapped location, when you touch the blue **information** icon, you can see all the details, even the pizza restaurant's phone number, address, and web site.

6. If you want directions to the restaurant, just touch **Directions to Here**, and a route is instantly calculated.

NOTE: If you touch the **Home Page** link, you will exit **Maps**, and **Safari** will start up. You will then need to restart **Maps** again when you're done.

Zooming In and Out

You can zoom in and out in the familiar way by double-tapping and pinching. To zoom in by double-tapping, just double-tap the screen as you would on a web page or picture.

Dropping a Pin

Let's say you're looking at the map, and you find something you'd like to set either as a bookmark or as a destination.

In this example, we are zooming in and looking around greater Boston. We stumble upon Fenway Park and decide it would be great to add it to our bookmarks, so we drop a pin on it, as shown in Figure 22–7.

1. Map a location or move the map to a location where you'd like to drop the pin.

2. Tap the lower-right corner of the map.

3. Tap **Drop Pin**.

4. Now, drag the pin around the map by touching and holding it. We move it right onto Fenway Park.

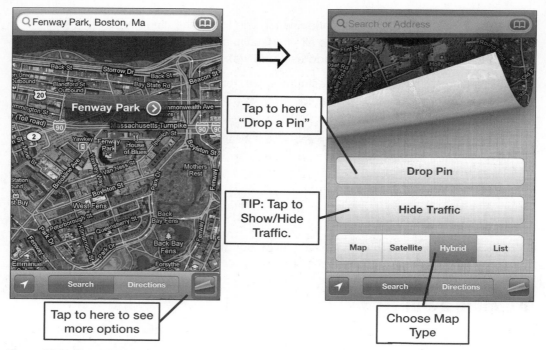

Figure 22–7. *How to drop a pin.*

TIP: How can you find the street address of any location on the map?

When you drop a pin, Google Maps will show you the actual street address. This is very handy if you find a location by looking at Satellite or Hybrid view but need to get the actual street address.

Dropping a pin is also a great way to keep track of where you parked, which is especially helpful in an unfamiliar location.

Using Street View

Google Street View (Figure 22–8) is really fun in **Maps** on the iPhone 4. Google has been hard at work photographing just about every address across the United States and elsewhere. The pictures are then fed into their database, and that's what shows up when you want to see a picture of your destination or waypoint.

NOTE: Google Street View is in a small number of countries now: much of North America, western Europe, Australia, and now South Africa.

If there is a Street View available, you will see a small icon to the left of the address or bookmark on the map—a small orange icon of a person.

In this example, Gary wants to check the Street View of his wife Gloria's store on Cape Cod.

1. In this case, to map the address, we tapped on the work address under Gloria's name on our Contacts list. We could have mapped it by typing an address in the search window, by searching for a type of business, or by touching the address in the **Contacts** app.

2. To the left of Gloria's name is the **Street View** icon.

3. We tap the icon to immediately shift to a Street View of the address.

4. What is very cool is that we can navigate around the screen in a 360-degree rotation by swiping left, right, or even up or down, looking at the places next to and across the street from our destination.

To return to the map, we just touch the lower-right corner of the screen.

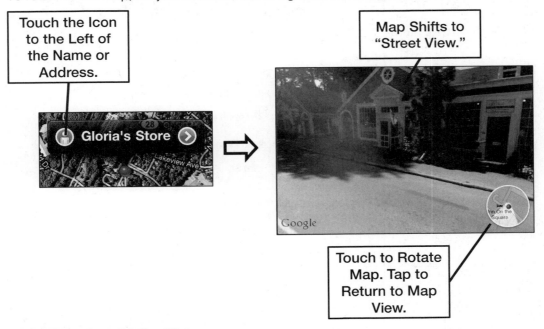

Figure 22–8. *Using Google Street View.*

Getting Directions

One of the most useful functions of the **Maps** program is that you can easily find directions to or from any location. Let's say we want to use our current location and get directions from Gary's wife's store to Fenway Park in Boston.

Tap the Current Location Button First

To find directions to or from your current location, you don't have to waste time typing your current address—the iPhone will assume you want directions from where you are unless you specify otherwise. You may need to repeat it a few times until you see the blue dot on the screen.

Now you can do one of two things:

- Tap the **Directions** button at the bottom.

- Touch the blue **arrow** as we did above and then select **Directions from Here** (see Figure 22–9).

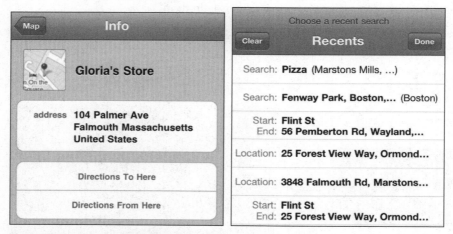

Figure 22–9. *Choosing* **Directions From Here** *and then* **Recents**.

Choosing Start or End Location

1. Touch the blue **arrow** icon above the pin.

2. Tap **Directions From Here**.

3. We could tap **Bookmarks**, **Recents**, or **Contacts** to find our destination.

4. In this case, we tap **Bookmarks**.

5. Tap **Fenway Park**.

> **NOTE:** As soon as you touch the **Directions From Here** button, your recent searches will be automatically displayed as in Figure 22–9. You can also touch the **Destination** box and type in a destination.

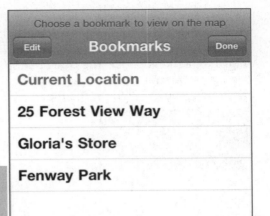

6. After we select Fenway Park from **Bookmarks**, the routing screen takes us to an overview screen.

7. A green pushpin is dropped at the start location, and a red one is dropped at the end location—in this case, Fenway Park.

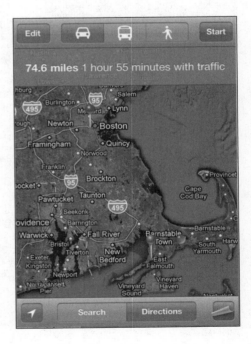

Looking at the Route

Before you start the trip, you will see a **Start** button in the lower-right corner of the screen. Tap the **Start** button, and the routing directions begin. The **Start** button changes to **arrow** icons that allow you to move between the steps in the trip.

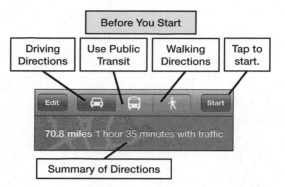

As Figure 22–10 shows, you can look at the route either as a path on the map or as a list.

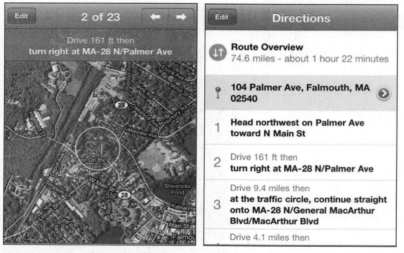

Figure 22–10. *Two ways of viewing directions.*

You can move the screen with your finger to look at the route, or just touch the arrows

at the bottom to show the route in step-by-step snapshots.

You can also touch the **List** button, which will show detailed step-by-step directions.

Switching Between Driving, Transit, and Walking Directions

Before you start your directions, you can choose whether you are driving, using public transportation, or walking by tapping the icons on the left side of the blue bar at the top of the directions screen, as shown in Figure 22–11.

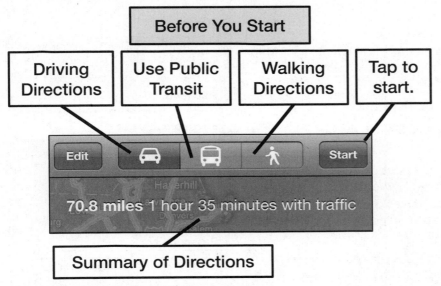

Figure 22–11. *Choosing your mode of transportation.*

Reversing the Route

To reverse the route, touch the **Reverse**   button, which is at the top between the **Start** and **End** fields. This can be useful if you're not great about reversing directions on your own or if your route uses lots of one-way streets.

Maps Options

Currently, the only setting that affects your **Maps** app is Location Services, which is critical for determining your current location.

1. Touch the **Settings** icon.

2. Tap the **General** tab in the left column.

3. Now find the **Location Services** switch about halfway down. Move this switch to the **ON** position so that **Maps** can approximate your location.

NOTE: Keeping the **Location Services** switch **ON** will reduce battery life by a small amount. If you never use Maps or care about your location, set it to **OFF** to save your battery life.

Settings	General	
About		>
Usage	16m	>
Network		>
Bluetooth	On	>
Location Services	On	>
Spotlight Search		>
Auto-Lock		>
Passcode Lock	Off	>

Set to "ON" so Maps can find your current location.

General	Location Services
Location Services	ON

Allow the apps below to determine your approximate location.

Using the Digital Compass

The iPhone 4 has a very cool digital compass feature built in. This can be helpful when you need to literally get your bearings and figure out which way is north.

Calibrating and Using the Digital Compass

Before you can use the digital compass, you need to calibrate it. You should need to calibrate the compass only the first time you use it.

1. Start **Maps** as you normally would.

2. Tap the current location button twice—it changes from to .

3. You'll see a digital compass appear on the screen, as shown in Figure 22–12.

4. The first time you use the digital compass, the calibration symbol appears on the screen .

5. Move your iPhone 4 in a figure-eight pattern, as shown on the screen.

> **NOTE:** The iPhone 4 may ask you to move away from any source of interference while you go through the calibration process.

6. Hold your iPhone 4 level to the ground. If you calibrated it successfully, the compass will rotate and point north.

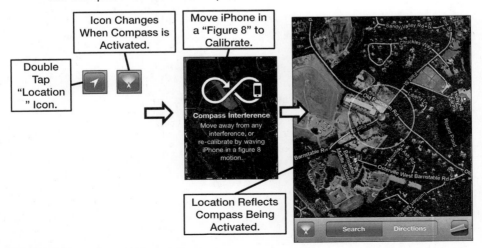

Figure 22–12. *Using the digital compass.*

Chapter 23

Eliminate Your Paper Notes

In this chapter, we will give you an overview of the **Notes** app, which you can use to write notes, make grocery lists, and make lists of movies you'd like to watch or books you'd like to read. We will show you how to organize and even email notes to yourself or others. Ideally, we hope that Notes will become so easy on the iPhone that you can eventually get rid of most, if not all, of your paper sticky notes!

Later in this chapter we will also give you a view of an excellent, and free, alternative to the **Notes** app called **Evernote**. There are various free or low-cost notes apps in the App Store. With Evernote, you can tag and organize your notes, add pictures to notes, add voice notes, and show the location where you originally wrote your note. Another nice thing about Evernote is that it will auto-synchronize your notes with the Evernote web site (so you can manage notes from your computer), and many other mobile devices you might own.

TIP: The **Notes** app that comes with the iPhone is pretty basic and utilitarian. If you need a more robust notes application that can sort, categorize, import items (PDF, Word, and so on), have folders, search, and more, you should check out the App Store on your iPhone. Do a search for "notes," and you will find at least a dozen notes-related apps ranging from free to $0.99 and up.

The Notes App

If you are like many people, your desk is filled with little yellow sticky notes—notes to do everything imaginable. Even with our computers, we still tend to leave these little notes as reminders. One of the great things about the iPhone is that you can write your notes on familiar yellow notepaper, and then keep them neatly organized and sorted. You can even email them to yourself or someone else to make sure that the information is not forgotten. You can also backup your notes using iTunes and, if you choose, sync notes to your computer or other web sites such as Google.

The **Notes** app on the iPhone gives you a convenient place to keep your notes and simple "to-do" lists. You can also keep simple lists, such as a grocery list, or a list for other stores, such as a hardware or pet store. If you have your iPhone with you, you can add items to these lists as soon as they occur to you, and they can be accessed and edited at any time.

Sync Notes

You can sync notes with your computer or other web site using the methods we show you in Chapter 3: "Sync Your iPhone with iTunes" and Chapter 4: "Other Sync Methods." In Figure 23–1, we synced using iTunes from the notes stored in Microsoft Outlook to the **Notes** app on our iPhone. The nice thing about syncing notes is that you can add a note on your computer and have it just "appear" on your iPhone. Then when you are out and about, you can edit that note and have it synced back to your computer. No more re-typing or remembering things. You always have your iPhone with you, so taking notes anywhere, anytime, can be a great way never to forget anything important.

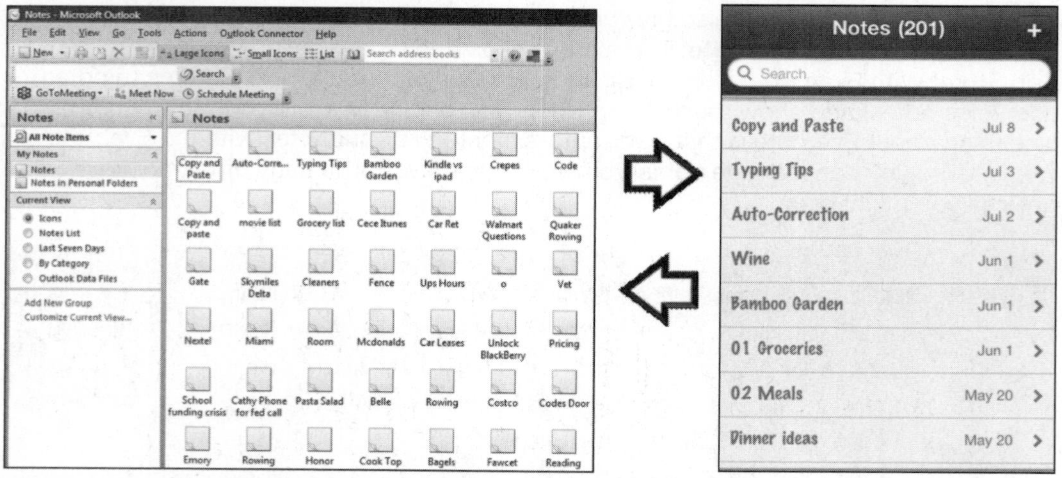

Figure 23–1. *Syncing notes between Microsoft Outlook and the iPhone **Notes** app using iTunes.*

Getting Started with Notes

Like all other apps, simply tap the **Notes** icon to start it (see Figure 23–2).

After starting the **Notes** app, you see what looks like a typical yellow note pad.

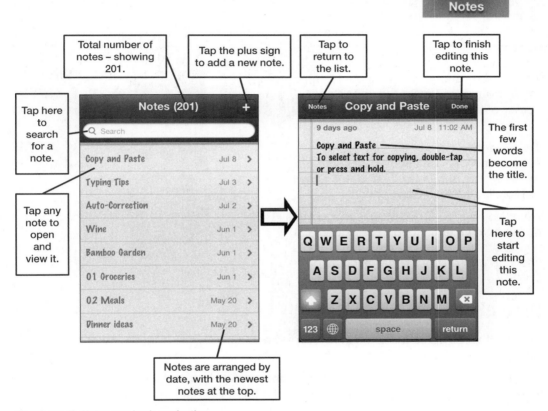

Figure 23–2. *Notes app basic navigation.*

Multiple Notes Accounts

If you happen to be syncing at least one IMAP email account and your computer using iTunes, then you will see that your notes from each of these accounts are kept separate. This is very much like how your contacts are kept in separate groups by email account and how your calendars are kept separate by email account.

In order to see multiple notes accounts, you have to set a switch in the account setup screen.

When you setup your IMAP email account, in **Settings** > **Mail,Contacts,Calendars**, you will see options to turn Notes syncing on or off. In order to see these notes accounts, you have to set the **Notes** switch to **On**, as shown for this Gmail account.

To view the various notes accounts, tap the **Accounts** button in the upper left corner of the **Notes** app.

Then, on the next screen, you can tap selections to view **All Notes**, or your notes for each account. In this image, the Gmail or MobileMe account are options.

Notes you add to an individual account will be kept with that account. For example, If you add notes to Gmail, then those would show up only on your Gmail account.

How Are My Notes Sorted?

You see that all notes are listed in reverse chronological order, with the most recently edited notes at the top and the oldest at the bottom.

The date that is shown is the last time and date that the particular note was edited, not when it was first created. So you will notice the order of your notes moving around on the screen.

This sorting can be a good thing because your most recent (or frequently edited) notes will be right at the top.

> **TIP:** If you want a nice app to keep track of your to-do lists, **Things for iPhone** is a very nice task and to-do app. It is currently US $9.99 in the App Store.

Adding a New Note

To start a new note, tap the plus sign **+** in the upper right-hand corner. See Figure 23–3.

The notepad is blank, and the keyboard pops up for you to begin typing.

TIP: You can tilt your iPhone on its side to see the larger keyboard.

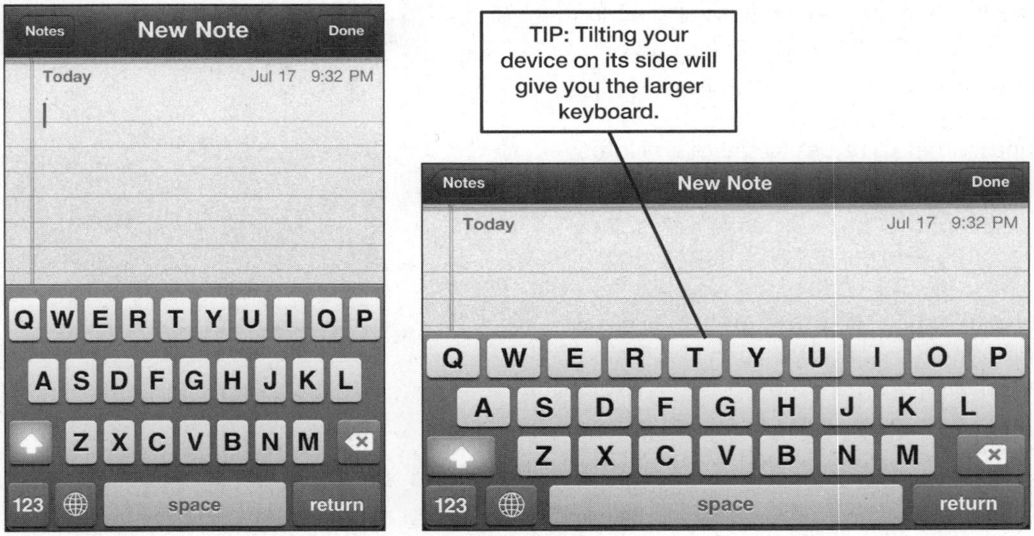

TIP: Tilting your device on its side will give you the larger keyboard.

Figure 23–3. *Adding a new note and using the larger keyboard.*

Adding a Title to the Note

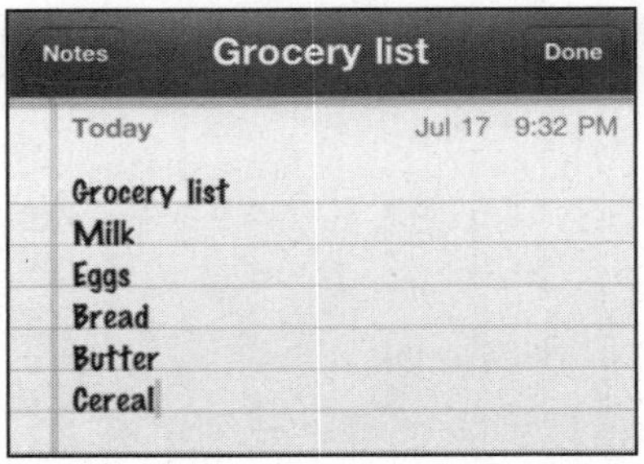

The first few words you type before you hit the **Return** key will become the title of the note. So think about what you want as the title, and type that first. In the image shown, **Grocery list** becomes the title of the note.

Put a new item on each line, and tap the **Return** key to go to the next line.

When you are done, touch the **Notes** button in the top left-hand corner to return to the main Notes screen.

Viewing or Editing Your Notes

Your notes appear in the list as tabs to touch. Touch the name of the note you wish to view or edit. The contents of the note are then displayed.

You can scroll in Notes as you do in any program. You will notice that the date and time the note was last edited appear in the upper right-hand corner.

When you are done reading the note, just touch the **Notes** button in the top left-hand corner to return to the main Notes screen.

To advance through multiple notes, just touch the arrows at the bottom of the screen. Touch the **Forward** arrow. The page turns, and you can see the next note. To go back, just hit the **Back** arrow.

Editing Your Notes

You can easily edit or change the contents of a note. For example, you might keep a "Things to Do" note and quickly edit it when you think of something else to add to the list (or when your family reminds you to get something from the store).

Touch any note in the list to open it.

Then tap the screen anywhere; the cursor moves to that spot for editing.

If you double-tap a word, the blue handles used to copy and paste appear. Just drag the handles to select text.

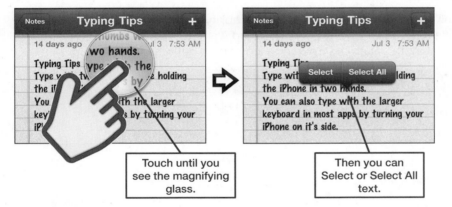

If you touch and hold your finger on a word, a magnifying glass appears, so you can find the exact spot you are looking for. See Figure 23–4.

Release your finger, and the **Select** menu appears. Choose **Select** or **Select All**.

Figure 23–4. *Selecting text in a note.*

You can also use the **Delete** key to delete a word or a line after selecting it—that is the fastest way to delete a number of words or lines of text.

> **TIP:** Using the copy handles is the best way to select a large amount of text; it is faster and more precise.

When done editing, touch the **Notes** button to return to the list.

Deleting Notes

To delete a note, tap it to open it from the main Notes screen and then touch the **Trash Can** icon at the bottom. See Figure 23–5.

The iPhone prompts you to delete the note or cancel.

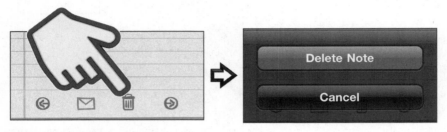

Figure 23–5. *Deleting a note.*

Emailing a Note

One of the **Notes** app's convenient features is the ability to email a note, as shown in Figure 23–6. Let's say you wrote a grocery note and wanted to email it to your spouse. From the text of the note, touch the **Envelope** icon at the bottom of the screen.

Figure 23–6. *Emailing a note.*

Now you see the Compose New Mail screen, with the subject as the title of the note and the body of the message as the contents of the note. Address and send the note as you would any other email message. Touch the **To** line of the email, touch the sign, and find the contact you wish to use. You can also start typing someone's name or email address and then choose from the pop-up list of names below.

Once you're done typing, tap **Send** to send the note on its way.

> **TIP:** Hitting space twice automatically inserts a period. Holding down a character gives you accent/variant options. Tapping the numbers toggle puts you in numbers entry mode and leaves you there. Sliding from the number toggle to the character you want and then letting go inserts the character. It also automatically switches you back to alphabet mode.

Creating a New Calendar Event from an Underlined Day and Time

If you type in the words "tomorrow morning" in a note and save it. The next time you open that note, you will see that the words have been underlined. If you touch and hold the underlined words, you will see a button asking if you want to Create Event. Tap the button to create a new calendar event for tomorrow morning.

> **TIP:** Whenever date and time words are underlined, the iPhone recognizes them as potential calendar events. This works in notes, email messages and other places on your iPhone.

An Alternative Note App: Evernote

A visit to the App Store will show you several note-taking and organizing apps designed for the iPhone. Prices range from free to about US $20.00.

A good free notes app is called **Evernote**. Evernote is great because you can track just about anything with it: text notes, pictures you snap, voice notes, copies of Safari web pages, documents—almost anything you can imagine. Also, when you enter a note in Evernote on your iPhone, you can automatically synchronize it with your Mac, PC, iPad, BlackBerry, or other mobile device. The same goes for notes you enter on your Mac, PC, or other devices—they all sync to your iPhone. All text is searchable, and you can even "geo-locate" (have your iPhone tie your GPS location to where you originally created each note) using Evernote.

Getting Started with Evernote

Start by going to the App Store and downloading Evernote. See Chapter 26: "The Amazing App Store" for help getting apps.

Once Evernote is downloaded and installed, you need to touch the **Evernote** icon to start the application.

The first time you use Evernote, you will be prompted to sign up for a free account. Type in your email address and set a password, and you are ready to start.

Create an account Sign in

EVERNOTE®

Register for Evernote

Did you forget your password?

Email address*

Martin@madesimplelearning.com

Username*

mtrautschold1

Available

Password*

••••••••

Confirm password*

••••••••

Adding and Tagging Notes

After logging in, you see the New Note screen (you know you are on this screen because the New Note soft key is highlighted in the lower left corner).

The New Note screen of Evernote gives you various options for adding a new note.

- **Text** (type a text note)
- **Snapshot** (take a picture with your iPhone camera)
- **Camera roll** (select a picture from your saved pictures to add as a note)
- **Voice** (record a voice note)

Just tap the type of note you want to add.

Text Notes

Tap the **Text** icon to start typing a text note.

Give your note a unique title and then add some tags to the note. These tags are used to help organize your notes, and they can be useful when searching through your notes.

You can add tags by typing them, separated by commas.

> **TIP:** If you are consistent about your tags, you can easily sort and find notes by your tags.

Or, if you already have typed a few tags on other notes, you can tap the ⊙ next to the tags and select from existing ones.

> Tags: book, iPhone, work   ⊙

Selecting tags from the list is easier, and it helps you avoid making mistakes when typing any of your tags.

Snapshot

This will bring up your camera so you can grab a picture and save it as a note. The picture is also geo-tagged with your current GPS location in Evernote to track where you took it. You can even take a picture of a document and have Evernote find words in the image of the document. See the "Searching for Notes" section in this chapter.

> **TIP:** Remember that you can flip your camera around to the front-facing camera on your iPhone so you can snap a picture of yourself or you and a friend or loved one!

Camera Roll

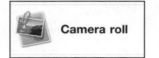

Tap **Camera roll** from the New Note screen to select an image from your camera roll to add as a new note.

Voice Notes

Tap **Voice** to record a voice note and add it to your list of notes. Remember, you can record your voice or any sounds around you, such as the sounds of the ocean, a running river, the wind, or even your niece's piano recital.

When you tap the **Voice** icon, you are given a 3-second countdown before the voice recorder starts recording. When you are done recording, you press the green triangle button to save this as a new note.

To erase the note and start over, press the red X button (Discard).

To stop recording, press the square **Stop** button.

You don't name the note when you record it—this is so you can do it completely hands-free.

What you need to do is to go into your notes list view in Evernote and edit the voice notes you created to give them names and tags. We will show you how to edit a note. Each voice note is titled as an **Untitled audio note**. See the "Editing Rich Text" section for more on editing an audio or voice note.

Refresh, Email, Delete, or Edit a Note

When you are viewing a note, you have four options, shown as soft keys along the bottom of each note.

Tap the **Refresh** icon at the left end of the soft keys to make sure you have the most up-to-date version of this note from the server.

To delete the note, tap the **Trash Can** icon.

You can also email your notes by touching the **Envelope** icon at the bottom of the screen, just as you can in the **Notes** app.

To edit a note, just touch the **Pencil** icon at the bottom of the screen. This brings up the editing screen.

When you are done editing, tap the **Save** button in the upper right corner.

Editing Rich Text Notes (Voice and Picture)

When you edit a rich text note, such as a picture or voice note, you will receive a warning message about rich text notes, shown here.

This warning applies only if you want to type text in the body of the note.

If you are only adding a title and assigning tags, you don't need to worry about it.

However, if you are typing text, we recommend selecting **Append**, which will add your changes to your existing note.

Note Grouping

You have various options for customizing the way you group your notes in Evernote on your iPhone.

1. To view your notes, tap the **Notes** soft key along the bottom.

2. In order to change the way your notes are grouped, tap the information button in the upper right corner. See Figure 23–7.

3. On the Note Grouping screen, you can group the notes by date created, updated, title, notebook, city, and country (using their geographic location).

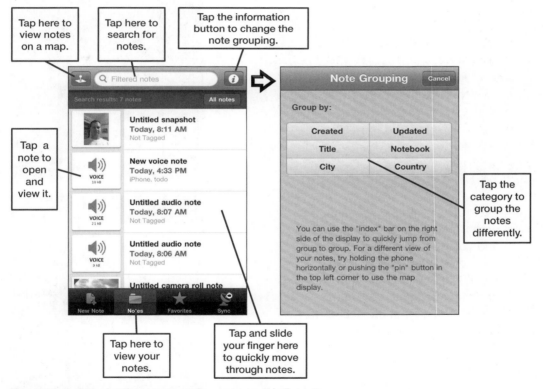

Figure 23–7. *Changing the way your notes are grouped in Evernote.*

Searching for Notes

Evernote provides you quite extensive and flexible searching features. You can even search for text contained in images. Next we show you how we were able to find the word **Client** in a picture we just snapped with our iPhone of a fax cover page.

1. Tap the **New Note** soft key, and then tap **Snapshot** to take a picture of any document with text on it. In this case, we took a picture of a fax cover page.

2. Tap the **Notes** soft key and tap the search notes field at the top of the page.

3. Press the **Search** key at the bottom right.

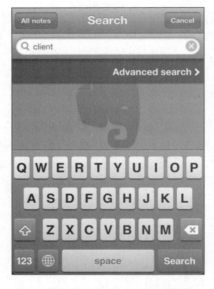

> **TIP:** If you are searching for text in an image, and your basic search did not work the first time, you may need to tap **Advanced search >** under the search window. Then tap **Other** at the very bottom and select **Images** under the **Contains** heading near the bottom of the page.

4. Evernote should then scan all your notes, including text in images, to find your results. In this case, we were presented with a single result—the picture of the fax cover page that contained the word **Client**. Notice that the search word is highlighted in the image.

The Evernote Places View

One cool Evernote view is the **Places View**. If you allow Evernote to use your location, Evernote will tag all your notes by the place where you originally created your note. For example, if you traveled to another state, province, or country, Evernote would track that you took notes in that particular region.

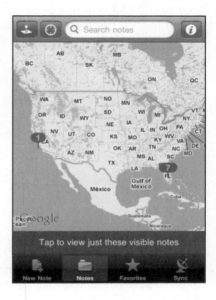

The image here shows one note taken in California and seven notes taken in Florida.

To view these notes, just tap the markers (push pins).

Evernote Synchronization and Settings

Tap the **Sync** soft key to view your synchronization settings.

The free account type is limited by the amount of information you can store on Evernote servers. If you use the application lightly, or mainly for text notes, the free version should be fine. If you use a lot of images or voice notes, then you will want to check out the premium version.

If you scroll down the Synchronization screen, you can check out your total usage of your free (or paid) account.

> **TIP**: Set **Upload on WiFi only** to **On** to reduce your 3G cellular data usage plan charges. This is very helpful if you are on a limited 3G data plan.

Upload on WiFi only	OFF
When switched on, notes will only be uploaded when connected via WiFi.	

Clear cache

Current Monthly Usage

Monthly upload allowance	40 MB
Current usage	1.52 MB
Days left in cycle	23

The free account gives you 40 MB of data, which is more than 50,000 text notes, but many fewer voice and picture notes. Tap the **Approximate notes remaining** option to get a feel for how many picture or voice notes this might include.

If you are running out of space, then you might want to upgrade by touching the **Go Premium** option in the top of the Synchronization window.

Approximate notes remaining	>

About Evernote

About Evernote	>
Technical Support	>
Legal	>

Evernote 3.3.5
Copyright © 2010 Evernote Corporation.

New Note   Notes   Favorites   Sync

Viewing or Updating Evernotes on Your Computer or Other Mobile Device

As we mentioned, all your notes get synced to the Evernote web site wirelessly and automatically. You can then log in to your account from your PC, Mac, iPhone, or BlackBerry to check out or update your notes. See Figure 23–8. This is a great feature if you have multiple devices, and you would like to stay up-to-date or add notes from any of them.

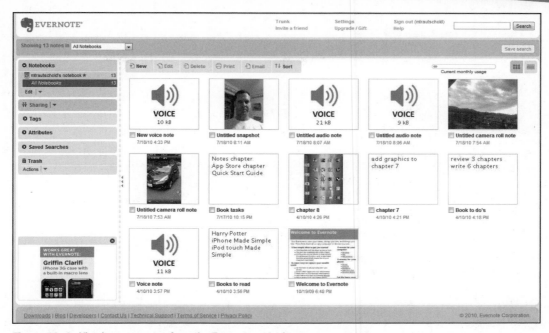

Figure 23–8. *Viewing your notes from the Evernote web site on your computer.*

Chapter 24

Utilities: Clock, Calculator, Compass, and Weather

The iPhone is very useful for a great number of things. Some of the most simple things and apps are those you might find yourself using quite frequently. Your iPhone comes pre-loaded with a few utilities that should prove quite useful.

In this chapter, we will show you how to use your clock, set alarms, and use the timer. We will also show you the features of the built-in calculator and compass.

Lastly, we will show you not only how to configure the built-in **Weather** app, but also a couple of other free weather apps you might want to add to your iPhone 4.

You might want to see what time it is in London, Tokyo or any other city around the world. You might want a wake-up alarm clock. How about a count-down timer to tell you when the pasta is finished boiling or a stopwatch to time how long it takes to get something done? All these can be done in the **Clock** app.

How about calculating the tip on your meal, or other simple, everyday calculations—what would 120 licenses of our Made Simple videos cost a company at $15.95 each? Use the calculator.

You may find yourself a bit "lost" and need to literally get your bearings. The built-in **Compass** app can help you do just that.

How about the weather for the next few days in your city, or any city in the world? Use the **Weather** app.

TIP: You might find some of these apps already in a folder on your Home screen, called **Utilities**. The **Utilities** folder will be there on new iOS 4 devices or clean upgrades to iOS 4. If not, we suggest moving the apps into a folder and naming that folder **Utilities** so all your utility apps can be in one place. See Chapter 7: "Organize Your iPhone: Icons and Folders," to learn how to do this.

The World Clock App

Touch the **Clock** icon to launch the Clock.

Immediately, you see the World Clock feature. Usually, the standard clock is for Cupertino, CA—but you can easily add to that or delete it.

Adding a New World Clock Entry

It is very easy to add new entries to the **Clock** app.

1. Touch the "+" sign in the upper right-hand corner and the keyboard will pop up.

2. Type in the name of a city.

3. As you type, the iPhone will show you entries that match your letters.

4. When you see the city you want, tap it to select it.

5. Once you do this, the new city is automatically added to the World Clock list. See Figure 24–1.

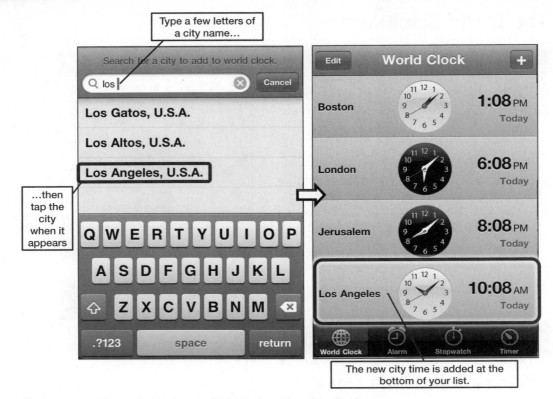

Figure 24–1. *Adding new cities into the World Clock section of the* **Clock** *app.*

Re-sorting or Deleting World Time Entries

1. Just touch the **Edit** button in the top left of the screen.

2. You will notice that each entry now has a red "-" sign.

3. When you touch the minus sign, it will rotate 90 degrees and a red **Delete** button will appear to the right.

4. Touch **Delete** and that particular World Clock entry will no longer be in the list.

To move a World Clock entry, do the following:

1. Touch and drag the three bars you see to the right of each entry.

2. Drop or let go of the entry when you have it in the correct location.

The Alarm Clock

The alarm clock feature is very flexible and powerful on the iPhone. You can easily set multiple alarms. For example, you might set an alarm to wake you up on weekdays, and a separate one on weekends. You can even set a separate alarm to wake you up from your Tuesday and Sunday afternoon nap at 3:00pm.

To get started, tap the **Alarm** icon in the lower row of soft keys.

If you have alarms set, they will be displayed. If there are no alarms, tap the "+" sign in the upper right-hand corner to add a new one.

Adjust the time of the alarm by rotating the dials at the bottom of the screen.

If this is a one-time alarm, then leave the Repeat set at **Never**. This setting will cause the alarm to automatically be set to **Off** after it rings.

Repeat	Never >

If the alarm does repeat, then adjust the repeating function of the Alarm by touching the **Repeat** tab. Touch the days of the week you would like the Alarm to be active.

Every Monday

Every Tuesday ✓

Every Wednesday

Every Thursday

Every Friday

Every Saturday

Every Sunday

TIP: You may touch as many or as few days as you want.

Sound	Marimba >

Adjust the sound the alarm makes by touching the **Sound** tab and then choosing an alarm sound from the list.

For silent alarms, set the sound to **None** at the top of the list to have an on-screen silent alarm—no sound will be made.

Tap **Back** when you are done.

Standard	
Marimba	
Alarm	
Ascending	
Bark	
Bell Tower	✓
Blues	
Boing	
Crickets	

To enable the **Snooze** feature—make sure the **Snooze** switch is in the default **On** position.

NOTE: The pre-set snooze time is 10 minutes and could not be changed as of the writing of this book.

Snooze	ON

You can re-name your alarm by touching the **Label** tab. The keyboard will launch and you can type in a new name for that particular alarm.

Give your alarm a name that is easy to recognize.

Give your alarm a name that is easy to recognize.

NOTE: If you want to use this feature to wake up in the morning at different times on different days, you will need to set an alarm for each day of the week following the procedure.

Will an alarm turn on my iPhone? **No**. If your iPhone is completely powered-off, the alarm will not turn it back on. However, if your iPhone is just in sleep mode (see Chapter 1: "Getting Started"), then your alarms will ring just fine.

Using the Stopwatch

The iPhone comes with a built-in stopwatch, which can be a very handy feature. Just touch the **Stopwatch** icon along the bottom row of the **Clock** app.

This is a very simple app. To start the stopwatch, tap the **Start** button and the clock will start to run.

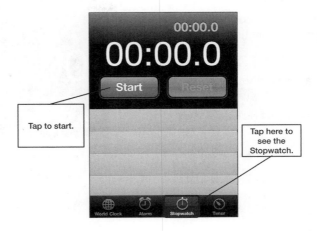

Tap to start.

Tap here to see the Stopwatch.

Showing "Lap" Times

You can either stop or lap the stopwatch after you start it.

Just touch the **Lap** button as if you were timing a sporting event like a track race.

1. Each lap time is shown in the list.

2. Drag them up/down to see all the lap times. When you are done, tap **Stop**.

Stopping and Resetting

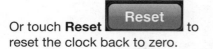

Touch the red **Stop** button to stop
the clock at any time.

You can then continue the timing by
touching **Start** again.

Or touch **Reset** to
reset the clock back to zero.

Using the Countdown Timer Feature

Need to take something out of the oven in 30
minutes?

Need to take the pasta out in 8 minutes, but
don't have a kitchen timer available?

Need to remember to turn off the sprinkler in 1
hour?

All these are perfect reasons to use the Timer,
which gives you a great count-down timer.

Setting the Timer

Tap the **Timer** soft key inside the **Clock** icon to see the timer screen.

1. Slide the dials at the top with your finger, setting the hours and/or minutes.

2. In the screenshot here, we have the timer set for 30 minutes.

To change the sound you hear when the countdown timer reaches 0:00, touch the **When Timer Ends** tab.

Choose any other sound from the list of sounds and touch the **Set** button when you are done.

Turning Off (Sleeping) Your iPod After a Set Time

A great thing to be able to do is to set your iPod to turn off (go into sleep mode) at a set time.

Say you want to have your music play for 30 minutes and then turn off automatically. This is a good thing to set when you are going to sleep and want to listen to music but don't want to be bothered turning off your **iPod** app.

Sleep Timer button.
TIP: Use this setting so you can go to sleep and have your iPod app turn off after the amount of time you set on the Timer.

Starting the Timer

Once you have the time and sound set, just touch the green **Start** button to start the timer.

The screen will display a digital clock counting down to zero. You can cancel the timer at any time by simply touching the red **Cancel** button.

The Calculator App

One more very handy app included on your iPhone is the **Calculator** app. The iPhone Calculator can handle almost anything a typical family can throw its way, performing both basic and scientific calculations.

Viewing the Basic Calculator (Portrait Mode)

 Click on the **Calculator** icon to start the **Calculator** app.

In portrait mode (vertical) view, the **Calculator** application is a "basic" calculator. All functions are activated by simply touching the corresponding key to perform the desired action.

Need to store something in memory? Use the following keys to do so:

- M+ to add it into memory
- M- to subtract the number from memory
- MC to clear memory
- MR to recall the number in memory to the screen

Viewing the Scientific Calculator (Landscape Mode)

Just turn the iPhone sideways into landscape mode (horizontal) view and the accelerometer in the iPhone transforms the calculator into a scientific calculator. The keys become smaller, and the new scientific keys are added along the left-hand side of the calculator.

Turn the calculator back to its vertical position, and it will return to its basic functions.

The Compass App

Your iPhone 4 has a built-in digital compass, which can be very helpful when you are lost and need to get your bearings. Sometimes, even a good GPS app doesn't tell you where true north is located.

Compass

The **Compass** app is very simple, but very powerful.

1. Touch the **Compass** icon to start the **Compass** app.

2. Calibrate the compass (if asked) in a figure-eight movement as shown on the screen.

3. Once the compass is calibrated, just move around and notice the compass reading on the screen. (See Figure 24–2.)

4. To see your location on the map, touch the arrow in the lower left-hand corner and your location will be shown in the **Maps** app. You will need to exit the **Maps** app and restart the **Compass** app if you choose this option.

5. Touch the **Information** icon to choose whether your compass is calibrated to true north or magnetic north.

CAUTION: If your iPhone is near a computer, the compass might be receiving interference. When this happens, you get a warning to move away from a computer or to recalibrate the compass as described.

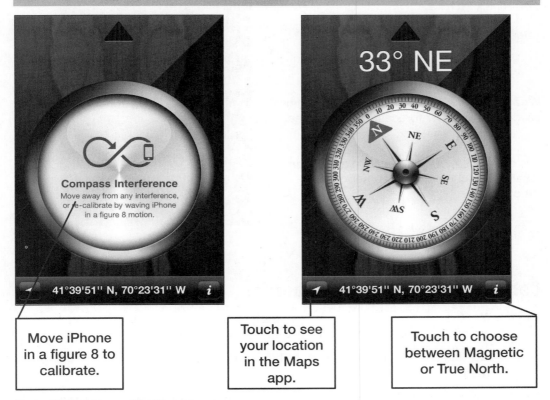

Move iPhone in a figure 8 to calibrate.

Touch to see your location in the Maps app.

Touch to choose between Magnetic or True North.

Figure 24–2. *Features of the Compass app.*

The Weather App

The iPhone comes with a very useful and easy-to-use **Weather** app built in.

After you set it up, a quick touch of the

Weather icon will show you the next six days of weather forecasts for your area.

It is easy to set up your location and other locations to check their weather on the **Weather** icon.

Getting Started with "Weather"

Tap the **Weather** icon. Unless you live in Cupertino, California, the default weather settings are not for your area. You will need to add your location.

1. Touch the small "*i*" in the lower right-hand corner to go to the Weather settings screen.

2. If the town selected is not one you wish to keep track of, just touch the red "minus" sign and you will be prompted to delete the location. See Figure 24–3.

Touch here to add a
new location.

Touch here to add
or edit your
weather locations.

Switch between
Fahrenheit and
Celsius here.

Figure 24–3. *Adding or editing your weather location.*

Adding a New Location

1. Just touch the "plus" sign in the upper left corner to add a new location.

2. Type in the name of the city or town or the zip code (the iPhone will start to display towns it thinks you are trying to type).

3. If it does not display suggestions as you type, touch **Search** after you type in your town.

4. When you see the town you want, just touch it.

You will be taken back to the Weather settings screen.

If it looks OK to you, just touch **Done** in the upper right-hand corner.

Deleting a Weather Location

To delete a weather location, do the following:

1. First get into the Weather settings screen by tapping the "i" in the lower right corner of the weekly weather screen.

Then tap the red minus sign to the left of the location name so you see the **Delete** button appear.

Finally, tap **Delete** and confirm to remove the location.

Tap **Done** in the upper right corner to complete your changes.

To delete a location, first tap here...

...then tap Delete.

Re-ordering the Locations in Weather

You can re-order the locations so your most important location is first on the list.

To re-order entries, touch and drag the

three bars  you see to the right of each entry.

Drop or let go of the entry when you have it in the correct location.

Tap **Done** in the upper right corner to complete your changes.

Touch and Drag up/ down to re-order

Moving Between Weather Locations

Once you have Weather set up for your various locations, you can then swipe from screen to screen, seeing the weather in all the cities you chose.

Touch and drag your finger across the screen to advance to the various Weather locations.

Other Weather Apps

The **Weather** app bundled with the iPhone 4 is certainly functional, but there are other alternatives. Most of the weather apps are free in the App Store, and some offer premium versions for a modest fee.

> **NOTE**: Most of the free weather apps are supported by ads in the app. For the most part, these are not intrusive.

The easiest way to find alternative weather apps is to go to the App Store and touch the **Categories** icon at the bottom. There is a separate category of the store simply called Weather. In the Weather category, touch **Top Free** at the top and then search for apps. See more about downloading apps in Chapter 26: "The Amazing App Store."

The Weather Channel

The Weather Channel is certainly one of
the weather authorities today. **The
Weather Channel** app takes a similar
approach to the **Weather** app on the
iPhone.

When you first start the app, you will input
your zip code or address so a custom
home page with your weather can be
created. The home page shows the current
weather, with soft keys for **Hourly**, **36
Hour**, and **10 Day** forecasts.

Along the very bottom are four icons:
Weather, **Map**, **Severe**, **Video**, and **Info**
(which gives indices). Each is fairly
explanatory of the features contained.

AccuWeather

Another of the weather authorities,
AccuWeather, has put together a very
comprehensive weather app for the
iPhone.

Download the app from the App Store as we explained earlier.

You will be prompted to use your location for determining local weather—we recommend allowing AccuWeather to do this.

The home page of the app shows you the current temperature and conditions with a graphic of what the sky should look like. Like **The Weather Channel** app, there are soft keys to show different views.

The upper level of soft keys at the bottom of the screen shows buttons for **Current**, **Hourly**, and **15 Day** forecasts. There is also a soft key for **Indices**.

Below that are the main function keys of the app, **Weather**, **Radar**, **Video**, **Risk**, **Alarms**, and **Alert**.

iTunes on Your iPhone 4

In this chapter, you will learn how to locate, buy, and download media using the **iTunes** app right on your iPhone 4. With iTunes, you will be able to download music, movies, TV shows, podcasts, audiobooks, and free educational content from leading universities with iTunes U. You will also learn how to redeem iTunes gift cards.

Some of us still remember going to the record store when that new single or album came out. It was an exciting feeling, browsing through all the vinyl albums, then tapes and CDs, and looking at all the music we wanted.

Those days are pretty much long gone with the iPhone 4. All the music, movies, TV shows, and more are available right from the iPhone 4 itself.

iTunes is a music, video, TV, podcast, and more store—virtually every type of media you can consume on your iPhone 4 is available for purchase or rent (and often for free) right from the iTunes store.

Getting Started with iTunes on the iPhone 4

Earlier in this book, we showed you how to get your music from iTunes on your computer into your iPhone 4 (see Chapter 3). You can also learn more about using iTunes on your computer in Chapter 26. One of the great things about iTunes is that it is very easy to buy or obtain music, videos, podcasts, and audiobooks, and then use them in minutes right on your iPhone 4.

The iPhone 4 allows you to access iTunes (the mobile version) right on your device. After you purchase or request free items, they will be downloaded to your **iPod** app on the iPhone 4. They will also be automatically transferred to your iTunes library on your computer the next time you perform a sync, so you can also enjoy the same content on your computer.

A Network Connection Is Required

You do need an active Internet connection (either Wi-Fi or 3G/cellular) in order to access the iTunes store. Check out Chapter 5 to learn more about network connectivity.

Starting iTunes

When you first received your iPhone 4, **iTunes** was one of the icons on the first Home screen page. Touch the **iTunes** icon, and you will be taken to the mobile iTunes Store.

NOTE: The **iTunes** app changes frequently. Since the **iTunes** app is really a web site, it is likely to change somewhat between the time we wrote this book and when you are looking at it on your iPhone 4. Some of the screen images or buttons may look slightly different than the ones shown in this book.

Navigating iTunes

iTunes uses icons similar to other programs on the iPhone 4, so getting around is quite easy. There are three buttons at the top and seven icons or soft keys at the bottom to help you. Look at Figure 25–1 to see the soft keys and features. Scrolling is just like scrolling in any other program; move your finger up or down to look at the selections available.

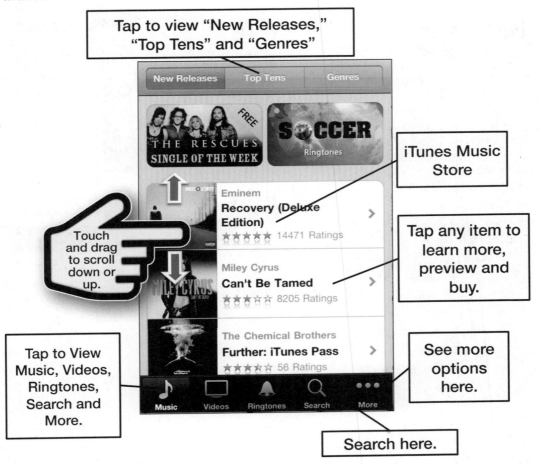

Figure 25–1. *The iTunes layout*

Finding Music with New Releases, Top Tens, and Genres

Along the top of the iTunes music store screen are three buttons: **Featured**, **Top Charts**, and **Genius**. By default, you are shown the **Featured** selections when you start iTunes.

Top Tens: The Popular Stuff

If you like to see what is popular in a particular category, you will want to browse the **Top Tens** category. Tap **Top Tens** at the top, and then tap a category or genre to see what is popular for that category.

> **CAUTION:** These songs or videos are selling well, but that doesn't mean that they will appeal to you. Always give the item a preview and check out the reviews before you pay for it.

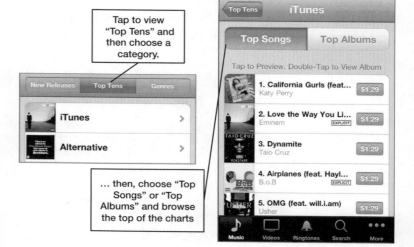

Tap to view "Top Tens" and then choose a category.

... then, choose "Top Songs" or "Top Albums" and browse the top of the charts

Genres: Types of Music

Touch the **Genres** button to browse music based on a genre. This is particularly helpful if you have a favorite type of music and would like to browse just that category.

There is quite an extensive list of genres to browse; just scroll down the list as you would in any other iPhone 4 app.

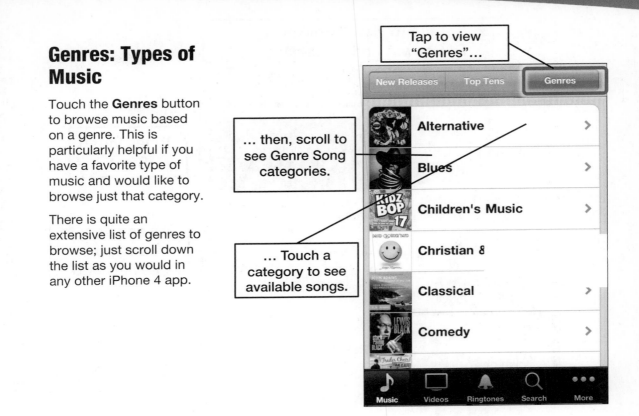

Tap to view "Genres"...

... then, scroll to see Genre Song categories.

... Touch a category to see available songs.

Go ahead and browse through the music until you see something that you would like to preview or buy.

Browsing for Videos (Movies)

Touch the **Movies**, **TV Shows** or **Movie Videos** buttons on the top to browse all the video-related items (see Figure 25–2).

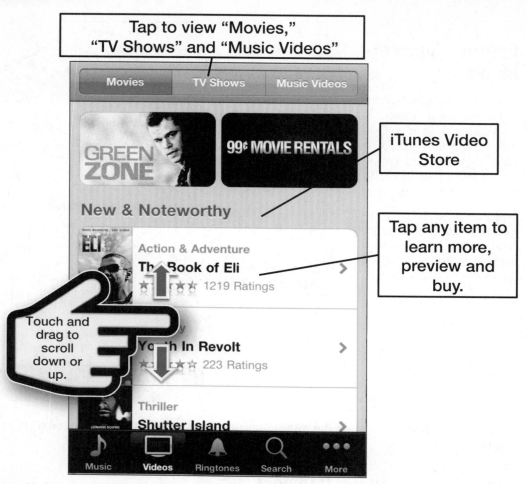

Figure 25–2. *Browsing the Videos category in iTunes on your iPhone 4*

You can also use your finger to scroll all the way to the bottom of the page to check out the links there, including these links in particular:

- **Top Tens**
- **Genres**

Tap on any movie or video to see more details or preview the selection. You have the option to rent or buy some movies and TV shows.

Rentals: Some movies are available for rent for a set number of days.

> **NOTE:** The rental period in the US is 24 hours and the rental period in Canada is 48 hours. Other countries may vary slightly.

Buy: This allows you to purchase and own the movie or TV show forever.

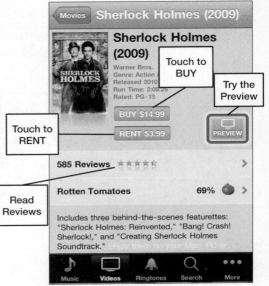

Finding TV Shows

When you're done checking out the movies, tap the **TV Shows** button at the top to see what is available from your favorite shows (see Figure 25–3).

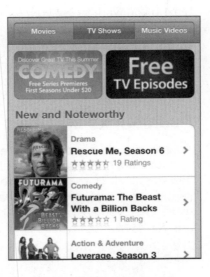

When you tap on a TV series, you will see the individual episodes available. Tap any episode to check out the 30-second preview. See Chapter 16 for more on watching videos. When you're finished with the preview, tap the **Done** button.

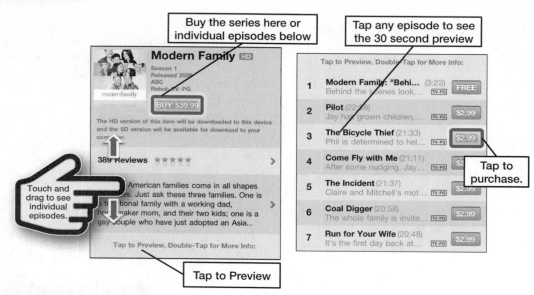

Figure 25–3. *Buying a TV season or episode*

When you are ready to buy, you can choose to buy an individual episode or the entire TV series. Many, but not all, TV series allow you to purchase individual episodes.

Maybe you want to get your fix of *Modern Family* and see the pilot episode that you missed. You can do this quickly and easily on your iPhone 4.

NOTE: There is also a **Free TV Episode** category, where you can get samples and bonus content.

Audiobooks in iTunes

Audiobooks are a great way to enjoy books without having to read them. Some of the narrators are so fun to listen to, it is almost like watching a movie. For example, the narrator of the Harry Potter series can do dozens of truly amazing voices. We recommend that you try out an audiobook on your iPhone 4; audiobooks are especially great when you are on an airplane and want to escape from the rest of the passengers, but don't want to have the light on.

TIP: If you're a big audiobook listener, getting an Audible.com subscription can get you the same content at cheaper prices.

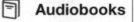

If you are an audiobook aficionado, be sure to check out the audiobooks in iTunes.

You can use the top three buttons to browse the audiobooks in iTunes:

- **Featured**
- **Top Tens**
- **Categories**

Touch "More" then touch the "Audiobooks" tab then touch Featured, Top Tens or Categories.

iTunes U: Great Educational Content

If you like educational content, then check out **iTunes U**. You will be able to see whether your university, college, or school has its own section.

One good example we discovered in just a few minutes of browsing around was a panel discussion with three Nobel Prize–winning economists moderated by Paul Solman (Economic correspondent for the PBS News Hour). You can find the podcast in **iTunes U** ➤ Universities & Colleges ➤ Boston University ➤ BUNIVERSE - Business ➤ Audio. Like much of the content in **iTunes U**, it was free!

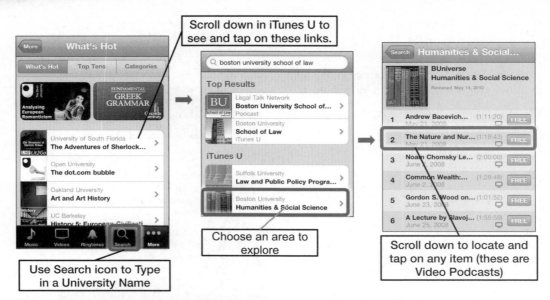

Figure 25–4. *You can search for a particular university, then browse iTunes U by that university.*

If you are in a location with a good wireless signal, you can tap the title of the audio or video item, and then listen to or watch it streaming (see Figure 25–5). If your signal gets interrupted, however, you will lose your place in the video. There are many advantages to actually downloading the file (if possible) for later viewing, not least of which is that you get more control of the video-watching experience.

NOTE: iTunes audio streaming, like audio podcasts, uses the new background audio multitasking API in iOS4 and allows you to interrupt a streaming podcast to check email and then go right back to it.

Download for Offline Viewing

If you know you are going to be out of wireless coverage for a while, such as on an airplane or in the subway, you will want to download the content for later, offline viewing or listening. Tap the **Free** button to change it to a **Download** button, and then tap it again. You can then monitor the download progress (some larger videos may take ten minutes or more to complete) by tapping the **Downloads** button at the bottom right of the screen. When the download is complete, the item will show up in the correct area in your **iPod 4** app.

NOTE: Any file larger than 20MB cannot be downloaded over the 3G network; you must use Wi-Fi for larger files.

Searching iTunes

Sometimes you have a good idea of what you want, but you are unsure where it is located or perhaps you don't feel like browsing or navigating all the menus. The Search tool is for you.

Up in the top right-hand corner of the **iTunes** app, as in virtually every other iPhone 4 app, you have a search window.

Touch **Search**, and the search window and the on-device keyboard will pop up. Once you start typing, the iPhone 4 will begin to match your entry with possibilities.

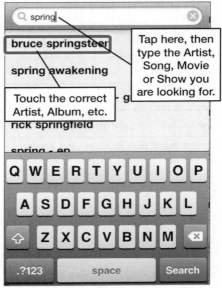

Tap here, then type the Artist, Song, Movie or Show you are looking for.

Touch the correct Artist, Album, etc.

Type in the artist, song name, video name, podcast name, or album you are searching for, and the iPhone 4 will display detailed matches. Be as general or as specific as you would like. If you are just looking to browse all particular songs by an artist, type the artist's name. If you want a specific song or album, enter the full name of the song or album.

When you locate the song or album name, simply touch it and you will be taken to the purchase page.

Purchasing or Renting Music, Videos, Podcasts, and More

Once you locate a song, video, TV show, or album, you can touch the **Buy** or (if you see it) **Rent** button. This will cause your media to start downloading. (If the content is free, then you will see the **Free** button, which you tap to turn into a **Download** button.)

We suggest you view or listen to the preview, as well as check out the customer reviews first, unless you are absolutely sure you want to purchase the item.

NOTE: You can also purchase ringtones for your phone from the iTunes store. Make sure to check out Chapter 10, where we show you how to create your own ringtones for free!

Previewing Music

Touch either the title of the song or its track number to the left of the song title; this will flip over the album cover and launch the preview window.

You will hear a representative clip of 30 seconds of the song.

Touch the **Stop** button and the track number will again be displayed.

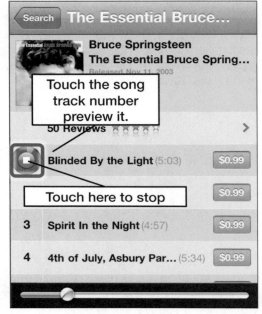

Check Out Customer Reviews

Many items in iTunes offer customer reviews. The reviews range from a low of one star to a high of five stars.

> **CAUTION:** *Be aware that the reviews can have explicit language.* Many of the reviews are clean; however, some do contain explicit language that may not be caught by the iTunes store right away.

Reading the reviews might give you a fairly good idea of whether you would like to buy the item.

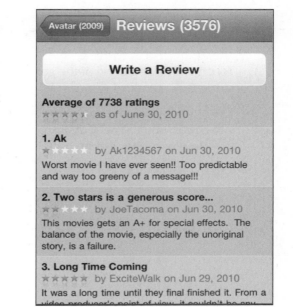

Previewing a Video, TV Show, or Music Video

Pretty much everything on iTunes offers a preview. Sometimes you will see a **Preview** button, as with music videos and movies. TV shows are a little different; you tap the episode title in order to see the 30-second preview.

We do highly recommend checking out the reviews, as well as trying the preview before purchasing items on iTunes.

Typical movie previews or trailers will be longer than 30 seconds. Some are two and a half minutes or longer.

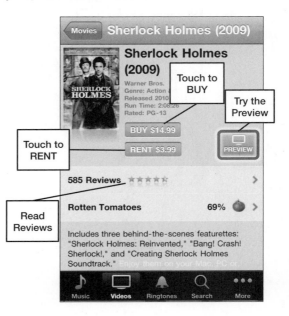

Purchasing a Song, Video, or Other Item

Once you are sure you want to purchase a
song, video, or other item, follow these steps
to buy it.

1. Touch the **Price** button of the song
   or the **Buy** button.

2. The button will change and turn
   into a green **Buy Now**, **Buy Song**,
   Buy Single, or **Buy Album** button.

3. Tap the **Buy** button.

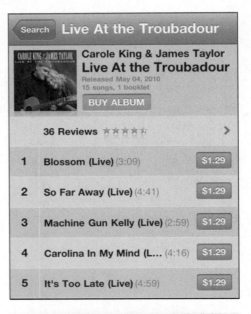

4. You will see an animated icon
   jump into the shopping cart.
   Type in your iTunes
   password and touch **OK** to
   complete the sale.

Touch the **More** button in the lower right-hand corner to see the download progress for each song on the album.

The song or album will then become part of your music library, and it will be synced with your computer the next time you connect your iPhone 4 to iTunes on your computer.

After the download is complete, you will see the new song, audiobook, podcast, or iTunes U podcast inside the correct category within your **iPod** icon.

> **NOTE:** Purchased videos and iTunes U videos go into the **Videos** section of the **iPod** app on your iPhone 4.

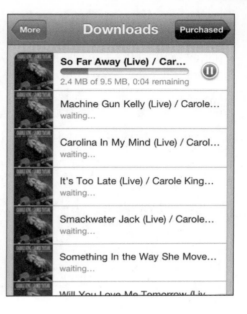

Podcasts in iTunes

Podcasts are usually a series of audio segments; these may be updated frequently (such as hourly news reports from National Public Radio) or not updated at all (such as a recording of a one-time lecture on a particular topic).

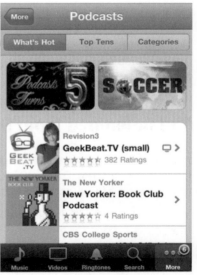

You can use the top three buttons to browse the podcasts in iTunes:

- **What's Hot**
- **Top Tens**
- **Categories**

Downloading a Podcast

Podcasts are available in video and audio varieties. When you locate a podcast, just touch the title of the podcast (see Figure 25–5). Luckily, most podcasts are free. If it is free, you will see a **Free** button instead of the typical **Buy** button.

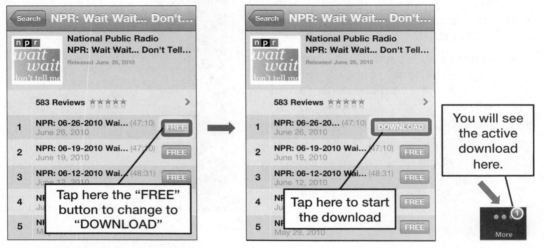

Figure 25–5. *Downloading an NPR podcast*

When you touch the button, it turns into a green button that says **Download**. Touch **Download**, and an animated icon jumps into your **Downloads** icon at the bottom bar of soft keys. A small number displayed in red reflects the number of files downloading.

The Download Icon: Stopping and Deleting Downloads

As you download items, they appear in your Downloads screen. This behavior is just like the behavior of iTunes on your computer.

You can touch the **Downloads** icon along the bottom row to see the progress of all your downloads.

Where the Downloads Go

All of your downloads will be visible in either your **iPod** icon or your **More** icon, organized by category. In other words, if you download a podcast, you will need to go into your **iPod** icon, touch **More**, and then the **Podcasts** tab to see the downloaded podcast.

Sometimes, you decide that you do not want the all downloads you selected. If you want to stop a download and delete it, swipe your finger over the download to bring up the **Delete** button, and then tap **Delete** (see Figure 25–6).

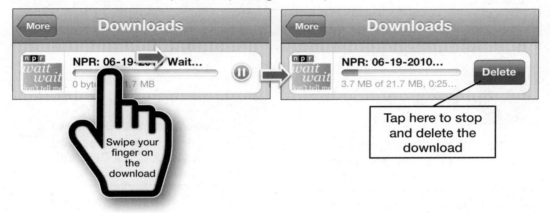

Figure 25–6. *Deleting a file while downloading*

Redeeming an iTunes Gift Card

One of the cool things about iTunes on your iPhone 4 is that, just as with iTunes on your computer, you can redeem a gift card and receive credit in your iTunes account for your purchases.

At the bottom of the **iTunes** screen, you should see the **Redeem** button (see Figure 25–7).

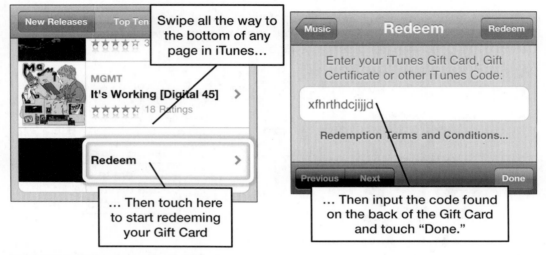

Figure 25–7. *Redeeming an iTunes gift card*

Tap the **Redeem** button to start the process of entering your iTunes gift card number for an iTunes store credit.

Chapter 26

The Amazing App Store

You have just seen how easy it is download music, videos, and podcasts from iTunes right to your iPhone. We have also shown you how to download iBooks from the iBooks store.

It is just as easy to download new applications from Apple's amazing **App Store**. Apps are available for just about any function you can think of: games, productivity tools, social networking, and anything else you can imagine. As the advertising says, *There's an app for that*.

In this chapter, you will learn how to navigate the **App Store**, as well as how to search for and download apps. You will also learn how to maintain and update your apps once they are downloaded onto your iPhone.

NOTE: If you purchase a new, unlocked iPhone 4 while travelling and bring it home to a country where it's not yet sold, then there's a good chance you may not be able to use your iPhone to purchase apps specifically designed for the iPhone 4 in your home country from the **App Store**. The work-around is to buy iPhone apps on the desktop version of **iTunes** (which does work) and sync them over.

Learning More About Apps and the App Store

In this chapter, we will focus on the **App Store** that you can access on your iPhone. However, you should remember that you can also shop at the **App Store** using the **iTunes** program on your Mac or PC (see Figure 26–1).

Figure 26–1. *Accessing the App Store from the iTunes program on your computer or the* **App Store** *icon on your iPhone.*

In a very short amount of time, the **App Store** has exploded in popularity. There are apps for just about anything you can imagine. Apps come in all prices; in many cases, the apps are even free!

The following interesting **App Store** statistics are provided courtesy of the www.148apps.biz web site. These stats were copied from the web pagehttp://148apps.biz/app-store-metrics/ when it was updated on July 18, 2010:

In July 2010, there were almost 600 apps submitted every day! (*Author's note:* By the time you read this, there will likely be more than 250,000 apps in the store.)

- COUNT OF ACTIVE APPLICATIONS IN THE APP STORE
    - Total Active Apps (currently available for download): 233,638
    - Number of Active Publishers in the U.S. App Store: 46,267
- APPLICATION PRICE DISTRIBUTION
    - Current Average App Price: $3.05
    - Current Average Game Price: $1.28
    - Current Average Overall Price: $2.79

Where to Find Apps News and Reviews

You can find reviews for many apps in the **App Store** itself, and we recommend you check out the **App Store** reviews. However, sometimes you will probably want more information from expert reviewers. If so, blogs are a great place to find news and reviews.

Here is a list of Apple iPhone- and iPod-related blogs with reviews of apps:

- The iPhone Blog: www.tipb.com

- Touch Reviews: www.touchreviews.net

- Touch My Apps: www.touchmyapps.com

- The Unofficial Apple Weblog: www.tuaw.com

- Cult of Mac: www.cultofmac.com

- App Smile: www.appsmile.com

App Store Basics

With a little time, you should find the **App Store** to be quite intuitive to navigate. We'll cover some of the basics for getting the most out of the **App Store**, so that your experience will be as enjoyable and productive as possible.

> **NOTE:** App availability varies by country. Some apps are only available in some countries, and some countries may not have certain games sections due to local ratings laws.

A Network Connection Is Required

After you set up your **App Store** (**iTunes**) account, you still need to have the right network connectivity (either Wi-Fi or 3G) to access the **App Store** and download apps. Check out Chapter 5: "Wi-Fi and 3G Connectivity" to learn how to tell whether you are connected.

Starting the App Store

The **App Store** icon should be on your first page of icons on the **Home** screen. Tap the icon to launch the **App Store**.

The App Store Home Page

We'll look at several parts of the App Store Home page: the Top Bar, middle content, and the bottom soft keys.

We'll look at the Top Bar first. At the top of the page shown in Figure 26–2, you will see three buttons: **New**, **What's Hot**, and **Genius**. Tap any of these to change the view.

> **TIP: Genius** is a fairly new feature in the App Store. Once you enable it and agree to the terms and conditions, the **Genius** feature suggests apps you might like based on apps you have already downloaded and installed on your iPhone. It can be quite a nice way to filter through the hundreds of thousands of apps to find the ones that might interest you.

The middle of the page is your main content area. This main content area shows you a list of apps or the details of a specific app when you are viewing one app. You can swipe up or down to view more apps in a list or details for a specific app. You can swipe left or right when viewing screen shots. On this **Featured** apps page, you will notice that there are a few large icons at the top. Clicking these icons will show you either types of apps or individual apps. Below the larger icons you have to swipe down), you will see a number of featured apps.

The bottom of the **App Store** page has five soft key buttons:

- **Featured**: Shows apps that have been highlighted by the **App Store** or by the app developers.

- **Categories**: Shows a list of categories used to organize the apps, so you can browse by category.

- **Top 25**: Shows top selling or top downloaded apps.

- **Search**: Finds an app using entered search terms.

- **Updates**: Lets you update any apps you have installed.

You can tell that Figure 26–2 is showing **Featured** apps because the **Featured** soft key is highlighted on the bottom row of soft keys. Also, scrolling is handled the same way as in **iTunes** and in other programs—just move your finger up and down to scroll through the page.

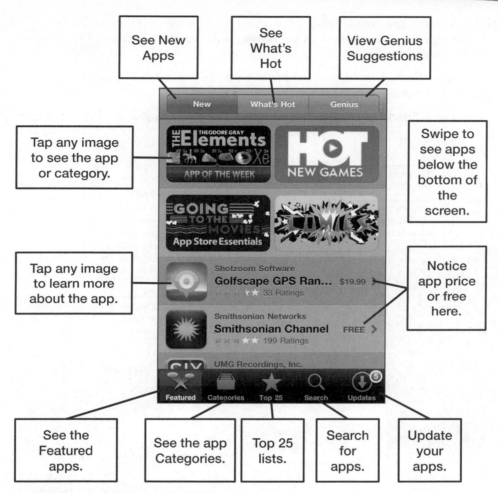

Figure 26–2. *Layout of the App Store Home page.*

NOTE: The **App Store** is essentially a web site, so it changes frequently. Some of the details and nuances of the **App Store** might be a bit different after this book goes to print.

Viewing App Details

If you see an app in a list that looks interesting, tap it to learn more. The Details screen for the app includes its price, a description, screen shots, and reviews (see Figure 26–3). You can use this information to help you determine whether the app will be a good choice for you.

Swipe down to read more details about the app on the **Info** page. Swipe left or right to view more screen shots of the app. Tap the **Rating** button near the bottom to read all the reviews for an app.

You can also see other details about the app, such as its file size, its version number, and developer information near the bottom of the **Info** page.

You can also **Tell a Friend** or **Report a Problem** using the buttons at the bottom of the screen.

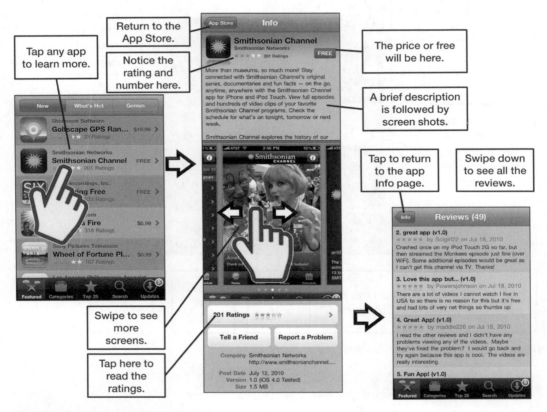

Figure 26–3. *Viewing details about an app.*

Finding an App to Download

If you want to search for an app to download, begin by looking around in the default view, which shows the **Featured** apps. Scroll down the page to see all the featured apps.

NOTE: As with **iTunes**, you can only download apps less than 20MB in size while on 3G. Downloading larger file sizes requires a Wi-Fi connection.

Viewing the New Apps

The default view in the **App Store** shows new and featured apps. This is the view shown back in Figure 26–2. You can tell that this view shows new featured apps because the

Featured soft key ![Featured] is highlighted at the bottom of the screen, and the **New**

button ![New] at the top of the page is pressed.

Viewing What's Hot

Touch the **What's Hot** button at the top of the screen, and the "hottest" apps in the store will be shown on the screen. Again, just scroll through the hottest apps to see if something catches your eye.

NOTE: The fact that an app is in the "What's Hot" category does not necessarily mean you will also believe it is useful or fun. Check out the app descriptions and reviews carefully before you purchase anything.

Genius

The third button at the top of the **Featured** apps section is the **Genius** feature. This feature works like the identically named feature in **iTunes** used on your computer for music. For example, it displays apps you might like based on apps you already have installed on your iPhone.

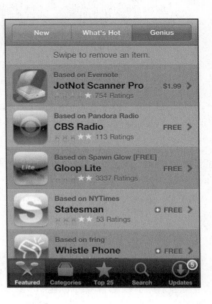

> **NOTE:** The first time you use the **Genius** feature, you will have to accept the terms and conditions presented before the feature will be enabled.

Based On

Notice that there is a **Based on (app name)** label above each app. This label shows you that the suggested app was based on a specific app you've installed on your iPhone. For example, the **CBS Radio** suggestion was based on the fact that **Pandora Radio** is installed. We didn't know about CBS Radio, but maybe we'll give it a try based on this recommendation.

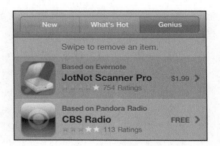

Swipe to Remove

If you do not like a Genius suggestion, then you can swipe left or right on it to bring up the **Delete** button, just as you would to remove email or other items from lists on your iPhone 4. Tap the **Delete** button to remove that app from the list.

Disable Genius Feature

To disable the **Genius** feature, you need to go into your **App Store** settings. See the "App Store Settings" section later in this chapter to learn how to disable this feature.

Categories

Sometimes, all the choices presented can be a bit overwhelming. If you have a sense of what type of app you are looking for, touch the **Categories** button along the bottom row of soft keys (see Figure 26–4).

The current categories available are shown in Table 26–1.

Table 26–1. *The App Store Category Listing*

▪ Games	▪ Reference	▪ Finance
▪ Entertainment	▪ Travel	▪ Education
▪ Utilities	▪ Sports	▪ Weather
▪ Social Networking	▪ Navigation	▪ Books
▪ Music	▪ Healthcare & Fitness	▪ Medical
▪ Productivity	▪ News	
▪ Lifestyle	▪ Photography	

NOTE: The categories listed are fluid and change over time, so it is possible that the categories you see will have changed by the time this book finds its way into your hands.

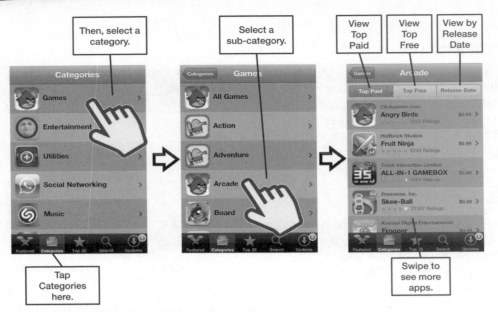

Then, select a category.

Select a sub-category.

View Top Paid

View Top Free

View by Release Date

Tap Categories here.

Swipe to see more apps.

Figure 26–4. *Viewing apps by category – Games, in this example.*

Looking at the Top 25 Charts

Touch the **Top Charts** soft key along the bottom row, and the **App Store** will change the view again. This time it will show you the top 25 paid, free, and top-grossing apps. Just touch one of the **Top Paid, Top Free**, or **Top Grossing** buttons at the top to switch between the views.

> **NOTE:** The **Top Grossing** category refers to the highest money-making apps, which is sales volume times selling price. This view will help more expensive apps get up higher in the charts. For example, a $4.99 app that sells 10,000 units will rank much higher on the **Top Grossing** chart than a $0.99 app that sells the same number of units.

Searching for an App

Let's say you have a specific idea of the type of app you want to find. Touch the **Search** soft key and type in either the name of the program or the type of program.

So, if you are looking for an app to help you with rowing, just type in *rowing* to see what comes up.

You may see some suggested search terms appear; tap these to narrow your search.

Tapping **Rowing Stats** in the suggested search terms yielded only one result.

We want to see all the rowing-related apps, so we tap in the **Search** bar and use the **Backspace** key to erase the word *Stats*. Next, we tap the **Search** button in the lower right corner to see a broader list of rowing-related results.

> **TIP:** If you row on the water (instead of only on a rowing machine), you might want to check out **SpeedCoach Mobile**, which sells for $64.99. There is also a free (at the time of writing) alternative called **iRowPro**.

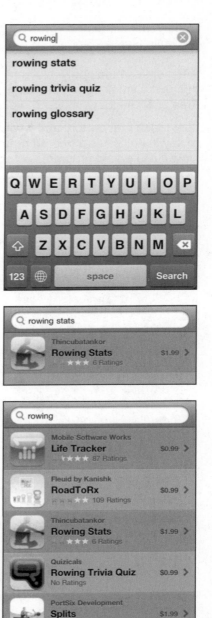

Downloading an App

Once you find the app you are looking for, you can download it right to your iPhone, as shown in Figure 26–5.

After locating the app you want to buy, notice the small button that says either Free or $0.99 (or whatever the price is).

Just touch that button, and it will change to say Install if it is a free program or Buy Now if it is a paid program.

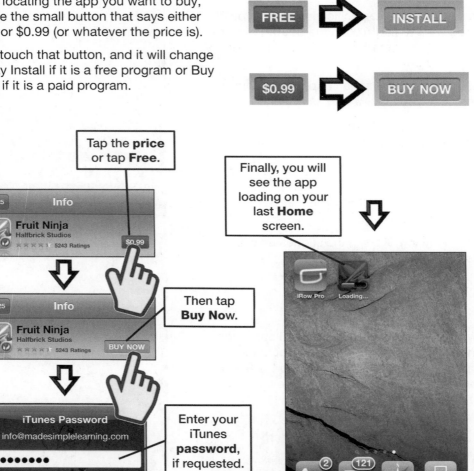

Figure 26–5. *Buying an app or downloading a free app.*

Once you have read the reviews and the app description (and perhaps visited the developer support site), go ahead and download or purchase the app. Once you tap the **Download App** button, you will be prompted to input your **iTunes** password.

Input your password and tap **OK**; the app will be downloaded to your iPhone, as shown in Figure 26–4.

Finding Free or Discounted Apps

After browsing around, you will notice a couple of things about the **App Store**. First, there are lots of *free* apps. Sometimes, these are great applications. Other times, they are not so useful—but they can still be fun!

Second, you will notice that there will be sales for some of the apps, while other apps will become less expensive over time. So if you have a favorite app and it costs $6.99, it is likely that waiting a few weeks or a month might result in a lower price.

Maintaining and Updating Your Apps

Often, developers will update their apps for the iPhone. You don't need to use your computer to perform the update—you can do it right on your iPhone.

You can even tell if you have updates, and how many, by looking at the **App Store** icon. The one shown here has five app updates available for you to download.

Once you enter the **App Store**, tap the right-most icon on the bottom row. This is the **Updates** icon.

If you have apps with updates available, there will be a small number indicated in red. This number corresponds to the number of apps with updates.

When you touch the **Update** button, the iPhone shows you which apps have updates.

To get your updates, you could touch an individual app. However, it is easier to touch the **Update All** button

in the upper right corner to have all your apps updated at once. The iPhone will leave the **App Store**, and you can see the progress of the updates in the little status bars. All apps updating will have icons that look grayed out.

Some status messages will show **Waiting**, while others will show **Loading** or **Installing**. When the update is complete, all your icons will return to their normal colors.

> **NOTE:** You will need to relaunch the **App Store** to get back in. The update process takes you completely out of the store.

App Store Settings

As with other apps, your settings for the **App Store** are located in the **Settings** app. You can check which account is logged into the store, log out, turn off the **Genius** feature, view your iTunes account, and work with your newsletter subscriptions.

> **TIP:** If you want to prevent someone from buying apps on your iPhone using your iTunes account, you would want to **Sign Out** of iTunes using the steps below.

Follow these steps to change a setting for the **App Store** program:

1. Tap the **Settings** icon.

2. Scroll down and tap **Store**. Notice that you can see the account you are logged in with at the top of this screen.

3. Tap **Sign Out** if you wish to log out of **iTunes**. For example, you might be giving this iPhone to someone whom you do not want to buy apps using your iTunes account.

4. Tap **View Account** to see details of your account (you will need to sign in).

The figure to the right shows your account information. Tap **Payment Information** to adjust your billing information (credit card type, number, etc.).

5. Tap **Billing Address** to update your address.

6. Tap **Change Country** to change your country.

7. Scroll down to see more settings.

8. You can **Turn Off Genius for Apps** or **Turn it On** using the button. Or, you can **Subscribe** or **Unsubscribe** to the iTunes newsletter from this dialog.

9. Tap **Done** in the upper right corner when finished.

Settings   **Store**

Account: info@madesimplelearning.com

View Account

Sign Out

Account   Done

Edit Account Info

apple ID   **info@madesimplelearning**

Payment Information & Billing Address

payment info   **Visa** **** **** **** **6962**

billing address   **Mr. Martin Trautschold 25 Forest View Way Ormond Beach, FL 32174 (386) 5068224**

Change Country or Region

United States

Genius

Turn Off Genius for Apps

iTunes Newsletters and Special Offers

Subscribe   **Unsubscribe**

Apple uses industry-standard encryption to protect the confidentiality of your personal information.

Terms of Service   **Privacy Policy**

Chapter 27

Games and Fun

Your iPhone 4 excels at many things. It is a multimedia workhorse, and it can keep track of your busy life. Your iPhone 4 particularly excels in two areas: as a gaming device and for displaying iPhone iOS4-specific apps that take advantage of the beautiful, high-resolution touch screen. You can even find versions of popular games for the device that you might expect to find only on dedicated gaming consoles.

The iPhone 4 brings many advantages to portable gaming: the high definition (HD) screen delivers for realistic visuals; the high quality audio provides great sound effects; and the gyroscope and the accelerometer allow you to interact with your games in a way that many PCs and dedicated gaming consoles (outside of the Wii) don't. For example, in racing games, the last feature lets you steer your car by turning the iPhone 4 as you hold it.

The iPhone 4 is also great for lots of other fun stuff like following your local baseball team and even using the iPhone as a musical instrument with great apps like Ocarina (which we show you later in the chapter.)

NOTE: We have written many books on the BlackBerry smartphones, and we have many BlackBerry devices lying around the house. The BlackBerry smartphones don't disappear into our children's rooms; rather, the iPhone 4 is the device that our children (and our spouses) have decided is fun enough to grab. We routinely discover that the iPhone 4 has disappeared from its charger and have to yell out, "Where is my iPhone 4? I need to finish this book!"

Using the iPhone 4 As a Gaming Device

The iPhone 4 includes a built-in accelerometer and *gyroscope*, which is essentially a device that detects movement (acceleration) and tilt.

Combine the accelerometer with a fantastic screen, lots of memory, and a fast processor, and you have the makings of a great gaming platform. With literally thousands of gaming titles to choose from, you can play virtually any type of game you wish on your iPhone 4.

With iOS 4, if a game supports multitasking, you can even take a phone call and come back to the exact place you left off. This means no more restarts!

> **NOTE:** Some games do require that you have an active network connection, either Wi-Fi or 3G, to engage in multiplayer games.

With the iPhone 4, you can play a driving game and use the iPhone 4 itself to steer. You do this simply by turning the device. You can touch the iPhone 4 to brake or tilt it forward to accelerate.

This game is so realistic that it might make you car sick!

"Real Racing HD"

Tap to Brake

Tilt the iPad left/ right to steer the Car

Lean forward to accelerate

Or, you can try a fishing game, where you case and reel in fish from the perspective of being on a boat!

"Flick Fishing"

Wind with your finger to reel in your fish

If music/rhythm games are your thing, then you will find many such programs in the App store. Popular console games such as **Rock Band**, **Guitar Hero**, and others have been ported to the iPhone.

On some games such as the new Guitar Hero, you really have to "strum" to keep pace and score points.

The iPhone 4 also has a very fast processor and a sophisticated graphics chip. Bundling these together with the accelerometer gives you a very capable gaming device.

Acquiring Games and Other Fun Apps

As is the case for all iPhone 4 apps, games can be found at the App Store (see Figure 27-1). You can get them either through iTunes on your computer or through the device's App Store.

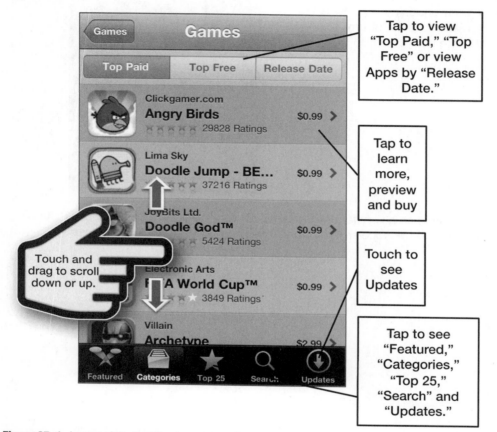

Figure 27-1. *Layout of the App* Store's *game section.*

To get a game, fire up the App Store as you did in the previous chapter. Next, use the **Categories** icon to go to the **Games** tab. You will also find many games in the **Featured** section of the App store, as well as in the **New and Notable** section. Figure 27–2 shows the app purchase page for a game available for the iPhone 4.

Touch on "Games."

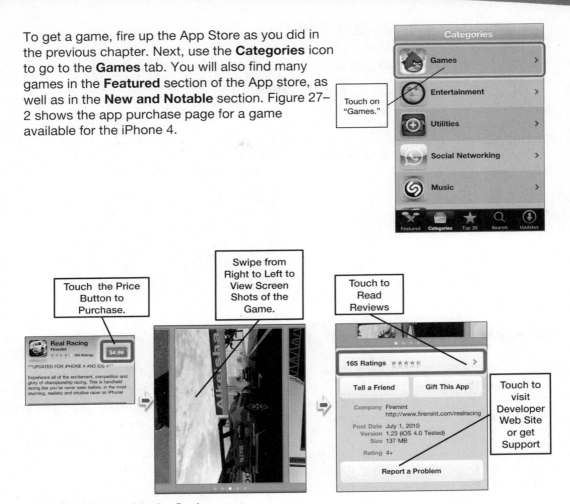

Figure 27–2. *Layout of the App Purchase page.*

Reading Reviews Before You Buy

Many of the games have user reviews that are worth perusing. Sometimes, you can get a good sense of the game before you buy it. If you find a game that looks interesting, don't be afraid to do a simple Google search to see whether any mainstream media outlets have performed a full review.

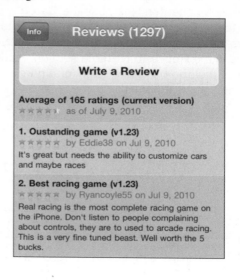

Looking for Free Trials or Lite Versions

Increasingly, game developers are giving users free trials of their games to see if they like them before they buy. You will find many games have both a Lite version and a Full version in the App Store.

Some "free" games are supported by the inclusion of ads within the game. Other games are free to start, but require in-app purchases for continued play or additional features.

Being Careful When You Play

You might use the iPhone 4 to cast your line in a fishing game, as you would in real life. You can also move around a bit in driving and first-person shooter games. So be mindful of your surroundings as you play! For example, make sure you have a good grip on your device, so it doesn't slip out of your hand; we recommend a good silicone case to help with this.

CAUTION: Games such as **Real Racing** can be quite addictive!

Two-Player Games

The iPhone 4 really opens up the possibility for two-player gaming. In this example, we are playing checkers against one another, using the iPhone 4 as a game board.

You can find similar two-person gaming apps for other board games, such as chess or checkers.

Online and Wireless Games

The iPhone 4 also allows online and wireless, peer-to-peer gaming (if the game supports it). Many new games are incorporating this technology. In **Scrabble**, for example, you can play against multiple players on their own devices. You can even use the iPhone 4 as your game board and up to four individual iPhones as wireless "racks" to hold the letters of all the players. Just flick the letters off the rack, and they go onto the board – very cool!

In this example, I selected **Online** from the **Real Racing** menu. I now have the option to either play against another opponent through Wi-Fi or to join an online league race.

NOTE: If you just want to play against a friend who is nearby, select Wi-Fi mode for multiplayer games. If you just want to play against new people, try going online for a league race or game.

Playing Music Games with Your iPhone 4

The iPhone 4's relatively large screen means that you can even install a piano keyboard on your iPhone 4 and play music. There are a number of music-related games available; check out the **Music** subcategory of the **Games** category in the iTunes Store to see what's available.

One of the apps that was in the Top 5 of the **Paid iPhone 4** apps category when we were writing this book was **Ocarina** , which turns your iPhone into a flute-like instrument for just US $0.99.

Download the app and just have fun with it!

If you have children, they might enjoy it, as well.

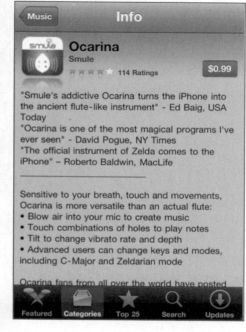

> **NOTE:** This app wants to know your location, so it can tell people around the world where you are when they hear you play. You can always say "No" when it asks you for permission.

Playing Songs from the Songbook

To use Ocarina, begin by tapping the **Menu** button in the center and select **Info**. You can find out where to go to get music to play. You can visit http://Ocarina.smule.com to acquire tutorials and music. With Ocarina, you blow into your microphone and place your fingers on the circles, just as you would for a recorder (see Figure 27–3).

> **TIP:** Begin by trying out the tutorial that teaches the notes of the scale. Next, you can try playing a song or just "freestyling."

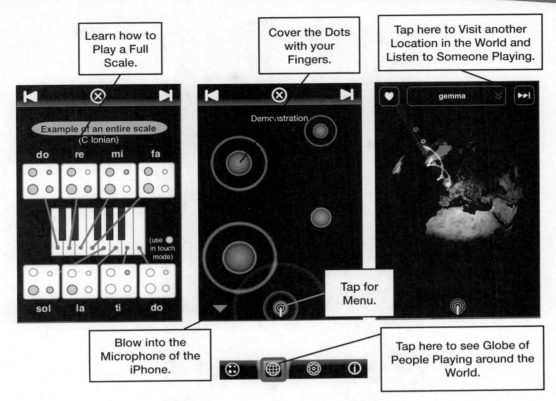

Figure 27–3. *Ocarina's controls and menu.*

The World View

Tap the **Menu** button and select **World** (see Figure 27–4). This shows you a globe with people happily "making music" in various places around the world.

If you like the way someone is playing, then hit the **Heart** icon. If you do not like the music you're hearing, then hit the **Next** icon (the two right arrows).

If you like the way someone plays, click here.

If you do not like the way someone plays, click here to skip to the next person.

Watch people playing Ocarina and their locations.

Click here to go to the Menu.

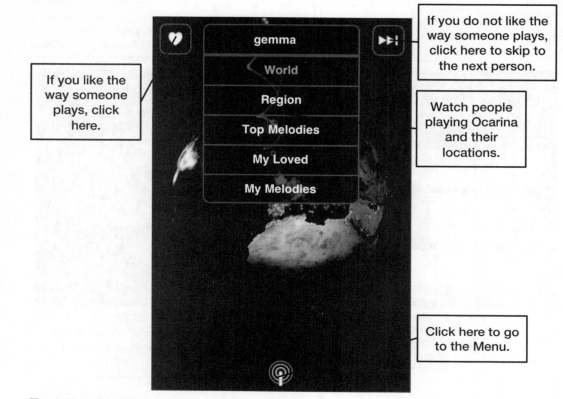

Figure 27–4. *Ocarina's world view – watching others play Ocarina.*

Other Fun Stuff: Baseball on the iPhone 4

There are many great apps that can provide you with endless hours of entertainment on the iPhone 4. Since the iPhone 4 was released on opening day of the Major League Baseball season, it is appropriate to highlight an app that was honored as the first "App of the Week" in the iPhone 4 App Store.

At Bat 2010 for iPhone 4 is a US $14.99 application that is well worth the entry fee for any baseball fan. It also highlights the iPhone 4's capabilities.

The main view of the app changes based on whether there are baseball games currently being played. When you first register the app, you pick your favorite team. The favorite team on the iPhone 4 in this example is set to the Red Sox. So, if this team is playing, then the view automatically goes to that team's game first. If the team is not playing, then it displays a recap of the team's previous game. Alternatively, it might list the details of the team's next game.

The main view during game time shows a batter at the plate (see Figure 27–5). This batter represents the real batter. Batters will switch sides of the plate, depending on whether the batter currently up hits from the left or right side of the plate. The current pitch count is shown above the plate, and the score is displayed at the top of the screen.

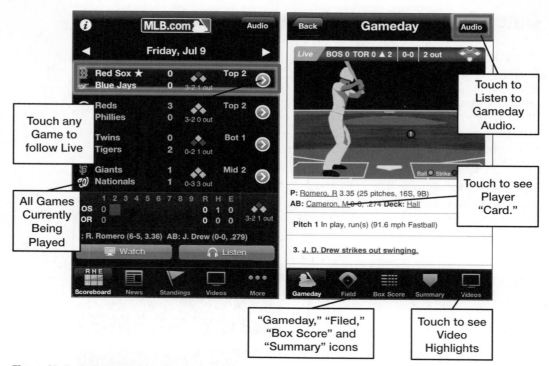

Figure 27–5. *At Bat 2010's layout.*

When you see a player at the plate or on base, you can touch the player's image to bring up his baseball card and view his stats.

If the game is being televised, there will be a **Watch** button at the lower left of the **Home** screen.

Touch the **Watch** button, and you will be taken to the MLB TV **Login** screen to watch the game.

Note: You need to have a separate MLB TV account to be able to watch live games.

You can touch the **Listen** icon to listen to the game day audio from either of the two cities playing a particular game.

You can touch the **Information** icon to adjust your favorite team, input your MLB TV subscription information (if you have one), or jump right to the MLB web site.

TIP: You can even allow notifications to be sent when something newsworthy occurs related to your favorite team. To do this, touch the **Information** icon and turn **Notifications** to **ON**.

To see video highlights of key plays of the game, just touch the **Videos** box in the lower right corner.

Touch any of the listed videos, and it will begin to play in the iPhone's **Video** player.

To jump to any other game that is being played, touch the **Back** button from the **Gameday** view and then touch the **Scoreboard** icon on the main page.

The options in this app are quite extensive, and the experience is immersive. This is a great way to follow your favorite teams, wherever you might be.

Chapter 28

Social Networking

Some of the most popular places to "connect" these days are those sites that are often called social networking sites—places that allow you to create your own page and connect with friends and family to see what is going in their lives. Some of the biggest web sites for social networking are Facebook, Twitter, and LinkedIn.

In this chapter, we will show you how to access these various sites. You will learn how to update your status, "tweet," and keep track of those who are both important or simply of interest to you.

Facebook

Facebook was founded in February of 2004. Since that time, it has served as the premier site for users to connect, re-connect, and share information with friends, co-workers, and family. Today, over 400 million people use Facebook as their primary source of "catching up" with the people who matter most to them.

> **NOTE: You cannot play Facebook games inside the Facefook app on your iPhone 4.** This may disappoint you if you are a big Facebook game player. At publishing time, you could not play any Facebook games, such as FarmVille and Mafia Wars, on your iPhone 4. However, you can often get the same games, including FarmVille, from the App Store and connect them to your Facebook computer version to keep your place.

On your iPhone 4, you have three primary ways of accessing your Facebook page as of publishing time:

1. Use Safari to go to the standard (full) web site: www.facebook.com.

2. Use Safari to go to the mobile site: touch.facebook.com.

3. Use the iPhone 4 **Facebook** app.

NOTE: The iPhone 4 app is a bit more limited than the full web site, but it is much easier to navigate.

Different Ways to Connect to Facebook

You can access Facebook by using the iPhone app or using one of two Facebook web sites in your Safari browser. For our purposes, we will focus on the **Facebook** app for the duration of this chapter.

Downloading and Installing the Facebook App

In order to find the app, use the **Search** feature in the App Store and simply type in **Facebook**.

You can also go to the Social Networking category in the App Store and find the official **Facebook** app as well as many other Facebook-related apps.

NOTE: Some of the apps may look like "official" Facebook apps and they do cost money. The only "official" app is the iPhone/iPod app mentioned.

In order to connect to your account on Facebook, you will need to locate the icon you just installed and click on it. We use the example of Facebook here, but the process is very similar for the rest of the apps.

Once Facebook is successfully downloaded, the icon should look something like this.

The Facebook App

To get the **Facebook** app installed on your iPhone 4, start up the **App Store** and search for Facebook. Tap the **Install** button from the **Facebook** app listing.

Facebook App Basics

Once Facebook is downloaded and installed, the first thing you will see is the login screen. Input your account information—your email address and password.

After you log in the first time, you will see a **Push Notifications** warning message.

Click **OK** if you want to allow these messages, which can be pokes from other Facebook friends, notes, status update notifications, and more.

Once you log in, you will see the Facebook screen shown in Figure 28-1. Tap the **Facebook** logo to navigate around the app.

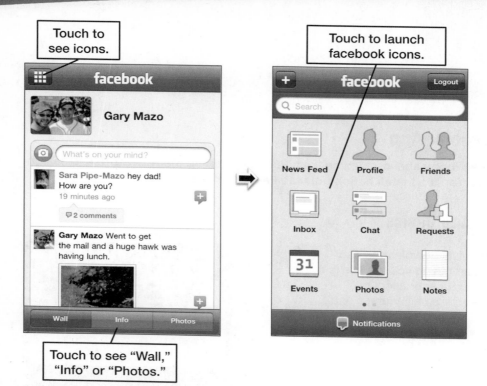

Figure 28-1. *Using the* **Facebook** *app.*

Navigating Around Facebook

Toggle between the **Navigation** icons and your current location by tapping the word **Facebook** at the top of the page.

For example, if you are in the **News Feed** and tap **Facebook**, you will see all the icons. Tap **Facebook** again and you will return to the **News Feed**.

From the icons page, you can access your **News Feed**, **Profile**, **Notifications**, **Upload a Photo**, **Friends**, **Requests**, **Events**, **Chat**, or **Inbox**.

Communicating with Your Friends

1. Tap **Facebook** at the top to see all the icons.

2. Tap the **Friends** icon and your list of friends is displayed.

3. Touch the Friend and you will go to his or her Facebook page, where you can then write on the **Wall** and see your friend's **Info** or **Photos**.

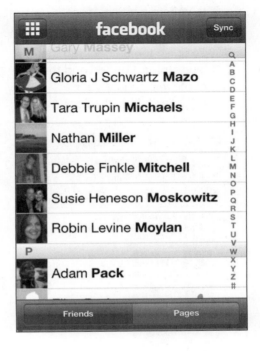

Uploading Pictures with the Facebook App

An easy and fun thing to do with Facebook is to upload pictures. Here, we show you how to upload pictures in the **Facebook** app.

1. From the Facebook main icons, tap **Photos**.

2. Choose an album, such as Mobile Uploads.

3. Tap the **Camera** next to the *What's on your mind?* Box. Then tap the **Take Photo or Video** to snap a picture or take a video to upload. Or, tap **Choose From Library** to navigate through the pictures on your iPhone 4 until you find the

picture you wish to upload.

4. Next, tap **Write a caption...** to write a caption, if so desired.

5. To finish the upload, tap the blue **Upload** button and the photo will go into your "Mobile Uploads" folder.

> **NOTE**: When you upload a photo, the image quality won't be the same as it was originally on your iPhone.

Facebook Notifications

Depending on your settings for Facebook push notifications, you can be inundated by updates, wall posts, and invitations. If you don't have too many Facebook friends and you want to know when someone is writing something on your wall or commenting on a post or picture, just set your push notification to **On**, as we show you here.

When a notification comes in, it will appear on your screen—even if your phone is locked.

In this example, Gary's daughter posted on his wall while his phone was locked. The message appeared on his screen and the **Slide to unlock** button was replaced by a **Slide to view** button.

Sliding the button to the right launched the **Facebook** app and Gary could respond to the message.

Sara's message is now at the top of Gary's wall, and the notification of her post is also highlighted at the bottom of the screen.

Settings to Customize Your Facebook App

Here's how to adjust settings for the **Facebook** app:

1. Tap the **Settings** icon.

2. Tap **Facebook** in the left column.

3. You can now adjust various options:

    Shake to Reload feature, which reloads or updates the page when you shake your iPhone 4

    Vibrate feature, for when notifications are sent

    Push Notifications: These features have simple **On/Off** toggle switches. Touch **Push Notifications** to see the detailed switches on the next screen.

Push Notifications settings screen for the **Facebook** app:

Touch each switch to set it **On** or **Off**.

For each switch that is in the **On** position, you will receive Push Notifications when something changes—for example, when you receive a message that somebody has confirmed you as a friend, tagged you in a photo, or commented on your Wall.

> **TIP**: The **Facebook** app will bring in Facebook profile pictures to your Contacts list. This can be quite humorous depending on the pictures.

LinkedIn

LinkedIn has core functionality very similar to Facebook, but tends to be more business- and career-focused, whereas Facebook is more personal friends– and game-focused. With LinkedIn, you can connect and re-connect with current and past business associates, send messages, see what people are up to, have discussions, and more.

As of publishing time, the status of LinkedIn was very similar to Facebook. You can go to the regular LinkedIn site on the Safari browser, or download the **LinkedIn** app for the iPhone.

Which is better? We liked the **LinkedIn** app for the iPhone slightly better than the full LinkedIn.com site in Safari. It was easier to navigate using the **LinkedIn** app with the large buttons, but you could see more on the screen in the Safari version. We recommend giving both options a try and see which you like better—it is really a personal preference.

Downloading the LinkedIn App

Similar to downloading Facebook, start up the App Store on your iPhone 4. Type **LinkedIn** in the search window and locate the app. It is free, so tap the **FREE** button to install it.

Logging In to LinkedIn App

Once the app is installed, click on the **LinkedIn** icon and enter your login information.

Navigating Around the LinkedIn App

LinkedIn has an icon-based navigation similar to Facebook. Tap any icon to move to that function, and then tap the **Home** icon in the upper left corner to return to the Home screen. See Figure 28-2.

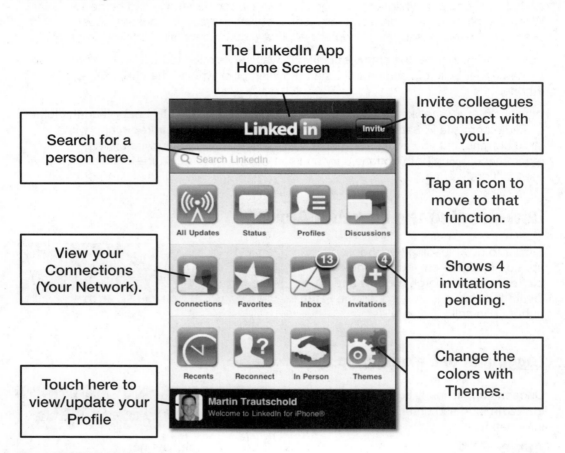

Figure 28-2. *LinkedIn* app home page.

Communicating with LinkedIn Connections

One of the things you will most likely do
the most with the **LinkedIn** app is
communicate with your connections. The
easiest way to do that is the following:

1. Touch the **Connections** icon.

2. Scroll through your connections or type in a connection name in the search box.

3. Touch the contact you are looking for.

4. Touch the **Send** icon  in the upper right-hand corner and then choose
   Send Message.

Twitter

Twitter was started in 2006. Twitter is essentially an SMS (text message)–based social networking site. It is often referred to as a "micro-blogging" site where the famous and not-so-famous share what's on their mind. The catch is that you have only 140 characters to get your point across.

With Twitter, you subscribe to "follow" someone who "tweets" messages. You might also find that people will start to "follow" you. If you want to follow us, we are @garymadesimple on Twitter.

Making a Twitter Account

Making a Twitter account is very easy. We do recommend that you first establish your Twitter account on the Twitter web site, `www.twitter.com`. When you establish your account, you will be asked to choose a unique user name—we use @garymadesimple—and a password.

You will then be sent an email confirmation. Click on the link in your email message and you will be taken back to the Twitter web site. You can choose people to "follow," make "tweets" on the web site, and also read tweets from your friends.

Twitter Options for the iPhone 4

There are many options for using Twitter on the iPhone 4. The easiest way to follow others and to tweet is to use one of the Twitter apps from the App Store.

There are many Twitter apps from which to choose. For purposes of this book, we are highlighting two specific Twitter apps, **TweetDeck** and **Twitter**. Both are very well designed and easy to use.

NOTE: Twitter has recently purchased the makers of **Tweetie** and **Tweetie 2**, and the "official" **Twitter** app for iPhone has a strong resemblance to those apps.

Downloading a Twitter App

Go to the App Store, touch **Categories**, and choose **Social Networking**. You should see both **TweetDeck** and **Twitter** in the **Featured** section. If not, simply touch the **Search** window and type in either app name.

Download the app as you would any other app to the iPhone 4.

Starting Any Twitter App for the First Time

Touch either app icon and the program will start. The first time using either Twitter app will require you to sign in to Twitter. Your user name is the one you picked when you first signed up for Twitter.

Using TweetDeck

TweetDeck gives you a very clean Home screen. It uses a **Column** view so you can easily scroll through the **Friends**, **Mentions**, and **Direct Message** screens. To make one screen the **Active** screen, just touch it.

Usually, the second screen contains the **Mentions**, which are responses to your tweets—almost like a text message conversation.

> **NOTE**: You can have more than three columns. Just touch the **Add Column** button at the bottom and scroll the available columns to add to your Twitter home page.

The controls for TweetDeck are along the bottom. There are five icons available to you. See Figure 28-3.

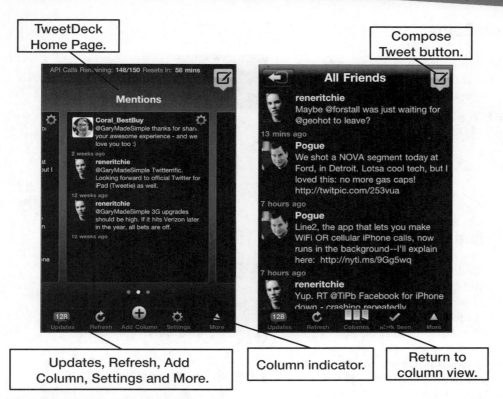

TweetDeck Home Page.

Compose Tweet button.

Updates, Refresh, Add Column, Settings and More.

Column indicator.

Return to column view.

Figure 28-3. *Layout of TweetDeck home page.*

Accounts and Settings

There are several adjustable fields in the **Accounts and Settings** section of the app. Touch the **Manage Accounts** tab to add or edit your Twitter account.

Touch the **Sign into an Account** to sign in to another Twitter account you may have. Just touch the tab and input your username and password.

Touch the **Settings** tab to adjust auto correction, auto capitalization, and sound options. You can also choose your picture service if you have a specific service for uploading pictures to Twitter.

Refresh Button

Touching the **Refresh** button simply refreshes your tweets.

> **NOTE:** If you select the **Shake Refresh** option in the settings, you can just "shake" the iPhone to refresh tweets.

Add Column Button

The **Add Column** button adds another column onto your Twitter Home screen. Just slide from right to left to advance from one column to the next. The "dots" at the bottom indicate how many screens you have to move through. You can add a column for **Search**, **Direct Messages**, **Mentions**, **Favorites**, **Twitter Trends**, **Twitter Lists**, **Twitter Search**, and **All Friends**.

Composing a Tweet

Touch the **Compose Tweet** icon and the tweet composition screen is displayed. Your Twitter ID is in the "From" line and you have 140 characters to express what is on your mind.

When you are done, just touch the **Send** button in the upper right-hand corner.

Reading and Replying

Touch a tweet to bring it to the main screen. In addition to the tweet being nice and large, you can touch on a link within the tweet to launch the web view. If you want to view the link in Safari, just touch

the **Safari** button.

> **NOTE:** When you view the link in Safari, you can quickly jump back to **TweetDeck** by double-clicking your **Home** button and using the App Switcher bar.

Along the top and the bottom of the tweet window, you will see six icons; **@Reply/all**, **send DM**, **retweet**, **email tweet**, **send RE:** and **+favorite**.

@reply/all	send DM	retweet

Maybe @forstall was just waiting for @geohot to leave?

3 hours ago from Tweetie for Mac

email tweet	send RE:	+favorite

Each will bring up an additional window and the onscreen keyboard for you to type your reply, forward the tweet, send a direct message to the author, email the tweet, or set it as a favorite.

Using Twitter

The "official" **Twitter** app takes a streamlined approach to using Twitter. The Home screen shows you the tweets from those you are following. The full message is nice and large.

Along the bottom are five icons, the first being the main **Twitter** feed. The other icons are **Mentions**, **Direct Messages**, **Search**, and the **More** button, which takes you to your **Profile**, **Favorites**, **Drafts**, **Lists**, and **Accounts and Settings**.

The **Compose Tweet** icon is in the top left-hand corner. See Figure 28-4.

Figure 28-4. *Layout of Twitter home page.*

Refreshing Your List of Tweets

To refresh your list of tweets, just pull down the main page and you will see the **Pull down to refresh** notification at the top. Once the page is pulled down, you will see a **Release to refresh** note. Release the page and it will refresh the tweets.

Your Twitter Profile

Touch the **More** button and then touch **My Profile** and your Twitter profile is displayed.

To see your tweets, just touch **Tweets**.

To see those tweets you have labeled as favorites, touch the **Favorites** button.

To see those individuals whom you are following, touch the **Following** button.

> **NOTE**: The number corresponding to your followers, those you are following, and your tweets is displayed above the title of the button.

Scroll down the page to see your **Retweets**, **Lists**, and **Services** to which you can subscribe.

Compose Button

Touch the **Compose** button  and the New Tweet screen pops up. The character counter will count down from 140 as you type your message.

Options within Tweet

From your Twitter Home screen, just touch one of your tweets for options. You can **Reply**, **Retweet**, **Set as Favorite**, **Send Link**, or **Email the Tweet**. Just touch the corresponding button to the action.

Details for the Link and Mail options are launch shown in Figure 28-5.

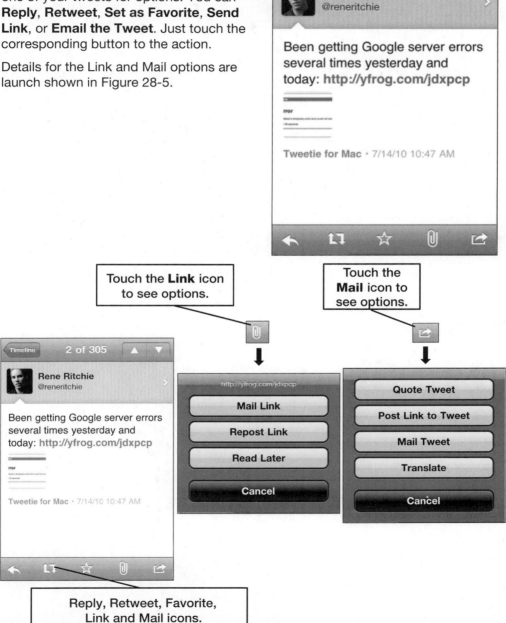

Figure 28-5. *Options within a tweet in the launch **Twitter** app.*

Chapter 29

Troubleshooting

The iPhone is usually highly reliable. Occasionally, like with your computer or any complicated electronic device, you might have to reset the device or troubleshoot a problem. In this chapter, we give you some useful tools to help get your iPhone back up and running as quickly as possible. We start with some basic quick troubleshooting and move into more in-depth problems and resolutions in the "Advanced Troubleshooting" section.

We also cover some other odds and ends related to your iPhone and give you a list of resources where you can find more help with your iPhone.

Basic Troubleshooting

First, we will cover a few basic tips and tricks to get your iPhone back up and running.

What to Do If the iPhone Stops Responding

Sometimes, your iPhone won't respond to your touch—it freezes in the middle of a program. If this happens, try these steps to see whether the iPhone will start responding (Figure 29-1):

1. Click the **Home** button once to see whether that exits the app to the **Home** screen.

2. If one particular app is causing trouble, try double-clicking the **Home** button to open the **App Switcher** bar. Then press and hold *any* icon in the **App Switcher** bar until they all shake and a red circle with a minus sign appears in the upper-left corner of the icon. Tap the red **circle** icon to close the app.

3. If the iPhone continues to be unresponsive, try pressing the **Sleep/Power** key until you see **Slide to Power Off**. Then press and hold the **Home** button until you return to the **Home** screen—this should quit the program.

4. Make sure your iPhone isn't running out of power. Try plugging it in or attaching it to your computer (if it's plugged in) to see whether it will start to respond.

5. If holding the **Home** button doesn't work, you will need to try to turn off your iPhone by pressing and holding the **Power/Sleep** button for 3–4 seconds. Then slide the **Slide to Power Off** slider at the top of the screen. If you cannot power off the iPhone, then see the following instructions about how to reset the iPhone.

6. After you power off the iPhone, wait a minute or so, and then turn on the iPhone by holding the same **Power** button for a few seconds.

7. You should see the Apple logo appear on the screen. Wait until the iPhone starts up, and you should be able to access your programs and data.

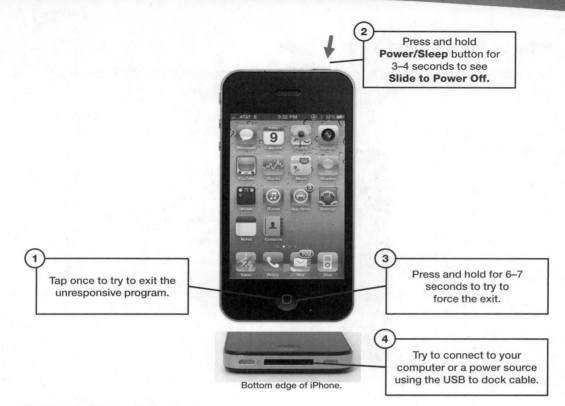

2 Press and hold **Power/Sleep** button for 3–4 seconds to see **Slide to Power Off.**

1 Tap once to try to exit the unresponsive program.

3 Press and hold for 6–7 seconds to try to force the exit.

4 Try to connect to your computer or a power source using the USB to dock cable.

Bottom edge of iPhone.

Figure 29-1. *Basic troubleshooting steps.*

If these steps don't work, you will need to reset your iPhone.

How to Hard-Reset Your iPhone

Resetting your device is your last response to an unresponsive iPhone. It is perfectly safe, and it usually fixes many problems. See Figure 29-2.

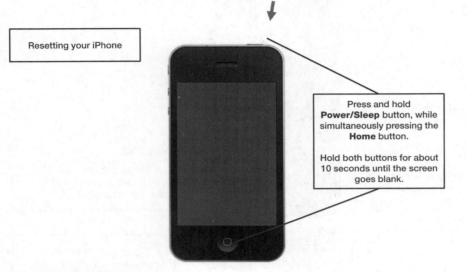

Resetting your iPhone

Press and hold **Power/Sleep** button, while simultaneously pressing the **Home** button.

Hold both buttons for about 10 seconds until the screen goes blank.

Figure 29-2. *Resetting your iPhone.*

The steps to hard-reset your iPhone are as follows:

1. Using two hands, press and hold the **Home** button and the **Power/Sleep** button at the same time.

2. Keep both buttons held down for about 8–10 seconds. You will see the **Slide to Power Off** slider. Ignore that, and keep holding both buttons until the screen goes blank.

3. After a few more seconds, you should see the Apple logo appear. When you see the logo, just release the buttons, and your iPhone will be reset.

How to Soft-Reset Your iPhone

There are various things you can reset in the **Settings** app, from the **Home** screen layout to the network settings to all the data on your device.

1. Tap the **Settings** icon.

2. Tap **General**.

3. Swipe up to see the bottom of the page.

4. Tap **Reset**.

5. Tap **Reset All Settings** to reset the network, keyboard, **Home** screen layout, and location warnings. Tap **Reset** to confirm in the pop-up window.

6. Tap **Erase All Content and Settings** to erase everything from your iPhone. Then tap **Erase** to confirm in the pop-up window.

7. Tap **Reset Network Settings** to clear all your Wi-Fi (and 3G) network settings.

8. Tap **Reset Keyboard Dictionary** to reset the spelling dictionary.

9. Tap **Reset Home Screen Layout** to return to the factory layout, from when you first received your iPhone.

10. Tap **Reset Location Warnings** to reset the warning messages you receive about allowing apps to use your current location.

No Sound in Music or Video

Few things are more frustrating than hoping to listen to music or watch a video, only to find that no sound comes out of the iPhone. Usually, there is an easy fix for this problem.

1. Check the volume by using the **Volume Up** key in the upper-left edge of your iPhone. You might have accidentally lowered the volume all the way or muted it.

2. If you are using wired headphones from the headphone jack, unplug your headphones, and then put them back in. Sometimes, the headset jack isn't connected well.

3. If you are using wireless Bluetooth headphones or a Bluetooth stereo setup:

   a. Check the volume setting (if available on the headphones or stereo).

    b. Check to make sure the Bluetooth device is connected. Tap the **Settings** icon. Tap **General**, and then tap **Bluetooth**. Make sure you see your device listed and that its status is **Connected**. If it is not connected, then tap it and follow the directions to pair it with the iPhone.

> **NOTE:** Sometimes you may actually be connected to a Bluetooth device and not know it. If you are connected to a Bluetooth Stereo device, no sound will come out of the actual iPhone.

4. Make sure the song or video is not in Pause mode.

5. Open the iPhone music or video controls. Double-clicking the **Home** button should open the **App Switcher**. Swipe from left to right to see your iPod controls. Verify the song is not paused or the volume is not turned down all the way, as shown here.

6. Check the **Settings** icon to see whether you (or someone else) has set the **Volume Limit** on the iPhone.

    a. Tap the **Settings** icon.

    b. Swipe down the page, and tap **iPod**.

    c. See whether **Volume Limit** is **On**.

    d. Tap **Volume Limit** to check the setting level. If the limit is unlocked, simply slide the volume to a higher level.

    e. If it is locked, you need to unlock it first by tapping the **Unlock Volume Limit** button and entering the four-digit code. See Figure 29-3.

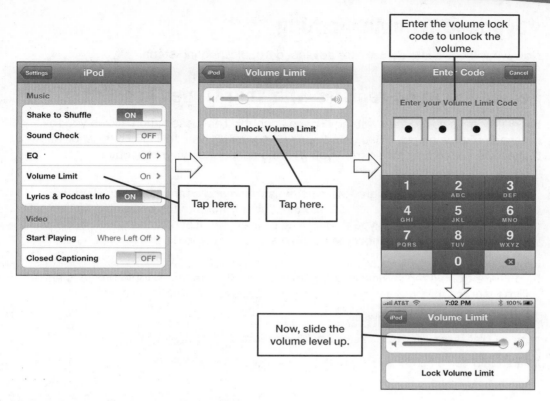

Figure 29-3. *Checking the volume limit in settings.*

If none of these steps helps, check out the "Additional Troubleshooting and Help Resources" section later in this chapter. If that doesn't help, then try to restore your iPhone from a backup file using the steps in the "Restore Your iPhone from a Backup" section in the chapter. Finally, if that does not help, then contact the store or business that sold you your iPhone for assistance.

If You Can't Make Purchases from iTunes or the App Store

You have this new, cool device, and let's say you go to the **iTunes** Store or the **App Store**. What if you receive an error message or you are not allowed to make a purchase? What do you do now?

1. Both stores require an active Internet connection. Make sure you have either a Wi-Fi connection or a cellular data connection. For assistance, check out Chapter 5: "Wi-Fi and 3G Connectivity."

2. Verify you have an active iTunes account. We show you how to set up a new iTunes account in the "Create an iTunes Account" section of Chapter 30: "Your iTunes User Guide."

Advanced Troubleshooting

Now we will delve into some more advanced troubleshooting steps.

Remember to Re-register with Your iTunes Account

Every iPhone is associated with an **iTunes** account. That association allows you to purchase **iTunes** music, videos, and apps from your iPhone. It is also this association that allows you to play music from your **iTunes** account on your computer on your iPhone.

Sometimes, your iPhone might "lose" its registration and connection with **iTunes**. Usually, this is a very simple fix. Just connect your iPhone to the computer via the USB cable, and **iTunes** will walk you through the process of reassociating your iPhone with your **iTunes** account. We show the detailed steps of how to do this in Chapter 1: "Getting Started."

If you have trouble registering your iPhone through **iTunes**, then Apple provides an online resource that you can get to from your computer or iPhone web browser.

Type this into your web browser:

`https://register.apple.com/cgi-bin/WebObjects/GlobaliReg.woa`

You should see a screen similar to the one shown in Figure 29-4.

Figure 29-4. *The online registration site from Apple's login page.*

1. Complete the information, enter your Apple ID and password, and click **Continue**.

2. Depending on what you are registering, select either **One product** or **More than one product**. In this case, we chose **One product** (Figure 29-5).

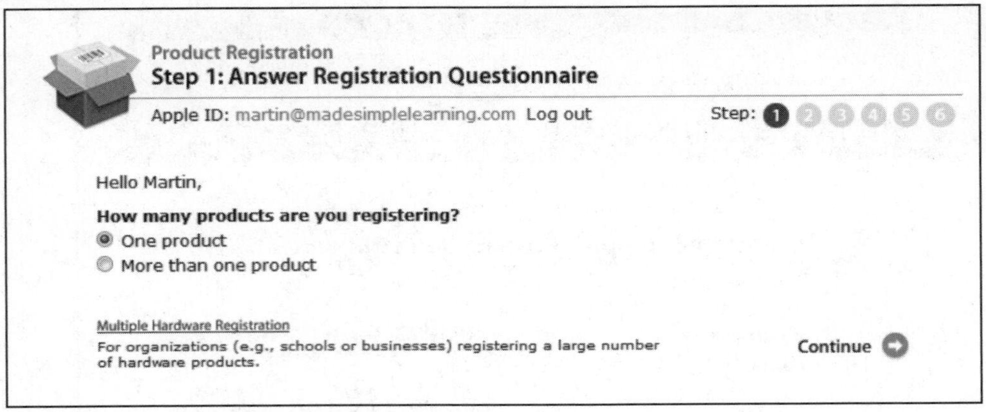

Figure 29-5. *Step 1 on Apple's online registration site.*

3. Now, choose the category, product line, and product. In this case, we chose **iPhone** category, **iPhone** product line, and **iPhone 4**. This moved us through steps 2–4 at once (Figure 29-6).

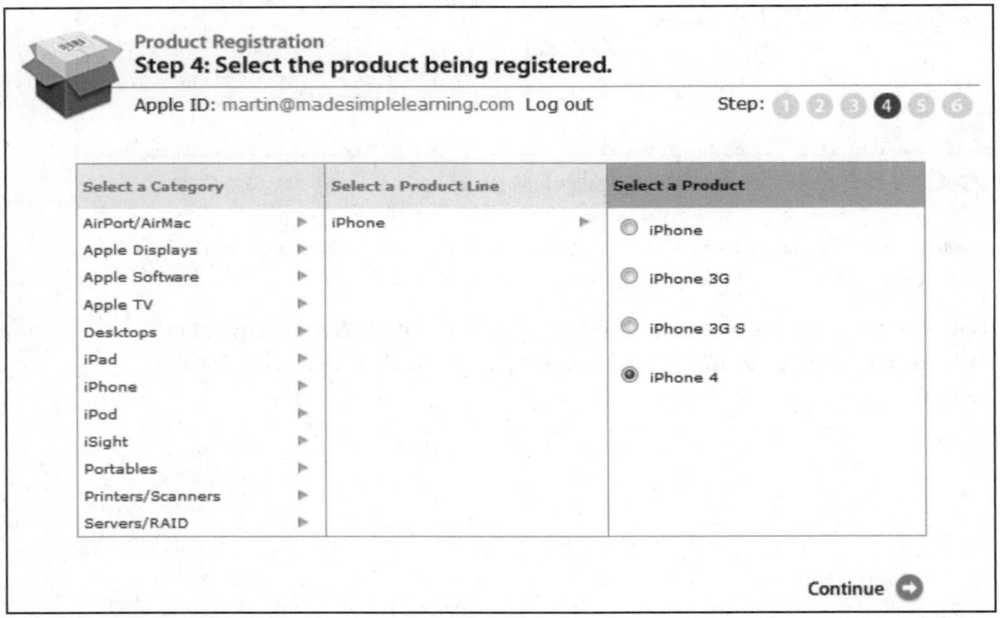

Figure 29-6. *Steps 2–4 on Apple's online registration site.*

4. Now you need to enter your iPhone serial number and other information about how you will use the iPhone.

TIP: To locate the serial number, connect your iPhone to your computer, and load **iTunes**. Click your iPhone in the left nav bar, and click **Summary** in the top nav bar. The serial number is at the top of the **Summary** screen, as shown in Figure 29-7.

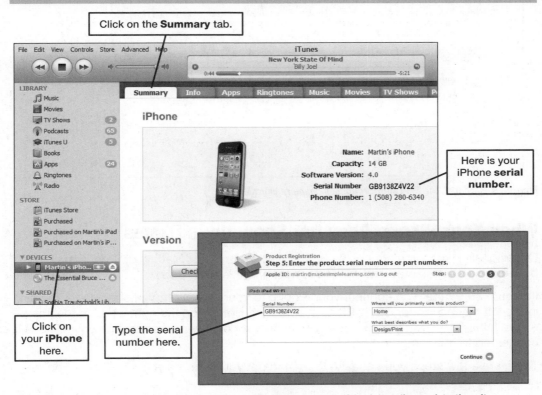

Figure 29-7. *Locating your iPhone serial number in **iTunes** and step 5 of Apple's online registration site.*

5. Now click **Continue**, and you should see the confirmation screen shown in Figure 29-8.

6. Click **Continue** to complete the registration of your iPhone.

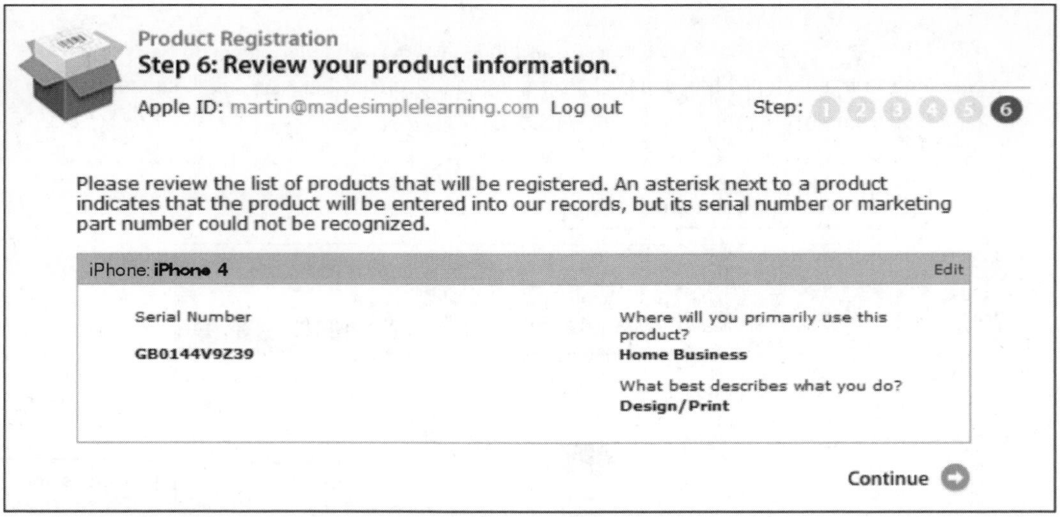

Figure 29-8. *Step 6, the final step, on Apple's online registration site.*

When Your iPhone Does Not Show Up in iTunes

Occasionally, when you connect your iPhone to your PC or Mac, your iPhone may not be recognized by **iTunes** and will not appear in the left nav bar.

In Figure 29-9, after you connect your iPhone to your computer, you should see it listed in the left nav bar under DEVICES as shown in the image on the right side. In the image on the left side, you will notice that there is no device shown, even though your iPhone is connected to the computer.

There are a few steps you can take to try and get your iPhone recognized so it appears in iTunes.

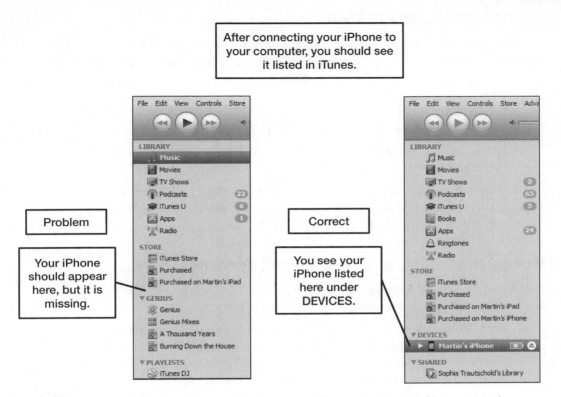

Figure 29-9. *Verifying your iPhone is listed in the left nav bar in **iTunes** when connected to your computer.*

1. Check the battery charge of the iPhone by looking at the battery level in the top right of the **Home** screen. If you have let the battery run too far down, **iTunes** won't see it until the level of the battery rises a bit.

2. If the battery is charged, try connecting the iPhone to a different USB port on the computer. Sometimes, if you have always used one USB port for the iPhone and switch it to another port, the computer won't see it.

3. If this still does not fix the problem, try disconnecting the iPhone and restarting the computer. Then, reconnect the iPhone to the USB port.

4. If this still does not work, download the latest update to **iTunes**, or completely uninstall and reinstall **iTunes** on the computer again. Just make sure if you choose this option that you back up all the information in **iTunes**.

We have included detailed steps showing you how to upgrade to the latest version of **iTunes** in the "Upgrade iTunes" section of Chapter 30: "Your iTunes User Guide."

Synchronization Problems

Sometimes, you might be having errors when synchronizing your iPhone with your computer (PC or Mac). How you work on the problem depends on your sync method.

Using iTunes to Sync

If you are using iTunes to sync your personal information, then follow these steps.

1. First, follow all the steps we outlined in the "iPhone Does Not Show Up in iTunes" section in this chapter.

2. If the iPhone still will not sync but you can see it in your **iTunes** left nav bar, go back to Chapter 3: "Sync Your iPhone with iTunes," where you can check your sync settings very carefully.

Using Apple's MobileMe or Microsoft Exchange to Sync

If you are using the **MobileMe** service or **Microsoft Exchange** method to sync your email and personal information, follow these troubleshooting steps.

1. Both **MobileMe** and **Exchange** sync require a wireless internet data connection in order to sync your email and personal information. Verify you have a live data connection by checking Table 1 found in the Quick Start guide "Reading the Connectivity Status Icons" section.

2. If you do not have a wireless data signal, then verify your Wi-Fi or 3G connection is setup correctly as we show in Chapter 5: "Wi-Fi and 3G Connectivity."

3. After you have your connection verified, you then need to check that your sync settings are correct on your computer and on your iPhone as shown in Chapter 4: "Other Sync Methods."

> **TIP:** Sometimes it is as simple as your password has changed. If this is the case, then make sure to correct your password on your iPhone for your sync settings. These are found by tapping your Settings icon, then tapping Mail, Contacts and Calendars. Finally, tap the account name and adjust the password.

Reinstalling the iPhone Operating System (with or Without a Restore)

Sometimes, you might have to do a clean install of your iPhone operating system to get your iPhone back up and running smoothly. If an update is currently available, like the 4.0.1 update that was available during the writing of this book, then this process will also result in upgrading your iPhone software.

TIP: This process is virtually identical to the process of updating your iPhone with a new version of the operating system.

During this process, you will have three choices:

- If you want to return the iPhone to its normal state with all your data, you will have to use the **Restore** function in **iTunes**.

- If you plan on getting a clean start and tying the iPhone to an **iTunes** account, you would use the **Setup a new iPhone** function at the end of this process.

- If you plan on giving away or selling your iPhone, then you would simply eject the iPhone from **iTunes** at the end of this process (before doing a restore or new setup).

CAUTION: This restore process will wipe your iPhone totally clean. You will need to resynchronize and reinstall all of your apps and enter your account information, such as e-mail accounts. This process could take 30 minutes or longer, depending on how much information you have synced to your iPhone.

To reinstall the iPhone operating system software with the option of restoring data to your iPhone from a previous backup, follow these steps:

1. Connect your iPhone to your computer, and load **iTunes**.

2. Click your **iPhone** in the DEVICES category in the left nav bar.

3. Click **Summary** in the top nav bar.

4. You will see the iPhone information screen. Click the **Restore** button in the middle screen, as shown here (Figure 29-10).

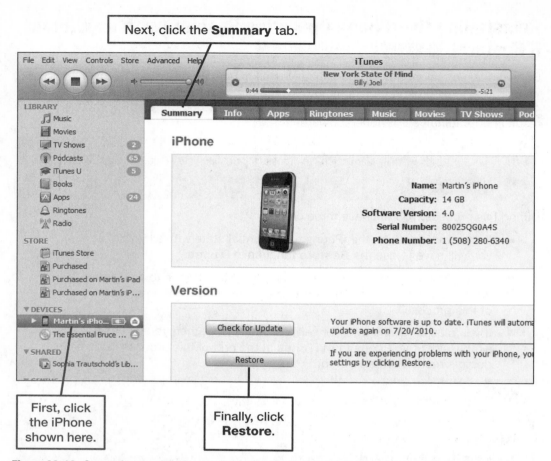

Next, click the **Summary** tab.

First, click the iPhone shown here.

Finally, click **Restore**.

Figure 29-10. *Connecting your iPhone and clicking the **Restore** button in **iTunes** in the **Summary** screen.*

5. Now you will be asked whether you want to back up. Click **Backup** just to be safe (Figure 29-11).

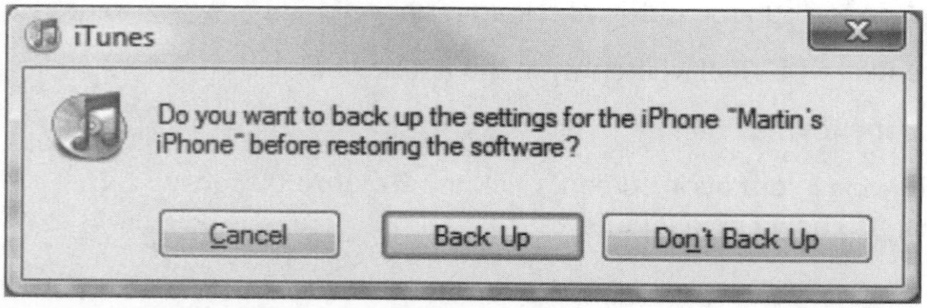

Figure 29-11. *Backing up before you restore in **iTunes.***

6. On the next screen, you are warned that all data will be erased. Click **Restore** or **Restore and Update** to continue (Figure 29-12).

Figure 29-12. *Backing up before you restore in **iTunes**.*

7. You will see an iPhone Software Update screen. Click **Next >** to continue (Figure 29-13).

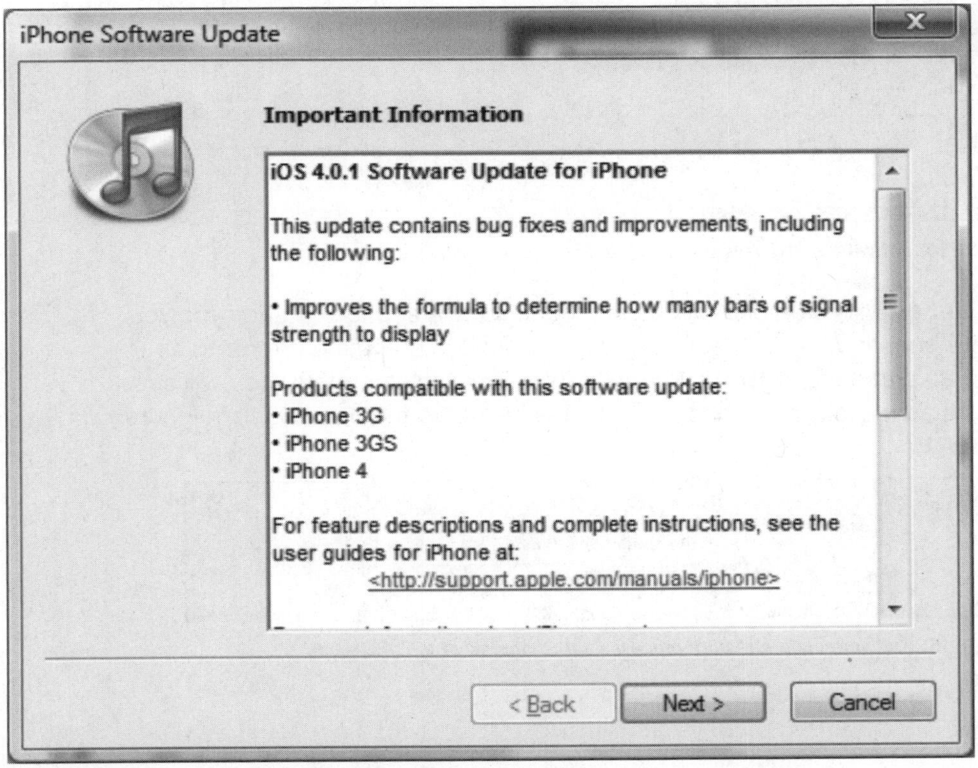

iPhone Software Update

Important Information

iOS 4.0.1 Software Update for iPhone

This update contains bug fixes and improvements, including the following:

• Improves the formula to determine how many bars of signal strength to display

Products compatible with this software update:
• iPhone 3G
• iPhone 3GS
• iPhone 4

For feature descriptions and complete instructions, see the user guides for iPhone at:
            <http://support.apple.com/manuals/iphone>

< Back   Next >   Cancel

Figure 29-13. *Beginning of the software update/restore process.*

8. You will see the Software License Agreement screen. Click **Agree** to continue and start the process (Figure 29-14).

iPhone Software Update   X

Safety Info: Read Important Product Information Guide before use:
www.apple.com/support/manuals/iphone

Software License Agreement

ENGLISH

IMPORTANT: BY USING YOUR iPHONE, YOU ARE AGREEING
TO BE BOUND BY THE FOLLOWING APPLE AND THIRD
PARTY TERMS:

A.   APPLE iPHONE SOFTWARE LICENSE AGREEMENT
B.   NOTICES FROM APPLE
C.   GOOGLE MAPS TERMS AND CONDITIONS
D.   YOUTUBE TERMS AND CONDITIONS

APPLE INC.
iPHONE SOFTWARE LICENSE AGREEMENT
Single Use License

Save...

< Back   Agree   Decline

Figure 29-14. *Software update/restore process: license agreement.*

9. **iTunes** will download the latest iPhone software, back up and sync your iPhone, and then reinstall the iPhone software completely, erasing all data and restoring your iPhone to its original "clean" state. You will see status messages at the top of **iTunes** similar to the one shown in Figure 29-15.

iTunes
Downloading 1 item
iPhone Software Update (6 minutes remaining)

Figure 29-15. *Software update/restore process: status window at top of **iTunes**.*

10. After the backup and sync, your iPhone screen will go black. Then the Apple logo will appear, and you will see a status bar under the logo. Finally, a small pop-up window will appear in **iTunes** to tell you the update process is complete. Click **OK** to be brought to the **Set Up your iPhone** screen.

    a. If you want to keep your iPhone clean (i.e., without any of your personal data), then select the top option, **Setup as a new iPhone**. You might want to use this option if you are setting up this iPhone for someone else (you will need their Apple ID and password).

    b. If you are giving away or selling your iPhone, simply click the **Eject** icon next to the iPhone, and you're done (Figure 29-16).

Figure 29-16. *Ejecting the iPhone if you are giving it away or selling it.*

    c. Select **Restore from the backup of:**, and verify the pull-down is set to the correct device.

11. Finally, click **Continue** (Figure 29-17).

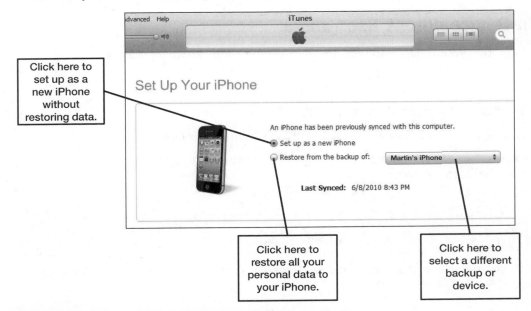

Figure 29-17. *Setting up as a new iPhone or restoring from a backup file.*

12. If you chose to restore, then after a little while you will see a **Restore in Progress** screen on your iPhone and a status window in **iTunes** saying "Restoring iPhone from backup…" with a time estimate.

13. Then you will see a little pop-up window saying "The settings for your iPhone have been restored." In a few seconds you will see your iPhone appear in the left nav bar under DEVICES in **iTunes**.

   a. If you sync your information with **iTunes**, all data will be synced now.

   b. If you use **MobileMe**, **Exchange**, or another sync process, you will probably have to reenter passwords on your iPhone to get those sync processes back up and running.

Additional Troubleshooting and Help Resources

Sometimes you may encounter a particular issue or question that you cannot find an answer to in this book. In the following sections, we provide some good resources that you can access from the iPhone and from your computer's web browser. The iPhone on-device user guide is easy to navigate and may provide you some quick information you seek. The Apple knowledgebase is helpful if you are facing a troubleshooting problem that is proving especially difficult to resolve. The iPhone/iPod touch-related web blogs and forums are good places to locate answers and even ask unique questions you might be facing.

On-Device iPhone User Guide

1. Open your Safari web browser to view the online user guide for your iPhone.

2. Tap the **Bookmarks** button ▢ in the bottom row of icons.

3. Swipe to the bottom of the list, and tap **iPhone User Guide**.

If you don't see that bookmark, then type this into the Safari address bar on your iPhone: help.apple.com/iPhone.

> **TIP**: To view the manual in PDF format from your computer, go to http://support.apple.com/manuals/iphone/.

Once you get to the user guide on your iPhone, you should see a screen similar to Figure 29-18.

The nice thing is that you already know how to navigate the guide. Tap any topic to see more information about that topic—either another list of subtopics or detailed information.

Read the topic, or tap another link to learn more.

Tap the button to the right of the screen to back out one level.

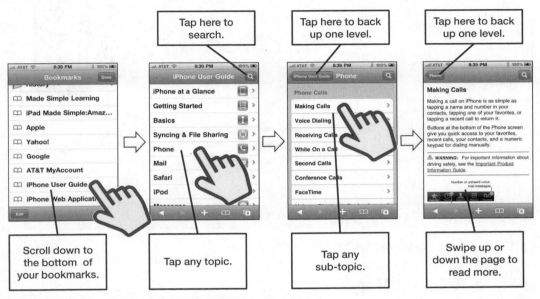

Figure 29-18. *Using the iPhone manual from Safari on your iPhone.*

The Apple Knowledgebase

On your iPhone or computer's web browser, go to this web page:

`http://www.apple.com/support/iphone/`

Then click a topic in the left nav bar, as shown in Figure 29-19.

Figure 29-19. *Apple Knowlegebase web site for the iPhone.*

iPhone-Related Blogs

One of the great things about owning an iPhone is that you immediately become part of a worldwide camaraderie of iPhone owners.

Many iPhone owners would be classified as "enthusiasts" and are part of any number of iPhone user groups. These user groups, along with various forums and web sites, serve as a great resource for iPhone users.

Many of these resources are available right from your iPhone, and others are web sites that you might want to visit on your computer.

Sometimes you might want to connect with other iPhone enthusiasts, ask a technical question, or keep up with the latest and greatest rumors. The blogs are a great place to do that.

Here are a few popular iPhone (and iPhone or iPod touch) blogs:

www.tipb.com

www.iphonefreak.com

www.gizmodo.com (iPhone section)

TIP: Before you post a new question on any of these blogs, please do a search on the blog to make sure your question has not already been asked and answered. Also, make sure you are posting your question on the right section (e.g., iPhone) of the blog. Otherwise, you may incur the wrath of the community for not doing your homework first!

Also, do a web search for "iPhone blogs" or "iPhone news and reviews" to locate more blogs.

Part IV

iPhone 4's Soulmate: iTunes

Your iPhone 4 is inextricably tied to iTunes—the e-commerce center of Apple. iTunes is not only where you buy music, videos and apps, it's also where you organize all of the great content you can use on your iPhone 4. We show you how to purchase exciting new content—and even how to find it for free. Learn something new with iTunes U or find related music and videos with the iTunes Genius feature. We even help you learn how to save money with iTunes Home Sharing.

Chapter 30

Your iTunes User Guide

In this chapter, we will show you how to do virtually everything you might want to do with iTunes. We help you get iTunes installed and updated. We will take you on a guided tour and describe all the great ways to organize and view your music and videos.

We'll also show you how to create normal playlists and smart playlists, how to use the **Genius** feature in iTunes, and how to save some money by using the **Home Sharing** feature. We will also show you how to import music CDs, DVDs, PDF or e-book files, and get album artwork for all your music. We will even teach you about the importance of authorizing computers to share content using iTunes. Finally, we will provide some useful iTunes troubleshooting tips.

> **NOTE:** If you are looking to set up your iPhone the first time, please check out Chapter 1: "Getting Started." If you are trying to sync your computer to your iPhone using iTunes, please check out Chapter 3: "Sync with iTunes."

If you need to install the **iTunes** software on your computer, please jump to the "Getting iTunes Software" section later in this chapter. If you already have the **iTunes** software installed, then go to the "Getting iTunes Updated" section to make sure you have the latest version.

> **TIP:** The **App Store** app (see Figure 30–1) on your iPhone is a separate icon, but on your computer it's included as a part of the **iTunes** computer program. You get to the **App Store** feature on your computer by clicking the **iTunes Store** link in the **Left** navigation bar.

Figure 30–1. *The iTunes screen showing the iTunes App Store.*

The iTunes User Guide Contents

This chapter has so much great material that we will give you an outline of everything it includes. The table that follows outlines the order you will find the relevant sections in this chapter:

Working with iTunes

What iTunes can do for you

Common questions

The iTunes guided tour

Changing views in iTunes

Playing songs, videos, and more

Finding things in iTunes

Creating a new playlist

The iTunes Genius feature

Home Sharing

iTunes Store and Account

Creating an iTunes account

Signing In to the iTunes store

Buying or getting free software from the App Store

Redeeming an iTunes gift card

Getting Your Stuff into iTunes

Importing music CDs

Importing movies from DVDs

Getting album artwork

Authorizing and deauthorizing computers

Getting & Updating iTunes

Getting iTunes software

Getting iTunes updated

Troubleshooting iTunes

What to Do if iTunes Auto Update Fails?

Getting your music back if your computer crashes

What iTunes Can Do

The **iTunes** app can do many things for you and your iPhone, including the following tasks:

- *Organize your media*: It provides a way to organize your media (both purchased and your own) into playlists and more.

- *Load your music CDs*: It lets you load up all your music CDs into **iTunes**, manage them with playlists, and sync them to your iPhone.

- *Buy media titles or download them for free*: In the **Media** sections of the **iTunes** app, you can purchase or download free music, movies, TV shows, podcasts, iBooks, PDF files, audiobooks, and educational content (from the iTunes U site).

- *Buy apps or download them for free*: In the **App Store** portion of the **iTunes** app, you can purchase or download free applications (*apps*) for your iPhone.

- *Share your media:* It lets you share your purchased music library (or portions of it) across all the computers in your home network. This can be a great money saver if your family has similar tastes in music and videos.

- *Play your media:* It serves as a great media player for your computer to play all your media, including music, videos, TV shows, and podcasts.

- *Sync media to iPhone*: It lets you transfer or synchronize your music, pictures, and video collections to your iPhone (see Chapter 3).

- *Organize and sync your apps*: It lets you manage and sync you're apps on your iPhone and arrange the app icons on your iPhone's various screens.

- *Sync personal information to your iPhone*: It lets you transfer or synchronize your personal information (e.g., addresses, calendar, and notes) between your computer and your iPhone.

- *Backup and restore your iPhone*: It lets you back up and restore your iPhone data.

Common Questions about iTunes

What follows is a list of frequently asked questions about **iTunes** for the iPhone, followed by short answers that address the core concern or issue raised by the question.

*Is the **iTunes** software on my computer the same as the **iTunes** app on my iPhone?*

The **iTunes** software on your computer does much more than the **iTunes** app on your iPhone. The **iTunes** software on your computer can do the job of four apps on your iPhone. For example, **iTunes** on your computer handles the following tasks, all of which require different apps on the iPhone: **iTunes**, **iPod**, **App Store**, and **iBooks**. The chart that follows gives you a quick overview of the differences between **iTunes** on your computer and **iTunes** on your iPhone, explaining how these functions are split.

You can do this with iTunes on your computer.	You use this app on your iPhone for the same functionality.
Organize and play your music, videos, TV shows, videos, and audio podcasts.	**iPod**
Purchase music and videos, as well as download podcasts.	**iTunes**
Purchase books.	**iBooks**
Purchase or download free apps.	 **App Store**

I have an iPad or another iPod; can I share music and videos with my new iPhone?

Yes! You can definitely keep listening to all your music and sharing all your videos on all of your Apple devices, including your new iPhone.

Can I use my existing iTunes software and account?

Yes! This is fine; you can use the same **iTunes** software already installed on your computer, as well as your existing iTunes account to set up your iPhone.

Can I use my purchased apps from my iPod touch, iPhone, or iPad?

Yes and no. Older iPhone and iPod touch apps will work; however, iPad-specific apps will not work on your iPhone.

> **TIP:** If you are an Apple Mac user, it is likely that the **iTunes** software is already installed on your computer, and it may already be in your **Bottom Dock**. If it is not there, then start your **Finder**, click **Applications** to locate the **iTunes** application, and start it.

The iTunes Guided Tour

After you have **iTunes** installed or updated, you're ready to take a quick guided tour of the **iTunes** interface on your computer (this is true whether you have a PC or Mac).

NOTE: If you need to install the **iTunes** software on your computer, please jump to the "Getting iTunes Software" section later in this chapter. If you already have **iTunes** installed, then go to the "Getting iTunes Updated" section to make sure you have the latest version.

When you first start **iTunes**, you will see the main window with the top controls to play your music or videos (see Figure 30–2). You will also see the **Left** navigation bar (nav bar), which lets you select from your library, Store, iPhone (when connected), shared media, **Genius** playlists, and your own playlists. The **Top** nav bar adjusts depending on what you have selected in the **Left** nav bar. Also, the center main window adjusts depending on selections from the **Left** nav bar, **Top** nav bar, and what is inside the main window itself.

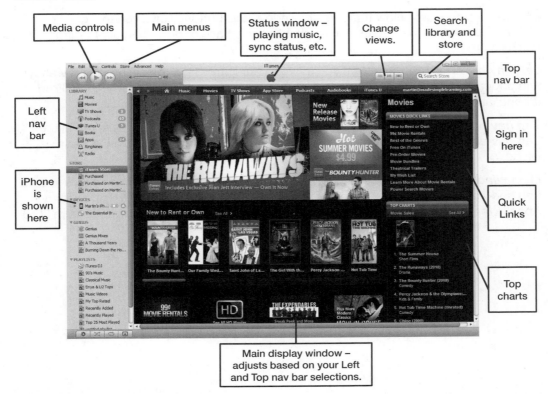

Figure 30–2. *The iTunes Main window.*

Starting from the top left of the main window, you can see the following menus, controls, windows, and other visual elements:

Main menus: These are located just above the media controls, and they provide access to all the actions **iTunes** can do through a logical and convenient set of menus. While a lot of the functionality in these menus is available in buttons and toolbars, these menus are where you'll find what you're looking for in a logical list.

Media controls: These buttons let you play, pause, or skip to the next song or video, as well as adjust the volume.

Status window: Located in the top, middle section of **iTunes**, this window shows you the status of what is currently going on (sync status, whether you're playing a song/video, or any other related messages).

Adjust views: These buttons allow you to adjust views between **List**, **Grid**, or **Cover Flow** views. (These are only active when you are in your own media libraries.)

Search: This box will search your library or the iTunes store for a particular song, video, TV show, or anything else based on the text you enter.

Sign In: Located just below the **Search** window, this button allows you to sign in or create a new Apple ID. (You use an Apple ID to purchase or download content from the iTunes store.)

Left nav bar: This nav bar allows you to view your library (e.g., music, videos, TV shows, and podcasts), the iTunes Store, any currently connected devices (your iPhone, iPod, iPhone, and so on), shared libraries, **Genius** mixes, and your own playlists.

Top nav bar: This set of buttons is adjusted based on what you have selected in the **Left** nav bar. Click any of these buttons to change the content shown in the **Main** window.

Main window: This is where you can see all the content based on your selections in the **Left** and **Top** nav bars. For example, if you selected your iPhone in the **Left** nav bar and **Apps** in the **Top** nav bar, you would see a screen similar to the one shown in Figure 30–3.

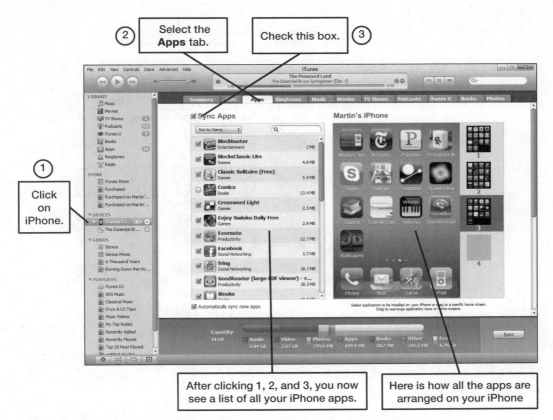

Figure 30–3. *The iTunes Main window changes based on Left and Top nav bar selections.*

Apple Video Tutorials for iTunes

In addition to all the information provided in this book, you can find some good video tutorials to help you start using the **iTunes** app from Apple. You can check these tutorials out from within the **iTunes** app by following these steps:

1. Go to the **Help** menu item and then to **iTunes Tutorials**. (This step is the same on a Mac or Windows PC.)

2. You should see a new window appear similar to the one shown in Figure 30–4. Tap any of the videos listed in the left column.

3. Press the **Click to Play** button in the center of the video in the **Main** window.

Click on a video topic here.

Click to start playing the video.

Click to close.

Figure 30–4. *The iTunes video tutorials.*

In the **iTunes** app, you can also configure your iPhone to sync with your personal information, data, and pictures, as we will explain later in this chapter. It is a good idea to familiarize yourself with the features of **iTunes** by going to www.apple.com/itunes/tutorials/ and watching the various iTunes tutorials.

Changing Views in iTunes

There are many ways to view your music, videos, and other media in **iTunes** on your computer. Getting familiar with these views on your computer will help you use your device in general because you will notice that your iPhone also has many of the same views. There are three customizable primary views: **List**, **Grid**, and **Cover Flow**.

List View

Click the left-most of the three view icons to see the **List** view (see Figure 30–5). You can re-sort the list by any column by clicking that column's heading. For example, to sort by name, you would click the **Name** column heading. To reverse the sort order, just click the same column heading again. This **List** view can be especially helpful for finding all the songs by a particular artist or on a particular album.

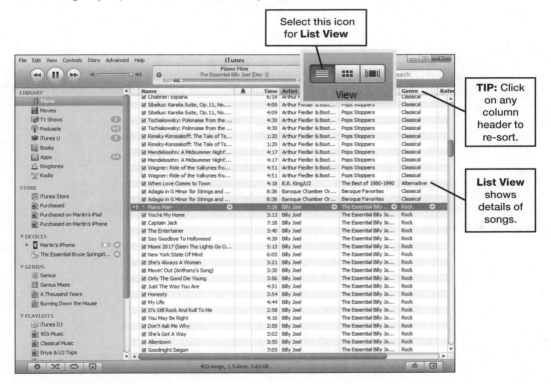

Figure 30–5. *The iTunes List view.*

Grid View

Click the middle icon to show the **Grid** view (see Figure 30–6). This is a very graphical view, and it is helpful if you want to quickly find album or poster art.

Figure 30–6. *The iTunes Grid view.*

Cover Flow View

Click the right-most icon to see **Cover Flow** view (see Figure 30-7). This is a fun view because it is visual, and you can quickly flip through the images using the slider bar to browse through the album covers. Like the **Album** view, this view provides an easy way to find an album when you know what the cover looks like.

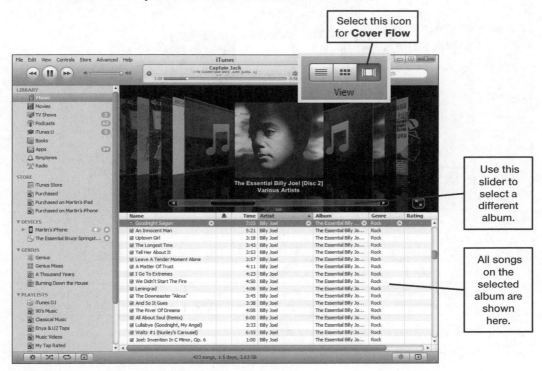

Figure 30–7. *The iTunes Cover Flow view.*

Playing Songs, Videos and More

If you are new to **iTunes**, these basic pointers can help you get around the app (see Figure 30–8):

- *Playing a song, video, or podcast*: Double-click an item to start playing it.

- *Controlling the song or video*: Use the **Rewind**, **Pause**, and **Fast Forward** buttons, in addition to the **Volume** slider in the upper left corner, to control the playback.

■ *Moving to a different part of the song or video*: Just click the diamond in the slider bar under the song name in the top of the window and drag it left or right, as desired.

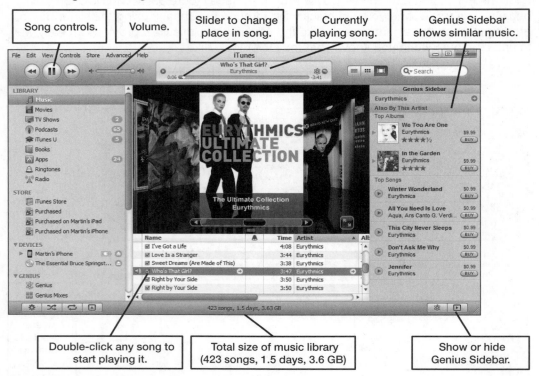

Song controls.

Volume.

Slider to change place in song.

Currently playing song.

Genius Sidebar shows similar music.

Double-click any song to start playing it.

Total size of music library (423 songs, 1.5 days, 3.6 GB)

Show or hide Genius Sidebar.

Figure 30–8. *Playing your songs, videos, and more in iTunes.*

Finding Things in iTunes

If your library does not already contain hundreds or thousands of songs and other media, it will soon! How do you quickly find that special song you are in the mood for right now? The quickest way to locate an individual song or video is to use the **Search** bar in the upper right corner of the iTunes app.

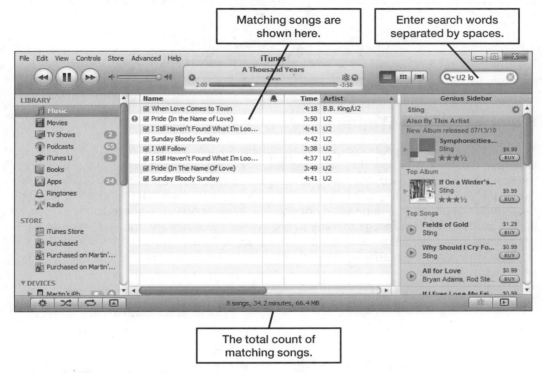

Figure 30–9. *Searching for media in iTunes.*

In the **Search** window, just start typing any part of a name in the following categories to find an item (see Figure 30-10):

- Artist name
- Album name
- Composer
- Song/video name

You will notice that, as soon as you type the first letter, **iTunes** will narrow your search results (shown in the **Main** window) by that letter. In this case, **iTunes** is finding all matching songs/videos that have the letter (or series of letters) that match any part of the artist, album, composer, or song/video name.

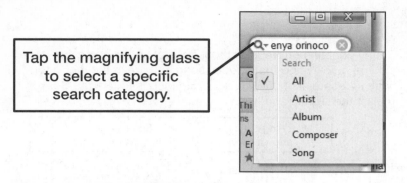

Tap the magnifying glass to select a specific search category.

Figure 30–10. *Narrowing the search categories by using the magnifying glass.*

Ways to Search iTunes

You can type any combination of words to match the item you are trying to find. For example, assume you know that the song you want has the word "love" in the title, and the song is by "U2." You could just type in those two words, separated by a space; "Love U2" will immediately show all matching items (see Figure 30–11). In this case, only two songs match, so you can quickly double-click the song you want to listen to. Search is also contextual. This means that if you are in your music library, the search function will search for music; whereas if you are in your apps library, the search will look only for apps. In every search, both your own library and the App Store web site will be searched.

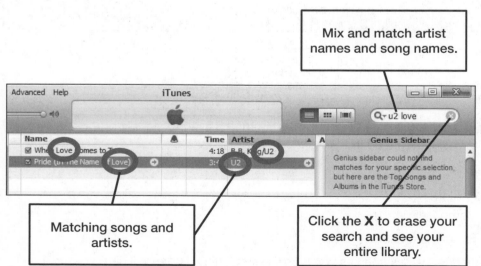

Mix and match artist names and song names.

Matching songs and artists.

Click the **X** to erase your search and see your entire library.

Figure 30–11. *Use two or more words separated by spaces to quickly narrow the search results.*

When you are done searching, hit the little **X** in the circle next to the search words to clear out the search and see all your songs and videos again.

Creating a New Playlist

You may be used to listening to all the music on a particular album, but you will soon find the benefits of creating your own custom playlists. These are lists of particular songs that you group together. You can create a **Normal** or a **Smart** playlist.

You can group playlists however you like, as in this example:

- Workout music
- Favorite U2 songs
- Traveling music

> **TIP:** You can create playlists in your **iTunes** library or directly on your iPhone. To create a playlist for your computer, click any existing playlist under the **Playlists** heading in the **Left** nav bar. To create a new playlist directly on your iPhone, click your iPhone listed under **Devices** in the **Left** nav bar. Depending on what you have highlighted in the **Left** nav bar, your new playlist will be created either on the computer or on the iPhone.

Creating a Normal Playlist

A **Normal** playlist is one in which you can drag-and-drop songs manually onto your new playlist.

Once you have decided whether to create your playlist on your iPhone or on your computer, you are ready to get started.

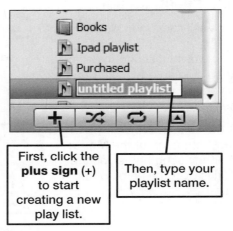

First, click the **plus sign** (+) to start creating a new play list.

Then, type your playlist name.

Follow these steps to create a new **Normal** playlist:

1. Press **Ctrl + N** (or **Command + N** on a Mac) to select a **New Playlist** from the **File** menu. Or, you can simply click the **New Playlist** button in the lower left corner of iTunes, as shown to the right.

2. Type the name of your playlist in the entry that appears in the **Left** nav bar.

> **TIP:** If you want to create a new playlist with songs very similar to another playlist, then right-click on the playlist and select **Duplicate**.

After creating and naming your playlist, you are ready to add songs to your new playlist (see Figure 30–12). To select from your entire library, click **Music** under the **Library** tab.

To select songs from an existing playlist, click that playlist.

Figure 30–12. *Locating songs to add to a playlist.*

Adding Individual Songs

You can easily add individual songs to your new playlist.

Click any individual song to select it, then keep holding down the **Mouse** key as you drag the song over to your new playlist.

To put the song into the playlist, drop it by letting go of the **Mouse** key when the song name you are dragging is over the name of the playlist.

Adding Multiple Songs or Videos (Not in a List)

You can add multiple items in two simple steps:

1. To add selected songs that are not listed sequentially, press and hold the **Ctrl** key (Windows) or **Command** key (Mac), then click the individual songs/videos. Once you are done selecting songs/videos, release the **Ctrl/Command** key.

2. After all the songs/videos are selected (highlighted), click one of the selected songs and drag-and-drop the entire selected group onto your playlist.

Press and hold the CTRL key (Windows) or COMMAND key (Mac) while clicking to select songs...

... then click and drag and drop the selected items on your new Playlist.

Adding a List of Songs or Videos

You can also add a list of songs/videos using a pair of steps:

1. To add a list of songs/videos that all at once in a continuous list, press and hold the **Shift** key. While pressing the **Shift** key, click the top item in the list and then click the bottom item. Both items clicked, as well as all the items between them, will be selected.

2. After all the songs/videos are selected (highlighted), click one of the selected songs and drag-and-drop the entire selected group onto your simple playlist.

Press and hold the SHIFT key and click on the top item...

After the list is selected, let go of SHIFT key then click to drag and drop the list on to your Playlist.

...while holding SHIFT, click on the bottom item to select the entire list.

Creating a New Smart Playlist

A **Smart** playlist is one that **iTunes** creates for you based on your selections. You can create a **Smart** playlist for your top 10 songs that you play all the time, specific artists, a specific genre, or even limit the playlist to a certain size based on the number of songs or their size (in MB or GB).

To start creating a **Smart** playlist, select **File ➤ New Smart Playlist**. Or, you can press **Ctrl + Alt + N** (Windows) or **Command + Alt + N** (Mac), and then select **New Smart Playlist** from the **File** menu.

Figure 30–13 illustrates that you have many options for creating a **Smart** playlist. All of the default playlists you see in **iTunes** are **Smart** playlists. Default categories include **90's Music**, **Classical Music**, **Music Videos**, **My Top Rated**, **Recently Added**, **Recently Played**, and **Top 25 Most Played**.

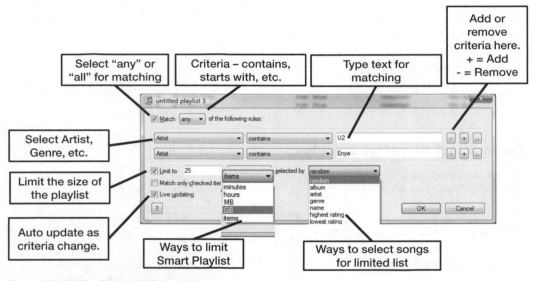

Figure 30–13. *The Smart playlist settings screen.*

Edit a Smart Playlist

The best way to get a feel for how the **Smart** playlist function works is probably to check out some of the preset **Smart** playlists.

To edit a **Smart** playlist, select **Edit Smart Playlist** from the **File** menu.

In Figure 30–14, you can see the **Smart** playlist for **90's Music**; you can also see that it will pull all **Music** and **Music Videos** that are from 1990 to 1999. Check out a few other default **Smart** playlists to start to learn how the myriad options interact to create a very powerful playlist function.

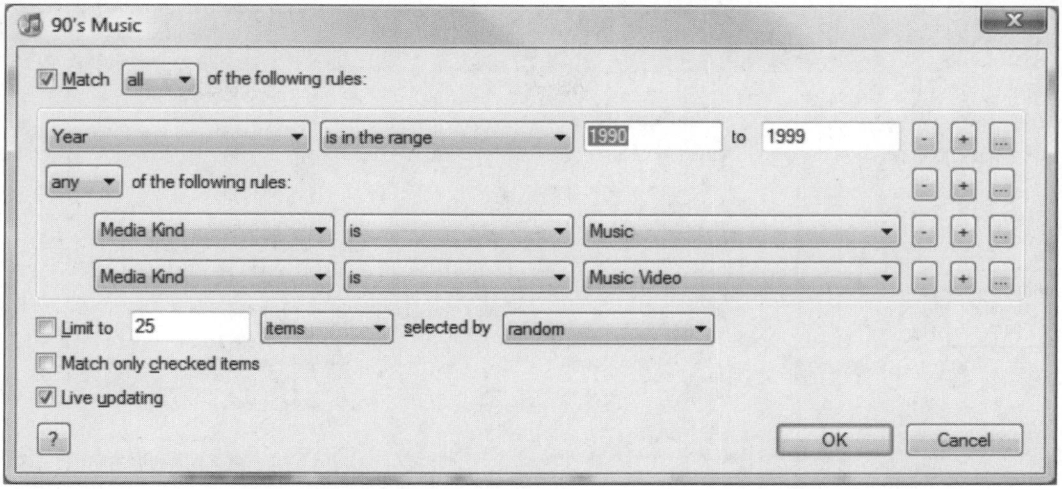

Figure 30–14. *The Smart playlist settings screen for 90's Music.*

> **NOTE:** The **Live Updating** feature of **Smart** playlists allows them to scan whenever you play a song or add any new media (e.g., songs, videos, and so on) to your library; it then includes any new songs that it deems may fit the criteria of the **Smart** playlist. This makes the playlists really dynamic.

The iTunes Genius Feature

The iTunes **Genius** feature can do all sorts of fun things to help enhance your music and video library in **iTunes**. You can take advantage of it by following these steps:

> **TIP:** You can use the **Genius** feature on your iPhone, but only after you have enabled it on your computer (as described in the steps that follow).

1. Click **Genius** in the **Left** nav bar, and then click the **Turn On Genius** button (see Figure 30–15). If you don't see the **Genius** item, then click **Store**, and then **Turn On Genius** from the **iTunes** menu.

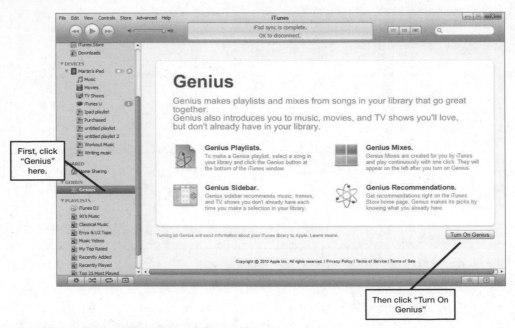

Figure 30–15. *Starting up the Genius feature in iTunes.*

2. If you are not already logged into the iTunes store, you will be asked to log in (see Figure 30–16). If you do not yet have an Apple ID, then please jump to the "Create an iTunes Account" section later in this chapter to learn how to create one.

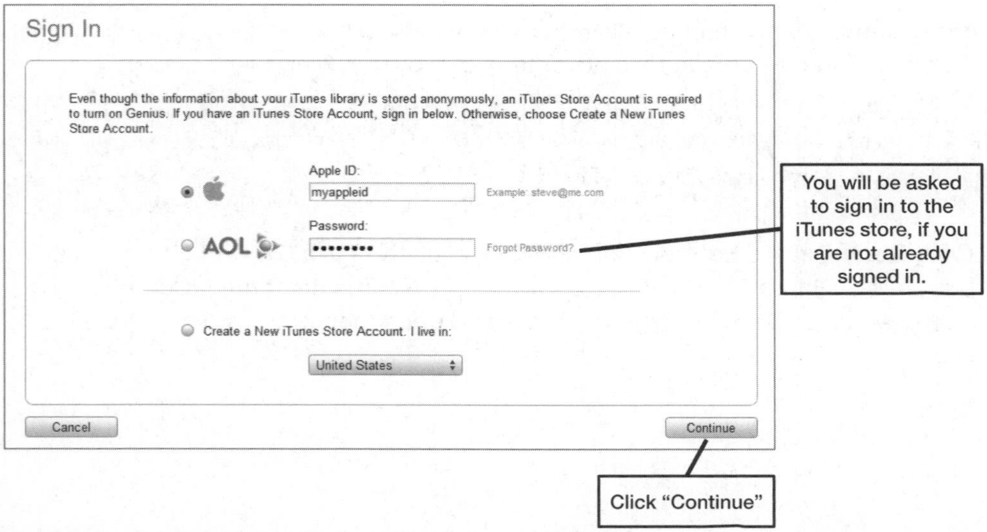

Figure 30–16. *Sign in using your Apple ID or AOL account to start the Genius feature in iTunes.*

3. Read and agree to the **Genius** license agreement to continue (see Figure 30–17).

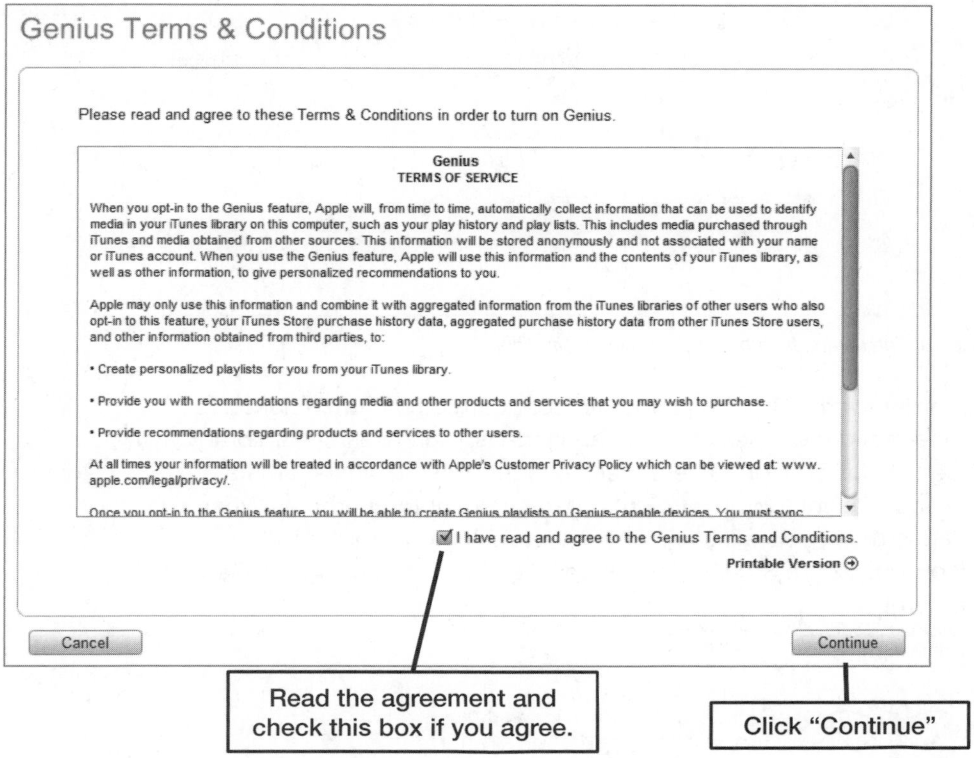

Genius Terms & Conditions

Please read and agree to these Terms & Conditions in order to turn on Genius.

Genius
TERMS OF SERVICE

When you opt-in to the Genius feature, Apple will, from time to time, automatically collect information that can be used to identify media in your iTunes library on this computer, such as your play history and play lists. This includes media purchased through iTunes and media obtained from other sources. This information will be stored anonymously and not associated with your name or iTunes account. When you use the Genius feature, Apple will use this information and the contents of your iTunes library, as well as other information, to give personalized recommendations to you.

Apple may only use this information and combine it with aggregated information from the iTunes libraries of other users who also opt-in to this feature, your iTunes Store purchase history data, aggregated purchase history data from other iTunes Store users, and other information obtained from third parties, to:

• Create personalized playlists for you from your iTunes library.

• Provide you with recommendations regarding media and other products and services that you may wish to purchase.

• Provide recommendations regarding products and services to other users.

At all times your information will be treated in accordance with Apple's Customer Privacy Policy which can be viewed at: www.apple.com/legal/privacy/.

Once you opt-in to the Genius feature, you will be able to create Genius playlists on Genius-capable devices. You must sync

☑ I have read and agree to the Genius Terms and Conditions.

Printable Version ⊕

Cancel
Continue

Read the agreement and check this box if you agree.

Click "Continue"

Figure 30–17. *The Genius license agreement in iTunes.*

4. Next, you will see a window on your screen for some time (longer if your library is large) that says the **Genius** feature is starting up (see Figure 30–18).

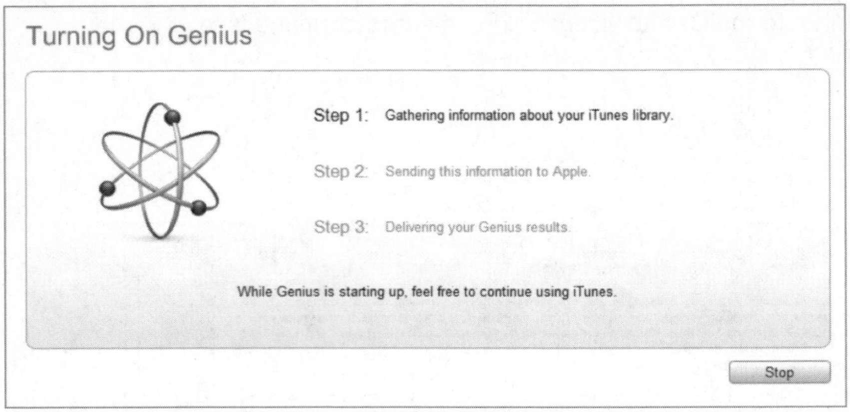

Turning On Genius

Step 1:   Gathering information about your iTunes library.

Step 2:   Sending this information to Apple.

Step 3:   Delivering your Genius results.

While Genius is starting up, feel free to continue using iTunes.

Stop

Figure 30–18. *The Genius feature getting turned on in iTunes.*

5.   In order for the **Genius** feature to work correctly, **iTunes** needs to understand the types of music and videos you have in your library. It will use this information to help make suggestions on similar artists or videos that you don't yet own, but might want to purchase. When this step is done, you will see a final success screen similar to the one shown in Figure 30–19. Now you are ready to start using the **Genius** feature!

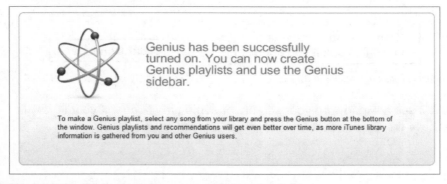

Genius has been successfully turned on. You can now create Genius playlists and use the Genius sidebar.

To make a Genius playlist, select any song from your library and press the Genius button at the bottom of the window. Genius playlists and recommendations will get even better over time, as more iTunes library information is gathered from you and other Genius users.

Figure 30–19. *The Genius feature successfully turned on in iTunes.*

You can think of the Genius feature as your "personal shopper" who knows your tastes and makes good recommendations (**Genius** suggestions). You can also think of the **Genius** feature as your "personal DJ" who knows the music that goes well together and will create a great playlist for you (**Genius** playlists).

Creating Genius Mixes and Playlists

Follow these steps to create a **Genius** mix and playlist:

1. Click a song in your library from that you would like to base the **Genius** mix and **Genius** playlist on.

2. Click the **Genius** button at the bottom of the **iTunes** screen, as shown in Figure 30–20.

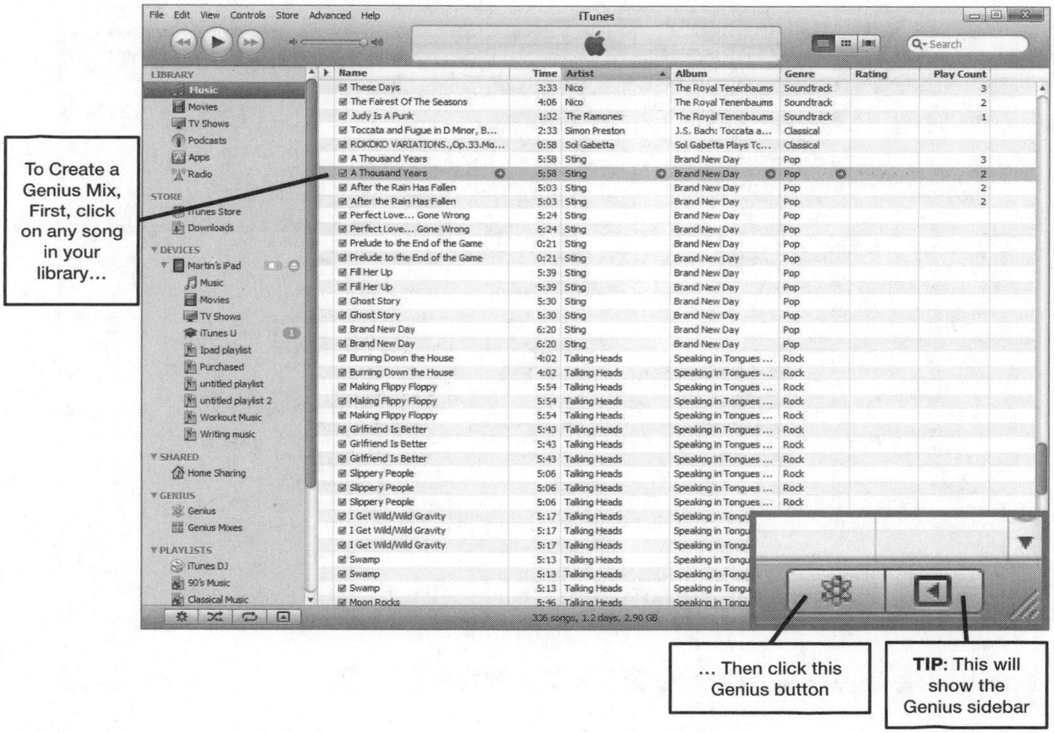

Figure 30–20. *Start creating a Genius mix that can be saved as a playlist.*

3. After you click the **Genius** button, the screen will immediately change to show you the **Genius** mix of all songs that **iTunes** thinks fit or match the type of song you selected (see Figure 30–21); these suggestions are based on computer algorithms and feedback from other iTunes users. You may be surprised at the list of music or even artists that you would not normally put together into a playlist.

TIP: Genius mixes and playlists provide a great way to keep your music library fresh, helping you to put together songs that go well together – often in combinations that you might not have thought about yourself.

The song you chose is at the top.

Change the number of songs here.

Keep clicking "Refresh" to see a new Mix of songs.

Click here to save this as a Playlist

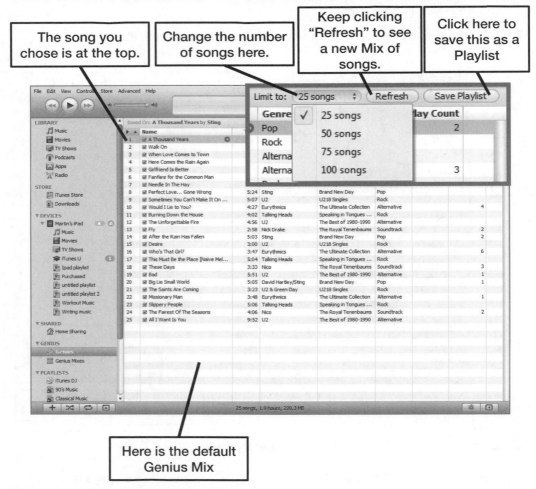

Here is the default Genius Mix

Figure 30–21. *The options for the Genius Mix screen.*

4.   On the **Genius Mix** screen (see Figure 30–21), you have options to change to 25, 50, 75, or 100 songs. Click the **Refresh** button to see a new (usually slightly different) mix/playlist.

5. If you like the mix and want to save it as a playlist, click the **Save Playlist** button in the upper right corner. Notice that the playlist is saved under the **Genius** section in the left column. The default name of the playlist is the name of the song you first clicked. You can change this name by double-clicking the playlist name. You will see it turn into editable text; from here, you can type a new name.

The Genius Sidebar

The other thing the **Genius** sidebar can do for you is make suggestions of related songs or videos to purchase from the iTunes store, based on the song or video you currently have highlighted from your library.

To view or hide the **Genius** sidebar, click the button in the lower right corner of **iTunes**, as shown in Figure 30–22.

Figure 30–22. *The Genius sidebar, showing recommendations and similar songs.*

Using the **Genius** sidebar, you can fill in your library with related songs or videos. If you get tired of the sidebar, then click the same button in the lower right corner to hide the **Genius** sidebar.

Turn Off Genius

To turn off the **Genius** feature (which will disable the **Genius** sidebar) and remove all your **Genius** mixes and playlists, select **Store** from the **iTunes** menu, and then choose **Turn Off Genius**.

Update Genius

If you have added a lot of music, videos, or other content to your **iTunes** library, periodically you will want to send an update to the **Genius** function in **iTunes**. To send this update, select **Store** from the **iTunes** menu, and then choose **Update Genius**.

The Home Sharing Feature

If you have several people in your home that use **iTunes**, and they are all connected together on a home network, then the **Home Sharing** feature will help you share your content (music, videos and more) across your computers with **iTunes** enabled. Follow these steps to take advantage of the **Home Sharing** feature:

1. *Pick the account to use for the **Home Sharing** feature*: All computers connected with the **Home Sharing** feature have to use the same iTunes account and password to log in and be connected. You will usually want to pick the account that has the most purchased content or the content you would like to share across all the computers.

> **NOTE:** Even though you can see other people's content and play it on **iTunes** on your computer, you need to import shared content into your own library if you want to enjoy it on your iPhone (or iPod or iPad). Keep in mind that shared content is for your personal enjoyment on your **iTunes** computer and your iPhone.

2. *Set up the **Home Sharing** feature and authorize each of the other computers*: You can get started with **Home Sharing** much as you do with the **Genius** feature. Click **Home Sharing** under the **Shared** heading in the **iTunes** app's **Left** nav bar, as shown in Figure 30–23.

NOTE: All versions of **iTunes** store videos and movies purchased or rented are protected by digital rights management (*DRM Protected*) using FairPlay. However, such DRM content can be played on up to five authorized computers (PC or Mac). Rented DRM content, such as a rented movie, must be physically transferred to one machine or device at a time. Protected music can be authorized on up to five computers, and music can be synced to a large number of mobile devices, as long as those mobile devices sync to only a single computer.

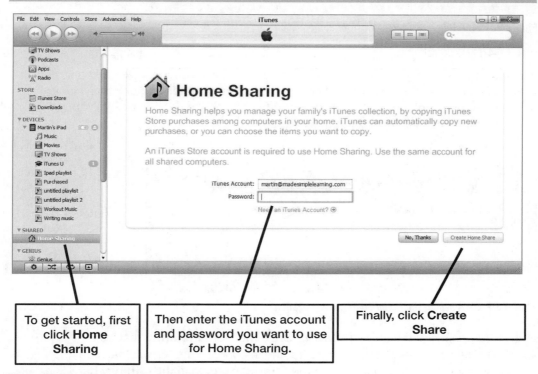

To get started, first click **Home Sharing**

Then enter the iTunes account and password you want to use for Home Sharing.

Finally, click **Create Share**

Figure 30–23. *Starting the Home Sharing feature.*

3. Repeat Step 2 on every computer you want to let access to your Home Shared content: Make sure that you use the same iTunes account on every computer; this could be a little confusing at first, but it's important to use the same account. On the other computers, you will probably have to authorize the computer to play iTunes content. The iTunes app will notify you if you need to authorize the computer by popping up a window similar to the one shown in Figure 30–24.

NOTE: Up to five computers that can be authorized as **Home Sharing** computers.

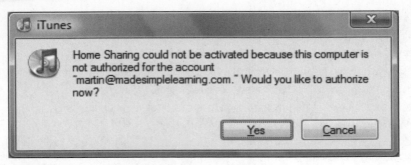

Figure 30–24. *A Home Sharing request for authorization.*

4. Click **Yes** to continue. Once authorization is complete, you will see a screen showing how many of your five total authorizations have been used up (see Figure 30–25). To learn more about authorizing or deauthorizing computers, see the "Authorize and Deauthorize Computers" section later in this chapter.

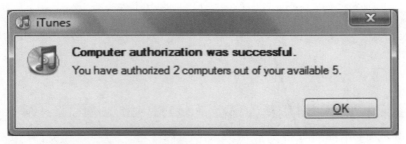

Figure 30–25. *A successful Home Sharing authorization.*

5. *Start enjoying the shared content*: Once the **Home Sharing** feature is enabled on at least two computers, the second computer will then see the shared content underneath the **Shared** heading in the **Left** nav bar in iTunes. To start viewing, playing, and importing this shared content, click the shared library, as shown in Figure 30–26.

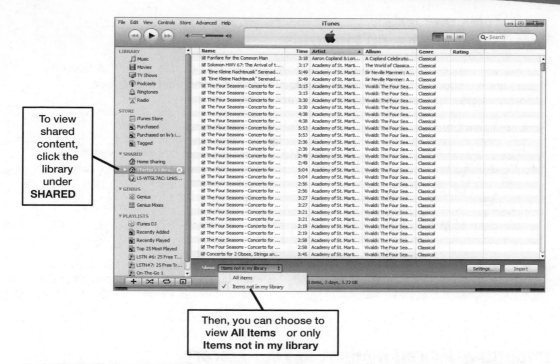

Figure 30–26. *Viewing a **Home Shared** library and filtering to view all items or those not in your own library.*

Filtering a Home Shared Library to Only Show Items Not in Your Library

Once you get up and running with a **Home Shared** library, you will notice that there is a switch at the bottom of the screen that allows you to show only those items that are not in your library (see Figure 30–26). This is a great way to quickly assess what you might need to add (i.e., *import*) to your library from the shared library.

Two Types of Shared Libraries

You will see two logos in the **Shared** category on the **Left** nav bar of iTunes. Each type of logo shows you whether the library is a fully shared library (the **House** logo) or a listen-only type of library (the **Stack of papers** icon).

Types of Shared Libraries	What this means
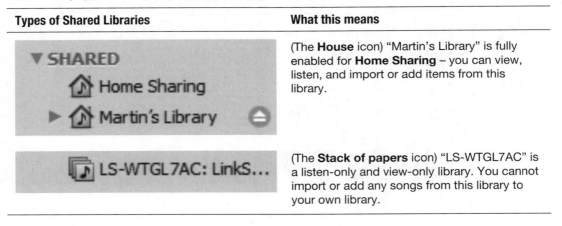	(The **House** icon) "Martin's Library" is fully enabled for **Home Sharing** – you can view, listen, and import or add items from this library.
	(The **Stack of papers** icon) "LS-WTGL7AC" is a listen-only and view-only library. You cannot import or add any songs from this library to your own library.

Importing Shared Content to Your Library

When you are viewing a **Home Shared** library, you can listen to anything in that library, as long as your computer has been authorized to do so. If you hit any authorization issues, please refer back to Chapter 3: "Sync Your iPhone with iTunes." In that chapter, we show you how to authorize your computers for iTunes.

You can manually drag-and-drop content to your library, or you can set up the **Home Sharing** feature to automatically import all new purchases from the **Home Shared** iTunes account.

Importing by Manually Dragging and Dropping

The drag-and-drop method for importing works well if you want to grab a few songs or videos from the shared library. Simply click the songs or videos to highlight them, and then drag them over to your library.

You can also click the songs/videos to highlight them, and then click the **Import** button in the lower right corner to do the same thing.

Automatically Importing of New Purchases

Follow these steps if you want to share all new purchases from the **Home Shared** iTunes account to the library on another device or computer automatically:

1. Click the **Home Sharing** library you would like to import from in the **Left** nav bar.

2. Click the **Settings** button in the lower right corner of the **iTunes** screen.

3. Now you will see a small window pop up that is similar to the one shown in Figure 30–27. Place a check next to the type of content you would like automatically transferred from the **Home Shared** library into your library. In Figure 30–27, all new music and movies purchased by the **Home Shared** iTunes account would automatically be imported and added to the iTunes account on this computer.

4. Click **OK** to save your **Home Sharing** settings.

Figure 30–27. *The Home Sharing Settings screen (transferring purchases automatically).*

To Toggle Home Sharing Off or On

Once you have enabled the **Home Sharing** feature, you may want to turn it off at some point. You do this by going to the iTunes **Advanced** menu and selecting **Turn Off Home Sharing**. To turn it back on, repeat this by going to the same **Advanced** menu and selecting **Turn On Home Sharing**.

Troubleshooting Home Sharing

Sometime you will see a "Computer Not Authorized" error, even though your computer has already been authorized on the **Home Sharing** account. Usually this happens because the content (e.g., song or video) that you are trying to view or listen to from the **Home Sharing** account was purchased by an account other than the **Home Shared** iTunes account. To correct this problem, follow these steps.

1. Locate the person in your home who originally purchased this song.

2. Ask him to authorize your computer. (If you hit any authorization issues, then you'll find Chapter 3: "Sync Your iPhone with iTunes" useful; this chapter explains how to authorize your computers for iTunes.)

3. Once your computer is authorized, you should be able to enjoy the music or video.

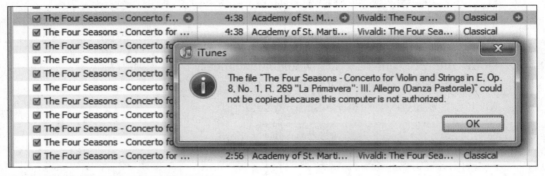

Figure 30–28. *The "not authorized" message.*

Create an iTunes Account

If you already have registered for an iTunes account using an Apple ID or AOL Screen Name, then you need to sign in (see the "Sign into the iTunes Store" section later in this chapter for information on how to do this).

If you want to buy or download free songs, books, apps, videos, TV shows, and more, you will need to acquire them from the iTunes store. You can do so by following these steps.

1. Click the **Sign In** button in the upper right corner, as shown in Figure 30–29. If you do not yet have an iTunes account, then click the **Create New Account** button and follow the instructions to create your new account. If you already have an account, enter your Apple ID or AOL screen name and password, click the **Sign In** button, and skip ahead five or six pages to the section called **Sign In to the iTunes Store**. This is where you'll enter you're Apple ID or AOL account details, if you have them.

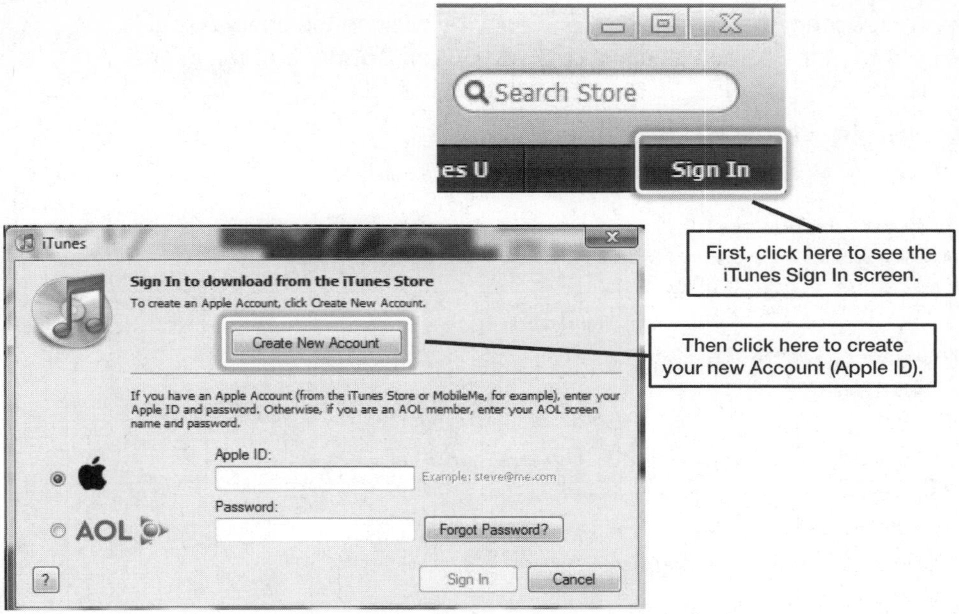

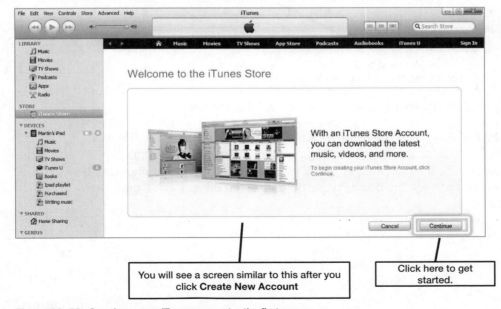

Figure 30–29. *The iTunes store Sign in screen – start creating a new account.*

2. When you click the **Create New Account** button, you will see a screen
   similar to the one shown in Figure 30–30. Click **Continue** to move on.

Figure 30–30. *Creating a new iTunes account – the first screen.*

3. Read and accept the Terms and Conditions by clicking the checkbox at the bottom of the screen (see Figure 30–31). Click **Continue** to move on.

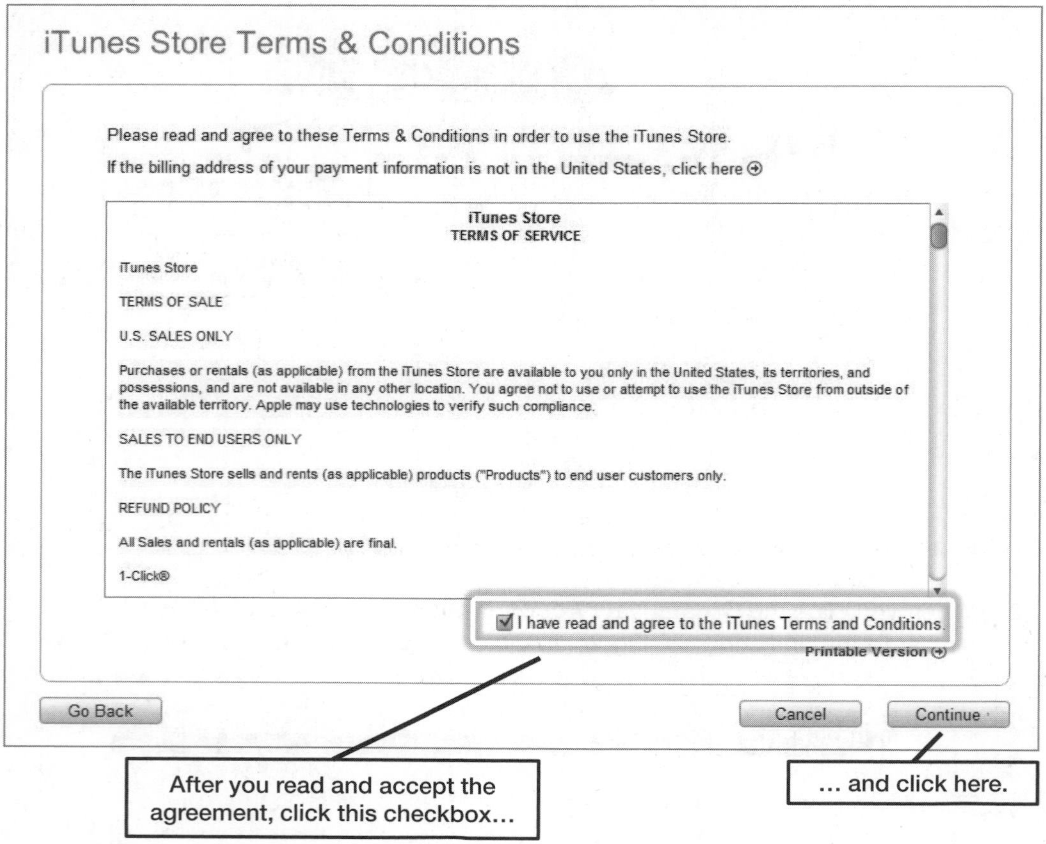

Figure 30–31. *Creating a new iTunes account – the Terms of Service screen*

4. On the next screen (see Figure 30–32), you set up your Apple ID (your login name for the iTunes store), your password, and your secret question and email preferences. If you do not want email notification, be sure to uncheck the boxes at the bottom of the page. Click **Continue** to move on.

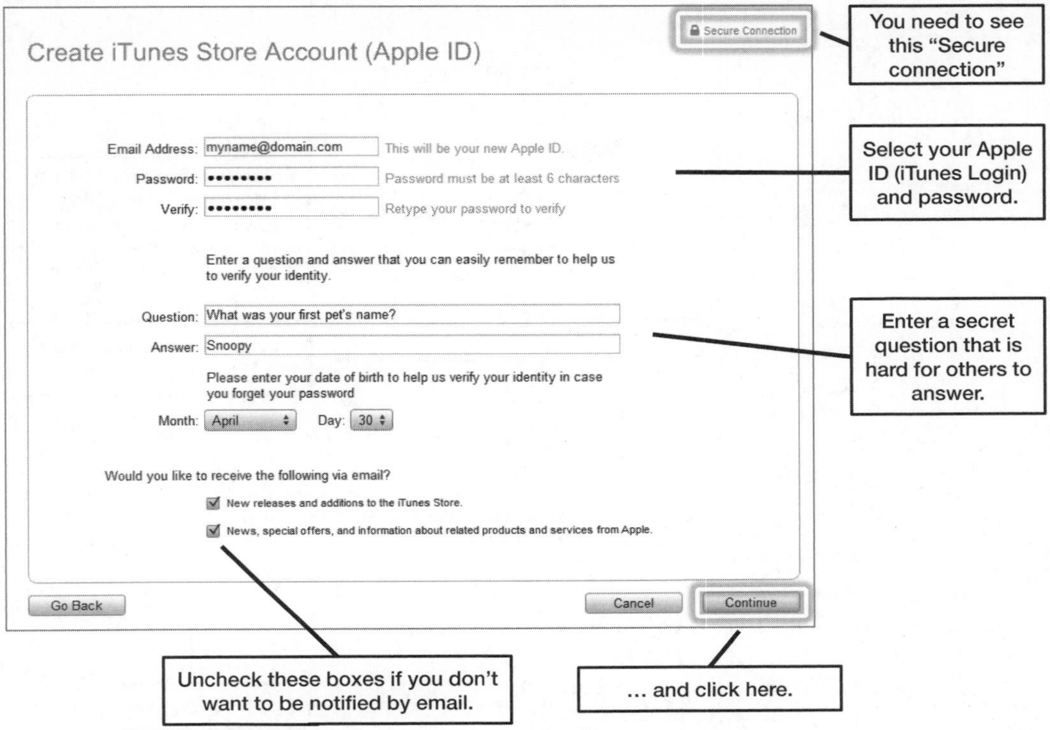

Create iTunes Store Account (Apple ID)

🔒 Secure Connection

> You need to see this "Secure connection"

Email Address: `myname@domain.com` This will be your new Apple ID.

Password: `••••••••` Password must be at least 6 characters

Verify: `••••••••` Retype your password to verify

> Select your Apple ID (iTunes Login) and password.

Enter a question and answer that you can easily remember to help us to verify your identity.

Question: `What was your first pet's name?`

Answer: `Snoopy`

> Enter a secret question that is hard for others to answer.

Please enter your date of birth to help us verify your identity in case you forget your password

Month: `April ⬍` Day: `30 ⬍`

Would you like to receive the following via email?

☑ New releases and additions to the iTunes Store.

☑ News, special offers, and information about related products and services from Apple.

[Go Back] [Cancel] [Continue]

> Uncheck these boxes if you don't want to be notified by email.

> ... and click here.

Figure 30–32. *Creating a new iTunes account – making an Apple ID account*

5. In the next screen (see Figure 30–33), you are asked to enter your billing information. Note that you can create a US-based account without billing information. Also, you can enter an iTunes gift card to receive credit, so you do not need to enter a credit card or PayPal account. This screen contains your preferred billing information, which will be used when you buy music, videos, and iPhone apps (from the **App Store** app on your iPhone). Click **Continue** to move on. Please note that the contents of this screen may vary slightly, depending on the country in which you are located.

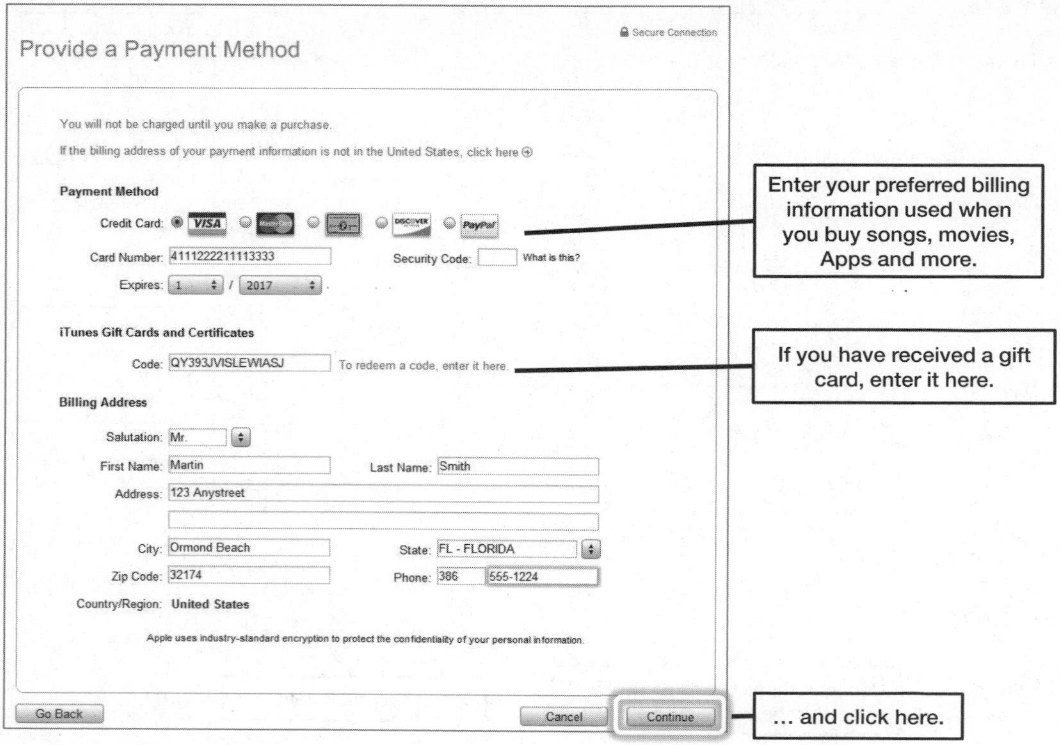

Figure 30–33. *Creating a new iTunes account – the Billing Information screen*

6. Depending on your locale, you may need to verify your county, province, or other local taxing authority (see Figure 30–34). Next, click **Done**.

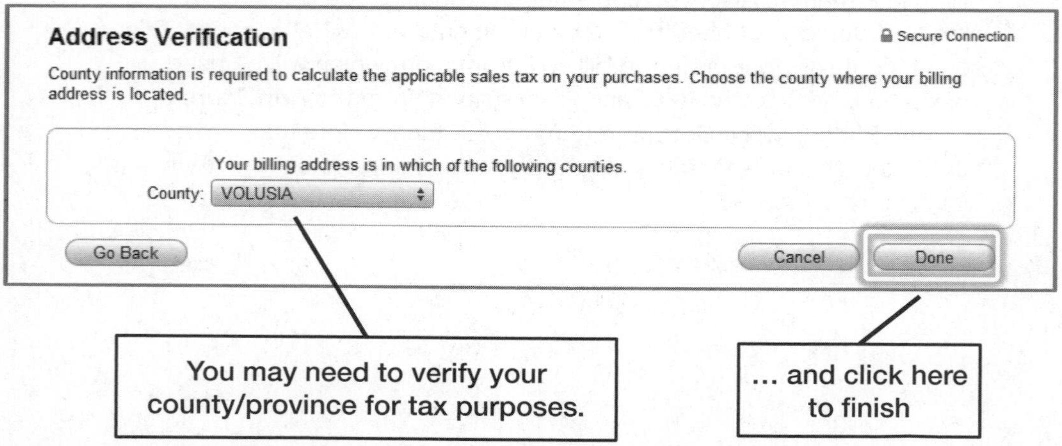

Figure 30–34. *Creating a new iTunes account – the Address Verification for tax purposes screen*

7. Now you should see a screen that asserts you have correctly set up your iTunes account; it should look similar to the one shown in Figure 30–35. Click **Done** to finish.

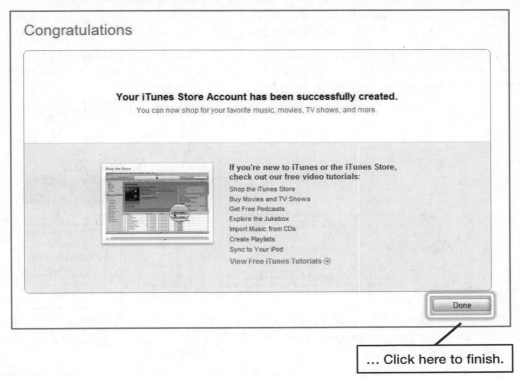

Figure 30–35. *Creating a new iTunes account – the Successful Completion screen*

Sign Into the iTunes Store

If you've successfully created an iTunes account, or you already own one, then the wonders of the iTunes store are now yours to explore! The following sections show you most of the things you can do once you're signed in. But first you need to sign in.

To do this, begin by clicking the iTunes **Sign In** button to take you to the **Sign In** screen, where you'll then be asked to enter your **Apple ID** and **Password**. Alternatively, you can enter your AOL Screen Name and Password:

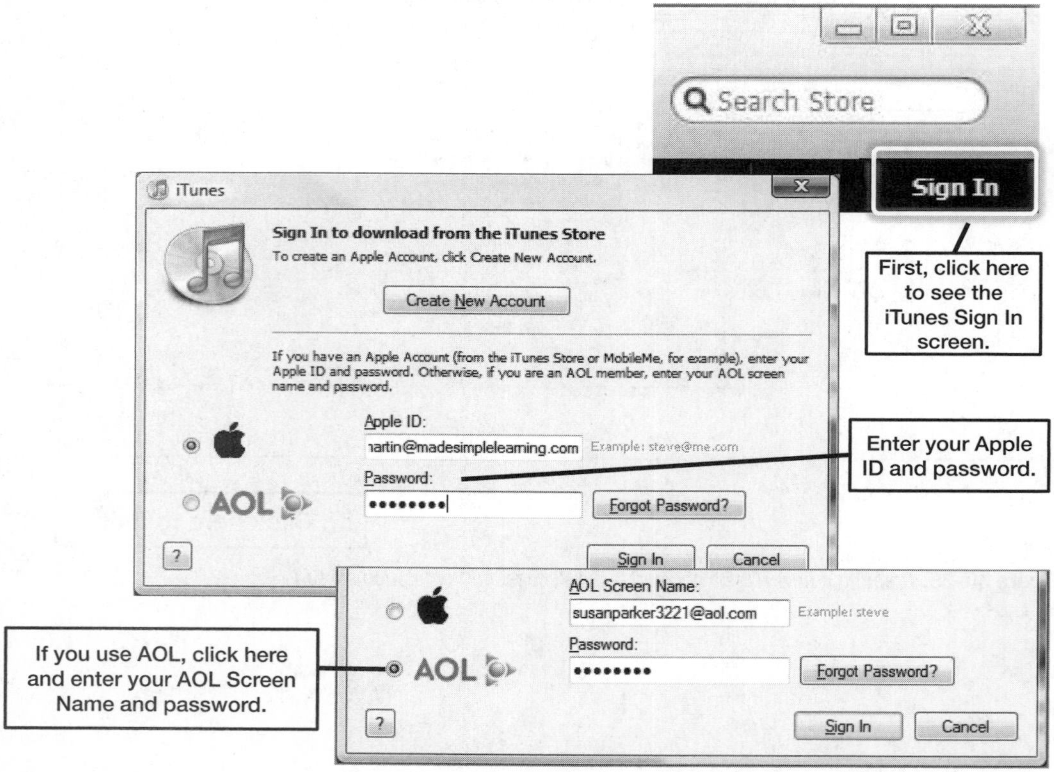

Figure 30–36. *Log in to iTunes using an Apple ID or an AOL screen name*

How to Know If You're Logged In to the iTunes Store

If you can see the **Sign In** button in the upper right corner of iTunes, then you know you are not logged in.

This shows you are not signed in. Click this button to Sign In.

If you can see your Apple ID (usually your email address) in the upper right corner instead of the **Sign In** button, then you are logged into the store.

When you are Signed In, you will see your Apple ID or AOL screen name here.

Getting to the iTunes Store

You can always get back to the iTunes store by clicking the **iTunes Store** link under **Store** in the **Left** nav bar.

Buy or Get Free Media from the iTunes Store

After signing in or creating a new account, you will be able to search the store for any artist, album, composer, or title.

Browse Store by Genre

If you prefer to browse by genre to locate songs, just click the **Genres** pull down button next to the **Music** option in the **iTunes Store** box. Select the genre you prefer.

The entire store will be tailored to show you songs from your selected genre.

To browse music by Genre, click here.

iTunes STORE   NEW AND NOTE

Music   Genres ⬦   Music

Movies
TV Shows
Music Videos   Alternative
Audiobooks   Blues
Podcasts   Children's Music
iTunes Latino   Christian & Gospel
iTunes U   Classical
iPod Games   Comedy
App Store   Country
                      Dance
MORE IN MOVI   Electronic
HD Movies   Hip-Hop/Rap
HD TV Shows   Jazz
TV Shows Ju   Latin
                      Pop
TOP TV EPISO   R&B/Soul
                      Reggae
1.   Rock
                      Singer/Songwriter
  The Goodh   Soundtrack
  Gossip Girl
2. Peter's Pr   Vocal
   Family Guy   World
3. Remembe
   One Tree Hi
4. If It's Only

To find all the songs by a particular artist, type that artist's name into the **Search** box in the upper right corner. You could also search by part or all of a particular song's name. Once you press the **Enter** key, you will be presented with all the matching items from the iTunes store (see Figure 30–37).

You can then navigate around and purchase individual songs with the **Buy Song** buttons at the bottom.

Type your favorite artist or song here...

Once you press the ENTER key, you will see the search results here and below.

You can purchase individual songs down here.

Figure 30–37. *Searching for and buying songs in the iTunes store*

After you click the **Buy Song** button, you will need to log in, unless you have previously instructed iTunes to keep you logged in for your purchases.

CAUTION: If you are at a public computer or are worried that anyone who might access your computer (e.g. your kids, spouse, or friends) would buy stuff without you knowing – then don't check the "Remember password for purchasing" box!

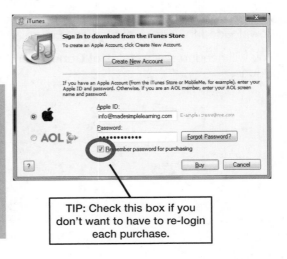

TIP: Check this box if you don't want to have to re-login each purchase.

After you log in, you will see this warning message if you have just clicked the **Buy** button.

If you don't want to see this dialog box every time you buy something, then check the box at the bottom of the dialog before clicking the **Buy** button.

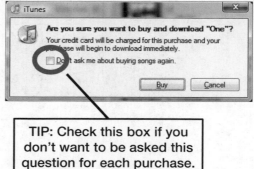

TIP: Check this box if you don't want to be asked this question for each purchase.

Now the song, video, or other item you purchased will be queued up to be downloaded to your local library in the **iTunes** app on your computer.

Making Sure All Items Are Downloaded

After you purchase a song, video, app, or other item from the App Store – or if you have just authorized this computer on your account – you should click the **Downloads** link that appears under the **Store** category heading in the left column.

Any items currently being downloaded will show a status bar in the **Downloads** main window. You will see a **Done** status message when the items are completely downloaded to your computer (see Figure 30–38).

You will need to see a status of **Done** before you can put the purchased item onto your iPhone.

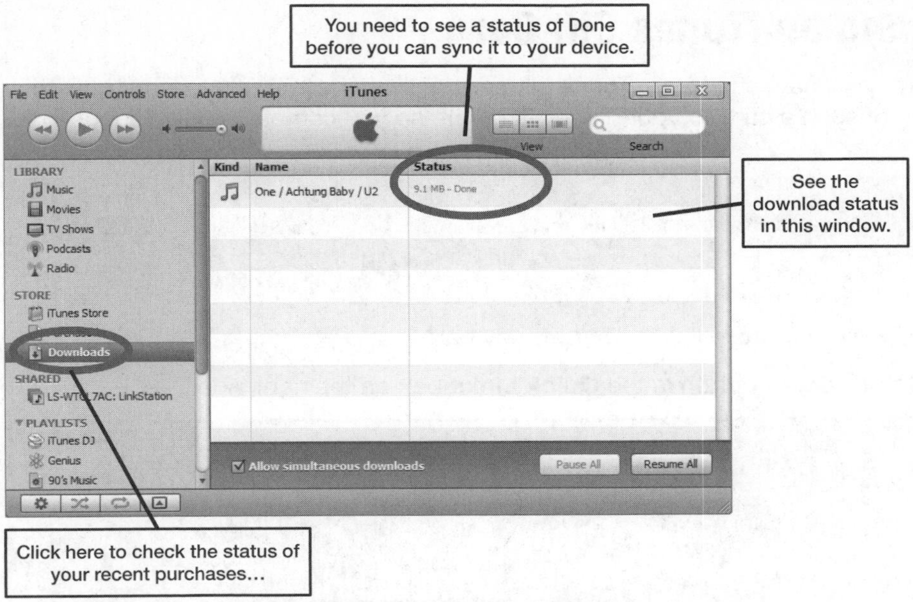

You need to see a status of Done before you can sync it to your device.

See the download status in this window.

Click here to check the status of your recent purchases...

Figure 30-38. *The iTunes Store – see the status of items purchased or downloaded*

If you see a popup window asking whether you want **iTunes** to download all your purchased items, then click **Yes**.

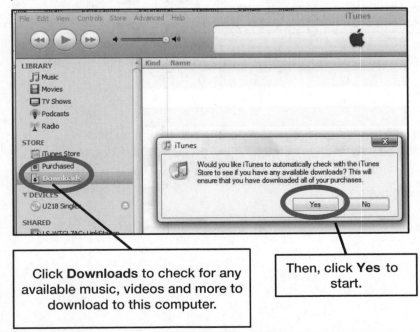

Click **Downloads** to check for any available music, videos and more to download to this computer.

Then, click **Yes** to start.

Figure 30-39. *iTunes asking to automatically check for previously downloaded items*

Redeeming an iTunes Gift Card

At some point, you may receive an iTunes gift card. Follow these steps to learn how to add the value of such a card to your iTunes account, so you can buy music, videos, and more"

> **NOTE:** iTunes gift cards are country specific. In other words, a US gift card will only work for a US iTunes account.

1. Click the **iTunes Store** link in the **Left** nav bar.

2. Click the **Redeem** button in the **Quick Links** box on the right side.

Figure 30–40. *Redeeming an iTunes gift card*

3. On the **Redeem** screen, you will need to enter the code from the back of the gift card. (You may need to scratch off the silver/gray covering to see the card's code.)

4. Click the **Redeem** button.

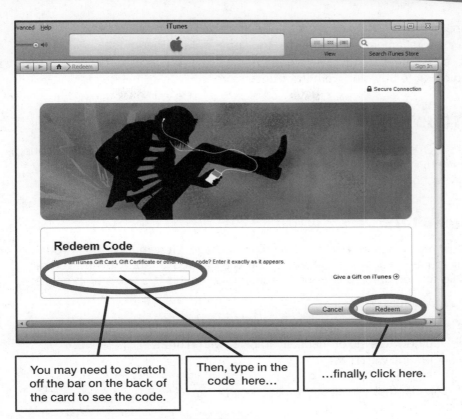

You may need to scratch off the bar on the back of the card to see the code.

Then, type in the code here...

...finally, click here.

Figure 30–41. *The iTunes Redeem Gift Card screen.*

5. To verify that the gift card is being applied to the correct iTunes account, you will need to sign in or re-enter your password.

6. Click the **Sign In** or the **View Account** button (if you're already signed in).

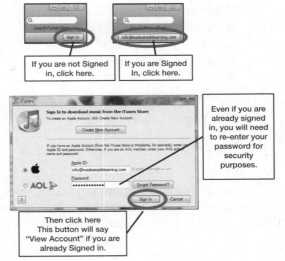

If you are not Signed in, click here.

If you are Signed In, click here.

Even if you are already signed in, you will need to re-enter your password for security purposes.

Then click here
This button will say "View Account" if you are already Signed in.

7. When the gift card has been successfully applied to your account, you will see the total amount of the card in the upper right corner of the **iTunes** screen, right next to your sign-in name. Now you can use this gift card credit to buy stuff from the iTunes store.

Getting Your Stuff into iTunes

If you have music CDs, DVDs, e-Books and PDF files you want to enjoy on your iPhone, you will first have to import them into your iTunes library on your computer. We show you how in this section.

Import Music CDs

If you are of legal drinking age, then it's likely that you have a few music CDs in your home library. If you are over 40, that likelihood goes up to 100%. So... how do you get all your best CDs loaded onto your iPhone? Accomplishing this is a two step process:

1. Load the CDs into iTunes.

2. Sync or manually transfer those CD songs to your iPhone. (Don't forget we show you how to sync or manually transfer with **iTunes** in Chapter 3: "Sync Your iPhone with iTunes.")

Here's a quick reminder that explains how to load one of your existing CDs into **iTunes**. This process requires only two simple steps:

1. Insert the CD into your computer's CD drive. You may see a popup inside **iTunes** that asks whether you would like to import the CD as shown.

2. Click **Yes** to import the CD.

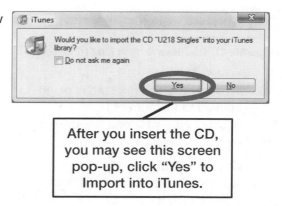

After you insert the CD, you may see this screen pop-up, click "Yes" to Import into iTunes.

If you did not receive this popup window, then you can manually start the CD import into **iTunes** by clicking the **Import CD** button in the lower right corner. You will also notice that the CD has appeared under the **Devices** list in the left column (see Figure 26–42).

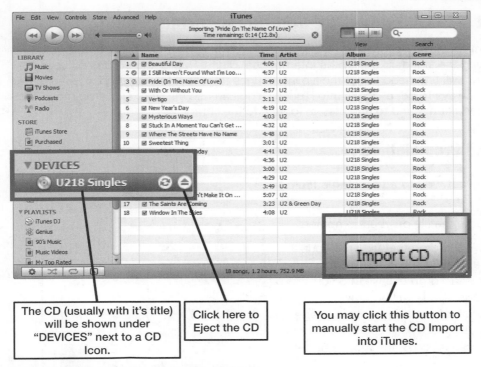

The CD (usually with it's title) will be shown under "DEVICES" next to a CD Icon.

Click here to Eject the CD

You may click this button to manually start the CD Import into iTunes.

Figure 30–42. *Working with a music CD inside iTunes*

Import Movies from DVDs

Some of the more recent DVDs and Blu-Rays you purchase have two versions of the movie: one for your DVD or Blu-Ray player and an extra digital copy that can be loaded automatically into **iTunes**.

Usually, you will see text on the outside of the DVD box that states there is an extra "Digital Copy for your Computer." You can check whether this copy exists by inserting the DVD into your computer's DVD drive and opening **iTunes**. If the digital copy exists, then iTunes will automatically detect it and ask whether you would like to import the movie.

> **CAUTION:** Most DVDs or Blu-Rays you own probably do not provide this extra digital version, which is meant to be loaded and watched on your computer or mobile devices. These standard DVDs or Blu-Rays are copy-protected and cannot normally be loaded into **iTunes**. However, if you do a web search for "load DVD into iTunes," you may find some software products (such as **Handbrake** at `http://handbrake.fr`) that allow you to *rip* or *burn* your DVDs into **iTunes**. We strongly urge you to obey copyright laws; if you use software like this, you should only use the DVD on your own computer or iPhone and never share the movie or otherwise violate the copyright agreement.

Import e-Book Files (PDF and iBook-format Files)

If you want to read a PDF file or e-book (in ePub format - the free and open e-book format using the standard set by the International Digital Publishing Forum) on your iPhone, you will first need to get the file into iTunes to sync it to your iPhone. There are a couple of ways to get e-books into iTunes. You can use the drag and drop method or use the menu command to add files or folders to the library.

Drag and Drop Method

This is a great way to add a single file or just a few files.

1. Locate the file on your computer.

2. Click and drag that file onto your library in iTunes. Let go of the mouse to drop this file into your library. A box will be drawn around your library as shown in the image to the right. When you see the box, you can let go of the mouse button.

3. Since the file is readable by the **iBooks** app, you should then see the file appear in the **Books** section of your library.

Use Menu Commands

Using menus works well if you have an entire folder or folders of files you want to move into iTunes.

> **TIP:** This method works for e-books and also other content such as music.

1. From the **iTunes** menu, choose File, then select **Add Folder to Library** to add an entire folder of content or **Add File to Library** if you have only one file to add.

2. Now navigate to the folder or file you wish to add and click **Select Folder** or **Open** (for a single file).

3. All iBooks-readable files will be added to **iTunes.**

	Edit View Controls Store Advanced Help	
	New Playlist	Ctrl+N
	New Playlist from Selection	Ctrl+Shift+N
	New Playlist Folder	
	New Smart Playlist...	Ctrl+Alt+N
	Edit Smart Playlist	
	Close Window	Ctrl+W
	Add File to Library...	Ctrl+O
	Add Folder to Library...	
	Library	▶

Getting Album Artwork

iTunes can automatically get the album art for most songs and videos; however, if you need to manually retrieve this artwork, follow these steps:

NOTE: You will need to have an iTunes account already and be logged in for this to work correctly.

1. Start **iTunes**.

2. Go to the **Advanced** menu.

3. Select **Get Album Artwork**.

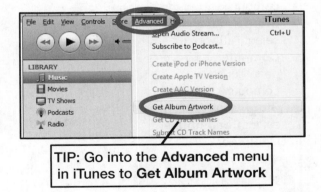

TIP: Go into the **Advanced** menu in iTunes to **Get Album Artwork**

Authorize and Deauthorize Computers to Play iTunes Media

You can authorize up to five different computers to play your iTunes media (e.g., music and movies).

Here's a question that you hear quite often: *Someone else has authorized my computer to play his songs; can I now load and listen to these "authorized songs" on my iPhone?*

The short answer is "maybe."

The answer is "no" for all songs purchased on iTunes prior to January 2009. It is also "no" for all songs purchased with DRM (*Digital Rights Management*) protection. These songs are tied specifically to one person's mobile device (iPad, iPod or iPhone).

The answer is "yes" for all songs purchased without DRM Protection enabled. Early in 2009, iTunes announced that it would start selling some songs and videos without DRM Protection, which means they can be played on multiple iPods and iPhones. Follow these steps to authorize or deauthorize your computer to be able to play songs on your computer, and possibly your iPhone, from someone else's iTunes library.

1. Start up **iTunes**.

2. To authorize a computer, go to the **Store** menu and select **Authorize Computer...** To deauthorize a computer, go to the **Store** menu and select **Deauthorize Computer...**

NOTE: You will need to know your iTunes or AOL username and password for this to work.

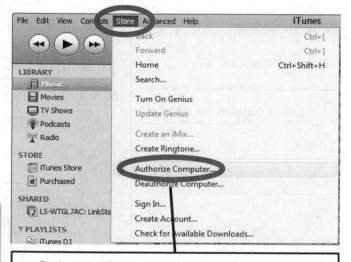

Go into the **Store** menu to **Authorize** or enable this computer to play your iTunes media.
TIP: You can authorize up to 5 computers.

3. Enter your Apple ID or, if you prefer, click the radio button next to AOL and enter your AOL screen name and password.

4. Next, click the **Authorize** or **Deauthorize** button.

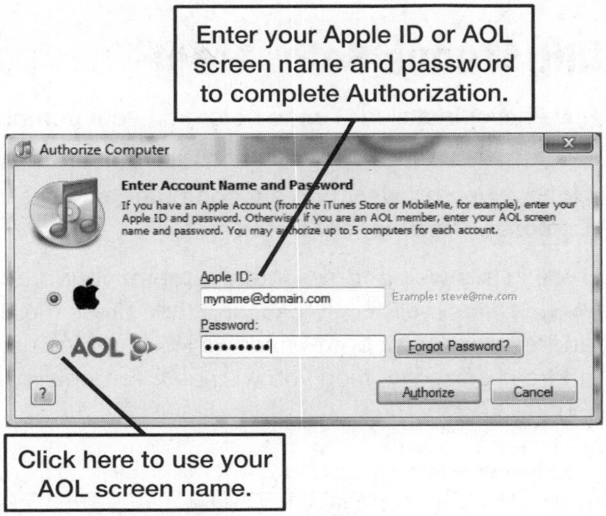

Enter your Apple ID or AOL screen name and password to complete Authorization.

Authorize Computer

Enter Account Name and Password

If you have an Apple Account (from the iTunes Store or MobileMe, for example), enter your Apple ID and password. Otherwise, if you are an AOL member, enter your AOL screen name and password. You may authorize up to 5 computers for each account.

Apple ID:

myname@domain.com   Example: steve@me.com

Password:

••••••••   Forgot Password?

AOL

Authorize   Cancel

Click here to use your AOL screen name.

Getting iTunes Software

If you have never installed **iTunes** before on your computer, you can download the software directly from the Apple's web site (www.apple.com) by following these steps:

1. Open a web browser on your computer, such as **Safari**, **Internet Explorer**, **Chrome**, or **Firefox**.

2. Type in this web address into the top of your browser: www.itunes.com/download, and then press the **Enter** key. This web address works for both Windows PC and Mac users. If you typed the address correctly, then you will see a screen similar to the one shown in Figure 30–43.

Figure 30–43. *The Apple iTunes software downloads web page*

3. Next, select the software that matches your computer's operating system, assuming that you're given a choice. (If you do not know what operating system version you are running, then please see the "Determining Your Windows PC Computer Operating System" sidebar later in this chapter for help.)

Determining Your Windows or Mac Computer Operating System Version

The instructions in the sidebars that follow will help you determine the specific version of the operating system on your Windows- or Mac-based computer.

Determining Your Computer's Windows Operating System

Follow these steps to determine which version of the Windows operating system your computer uses:

1. Click the **Start** button or the **Windows** logo in the lower left corner to bring up the **Start** menu.

2. Right-click **Computer** and select **Properties** from the popup menu.

3. You will then see a screen similar to the one shown in Figure 30–44. Notice that this computer is running "Windows Vista Home Premium" and that the System Type is a "64-Bit Operating System." This user in this figure would select "iTunes 9.1 for Windows (64-bit)" when downloading the **iTunes** software from the iTunes download page.

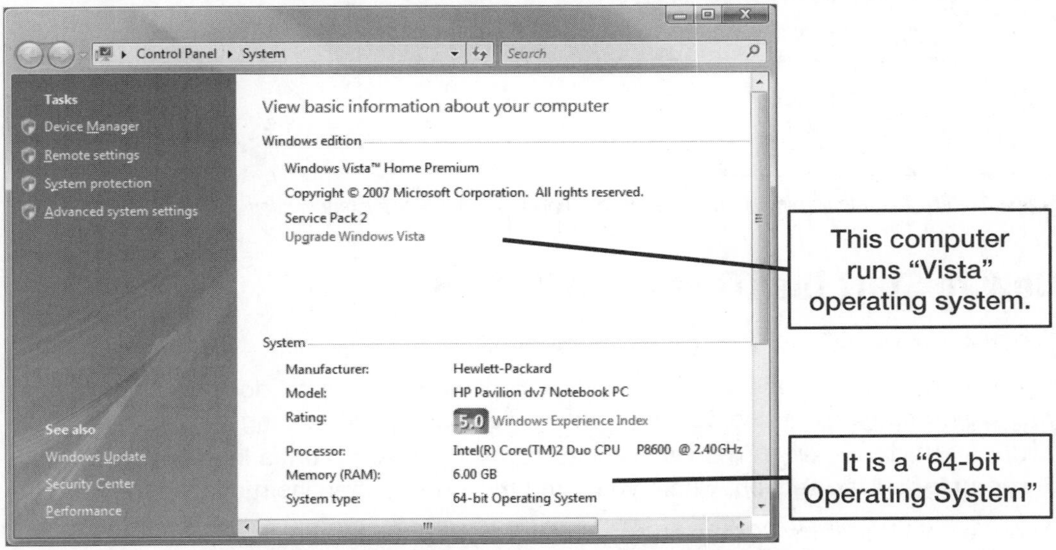

Figure 30–44. The Windows System properties page, which shows the operating system version

Determining Your Mac's Operating System

Follow these steps to determine which version of the Mac operating system your computer uses:

1. Click the **Apple** logo in the upper right corner and select **About This Mac** from the menu.

2. You will then see a screen similar to the one shown in Figure 30–45. The Mac in this screenshot is running OS X Version 10.6.2. Note that you can check for updates by clicking the **Software Update** button.

Figure 30–45. *The About This Mac window, which shows the operating system version*

How to Start the iTunes Installation

The next step is to install the iTunes application.

If you are on a Mac, then the install should start automatically; if it does not, then locate your **Downloads** folder and double-click the file that says something like iTunes_Install.dmg. Then skip ahead to this chapter's **iTunes Installation Screens for a Mac** section, where you'll find the step-by-step instructions.

If you're on a Windows PC, the steps you take to start the downloaded installation file vary a little, depending on your web browser. In the section that follows, we will walk you through the installation steps for the **iTunes** app with four popular browsers: **Google Chrome**, **Microsoft Internet Explorer**, **Apple Safari**, and **Mozilla Firefox**.

Google Chrome Browser

If you are using **Google Chrome** browser, follow these steps to install the **iTunes** app on your Windows PC:

1. Click the **Save** button at the bottom of the web browser screen.

2. When the download is complete, double-click `iTunesSetup.exe` or `iTunes64Setup.exe` to start the **iTunes** installation.

CAUTION: If you have previously downloaded an iTunes setup file, the more recently downloaded file name may have a number after it, such as `iTunes64Setup (1).exe`. You want to select the file with the highest number after it.

Microsoft Internet Explorer Browser

If you are using **Microsoft Internet Explorer** browser, follow these steps to install the iTunes application on your Windows PC:

1. Click the **Run** button in the **File Download-Security Warning** screen (see Figure 30–46).

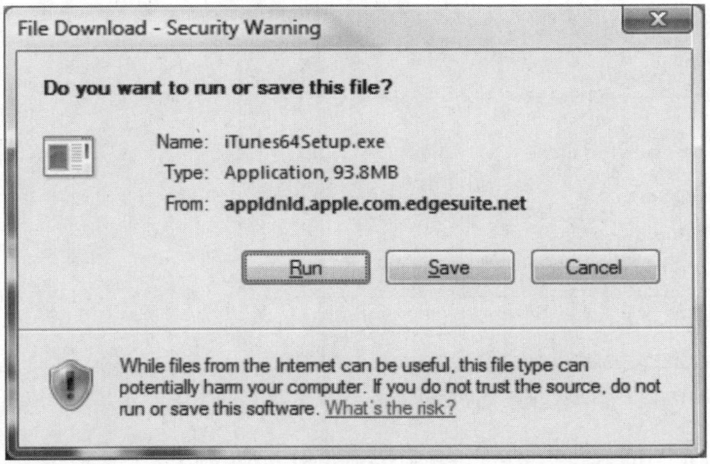

Figure 30–46. *The Internet Explorer File Download – Security Warning window*

2. To start the software installation of **iTunes**, you may need to answer another security question. If you see a window like the one shown in Figure 30–47, verify that the software name is "iTunes" and that the Publisher is "Apple Inc."

3. Click the **Run** button.

Figure 30–47. *The Internet Explorer File – Security Warning popup window*

Apple Safari Browser

If you are using **Apple Safari** browser on a Windows PC, follow these steps to install the **iTunes** app:

1. Click the **Run** button in the **File Download – Security Warning** popup window (see Figure 30–48).

Figure 30–48. *The Apple Safari File Download – Security Warning window*

2. To start the installation of iTunes, you may need to answer another security question. If you see a window like the one shown in Figure 30–49, verify that the software name is iTunesSetup.exe or iTunes64Setup.exe and that the publisher is "Apple Inc."

3. Click the **Run** button.

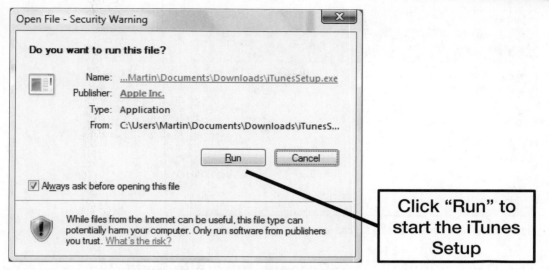

Figure 30–49. *The Apple Safari File Download-Security Warning window*

Firefox Browser

If you are using the **Firefox** browser, follow these steps to install the **iTunes** app on your Windows PC:

1. Click the **Save File** button in the opening iTunes.exe popup window (see Figure 30–50).

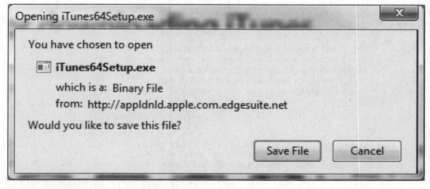

Figure 30–50. *The Firefox opening file pop-up window*

2. To start the installation of **iTunes**, double-click the iTunes setup file (it could be called iTunesSetup.exe or iTunes64Setup.exe) in the **Downloads** popup window, as shown in Figure 30–51.

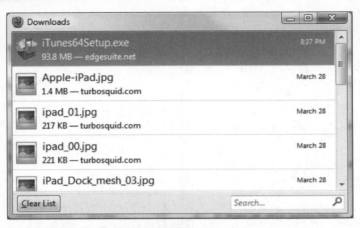

Figure 30–51. *The Firefox opening file popup window*

The iTunes Installation Screens for a Windows PC

Now that you have successfully downloaded and started the installation file, you should see a screen similar to the one shown in Figure 30–52. This screen will have a main heading that says something like, "Welcome to the iTunes Installer."

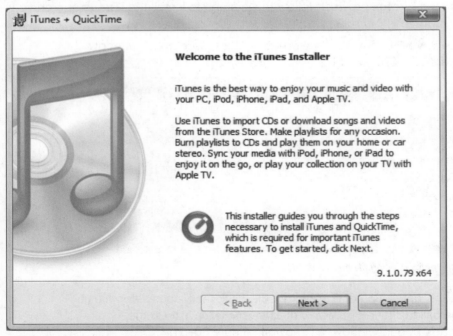

Figure 30–52. *The opening screen of the iTunes software installation process on Windows*

Follow these steps to complete the installation process (your **iTunes** version numbers will be higher than the ones shown in these images, this is OK):

1. Click the **Next** button and follow the steps presented by the wizard to install **iTunes**. If you see an error message about 32-bit or 64-bit versions, as shown in the images immediately below, please read the caution that follows because you may want to download another version of iTunes. This will bring up the License Agreement for the software (see Figure 30-53).

CAUTION: If you see a 64-bit warning message similar to this one, then please click the **No** button and return to the Apple site to download the 64-bit edition of iTunes. This version will be better suited for your computer. You can grab the file at this URL: `www.itunes.com/download`.

If you see this warning, then click "No" and return to the Apple site to download the "64-bit" edition of iTunes.

Figure 30-53. *The iTunes software installation software license screen (Windows).*

2. If you agree with the terms, click the radio button next to "I accept the terms in the license agreement" and click the **Next** button. This will bring up a dialog that presents a handful of installation options for the **iTunes** app (see Figure 30-54).

---

iTunes + QuickTime   ✕

Installation Options

Select folder where iTunes files will be installed and choose installation options.

☑ Add iTunes and QuickTime shortcuts to my desktop

☑ Use iTunes as the default player for audio files

☑ Automatically update iTunes and other Apple software

Default iTunes language: English (United States) ▼

Destination Folder

📁   C:\Program Files (x86)\iTunes\   Change...

< Back   Install   Cancel

Figure 30–54. *The iTunes software Installation Options screen (Windows)*

3. You can usually you can leave all the default settings alone, unless you have a specific reason to change them. Click the **Install** button to start the installation.

NOTE: If you have **Microsoft Outlook** or another email program running, you will be asked to stop it or restart it after the installation completes. We recommend stopping Outlook before installing **iTunes**.

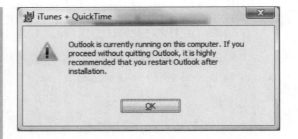

4. Once you have successfully installed **iTunes**, you will see a screen similar to the one shown in Figure 30–55. If you want to start up **iTunes** automatically, leave the box checked (again, see Figure 30–55).

Figure 30–55. *The iTunes software installation final success screen (Windows)*

5. Click the **Finish** button to close the installer.

iTunes Installation Screens for a Mac

Now that you have successfully downloaded and started the installation file on your Mac, you should see a screen similar to the one shown in Figure 30–56. This screen will have a main heading that says something like, "Welcome to the iTunes Installer." Follow these steps to complete the process:

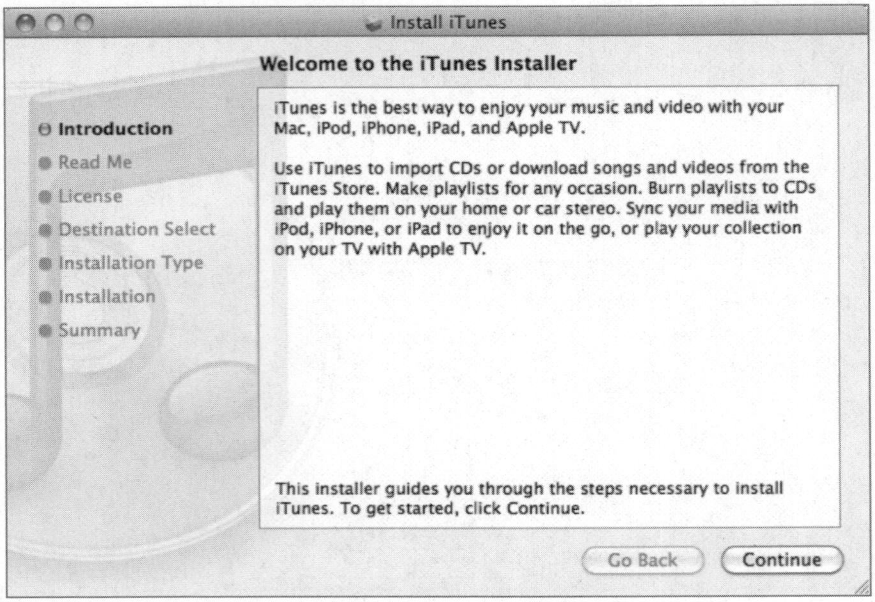

Figure 30–56. *The iTunes software installation wizard's first screen (Apple Mac)*

1. Click the **Continue** button to bring up the **What's new** screen.

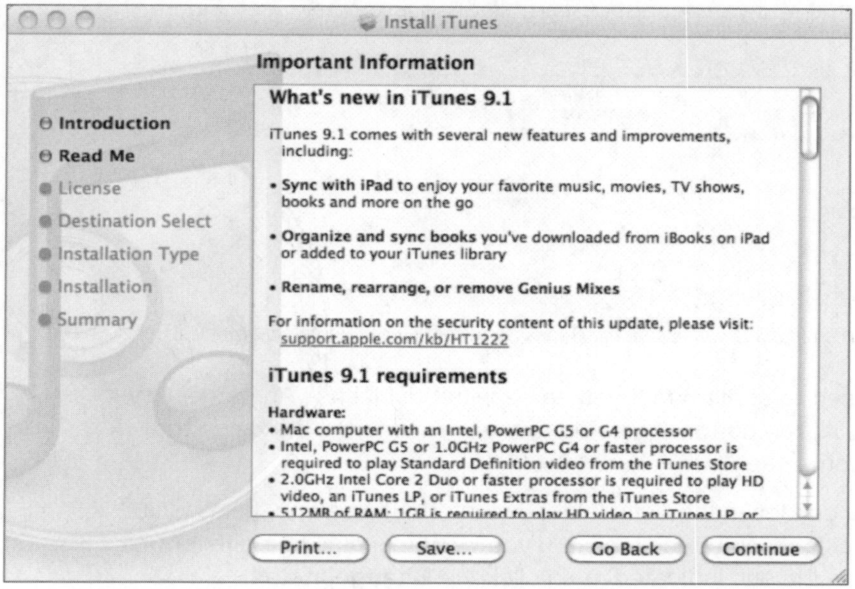

Figure 30–57. *The iTunes software installation What's New screen (Apple Mac)*

2. On the **What's New** screen, you can scroll down to check out what's new in the latest version of **iTunes**, as well as to see the system requirements (see Figure 30–58). Click **Continue** to move on.

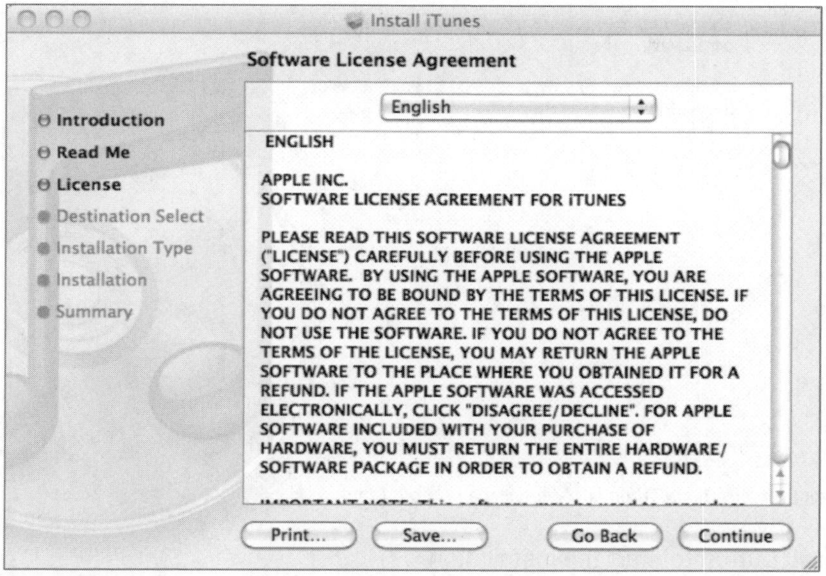

Figure 30–58. *The iTunes software installation Software License Agreement screen (Apple Mac)*

3. Read the License Agreement and click the **Continue** button to bring up the screen that lets you accept or reject license agreement (see Figure 30–59).

Figure 30–59. *The screen that lets you accept the iTunes Software License Agreement (Apple Mac)*

4. Now you need to confirm that you agree with the License Agreement by clicking the **Agree** button. Agreeing to the license terms brings up the final selection screen (see Figure 30–60).

5. Usually you can leave the default location information alone, unless you have a specific reason to change it. If you want to install to a different location than the one indicated, then click the **Change Install Location...** button and indicate your preferred location.

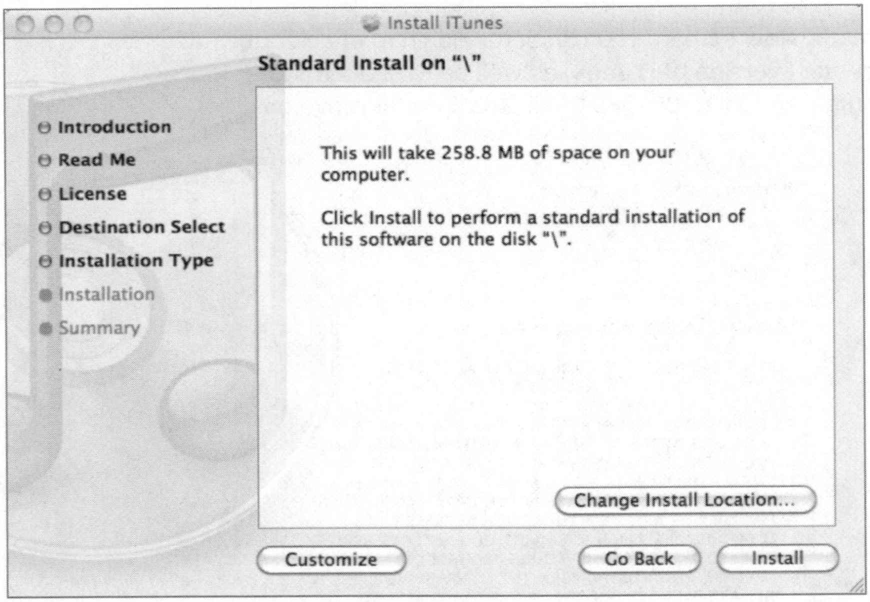

Figure 30–60. *The iTunes Software Installation Location screen (Apple Mac)*

6. Click the **Install** button to start the installation.

NOTE: If you have an email client such as **Entourage** or **Mail** running, you may be asked to stop it or restart it after the installation completes. We recommend stopping your email client before installing **iTunes**.

7. Once you have successfully installed iTunes, you will see a screen similar to the one shown in Figure 30–61.

Figure 30–61. The *iTunes software installation final success screen*

8. Click the **Close** button to close the installer.

Updating an Existing iTunes Installation

If you have previously installed **iTunes** on your computer, you should check for an updated version. Follow these steps to update your **iTunes** software:

NOTE: You will need **iTunes** version 9.2 or higher to sync with your iPhone. Next, we will show you how to make sure you have the most up-to-date version of **iTunes** on your computer.

1. Start the **iTunes** software.

2. Go to the **Help** menu (on your
    PC) or **iTunes** app (the left-
    most menu on the Mac) and
    then select **Check for
    Updates**.

3. If you are not using the latest
    version, then you will see a
    screen similar to the one
    shown to the right.

4. Click **Download iTunes** to be taken to the **Apple Software Update**
    screen (see Figure 30–62).

5. On the **Apple Software Update** screen, make sure the **iTunes** selection
    is checked. Next, uncheck any software you do not want to install and
    click the **Install** button in the lower right corner.

Uncheck anything you do not want to install.

Make sure iTunes is checked

Click to highlight a particular item above to see details here.

Then click this button.

Figure 30–62. *The Apple Software Update screen*

6.   You will then need to accept the Apple License Agreement by clicking **Next** and **Accept** for the software update to start downloading (see Figure 30–63).

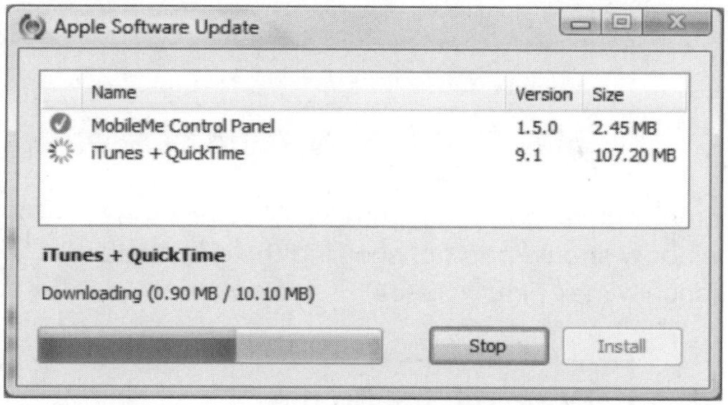

Figure 30–63. *The Apple Software Update download status screen*

> **TIP:** The software downloads can be 50 megabytes (MB) or more in size. We highly recommend performing the software downloads and updates from a high-speed Internet connection.

If everything goes smoothly, your **iTunes** app and related software should be automatically updated with the latest versions.

iTunes Troubleshooting

In this section, we will provide a few tips and tricks to help you deal with some common issues you might encounter when using **iTunes**. We also have an entire chapter devoted to troubleshooting (see Chapter 29) if you cannot find answers to the problems you encounter in this section.

What to Do If the iTunes Auto Update Fails

The automatic update may fail when you have the About iTunes.rtf text file open, or you have another related file open that cannot be closed by the installer automatically. If you locate and close the problem file, you should be able to retry the automatic update.

If you see a message similar to the one shown to the right, then you will have to manually install the update. Follow these steps to do so:

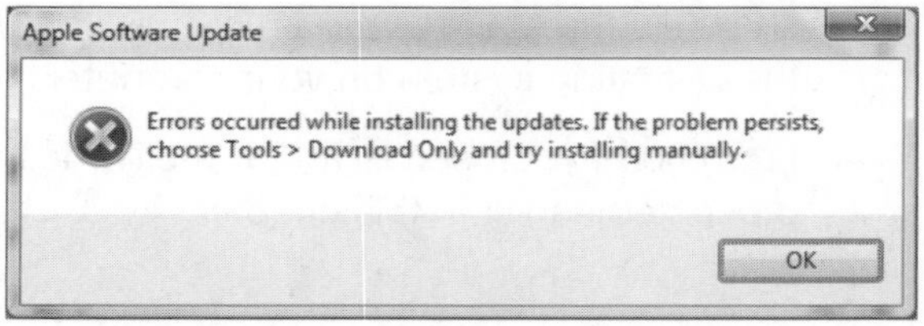

1. From the **Apple Software Update** screen, select the **Tools** menu and then **Download Only**.

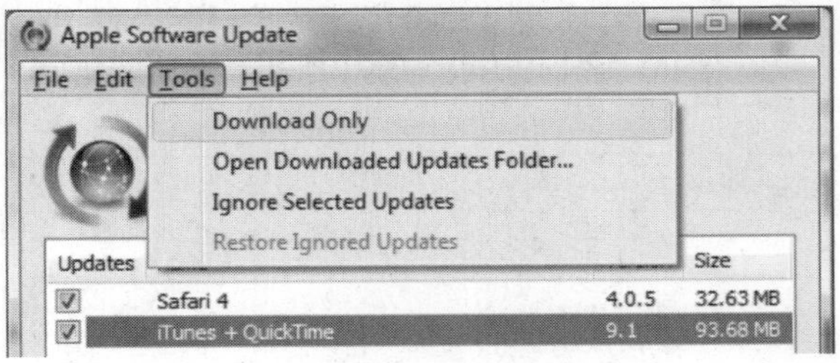

You will see the download status screen shown in Figure 30–63. Once the download is finished, a new window should pop up, showing the downloaded files ready for you to install manually (see Figure 30–64).

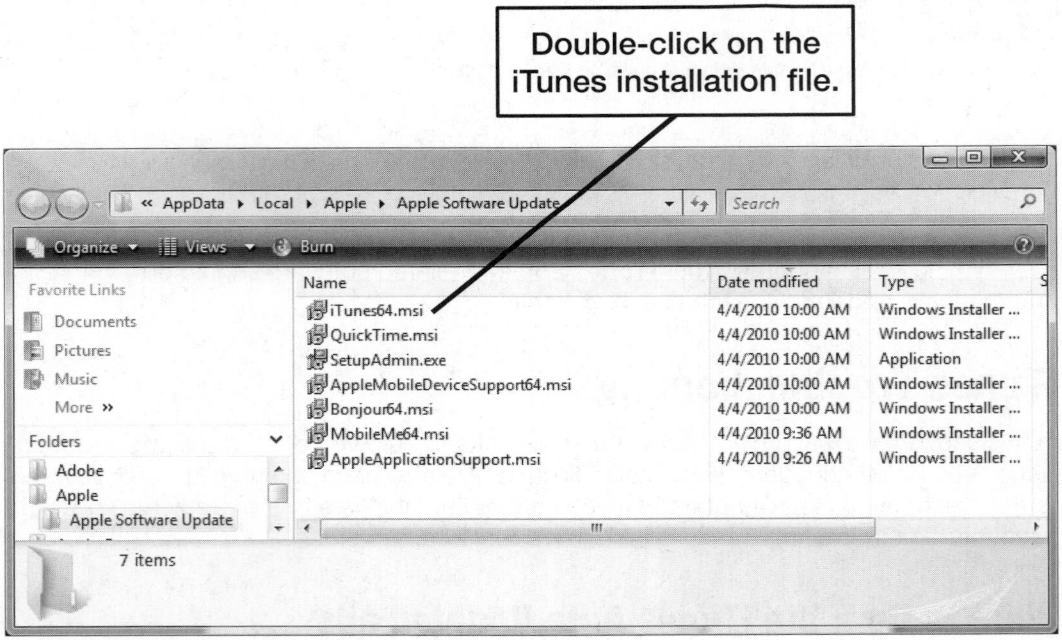

Double-click on the iTunes installation file.

Figure 30–64. *Apple Software Update manual install folder (Windows PC)*

2. To manually start the install, double-click the **iTunes** installer file, as shown in Figure 30–64. The file may be slightly different than the one shown in the figure (e.g., iTunes.msi or iTunes64.msi), depending on the operating system on your computer.

3. From here, you need to follow the iTunes installation screens that were presented earlier in this chapter.

Fixing the Apple ID Security Error

If you try to log in with your Apple ID, you might receive an error message at the top of the screen that looks similar to this one:

> To use this Apple ID you must first login to the My Info Web page then provide additional security information.

If this happens, then you will have to log in to the Apple Store web site, enter a Security Question/Answer, and then add the month and day of your birth.

To correct this error, follow these steps:

1. Open up a web browser on your computer and go to www.apple.com.

2. Click the **Store** link in the left portion of the **Top** nav bar, and then hover your mouse over the **Account** link in the upper right corner to see a dropdown list. Select **Account Information** from this list (see Figure 30–65).

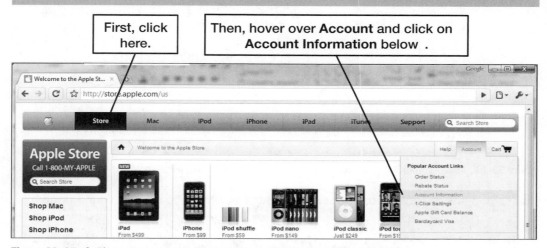

Figure 30–65. *Getting to your account information to correct your security information*

3. If you clicked **Account**, then you will need to select the **Change account information** link from the next screen.

4. Log in with your Apple ID and password (the one that caused the error above).

5. Most likely, your security question and answer or your birth month and date are blank. You need to add this information, type your password twice, scroll to the bottom of the screen, and then click the **Continue** button (see Figure 30–66).

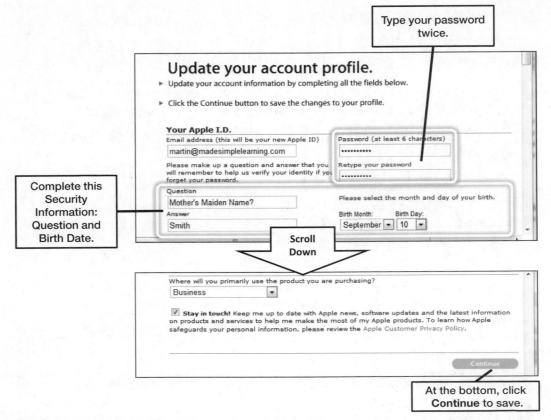

Figure 30–66. *Updating your Apple ID account's security information on the www.apple.com web site*

You should now be able to use your Apple ID and password to register your iPhone.

CAUTION: Apple will never send you an email asking you for your password or asking you to log in and enter your password. If you receive such an email, it might be a scam. Don't click on any links in such an email. If you are concerned about your iTunes account, log in through the **iTunes** app to manage it.

How Do I Get My Music Back if My Computer Crashes?

The good news is that you have a lot, or perhaps all, of your music on your iPhone. We can't help you about getting your computer back up and running in this book if the initial reboot isn't successful. However, we can tell you about how you can get your music back from your iPhone to your **iTunes** app, once your computer is running again!

So, if your only copy of your music, videos, and other content resides on your iPhone, iPod, or iPad, then you need to use a third-party tool to copy your music from that mobile device back into **iTunes** app on your computer, once you've got your computer up and running again.

Do a web search for "copy iPhone or iPod to iTunes" and you will find a number of both free and paid software tools to accomplish this task.

We recommend using a free trial of any software before purchasing it to make sure it will meet your needs.

This solution will also help if you encounter the problem where all your iPhone music is grayed-out when you view it from **iTunes**. In that case, you will need to copy all your iPhone music to **iTunes**, then start fresh with the sync steps or manual transfer steps described in Chapter 3: "Sync Your iPhone with iTunes."

CAUTION: Please do not use this third-party software to create unauthorized copies of music, videos, or other content that you have not legitimately purchased.

Index

■B

Making Technology Simple

iPhone 4
Free Email Tips

Since 2005, Made Simple Learning (**www.madesimplelearning.com**) has been successfully helping to make technology simple with our Made Simple guide books and our video tutorials.

Made Simple Learning is now offering some free iPhone 4 tips and tricks via email! We have selected 10 tips from our new book to help you get more out of your iPhone. Learning in small chunks is the best way to absorb new information and the email tips give you exactly that. We also offer free email tips for BlackBerry, iPhone/iPod Touch, iPad, and webOS devices.

Visit **www.madesimplelearning.com** and click on **Free Tips** to start receiving these informative tips.

Unlock the power of your iPad

Making Technology Simple

For You

Get Started Today!

1. Go to **www.madesimplelearning.com.**
2. Purchase any of our video tutorials or
   guide books right from our site.
3. Start learning in minutes.

For Your Organization

Get Started Today!

1. Request a quote by e-mail from:
   info@madesimplelearning.com
2. We set you up with a free trial.
3. Try before you buy.

What corporate customers say:

Videos Now™
3-minute Video Tutorials
About Your BlackBerry®
Viewed on your PC or Mac

Videos ToGo™
Mobile Video Training
About Your BlackBerry®
On Your BlackBerry®